How Effective Negotiation Management Promotes Multilateral Cooperation

Multilateral negotiations on worldwide challenges have grown in importance with rising global interdependence. However, they have recently proven slow to address them successfully. This book addresses the questions which have arisen from the highly varying results of recent multilateral attempts to reach cooperation on some of the critical global challenges of our times. These include the long-awaited UN climate change summit in Copenhagen, which ended without official agreement in 2009; and the Cancún summit one year later, where parties attained at least moderate tangible results; the first salient trade negotiations after the creation of the WTO, which broke down in Seattle in 1999 and were only successfully launched in 2001 in Qatar as the Doha Development Agenda; and the biosafety negotiations to address the international handling of living modified organisms, which first collapsed in 1999, before they reached the Cartagena Protocol in 2000. Using in-depth empirical analysis, the book examines the determinants of success or failure in efforts to form regimes and manage the process of multilateral negotiations.

The book draws on data from 62 interviews with organizers and chief climate and trade negotiators to discover what has driven delegations in their final decision on agreement, finding that with negotiation management, organizers hold a powerful tool in their hands to influence multilateral negotiations.

This comprehensive negotiation framework, its comparison across regimes and the rich and first-hand empirical material from decision-makers make this invaluable reading for students and scholars of politics, international relations, global environmental governance, climate change and international trade, as well as organizers and delegates of multilateral negotiations.

This research has been awarded the German Mediation Scholarship Prize for 2014 by the Center for Mediation in Cologne.

Kai Monheim researches on negotiations and international cooperation. He is Visiting Fellow at the Grantham Research Institute on Climate Change and the Environment, London School of Economics and Political Science, UK. He also works in management consulting at the Boston Consulting Group. He holds a Harvard Kennedy School Master in Public Policy and attained qualification as a lawyer in Germany.

Routledge Research in Global Environmental Governance

"Structures of power and interest, shaped by domestic politics, tightly constrain international negotiations. Yet *How Effective Negotiation Management Promotes Multilateral Cooperation* shows in fascinating and well-researched detail how the quality of negotiation leadership both varies a great deal across negotiations and affects the processes that ensue."

Robert O. Keohane, Professor of Public and International Affairs,
Princeton University

"The world faces twin challenges of managing climate change and fostering development. The policies to tackle these challenges are clear and many countries are already acting strongly as they see new markets and opportunities for low-carbon investment and growth. But we will do better as a world and accelerate action if we act together. This book considers in detail the essential elements of how we can manage complex multilateral negotiations better. It provides helpful tools to assist future organizers of global climate summits. It also offers helpful insight for students of multilateral negotiations."

Nicholas Stern PBA,FRS, IG Patel Professor of Economics and Government,
London School of Economics and Political Science, and Chair of the
Grantham Research Institute on Climate Change and the Environment

"A valuable addition to the growing number of studies that document and analyze the process of international negotiation. This book shows that state power and domestic politics are not the whole story. Leaders managing multilateral talks also can encourage or inadvertently scupper agreements. Future chairs can find here a practical map to the pitfalls."

John Odell, Professor Emeritus of International Relations,
University of Southern California

"Distilled into a readable policy brief, Kai Monheim's opus conveys a perceptive analysis of the "power of process" in guiding multilateral negotiations to constructive outcomes. While the national interests of the heavyweights remain the key drivers, Monheim's contrasting examples of successes and failures show that a skilful presiding officer, backed by an effective secretariat and working through transparent and inclusive consultations, can contribute to fashioning the broader consensus that confers legitimacy. This is valuable reading for aspiring conference presidencies."

Michael Zammit Cutajar, Executive Secretary of the UNFCCC Secretariat
from 1991 to 2002

How Effective Negotiation Management Promotes Multilateral Cooperation

The power of process in climate, trade, and biosafety negotiations

Kai Monheim

Routledge
Taylor & Francis Group

LONDON AND NEW YORK

First published 2015
by Routledge

2 Park Square, Milton Park, Abingdon, Oxon OX14 4RN
711 Third Avenue, New York, NY 10017, USA

Routledge is an imprint of the Taylor & Francis Group, an informa business

First issued in paperback 2016

British Library Cataloguing-in-Publication Data
A catalogue record for this book is available from the British Library

Library of Congress Cataloging-in-Publication Data
A catalog record for this book has been requested

ISBN: 978-1-138-79752-9 (hbk)
ISBN: 978-1-138-22590-9 (pbk)

Typeset in Goudy
by FiSH Books Ltd, Enfield

To future generations, with concern for the earth's climate

Contents

List of figures and tables

List of abbreviations

ACP	group of African, Caribbean and Pacific Countries
AIA	advance informed agreement
ALBA	negotiation group of Bolivia, Cuba, Ecuador, Nicaragua and Venezuela (Bolivarian Alliance for the Peoples of Our America)
AOSIS	Alliance of Small Island States
AWGs	ad hoc working groups
AWG-KP	Ad Hoc Working Group on Further Commitments for Annex I Parties under the Kyoto Protocol
AWG-LCA	Ad Hoc Working Group on Long-term Cooperative Action under the UNFCCC
BASIC	negotiation group of Brazil, South Africa, India and China
BSWG	Ad Hoc Biosafety Working Group
COP	Conference of the Parties
COP/MOP	Conference of the Parties serving as Meeting of the Parties to the Kyoto Protocol
DG	director-general of the World Trade Organization
EIG	Environmental Integrity Group consisting of Liechtenstein, Mexico, Monaco, South Korea, Switzerland
ExCOP	Extraordinary Conference of the Parties to the Convention of Biological Diversity
G-8	negotiation group of Canada, France, Germany, Italy, Japan, Russia, the United Kingdom and the United States
G-10	trade negotiation group of Iceland, Israel, Japan, Liechtenstein, Mauritius, Norway, South Korea, Switzerland, Taiwan
G-11	trade negotiation group of Argentina, Australia, Brazil, Canada, China, India, Japan, Mauritius, South Africa the United States and the European Union
G-20	negotiation group of Argentina, Australia, Brazil, Canada, China, France, Germany, India, Indonesia, Italy, Japan, Republic of Korea, Mexico, Russia, Saudi Arabia, South

	Africa, Turkey, the United Kingdom, the United States and the European Union
G-77	negotiation group of developing countries, founded by 77 members in 1964 and later expanded to more than 100 countries
GATT	General Agreement on Tariffs and Trade
GMO	genetically modified organism
ICA	international consultations and analysis
IPCC	Intergovernmental Panel on Climate Change
ICTSD	International Centre for Trade and Sustainable Development
LDCs	least developed countries
LMO	living modified organism
LULUCF	land use, land-use change and forestry
MRV/ICA	measurement, reporting and verification/international consulting and analysis
NAMA	nationally appropriate mitigation action
OECD	Organisation for Economic Co-operation and Development
OPEC	Organization of Petroleum Exporting Countries
REDD+	reducing emissions from deforestation and forest degradation in developing countries, including conservation
SBI	Subsidiary Body for Implementation
SBSTA	Subsidiary Body for Scientific and Technological Advice
TRIPS	Trade-related Aspects of Intellectual Property Rights
UNFCCC	United Nations Framework Convention on Climate Change
Umbrella Group	negotiation group of Australia, Canada, Japan, New Zealand, Norway, Russia, Ukraine and the United States
WTO	World Trade Organization

Acknowledgements

This book owes a lot to a number of institutions and individuals to whom I would like to express my deep gratitude. Above all, I thank my PhD supervisor Dr Robert Falkner of the Department of International Relations of The London School of Economics and Political Science, who has accompanied this research with tremendous intellectual advice and personal engagement from its first day on. He offered insightful and instant feedback on every kind of question that has arisen over the course of three years. I could not have imagined a better support for such a project.

The London School of Economics and the Grantham Research Institute of Climate Change and the Environment have been stimulating bases for this research. They generously provided the support to realize field research that draws on fresh evidence from climate and trade summits in Cancún, Durban, Doha, and Geneva, as well as from interviews in Copenhagen, Bonn, and Brussels. It allowed collecting feedback in conferences and workshops from the ECPR Joint Session in St Gallen to the ISA in San Diego. Besides, wonderful individuals fill these institutions that have made this long journey very pleasant. Institute Manager Ginny Pavey and Co-Director Simon Dietz of the Grantham Institute are only two of them.

I also want to thank the numerous academics who have so generously spent their precious time to give very helpful, direct feedback: Robert Keohane, Joseph Nye Jr and John Odell at the ISA in San Diego; Jonas Tallberg, John Vogler and Philipp Pattberg at ECPR sessions in St Gallen and Reykjavik; Stephen Woolcock, Jens Meierhenrich, Andrew Walter, Mathias Koenig-Archibugi, Mareike Kleine, Victoria de Menil and Verena Kroth at the LSE; Thomas Bernauer via '21st century' Skype feedback from the ETH; Andrew Bennett at his superb methodology summer course in Oslo; and Joanna Depledge and Fariborz Zelli at the start of this project. Long before this PhD, Brian Mandell and Ronald Heifetz taught me the importance of the non-rational part of (political) life in their negotiation and leadership classes, while Joe Nye passed on his passion for International Relations at the Harvard Kennedy School. They indirectly inspired this research.

The entire project though rests on the access to the chief negotiators, lead

UNFCCC and WTO officials, and seasoned observers. I am very grateful to all
62 of them, who largely preferred to remain anonymous due to their ongoing
political obligations. They generously gave time (of up to three hours!) despite
their busy schedules to share their experience and to thereby enable this analysis. Michael Zammit Cutajar was one of them, who provided enlightening input
and so kindly facilitated research access to the world of climate experts for this
study. Their staffs were often of invaluable help in arranging the interviews, such
as Esmeralda Fratta Dormond of the UNFCCC, to name only one. I finally owe
thanks to a major European delegation that supported this research by taking me
on board (and behind the scenes) at the Doha summit.

Finally, I deeply thank my parents Kristel and Rolf Monheim for the warmth
and endless support they have always given me, and for the respect and adora-
tion for this planet they have raised me with. My greatest fortune of all though
is my wife Myra, who is the understanding and loving sunshine of my heart,
together with our little precious gem, Linus.

Introduction

Multilateral negotiations aiming to advance cooperation on core worldwide challenges have grown in importance in our current age of increasing global interdependence. Over recent years, their outcomes have no longer only been determined by the preferences of a few powerful countries. Instead, new coalitions have emerged, and hitherto less powerful players are demanding that their voices also be heard. This has raised the need to facilitate broad consensus in order to reach agreements. In consequence, salient adaptations are needed to the way negotiations are managed.

The spectacular breakdowns of a series of multilateral negotiations over the past fifteen years have impressively demonstrated these changing dynamics. They have been a painful experience for policy-makers and citizens around the world, as well as a puzzle for the traditional scholarship in the field of international relations. The latter could not fully explain why the long-awaited UN climate change summit in Copenhagen ended without official agreement in 2009, while it succeeded only one year later in Cancún. Over 120 heads of state and government had travelled to Denmark to attend one of the largest summits ever but failed to achieve a historic comprehensive agreement on the global challenge of climate change that could cost the world dearly. Similarly, the first salient trade negotiations after the creation of the WTO broke down in Seattle in 1999, and were successfully launched only in 2001 in Qatar as the Doha Development Agenda. What factors drove these events? Or, why did the biosafety negotiations to address the international handling of Living Modified Organisms collapse in 1999, before they reached the Cartagena Protocol in 2000?

In all of these cases, fundamental power and interests constellations appeared to be constant in the brief time between the summits. So, these principal factors of two traditional political science theories – *neorealism* and *liberal institutionalism* – offer scant explanation for the initial failures and ensuing agreements, and leave us with a puzzle: did the summits in Copenhagen, Seattle and Cartagena possibly not (only) break down due to clashing interests or lack of support by powerful countries, but to ineffective negotiation management? As a lead UNFCCC Secretariat official suggested in an anonymous interview for this book in May 2011: 'The reason the Copenhagen Accord was not formerly adopted was bad negotiation management.'

This book addresses the puzzle created from these attempts by states to reach international cooperation. It thereby aims to contribute to the understanding of multilateral negotiations as a key step towards attaining such cooperation. The central question is whether and how the negotiation management of a multilateral negotiation by the organizers, such as the host government and the UN, alters the probability of agreement. In short, is there a 'power of process'? The work is embedded in the larger question that has intrigued scholars of international cooperation for decades: in the words of Osherenko and Young (1993: 2), 'What are the determinants of success or failure in efforts to form regimes dealing with specific issues?' Better understanding the dynamics triggered by negotiation management should add a missing piece to the knowledge of how multilateral negotiations evolve and conclude with varying degrees of success.

Chapter 1 introduces the argument about the role of negotiation management for multilateral cooperation. It details the four elements of negotiation management (transparency and inclusiveness, capability of the organizers, authority of the lead organizer, and the negotiation mode of arguing and bargaining) and their roots in contemporary academic thinking. Some fields of political science and negotiation analysis have partially addressed this kind of negotiation management, such as strands of regime theory, constructivism, general negotiation theory on arguing and bargaining, and those approaches that study the agency of bureaucracy and individuals, be they non-state actors such as the UN Climate Secretariat or be they a foreign minister and the supporting bureaucracy of a state that hosts a multilateral negotiation. This is where the book is located within the greater field of research on international cooperation, without an exclusive base in *one* theoretical corner. The entire point of the approach taken here is to combine insights from across these schools. In addition to the literature, exploratory interviews and observation at the UN climate summit in Cancún in 2010 informed the development of the argument.

Having fleshed out the argument, Chapter 1 briefly describes the research approach taken to evaluate the role of negotiation management. The book concentrates on the three case pairs of the above-mentioned negotiations on climate, trade and biosafety. All three negotiations were of high political importance: climate delegates negotiated about a first ever comprehensive global agreement on climate change; trade negotiators discussed the launch of a new post-GATT trade round; and biosafety talks addressed the rapidly expanding business with Living Modified Organisms. They dealt with highly complex global challenges and opportunities, and negotiated in global fora. All case pairs were situated in similar temporal circumstances between 1999 and 2010 of a post-Cold War and post-US hegemonic era with emerging developing countries as China or Brazil, and so their overall contextual conditions are comparable. The potential salience of details of the negotiation process demands the possibility of interviewing most key players in person for this research and hence suggested relatively recent cases. Moreover, the opportunity for participant observation and access to a wide range of actual participants of the climate case pair made the UN climate negotiations during the Danish and Mexican Presidencies in 2009 and 2010 an ideal focus case. Negotiations on trade and biosafety became secondary case pairs. *Within* each case pair, the negotiation management by the organizers of the first case is contrasted with that of the successive negotiation. The comparison *across* regimes then ensures maximal external validity of the findings.

The book turns to its heart in the following chapters on UN negotiations on climate change during 2009 and 2010. Chapter 2 provides an overview of the fall and rise of climate negotiations from Copenhagen to Cancún. It first offers an account of the long and winding road of the climate negotiations since the signing of the UN Framework Convention on Climate Change in 1992, and an introduction to the complex UN climate negotiation structure. It then tells the story of climate negotiations: from being on the brink by the end of 2009 to their recovery in 2010. These chronologies are mostly based on first-hand evidence from interviews with delegates, organizers, and observers, as well as participant observation at the time, and complemented by the detailed accounts of the *Earth Negotiations Bulletin*.

Chapter 3 takes on the primary task of testing the argument of this book on the 'power of process' against the vast empirical evidence from climate negotiations. It compares the negotiation management of the Danish and Mexican Presidencies and the UNFCCC Secretariat during the UN climate negotiations in 2009 and 2010. Among the key organizers in 2009 were Climate and Energy Minister Connie Hedegaard and Prime Minister Lars Løkke Rasmussen as successive Conference Presidents from Denmark and UNFCCC Executive Secretary Yvo de Boer. The Mexicans followed in 2010 with Foreign Minister Patricia Espinosa as Conference President and new UNFCCC Executive Secretary Christiana Figueres. The conditions for a decisive impact of negotiation management by the organizers are met for both years: interests overlapped only narrowly in the beginning of both Presidencies, so an outcome was possible but not at all certain; next, negotiations were consensus-based, so mere majorities would not be sufficient to conclude a deal. The book uses new evidence from interviews and participant observation, which was collected mostly at climate negotiations between 2010 and 2012. The database resulting from this field work contains 55 in-depth, semi-structured interviews on climate negotiations with senior delegates from key countries, high-level UNFCCC officials, and chief organizers of the Danish and Mexican Presidencies, complemented by participant observation at the climate summits in Cancún, Durban, and Doha.

Chapter 3 scrutinizes the four key negotiation management factors of:

1   transparency and inclusiveness;
2   the capability of the organizers;
3   the authority of the lead organizer; and
4   the negotiation mode of arguing and bargaining.

A two-step analysis examines the role each driver played during the negotiations. The first step checks the correlation between a factor and the respective negotiation outcome. For example, the process during the Danish Presidency was much less transparent and inclusive than during the Mexican one. This process factor correlated negatively and positively with agreement as a negotiation outcome, as Copenhagen collapsed without adoption of the compromise proposal, while Cancún succeeded in attaining the Cancún Agreements. The second step examines, through meticulous analysis of the historical process (process tracing), whether and how a negotiation management factor, here transparency and inclusiveness (or the lack of it), contributed to the outcome. All four negotiation management variables are studied through this two-step analysis, based on solid and original empirical data.

Having examined negotiation management as one core part of the argument, I proceed to evaluate alternative explanations for the outcomes in Chapter 4 (this adds the missing element to probe causality and maximizes the internal validity of the findings). The book thereby takes up the traditional International Relations theories, and scrutinizes to what extent they can (and seek to) explain the differences in negotiation outcomes. As we will see, hegemonic theory proves less able to explain these results, as power structures barely changed between both years. Further, the interests of countries generally provide the context in which delegates negotiate. In the climate case, they allowed the reaching of an agreement as they narrowly overlapped at the outset. Yet, the constellation of underlying political, economic, and environmental interests altered very little between 2009 and 2010, so how can they explain the difference in outcomes? Besides, what role was played by the increased risk that the UN climate process would be abandoned as negotiation forum should no agreement be reached again? Additional drivers may also come into play, such as the possibility of using the compromises from the earlier summit in Copenhagen as 'stepping stone' for Cancún, to name only one. The chapter concludes the analysis of the negotiation framework of the climate case pair, which is the focus of this book.

The aim of the next two chapters is to discover to what extent the argument on negotiation management holds in comparable multilateral settings (i.e. do we find its external validity?). The trade and biodiversity case pairs serve as such a comparison to assess the application of findings beyond climate negotiations. Chapter 5 covers trade negotiations on the bedevilled launch of the Doha Development Agenda. The spectacular breakdown of Seattle in 1999 was followed by the successful agreement on the Doha Development Agenda in 2001 in Qatar. As for climate change, the chapter compares the negotiation management of the organizers of both years: the US and Qatari host governments and the respective WTO officials at the time, with Mike Moore as WTO Director-General. Again, the analysis within each case first examines the four negotiation management elements and the respective summit outcomes, before it traces the specific steps of the negotiation process and searches for alternative explanations. Highly varying negotiation management of the hosts notwithstanding, political pressures after the terror attacks of 9/11 also appear as promising explanatory factors.

The rocky path to the Cartagena Protocol on biosafety, from the Cartagena chaos in 1999 to the historic agreement in Montreal in 2000, is depicted in Chapter 6. The biosafety negotiation case pair serves as the final comparison for the negotiation framework. The confirmation in a third regime would significantly support the argument proposed by this book. The expanding trade in Living Modified Organisms demanded states to act, yet negotiations for a biosafety agreement collapsed at the Cartagena summit in 1999. They only reached a successful conclusion in Montreal in 2000. The chapter contrasts negotiation management until 1999, led by Danish negotiation Chair Veit Köster and the Biodiversity Secretariat head Zedan, with that by Colombian Chair Juan Mayr and Zedan post-Cartagena until 2000. The analysis of their varying negotiation management indicators and respective summit outcomes is followed by the stepwise account of the decision-making process and alternative explanations.

Chapter 7 offers the final conclusions of this book. It first provides policy insights for the organizers of future multilateral negotiations by summarizing the key learnings from negotiation management across the three case pairs. This comparison reveals intriguing similarities between the cases, up to verbatim quotes of how process influenced the decision of parties to agree. After these 'lessons learnt', the chapter highlights the two academic contributions. First, the book supports and refines particular strands of International Relations and Negotiation Analysis based on extensive, first-hand data; it thereby strengthens the position of 'process' relative to 'structure' in International Relations theory. Second, it strengthens 'process' without neglecting structural explanations. It rather provides a framework, which integrates structural and negotiation management approaches, to better understand the emergence of international cooperation; the framework includes the detailed paths of effect on the outcome. Negotiation management may finally offer an additional element for future research in this important field. Overall, this book hopefully contributes to facilitate international cooperation on today's global challenges and opportunities.

Reference

Osherenko, Gail, and Oran R. Young. (1993) *Polar Politics: Creating International Environmental Regimes. Cornell Studies in Political Economy*. Ithaca, NY: Cornell University Press.

Chapter 1

The argument

How negotiation management alters multilateral cooperation

This book proposes that negotiation management may influence the course of multilateral negotiations. The first chapter lays out a framework for analysing multilateral negotiations and details the elements of negotiation management. The chapter finally sketches the research approach for those readers interested in the methodology underlying this book. I also shed some light on the exciting research journey to collect data from 62 lead practitioners of climate and trade negotiations from around the world. Overall, it provides a first idea of how this book refines and complements current insights on negotiations and multilateral cooperation.

The argument

In order to analyse comprehensively to what extent negotiation management explains the outcomes of multilateral negotiations on climate change, trade, and biosafety I suggest a comprehensive negotiation framework, which goes beyond mere structural approaches. This responds to the call of scholarship on multilateral cooperation to abandon overly parsimonious approaches (Keohane and Victor 2011; Mitchell 2010; Touval 2010; Woolcock 2011b). I rather acknowledge regime theory's finding that a multivariate approach best accumulates explanatory power (Osherenko and Young 1993; Underdal 2002): there is a 'need to look more at the process ("the how") as scholars have so far more focused on the conditions of regime creation ("the why")' (Jönsson 2002).

Falkner, for example, argues that the several perspectives of constructivism on discourse and of rationalist theories on structure and leadership only jointly explain agreement on the Cartagena Protocol on Biosafety (Falkner 2009). Similarly, Odell regrets the lacking integration of negotiation analysis, international political economy, and constructivism, and the 'still primitive' knowledge about international organization negotiations (Odell 2010: 628). With his synthesis of structure and process, Odell had earlier discovered process influence in the outcomes of ten bilateral economic negotiations (Odell 2000). A recent compendium of environmental regime creation confirms the trend towards process by distinguishing between structure, process, and institutional provisions

(Mitchell 2010: ch. 5). This negotiation framework therefore integrates structural and process explanations (Figure 1.1).

Let us turn to the argument underlying the framework, which holds that *the effective management of a multilateral negotiation by the organizers increases the probability of an agreement (Hypothesis 1, Figure 1.2): negotiation management is considered* effective *when negotiations are transparent and inclusive (Hypothesis 1.1), when organizers are highly capable (Hypothesis 1.2), when the lead organizer enjoys high authority (Hypothesis 1.3), and when the negotiation mode of arguing prevails (Hypothesis 1.4).*[1] Let us explain this argument in more detail.

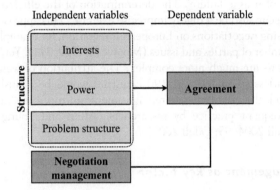

Figure 1.1 Negotiation management as additional independent variable

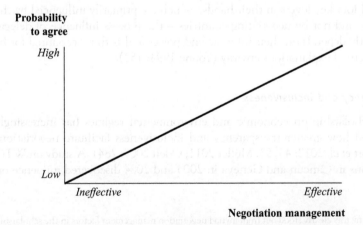

Figure 1.2 Effective negotiation management increases the probability of an agreement

1   The entire year of the Mexican Presidency of the UN climate negotiations before and during the Cancún summit is defined as one multilateral negotiation, for example. The organizers are the lead officials of the host country and of the treaty Secretariat.

Negotiated agreement as potential outcome

The outcome (or dependent variable) of such a round of multilateral negotiations is *negotiated agreement*. One successful example for such a 'negotiated agreement' of the climate change regime was the Kyoto Protocol, or with a much lower degree of commitment to action the Cancún Agreements. As an alternative to 'negotiated agreement', one could have chosen 'failure/success' or 'outcome efficiency' as variables to judge the outcome of multilateral negotiations. However, these are often subjective and blurry criteria, and thus not very helpful for a clear-cut analysis. A few people consider Copenhagen a 'success', while most perceive of it as a 'failure'. The determination of the efficiency of a negotiation outcome can also be a highly imprecise exercise. This approach may be possible for analysing negotiations on European integration, for example, that involve a limited number of parties and issues (Moravcsik 1999: 271). Yet, multilateral climate summits are much more complex. The attribution of weights to preferences on countless issues for over 190 countries would be a misleading simplification. Instead, the use of 'negotiated agreement' mirrors a less nuanced but more reliable frequent practice by researchers (Albin and Young 2012; Bernauer and Mitchell 2004: 95; Odell 2009).

Negotiation management as key factor

So, which drivers make a negotiated agreement more, or less, likely? The central argument of this book is that one key factor is the way in which these multilateral negotiations are managed. More precisely, the organizers of multilateral negotiations hold four key levers in their hands,[2] which are primarily influenced by the organizers, and not by negotiating countries – the process influence of delegations mostly depends on their interests and power and is thus accounted for by these structural explanations anyway (Young 1994: 152).

Transparency and inclusiveness

Recent scholarship on economic and environmental regimes has increasingly emphasized how greater transparency and inclusiveness facilitate negotiations (Davenport *et al.* 2012: 45, 53; Müller 2011; Odell 2009: 284). A study on WTO negotiations in Cancún and Geneva in 2003 and 2004 discovered influence on

---

2   These factors clearly stood out from myriad negotiation management factors in the scholarship on regimes, discourse, agency, and fair process, and in the exploratory interviews in Cancún. To be clear: this research considered myriad other variables. Each of the 62 climate and trade negotiation expert interviewees was queried on the influence of variables in addition to those hypothesized. Their answers are analysed under alternative explanations and may well rise to importance. Nevertheless, a controlled comparison demands to focus on a selection of variables. Those included in the framework stood out clearly from scholarship and the exploratory research phase.

an agreement through transparency, fair representation, fair treatment, and voluntary agreement (Albin and Young 2012: 46–8). Delegates expect respect for ground rules of UN diplomacy, although climate, trade, and biosafety negotiations are less institutionalized than EU decision making for instance (e.g. for economic diplomacy see Woolcock 2011a: 15–17), and thus have less detailed provisions on the required kind of negotiation process. Practitioners of the biosafety negotiations shared these findings (Köster 2002; Mayr 2002). The evidence collected in this book will examine the effect of transparency and inclusiveness on agreement probability.

What indicates transparency and inclusiveness of a negotiation (Figure 1.3)?[3] Information management on small group negotiations is a first aspect of transparency. These often consist of only 20 to 60 delegates and play a central role in reducing the complexity of parties and issues. Since the small group frequently addresses core areas, it becomes vital how well organizers inform the thousands of excluded delegates about its mandate, schedule, and participants. Transparency also varies with the handling of compromise text, which is meant to satisfy the key positions of as many countries as possible after endless negotiations. Given this text's importance, how broadly organizers inform about its origin, evolution, and conclusion becomes crucial. Transparency finally depends on how diligently organizers update parties on the overall negotiation progress and schedule. As thousands of negotiators are scattered over myriad formal and informal groups, hardly anyone has a grasp of all key moves.

Small group negotiations are also a first indicator of inclusion. Countries want to participate in these salient meetings or at least be represented by their

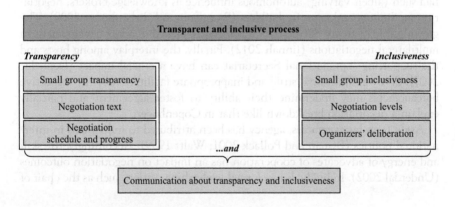

Figure 1.3 Indicators for transparency and inclusiveness

3   This process element refers to *all* negotiating parties, as major powers often enjoy more transparency and inclusiveness.

coalition members, which renders its selection process decisive. Second, negotiations occur across several levels, from experts up to heads of state and government. The integration of levels affects how expert negotiators and politicians perceive their inclusion. Third, organizers engage in extensive deliberation on parties' positions and solutions: how broadly do they reach out to countries to consider their views when facilitating compromise? Finally, the framing of a process as transparent and inclusive influences the perception of parties.

These indicators assess transparency and inclusiveness in *relative* terms by contrasting two negotiations in the same field, like Copenhagen and Cancún. A binary way qualification is unfeasible as complex multilateral negotiations are rarely fully transparent and inclusive (or not): 'Parties never know all that happens.'⁴ A small group that excludes thousands of negotiators can never be considered fully transparent and inclusive. Nonetheless, informing diligently about the group's details and allocating membership through an accepted process enhances its transparency and inclusiveness.

Capability of organizers

Research in the fields of bureaucratic theory, foreign policy analysis and transnational studies indicates that bureaucracies and individuals influence the process and outcome of multilateral negotiations (Mitchell 2002: 506). The negotiation framework builds on these approaches by proposing the negotiation management element of the capability of organizers. Bureaucratic theory and foreign policy analysis have long argued for an autonomous impact of administrations (Allison 1971; Barnett and Finnemore 1999: 707; Weber 1946). Transnational studies have specifically researched international bureaucracies and found that many had such (albeit varying) autonomous influence as knowledge brokers, negotiation facilitators and capacity builders (Biermann and Siebenhüner 2009). The growing role of treaty Secretariats was recently judged as a key development in multilateral negotiations (Jinnah 2012). Finally, the interplay among hosts and the supporting supranational Secretariat can have a crucial impact (Depledge 2007). So overall, internal strife and inappropriate facilitation by the respective bureaucracies may undermine their ability to foster agreement and partially explain a negotiation breakdown like that in Copenhagen.

Aside from bureaucracies, agency has been attributed to individuals in international politics (Byman and Pollack 2001; Waltz 1959). Accordingly, the skill and energy of advocates of cooperation has an impact on negotiation outcomes (Underdal 2002). Individuals in a formal leadership position, such as the chair of

---

4   UNFCCC Secretariat(4)-17.05.2011. Please note that this reference, and all such references in this and subsequent chapters, refer to the interviews carried out for this research. Please find the table of interviews in Appendix III. As interviewees spoke under condition of anonymity, their names and positions had to be deleted.

a multilateral negotiation, the head of a treaty Secretariat or the host country lead facilitator, have varied in their brokerage styles with respective impacts in several regimes, such as climate (Depledge 2005), trade (Odell 2005) and biosafety negotiations (Falkner 2002). While Moravcsik sees a greater effect by national than supranational leaders, such as in EU negotiations, he concedes that the mediating leeway of international bureaucracies and individual policy entrepreneurs is wider in the complex and chaotic settings of global negotiations (Moravcsik 1999: 300).

Connecting to this literature, this book integrates the capability of bureaucracies *and* their lead individuals into one negotiation management factor (similar: O'Neill *et al.* 2004), detailing their interaction and causal mechanism. Organizers are understood institutionally as the responsible host country's bureaucracy and the supporting treaty Secretariat, and individually as Conference President, chief advising official of the national administration, and head of the treaty Secretariat.[5]

Their capability is measured by criteria which are as objective as possible (Figure 1.4). This ensures that the assessment of capability remains *independent* of the negotiation outcome. It avoids a post-hoc rationalization with the risk of tautology in the sense that 'the Mexicans were capable because Cancún reached a negotiated agreement'.[6] The first set of objective criteria is the cultural and organizational or personal fit of organizers to the specific negotiation circumstances. Cultural fit applies to institutions and individuals and entails, for

5   Naturally, these organizations do not manage a multilateral negotiation with only a few people. Among others, the Chairs of key working groups (e.g. AWG-LCA or AWG-KP at the climate negotiations) and their treaty Secretariat counterparts also fulfil salient facilitating functions. Despite their obvious contribution, interviews and scholarship on Chairs have yielded that the Conference President, the host lead adviser, and the treaty Secretariat Executive Secretary are the primary agents among organizers with the widest responsibility and leverage for facilitation. Therefore, this research uses a narrow definition of individual organizers.

6   While these criteria are objective as such, one major source for assessing the capability of these institutions and individuals are the interviews with negotiators, UN officials, and observers. The input may therefore be subjectively coloured by the respondents' opinion about someone's capability. Three approaches alleviated this concern. First, answers are triangulated through an additional empirical basis of a form of participant observation. The author gathered a first-hand impression through in-person, one-on-one interviews with each of the eight assessed individuals of the Presidency and the UN of 40 to 120 minutes each – except for Prime Minister Rasmussen who rejected two interview attempts during 2011, and for Foreign Minister Espinosa whom the author observed during the two-week summit in Cancún. This direct exposure enhanced the author's understanding also on a subjective, cultural-personal side. This additional source provides higher authenticity for interpreting the interview data. Second, responses will not be directly used to determine whether an institution or individual was capable or not in a specific role. Rather, objective circumstantial facts from interviews, observation, and secondary material indicate the level of capability indirectly. On an individual level, for instance, information on the degree of prior multilateral experience of a Conference President reveals process expertise. Third, the wide range of interviewees triangulates responses from different negotiation groups and rivalling factions inside the organizing institutions.

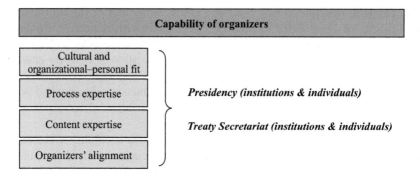

Figure 1.4 Indicators for capability of organizers

instance, the ability to: build bridges as a neutral facilitator, communicate in a not too directive and pushy way, keep a moderate level of activism, work behind the scenes, and create an inviting, unthreatening atmosphere. Organizational fit of institutions requires, above all, internal unity of the organizing institution with clear responsibilities. High personal fit is attributed to organizers that are *inter alia* empathic, approachable, open to listen, modest, and humorous, while still steering confidently. The second indicator is process expertise of the organizers on the dynamics of negotiations and their available facilitation 'toolkit', flowing especially from long-time multilateral negotiation experience. This is thirdly complemented by expertise on the negotiation substance. The alignment of organizers such as between the host country and Secretariat serves as the final indicator and assesses the relative degree of conflict.

Assessing capability is naturally not a binary exercise, but measures it in relative terms. For instance, alignment does not mean idealist harmony but implies a comparatively low degree of conflict between organizers. Alignment varies with alternating Presidencies.[7] 'There is always tension between the orderly way the Secretariat would go about negotiations and the new approaches by the hosts. At COP-15, this was less harmonious than in other COPs.'[8]

Authority of the lead organizer

Taking the scholarship on individual leadership as discussed in the previous section further, the degree of authority of the lead organizer has an additional, salient effect on negotiations beyond the element of capability of the responsible

7   UNFCCC Secretariat(3)-08.12.2010.
8   UNFCCC Secretariat(2)-04.12.2010.

institutions and its key individuals. For Depledge in her in-depth study of climate negotiations, the presiding officer is the most important variable (Depledge 2005). Others add the Chair's political capital as a key driver (Blavoukos and Bourantonis 2011), which also relates to his authority. The Chair has leverage to observe, formulate, and manipulate even in the strong institutional setting of the WTO (Odell 2005). For him, picking the situation-appropriate tool for the right level of restraint or proactive leadership seems crucial (e.g. on manipulation; *ibid.*: 441–5). Similarly, Tallberg brought evidence *inter alia* from trade negotiations on the importance of brokerage by the Chair, who uses informational and procedural assets (Tallberg 2010).

The concept of authority of the lead organizer and how it impacts the fulfilment of his role ties into this understanding of the Chair. The consensus-requirement of many multilateral negotiations in particular places abundant responsibility on a Chair to facilitate and to eventually declare such consensus, notwithstanding that the decision flows from an iterative process with the parties. The president must decide at one point in the turbulence of a final negotiation night whether parties have reached an agreement. So, the third management lever is the authority of the lead organizer.

As with capability, it is essential to assess authority of the lead organizer independent from the negotiation outcome, and to thus exclude tautology. Authority is indicated if delegates accept him or her widely, i.e. when the large majority of key negotiators overall trust the lead organizer in his or her negotiation role (Figure 1.5). Interview responses by negotiators and Secretariat officials were examined to what extent they express acceptance of the lead organizer *at the time* of the negotiations. Responses were triangulated with participant observation in Cancún, the UN video footage of the Copenhagen closing plenary, and secondary sources. Owing to the subjective nature of 'trust', answers are counted in a binary (not continuous) way of 'overall trusted or not', and 'ambiguous/undecided'. The diversity of the sample (cf. Table 1.1, section on data collection) controls for potential political biases of interviewees.

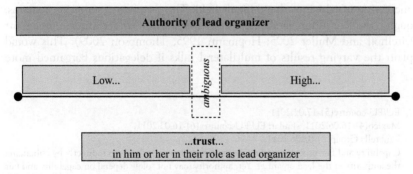

Figure 1.5 Indicator for authority of lead organizer

Finally, the process variables interact with each other. Many negotiators base their trust in the lead organizer on their perception of capability and the transparency and inclusiveness of the process. A former COP president put it in a nutshell: the president 'needs to know what he talks about. He needs to be trusted and to be neutral.'[9] Thus, the quality of work is often the foundation of legitimacy, like Espinosa's in Cancún.[10] An inclusive process further bolsters authority: 'It helped for Espinosa that the Mexicans had an open-door policy during the preparation time and the COP itself. Everyone appreciated this.'[11] This interaction, however, does not render 'authority' redundant, as the causal influence may work through multiple paths.[12]

Negotiation modes of arguing and bargaining

Finally, the negotiation modes of arguing and bargaining among delegations determine the influence of ideas on negotiations, and hence their outcome. This understanding builds on constructivist theory on the shaping of interests and positions of countries through ideas (e.g. Goldstein and Keohane 1993; Haggard and Simmons 1987). Regime theory (Mitchell 2010: 117; Osherenko and Young 1993: 13), conflict research (e.g. Wagner 2008), and general negotiation analysis (e.g. Sebenius 1992; Thompson 2009) have all underlined the importance of negotiation modes.

Generally, the negotiation mode of arguing enhances the generation and diffusion of ideas to render agreement more likely (Deitelhoff and Muller 2005; Hopmann 1995; Ulbert *et al.* 2004). It means a deliberative, truth-seeking approach to convince each other: 'true' Habermasian discourse influences parties' perception of an issue, the related interests, and eventually negotiation position (Ulbert *et al.* 2004: 34). In contrast, the mode of bargaining implies a demand- and threat-based exchange between parties to distribute pay-offs. Recent studies have addressed the prevailing uncertainty about the conditions and impact of these discourse modes (Risse and Kleine 2010). The synthesis of constructivist and rationalist strands of International Relations (Hopmann 2010), and even of general negotiation analysis (Odell 2010) has been one way of increasing insight into this difficult field. The common assumption remains, though, that arguing facilitates and bargaining undermines agreement (Deitelhoff and Muller 2005; Hopmann 1995; Thompson 2009). This would explain the varying results of multilateral talks if delegations bargained more

9   EU/EU-country(5)-17.02.2011.
10   Mexico(4)-16.06.2011, similar: EU/EU-country(6)-16.03.2011.
11   Umbrella Group(2)-02.06.2011.
12   Capability and fair process can directly impact on a process, but also indirectly by enhancing the authority of the lead organizer. Yet, authority may not solely depend on capability and fair process. So, the causal chain between authority and agreement may therefore differ from the direct routes of capability and fair process, and agreement.

when talks broke down, and argued constructively when they reached agreement. This study will shed light on the still underexplored causal link between discourse and outcome (O'Neill *et al.* 2004: 163).

How can we measure negotiation modes using the evidence collected on these negotiations? The type of discourse and its underlying assumptions and goals serve as primary indicators (Figure 1.6), and it proves useful to consider differences between preparatory and summit negotiations, and between negotiating groups. *Arguing* is indicated by a constructive discourse open to a change of minds based on facts and logical insights in order to find a joint solution. It largely reveals the underlying interests of the parties and lets ideas enter the process easily. Parties *bargain* when they mostly negotiate about the distribution of a fixed set of gains and burdens while assuming a zero-sum situation (e.g. distributing a given amount of 'carbon space' in the atmosphere among parties).[13] They merely state their positions without a willingness to engage in open-ended solution finding, and often claim a restrictive negotiation mandate.[14]

Finally, evidence from climate negotiations suggests that the organizers' negotiation management affects the negotiation mode of delegates.[15] If negotiators trust the organizing Presidency and Secretariat they are less anxious about

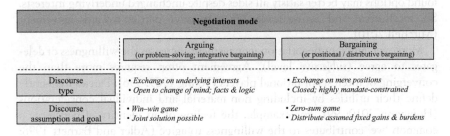

Figure 1.6 Indicators for negotiation modes of arguing and bargaining

13   Denmark(1)-02.12.2010: as routinely argued by China. A textbook example illustrates this well: two people want to use the one lemon they have. When they can't agree on who should get it, each receives one half (zero-sum bargaining). Revealing the interests underlying their positions, they would have found that one only wanted the lemon's juice to make lemonade while the other only needed the lemon's skin for baking cookies (win-win arguing, or integrative bargaining).

14   To counter the challenge to separate true arguing from a mere exchange of positions, the abundantly available interview responses were cautiously examined for evidence on objective arguing and bargaining indicators, as well as on internal motives that delegates expressed they had during the negotiations.

15   EU/EU-country(9)-26.05.2011, UNFCCC Secretariat(2)-04.12.2010, AWG/SB-Chair(2)-04.12.2010.

hidden agendas and secretive negotiations. This leads to more open-minded arguing.[16] In a situation of mistrust many negotiators perceive it safer to close up and stick to their positions. Further, informal settings, which organizers initiate outside the official negotiation process ahead of a summit, provide arguing space without the pressure of an outcome.[17] Their non-public set up and less crowded atmosphere additionally induce open exchange on interests and a true discourse on content.[18] At summits, smaller informal groups fulfil a similar function, in contrast to plenaries with the presentation of well-known positions.[19] Overall though, an overly exclusive process reduces arguing among *all* parties. Instead, organizers can also foster arguing by creating higher trust between delegates through a mostly transparent and inclusive process (references to social psychology: Albin and Young 2012: 40).

Connecting negotiation management and outcome

Negotiation management alters the probability of an agreement in two ways. When applied efficiently, it supports parties in reaching a zone of possible agreement where interests and proposals converge in an *objective* way. The compromise proposal is then superior to parties' best alternatives to a negotiated agreement (negotiation literature: Sebenius 1992; Thompson 2009). For example, organizers facilitate new proposals through a setting conducive to argument, where parties uncover joint preferences (Zartman and Touval 2010: 4). The new-found options may better satisfy all sides despite unchanged underlying interests. So, intellectual and active leadership can move parties towards agreement (Mitchell 2010).

Moreover, efficient negotiation management increases the willingness of delegates to agree (*subjective* level). Agreement often requires more than the converging of interests of rational players (Young 1989: 356). Parties frequently define their utilities by including non-material and individual considerations (Hopmann 2010: 99). For example, the feeling of an identity of parties as a common 'we' contributes to the willingness to agree (Adler and Barnett 1998: 32). Further, the notion of equality in a negotiation leads to 'kinship' among delegates, and thereby to reciprocal behavior (Müller 2011: 3; Zartman and Touval 2010: 233). Conciliatory moves then create trust alongside an objective overlap of interests (Jönsson 1993: 206). In sum, negotiation management alters the *willingness* by delegates to agree by addressing social and individual psychological concerns.

Finally, the condition for an influence of negotiation management is that the initial interests of countries neither mostly converge nor mostly collide at the

---

16   AWG/SB-Chair(4)-14.06.2011.
17   AWG/SB-Chair(3)-07.12.2010, BASIC(1)-04.12.2010.
18   G-77(1)-04.12.2010, UNFCCC Secretariat(3)-08.12.2010, EU/EU-country(3)-03.12.2010.
19   Denmark(2)-16.06.2011, G-77(3)-19.07.2011.

start of the negotiations (Figure 1.7). In this case of a tipping point of an originally narrow overlap of interests, effective negotiation management can crucially facilitate the converging of positions. In contrast, largely aligned parties agree independent of negotiation management, while even a perfect process cannot convince parties to agree when their interests clash. Interests then suffice to explain behaviour. Consensus-based decision-making further enhances the role of negotiation management. Otherwise, parties reach mere majorities more easily through coalition building and may neglect a few dissenting countries. Having laid out the argument concerning negotiation management, which role do structural circumstances, such as interests and power, play?

Interests, power and problem structure

The interests of countries and the distribution of power among them, as well as the structure of the issue under negotiation determine the context in which multilateral negotiations occur. The crucial question is to which extent they influence their outcomes. Do they suffice to explain the course of international cooperation?

Without doubt, the *interests of countries* strongly influence the reaching of an agreement. As we have seen, their initial constellation is one condition for the impact of negotiation management. Key factors to define preferences of countries are of a domestic nature, such as influence by business and civil society, and by the structure of political institutions. All three regimes concerned fundamental interests of most countries, such as climate change with far-reaching environmental, economic, societal, and even security ramifications. The book therefore examines any changes of interests that may explain the variance in outcomes.

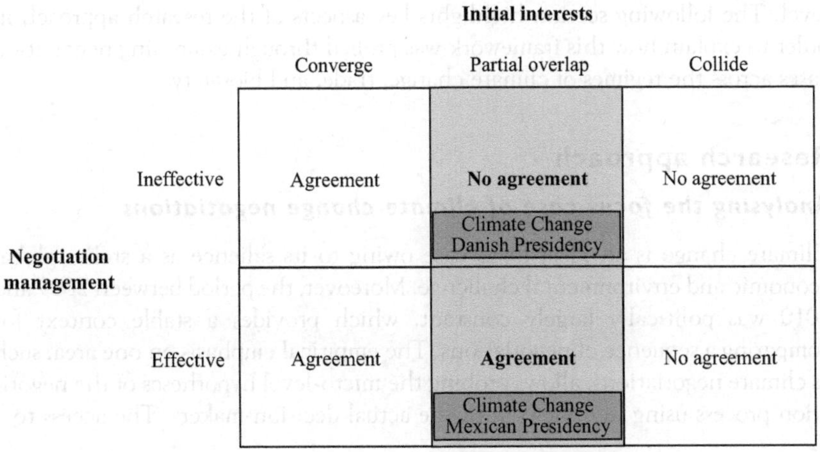

		Initial interests	
	Converge	Partial overlap	Collide
Ineffective	Agreement	**No agreement** Climate Change Danish Presidency	No agreement
Effective	Agreement	**Agreement** Climate Change Mexican Presidency	No agreement

(Negotiation management)

Figure 1.7 Condition for an influence of negotiation management

The *interests of the organizers* in being successful facilitators affect their negotiation management (Blavoukos and Bourantonis 2011). Given the expected neutrality on substance, the hosts seek reputational gains from a negotiation success in their country, like Japan with the Kyoto Protocol (Busby 2009: 86). Alternatively, the Cancún climate summit could 'give a profile to Mexico which it didn't have until then'.[20] This enhances soft power and countries fulfil their hosting role, as expected by rational and cognitivist theories. Supporting international organizations cater to their self-interest by deepening 'their' regime (e.g. Biermann and Siebenhüner 2009).

Besides interests, the changing *distribution of power between countries* may alter chances for reaching agreement. The book examines the role of power in negotiations on climate change, trade, and biosafety, and echoes recent voices that cast doubt on its traditionally assumed importance. Cooperation has been frequently established without hegemonic approval, such as the establishment of the International Criminal Court (Stiles 2009). For all regimes studied in this book, the different dimensions of power (such as military, political, economic) appear fairly constant and thus have difficulty in explaining outcome variance between two successive negotiation rounds.

Finally, the *structure of the 'problem'* under negotiation is similar for the fields of climate change, trade, and biosafety. The original idea would be that some policy areas are less amenable to cooperation than others (Rittberger and Zürn 1990). The three cases of this book, however, all address highly complex policy areas of salient economic, environmental, and even security importance. The challenges remain unaltered in the respective time periods, marginalizing this variable for the book.

To conclude, Figure 1.8 graphically summarizes the central argument about how multiple drivers shape the course of multilateral negotiations. It shows the key variables and how they affect agreement on an objective and a subjective level. The following section highlights key aspects of the research approach in order to explain how this framework was probed through examining negotiation cases across the regimes of climate change, trade, and biosafety.

Research approach

Analysing the focus case of climate change negotiations

Climate change is an ideal focus case owing to its salience as a stellar global economic and environmental challenge. Moreover, the period between 2009 and 2010 was politically largely constant, which provides a stable context for comparing a sequence of negotiations. The empirical emphasis on one area, such as climate negotiations, allows probing the micro-level hypotheses of the negotiation process using interviews with the actual decision-makers. The access to a

20   BASIC(5)-15.06.2011, similar: Mexico(4)-16.06.2011.

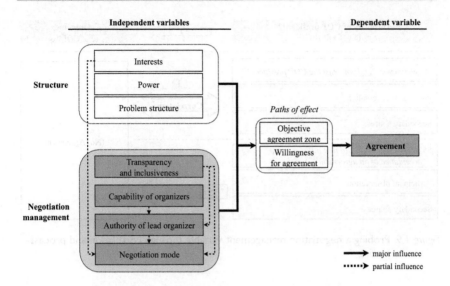

Figure 1.8 The negotiation framework integrates structure and negotiation management

wide range of participants and the opportunity for participant observation at the UN climate negotiations of 2009 and 2010 provided this empirical material.

A combination of qualitative methods probes the argument of this book. The within-case analysis examines the two negotiation rounds of the case pair of the Danish and Mexican Presidencies (the period of each negotiation Presidency delineates the cases). It first establishes the correlation between each negotiation management element and negotiation outcomes to assess their potential association. Process tracing then reconstructs the historical narrative of the causal chain to approximate probabilistic causality (Bennett 2004: 22, 35; Bernauer and Mitchell 2004: 96; Figure 1.9). The study sheds light on *several* causal paths that *jointly* increase agreement likelihood – as it is questionable to reiterate one causal chain in a linear way given the simultaneous work of myriad factors (George and Bennett 2005: 212). The search for alternative variables completes the process tracing.

To determine the 'value' of the variables (e.g. high versus low authority), hypotheses were translated into observable implications (King *et al.* 1994: 28). For example, the influence of 'authority of the lead organizer' on outcome could be observed in interviews, where negotiators provided clues about their (dis)trust of a Conference President, and how this affected their final decisions.

Having examined the negotiation management of the Danish Presidency of climate negotiations for example (within-case analysis), the ensuing comparison with the Mexican Presidency strengthens the confidence in the findings of the

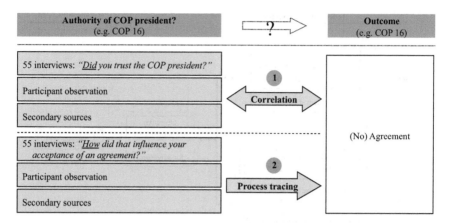

Figure 1.9 Probing a negotiation management variable through correlation and process-tracing

Danish Presidency. This approach is known as 'before–after' research design (Bennett 2004: 166), and divides a longitudinal case into two sub-cases (for trade: Odell 2009: 282). Its advantage is that one variance between subsequent negotiation rounds, like an altered process, can be better isolated for its impact on the change in outcome ('no agreement' versus 'agreement'), as the political structures may be fairly constant over the period of two Presidencies.

Comparing across regimes using trade and biosafety negotiations

The final step compares the climate change findings to other multilateral negotiations to allow for their generalization ('external validity'; Bernauer and Mitchell 2004: 84). This book uses the negotiations on trade in Seattle and Doha in 1999 and 2001 and on biosafety in Cartagena and Montreal in 1999 and 2000. The three case pairs are comparable with possibly largely constant structural circumstances and some shifts in negotiation management. This prima-facie notion is thoroughly scrutinized but serves as an indicator at the outset of the investigation. The trade and biosafety cases follow the same methodology of correlation and process-tracing, combined with the 'before-after' design of subsequent negotiations.

The case pair of the trade negotiations on the launch of the Doha round covers the negotiations that culminated in the 3rd and 4th Ministerial Conferences in Seattle and Doha. The breakdown in Seattle in 1999 was followed by negotiations at the WTO headquarters in Geneva and the agreement in Doha in 2001. The content of both negotiation phases towards Seattle and Doha was economically salient and contested: whether and how to launch a new round of trade liberalization as well as a review and refinement of existing trade rules. The selection of older cases would not have accounted for the increased multilateral complexity of myriad parties and countless issues of the late 1990s.

Similar to climate and trade, negotiations on a Biosafety Protocol were a land-mark in the evolution of the biodiversity regime that attracted political and academic attention. The case pair of the preparatory negotiations and summits of Cartagena in 1999 and Montreal in 2000 fits the failure–success sequence. The focus on a short time period reduces the variance of structural factors. As the outcome alters, changed negotiation management factors indicate their impact. The multitude of environmental, trade, and development interests make also the biosafety negotiations a negotiation challenge.[21]

To summarize the approach of this book, a framework was constructed by building on selected negotiation management literature and on exploratory interviews at the Cancún climate summit. The research then assessed the corre-lation of the framework variables for the Danish and Mexican climate negotiation Presidencies. Next, process-tracing approximated probabilistic causation. The comparison of the Danish and Mexican climate Presidencies through the 'before–after' research design further strengthened the internal validity of the findings. Finally, the application to the biosafety and trade case pairs probed its generalization. This combination of qualitative methods provides a solid basis to assess the impact of negotiation management on multilateral cooperation.

Collecting evidence around the world

Climate change negotiations

The evidence on climate negotiations was collected at the sidelines of multilat-eral negotiations around the world. Expert interviews and participant observation yielded the data to identify key management factors and to recon-struct political dynamics, often taking place behind closed doors. During interviews, open questions (e.g. 'Why did you not get an agreement in Copenhagen?') allowed for surprising findings, while the guided section ('How

21   Regarding methodological caveats, the case pairs were *not* selected according to the conform-ity of the dependent and independent variables with the hypothesis (George and Bennett 2005: 24), as we can only determine the value of the myriad variables after a thorough analy-sis of evidence. Furthermore, the collapse–agreement sequences entail the impact of a prior breakdown and of preceding work on the ensuing negotiation. However, only this sequence holds the negotiation goal constant. For instance, the Cancún climate summit finally sealed official agreement on a number of issues so that any negotiation afterwards would address a novel goal, which creates a different interest constellation. Yet in the most similar case design of a longitudinal case, the compared cases maintain their core setting and may only differ by one aspect, like negotiation management (*ibid.*: 81). The alternative explanations then capture additional implications of this sequence.

transparent were the negotiations?') ensured comparability of answers across interviews (cf. Appendix II). They were mostly held in person, such as at the Cancún summit in 2010, at the intersessional negotiations in Bonn and at COP-17 in Durban in 2011, or with former Danish Presidency members in Copenhagen in 2011.

In the end, climate interviews totalled 55, lasting one hour on average (cf. interview list in Appendix III). The number well exceeds the 20–30 considered as minimum for expert interviews (Burnham 2008: 234). Interviewees are politicians, officials, and observers from media and NGOs (Table 1.1). They include close to all lead representatives of the Danish and Mexican Presidencies, inter alia one COP-President and all chief advisers. On the UNFCCC side, the current and former Executive Secretaries and their lead officials participated, as did the facilitators of the main working groups of Copenhagen and Cancún. Respondents from parties are usually lead delegates from all major negotiation groups. They reflect the wide range of perspectives, such as from the US to Bolivia and from India to the EU.

Let us consider one caveat in the use of interviews. They reflect the perspective of delegates and organizers. As most still work in public policy, they have incentives to shape the discourse of current climate negotiations and the interpretation of past ones. For instance, was Copenhagen a success? Did the Mexican Presidency organize a transparent process? Respondents may not have revealed their entire knowledge of events or even spread misleading information.

Table 1.1 Interviews on climate negotiations with lead organizers, head negotiators, and observers (2010–12)

Organizers, facilitators, observers	n	Negotiation groups	n
Danish Presidency	7	ALBA (Bolivia, Cuba, Ecuador, Nicaragua, Venezuela)	2
Mexican Presidency	5	BASIC (Brazil, South Africa, India, China)	5
UNFCCC Secretariat	7	EIG (Liechtenstein, Mexico, South Korea, Switzerland)	1
Chair of an Ad-Hoc Working Group (AWG) or Subsidiary Body	4	EU Commission or EU member state	11
Observers	3	G-77 (non-ALBA/BASIC developing countries)	5
		Umbrella Group (Australia, Canada, Japan, New Zealand, Norway, Russia, Ukraine, US)	5
Total	26		29

Notes: *n* = number of interviewees. ALBA: Bolivarian Alliance for the Peoples of Our America; EIG: Environmental Integrity Group.

This research responded to the potential biases in multiple ways. Creating a large and diverse set of nearly 60 interviews is one salient remedy. The quantity and diversity of the data from all major and adversarial coalitions should capture all principal viewpoints. When the biases are politically motivated among conflicting coalitions, the respective reverse directions of opinion reveal these biases. Or, biases from one side are uncovered by more neutral sides, such as on the process and content expertise of the lead organizers. The ability to analyse the evidence in the databank by institutional origin of respondent allowed the systematic checking of biases on each answer category. Surprisingly, there is often consensus on questions across adversaries, such the transparency and inclusiveness of a process. Finally, anonymity and detailed hand-written notes instead of tape recording reduce the intentional bias of answers (Burnham 2008: 239).

Overall, primary data from interviews can mean more relevant and reliable information than secondary material from existing studies. For instance, the decision to agree is hypothetically also based on the *willingness* by the delegation. This willingness may stem from the participant's *subjective* assessment of process factors, such as its transparency and inclusiveness, and the authority of the lead organizer. Data on these kinds of questions is most reliably collected directly from the negotiators and organizers involved. How could other sources give more authentic answers about the (internal) perceptions of these people? So, interviews are best suited to gather data for these specific research questions, combined with participant observation and secondary sources.

Participant observation is used for the principal case of climate negotiations, and partially on trade, for generating hypotheses and triangulating interview data (Burnham 2008: 232; Gusterson 2008). The author attended the three climate summits in Cancún, Durban, and Doha between 2010 and 2012 (COP-16, 17, and 18). The academic observer position for the London School of Economics allowed for the observation of all plenary sessions and of open informal negotiations during the 2010 and 2011 negotiations. The neutrality as an observer during the first two summits ensured detachment of the research object with minimal bias and maximized candidness of interviewees. At the Doha climate summit, the author observed as researcher on a national European delegation. It provided unique access to closed-door preparations and negotiations, and thus allowed a first-hand, authentic verification of previous responses on negotiation dynamics. In sum, this book offers abundant and original, first-hand material on cooperation in the salient field of climate change.

Trade and biosafety negotiations

The evidence for the controlling case pair of trade negotiations relies on a wealth of secondary sources, such as meeting reports from the WTO and observer organizations as well as academic literature containing rich primary material (e.g. Jawara and Kwa 2003). The literature, for instance, includes an extensive first-hand account by then-WTO Director General Mike Moore (Moore 2003).

Table 1.2 Interviews on trade negotiations with lead organizers and head negotiators (2011–12)

Organizers	n	Negotiation groups	n
WTO	2	ACP	1
		EU member state	2
		G-10	2
Total	2		5

Notes: *n* = number of interviewees. ACP: Group of African, Caribbean and Pacific Countries; G-10: mixed group of advanced developed and developing economies.

Selected interviews with trade negotiators and WTO officials and participant observation at the 8th Ministerial Conference in Geneva in 2011 complement the secondary sources. Despite their small number of seven interviewees yielded rich data as they included high-ranking WTO officials, and senior negotiators from various countries (Table 1.2 and interview list in Appendix V). Respondents had good knowledge of the cases as they participated in, or were close to, the trade negotiations of 1999 and 2001. Tailored to this research design, questions paralleled the climate negotiation questionnaire to ensure comparability across regimes. Granting anonymity, all but one interview was conducted in-person to maximize candid responses. Nevertheless, the scope of the controlling trade and biodiversity cases is limited, so the data allows for indications but not always a detailed filling of each negotiation framework variable.

The biosafety case pair data stems primarily from the largest in-depth study on this milestone of the biodiversity regime (Bail *et al.* 2002). The editors ensured a broad range of perspectives with first-hand contributions by over 50 participants and analysts, such as the accounts of the Chairs of the preparatory negotiations, Veit Köster, and of the Cartagena and Montreal summits, Juan Mayr. This rich evidence and additional secondary sources allow saving financial and time resources for the main case pair of climate change and, to a lesser extent, for trade with its selected interviews and participant observation in Geneva. While the biosafety study does not substitute for the over 60 climate and trade interviews, it is still a sufficiently detailed source to extract the data of interest for the negotiation framework.

Conclusion

This chapter laid out the central argument of this book that negotiation management can change the course of multilateral cooperation, at least in those frequent cases where negotiations require consensus and where interests initially overlap only narrowly. Connecting to recent trends in scholarship and based on exploratory data, I propose a negotiation framework to assess the impact of negotiation management through a combination of methods that maximize the validity of findings. The cases of trade and biosafety negotiations probe the preliminary results from the focus case pair of climate change across regimes. Abundant and original evidence from interviews, participant observation, and secondary sources trace the key steps in the chain of events.

Chapter 2 provides the background to the climate case, which is at the heart of this book. Based on first-hand evidence from 55 climate negotiation insiders, it tells the story of the fall and rise of climate negotiations in 2010 and 2011, which culminated in the historical summits of Copenhagen and Cancún.

References

Adler, Emanuel, and Michael N. Barnett. (1998) *Security Communities*. Cambridge Studies in International Relations no. 62. New York: Cambridge University Press.

Albin, Cecilia, and Ariel Young. (2012) Setting the Table for Success – or Failure? Agenda Management in the WTO. *International Negotiation* 17: 37–64.

Allison, Graham Tillett. (1971) *Essence of Decision: Explaining the Cuban Missile Crisis*. New York: Little Brown.

Bail, Christoph, Robert Falkner and Helen Marquard. (2002) *The Cartagena Protocol on Biosafety: Reconciling Trade in Biotechnology with Environment and Development*. London: Earthscan.

Barnett, Michael N., and Martha Finnemore. (1999) The Politics, Power, and Pathologies of International Organizations. *International Organization* 53: 699–732.

Bennett, Andrew. (2004) Case Study Methods: Designs, Use, and Comparative Advantages Models. In *Numbers and Cases: Methods for Studying International Relations*, edited by Detlef F. Sprinz and Yael Wolinsky-Nahmias. Ann Arbor, MI: University of Michigan Press.

Bernauer, Thomas, and Ronald B. Mitchell. (2004) Beyond Story Telling: Designing Case Study Research in International Environmental Policy. In *Models, Numbers, and Cases: Methods for Studying International Relations*, edited by Detlef F. Sprinz and Yael Wolinsky-Nahmias. Ann Arbor, MI: University of Michigan Press.

Biermann, Frank, and Bernd Siebenhüner. (2009) *Managers of Global Change: The Influence of International Environmental Bureaucracies*. Cambridge, MA: MIT Press.

Blavoukos, Spyros, and Dimitris Bourantonis. (2011) Chairs as Policy Entrepreneurs in Multilateral Negotiations. *Review of International Studies* 37: 653–72.

Burnham, Peter. (2008) Elite Interviewing. In *Research Methods in Politics*, edited by Peter Burnham, Karin Gilland, Wyn Grant and Zig Layton-Henry. Basingstoke: Palgrave Macmillan.

Busby, John. (2009) The Hardest Problem in the World: Leadership in the Climate Regime. In *Cooperating without America: Theories and Case Studies of Non-Hegemonic Regimes*, edited by Stefan Brem and Kendall W. Stiles. London: Routledge.

Byman, Daniel L., and Kenneth M. Pollack. (2001) Let Us Now Praise Great Men: Bringing the Statesman Back In. *International Security* 25: 107–46.

Davenport, Deborah, Lynn M. Wagner and Chris Spence. (2012) Earth Negotiations on a Comfy Couch: Building Negotiator Trust through Innovative Processes. In *The Roads from Rio: Lessons Learned from Twenty Years of Multilateral Environmental Negotiations*, edited by Pamela S. Chasek and Lynn M. Wagner. Abingdon: Routledge.

Deitelhoff, N., and H. Muller. (2005) Theoretical Paradise – Empirically Lost? Arguing with Habermas. *Review of International Studies* 31: 167–79.

Depledge, Joanna. (2005) *The Organization of Global Negotiations: Constructing the Climate Change Regime*. London: Earthscan.

Depledge, Joanna (2007) A Special Relationship: Chairpersons and the Secretariat in the Climate Change Negotiations. *Global Environmental Politics* 7: 45–68.

Falkner, Robert. (2002) Negotiating the Biosafety Protocol: The International Process. In *The Cartagena Protocol on Biosafety: Reconciling Trade in Biotechnology with Environment and Development*, edited by Christoph Bail, Robert Falkner and Helen Marquard. London: Earthscan.

Falkner, Robert. (2009) The Global Politics of Precaution: Explaining International Cooperation on Biosafety. In *Cooperating without America: Theories and Case Studies of Non-Hegemonic Regimes*, edited by Stefan Brem and Kendall W. Stiles. Abingdon: Routledge.

George, Alexander L., and Andrew Bennett. (2005) *Case Studies and Theory Development in the Social Sciences*. Bcsia Studies in International Security. Cambridge, MA: MIT Press.

Goldstein, Judith, and Robert O. Keohane. (1993) *Ideas and Foreign Policy: Beliefs, Institutions, and Political Change*. Cornell Studies in Political Economy. Ithaca, NY: Cornell University Press.

Gusterson, Hugh. (2008) Ethnographic Research. In *Qualitative Methods in International Relations: A Pluralist Guide. Research Methods Series*, edited by Audie Klotz and Deepa Prakash. Basingstoke: Palgrave Macmillan.

Haggard, Stephan, and Beth A. Simmons. (1987) Theories of International Regimes. *International Organization* 41: 491–517.

Hopmann, P. Terrence. (1995) Two Paradigms of Negotiation: Bargaining and Problem Solving. *The ANNALS of the American Academy of Political and Social Science* 542: 24–47.

Hopmann, P. Terrence. (2010) Synthesizing Rationalist and Constructivist Perspectives on Negotiated Cooperation. In *International Cooperation: The Extents and Limits of Multilateralism*, edited by I. William Zartman and Saadia Touval. Cambridge: Cambridge University Press.

Jawara, Fatoumata, and Aileen Kwa. (2003) *Behind the Scenes at the WTO: The Real World of International Trade Negotiations*. 2nd edn. London: Zed Books.

Jinnah, Sikina. (2012) Singing the Unsung: Secretariats in Global Environmental Politics. In *The Roads from Rio: Lessons Learned from Twenty Years of Multilateral Environmental Negotiations*, edited by Pamela S. Chasek and Lynn M. Wagner. Abingdon: Routledge.

Jönsson, Christer. (1993) Cognitive Factors in Regime Dynamics. In *Regime Theory and International Relations*, edited by Volker Rittberger and Peter Mayer. Oxford: Oxford University Press.

Jönsson, Christer. (2002) Diplomacy, Bargaining and Negotiation. In *Handbook of International Relations*, edited by Walter Carlsnaes, Thomas Risse-Kappen and Beth A. Simmons. London: Sage.

Keohane, Robert O., and David G. Victor. (2011) The Regime Complex for Climate Change. *Perspectives on Politics* 9: 7–23.

King, Gary, Robert O. Keohane and Sidney Verba. (1994) *Designing Social Inquiry: Scientific Inference in Qualitative Research*. Princeton, NJ: Princeton University Press.

Köster, Veit. (2002) The Biosafety Working Group (BSWG) Process: A Personal Account from the Chair. In *The Cartagena Protocol on Biosafety: Reconciling Trade in Biotechnology with Environment and Development*, edited by Christoph Bail, Robert Falkner and Helen Marquard. London: Earthscan.

Mayr, Juan. (2002) Environment Ministers: Colombia. In *The Cartagena Protocol on Biosafety: Reconciling Trade in Biotechnology with Environment and Development*, edited by Christoph Bail, Robert Falkner and Helen Marquard. London: Earthscan.

Mitchell, Ronald B. (2002) International Environment. In *Handbook of International Relations*, edited by Walter Carlsnaes, Thomas Risse-Kappen and Beth A. Simmons. London: Sage.

Mitchell, Ronald B. (2010) *International Politics and the Environment*. London: Sage.

Moore, Mike. (2003) *A World without Walls: Freedom, Development, Free Trade and Global Governance*. Cambridge: Cambridge University Press.

Moravcsik, Andrew. (1999) A New Statecraft? Supranational Entrepreneurs and International Cooperation. *International Organization* 53: 267–306.

Müller, Benito. (2011) *UNFCCC – the Future of the Process: Remedial Action on Process Ownership and Political Guidance*. Oxford: Climate Strategies.

O'Neill, Kate, Jörg Balsiger, and Stacy D. VanDeveer. (2004) Actors, Norms, and Impact: Recent International Cooperation Theory and the Influence of the Agent-Structure Debate. *Annual Review of Political Science* 7:149-75.

Odell, John S. (2000) *Negotiating the World Economy*. Ithaca: Cornell University Press.

Odell, John S. (2005) Chairing a WTO Negotiation. *Journal of International Economic Law* 8: 425–48.

Odell, John S. (2009) Breaking Deadlocks in International Institutional Negotiations: The WTO, Seattle, and Doha. *International Studies Quarterly* 53: 273–99.

Odell, John S. (2010) Three Islands of Knowledge About Negotiation in International Organizations. *Journal of European Public Policy* 17: 619–32.

Osherenko, Gail, and Oran R. Young. (1993) *Polar Politics: Creating International Environmental Regimes*. Cornell Studies in Political Economy. Ithaca, NY: Cornell University Press.

Risse, Thomas, and Mareike Kleine. (2010) Deliberation in Negotiations. *Journal of European Public Policy* 17: 708–26.

Rittberger, Volker, and Michael Zürn. (1990) Towards Regulated Anarchy in East-West Relations. In *International Regimes in East-West Politics*, edited by Volker Rittberger. London: Pinter.

Sebenius, James K. (1992) Negotiation Analysis: A Characterization and Review. *Management Science* 38: 18–38.

Stiles, Kendall W. (2009) Introduction: Theories of Non-Hegemonic Cooperation. In *Cooperating without America: Theories and Case Studies of Non-Hegemonic Regimes*, edited by Stefan Brem and Kendall W. Stiles. Abingdon: Routledge.

Tallberg, Jonas. (2010) The Power of the Chair: Formal Leadership in International Cooperation. *International Studies Quarterly* 54: 241–65.

Thompson, Leigh L. (2009) *The Mind and Heart of the Negotiator*. 4th edn. Boston, MA: Pearson Education.

Touval, Saadia. (2010) Negotiated Cooperation and Its Alternatives. In *International Cooperation: The Extents and Limits of Multilateralism*, edited by I. William Zartman and Saadia Touval. Cambridge: Cambridge University Press.

Ulbert, Cornelia, Thomas Risse, and Harald Müller. (2004) Arguing and Bargaining in

Multilateral Negotiations. Paper presented to the Conference on Empirical Approaches to Deliberative Politics, European University Institute, Florence.

Underdal, Arild (2002) One Question, Two Answers. In *Environmental Regime Effectiveness: Confronting Theory with Evidence*, edited by Edward L. Miles. Cambridge, MA: MIT Press.

Wagner, Lynn M. (2008) *Problem-Solving and Bargaining in International Negotiations*. International Negotiation Series, no. 5. Leiden: Martinus Nijhoff.

Waltz, Kenneth Neal. (1959) *Man, the State, and War: A Theoretical Analysis*. New York: Columbia University Press.

Weber, Max. (1946) Bureaucracy. In *From Max Weber: Essays in Sociology*, edited by H. H. Gerth and C. Wright Mills. Oxford: Oxford University Press.

Woolcock, Stephen. (2011a) *European Union Economic Diplomacy: The Role of the EU in External Economic Relations*. Global Finance Series. Farnham: Ashgate.

Woolcock, Stephen. (2011b) Factors Shaping Economic Diplomacy: An Analytical Toolkit. In *The New Economic Diplomacy: Decision-Making and Negotiation in International Economic Relations*, edited by Nicholas Bayne and Stephen Woolcock. Farnham: Ashgate.

Young, Oran R. (1989) The Politics of International Regime Formation: Managing Natural Resources and the Environment. *International Organization* 43: 349–75.

Young, Oran R. (1994) *International Governance: Protecting the Environment in a Stateless Society*. Cornell Studies in Political Economy. Ithaca, NY: Cornell University Press.

Zartman, I. William, and Saadia Touval. (2010) *International Cooperation: The Extents and Limits of Multilateralism*. Cambridge: Cambridge University Press.

Chapter 2

The fall and rise of climate negotiations

From Copenhagen to Cancún

I will now sketch the protracted process of climate negotiations since the 1990s and explain the structure of these highly complex negotiations, which have involved thousands of delegates and hundreds of far-reaching issues. For the majority of this chapter, however, I will retell the suspenseful story of the Danish and Mexican Presidencies, from the 'fall' in Copenhagen to the 'resurrection' in Cancún.

The long and winding road since 1990

Climate negotiations have been evolving over two decades (for the following, see also Depledge 2005: 3). The UN General Assembly initiated the process in 1990, and the UN Conference on Environment and Development in Rio, known as the 'Earth Summit', adopted the UN Framework Convention on Climate Change two years later. At the first COP in 1995, developed countries agreed in the Berlin mandate on specifying emission reduction targets in a new Protocol. This landmark agreement was reached in 1997 when most development countries committed to reduce emissions by, on average, 5.2 per cent between 2008 and 2012 compared to the 1990 levels in the Kyoto Protocol. The Protocol allowed flexible implementation to achieve cost-efficient mitigation. Developed countries could set up an emission trading system, and reduce emissions through projects in developing countries counting towards their own reduction commitments (Clean Development Mechanism) and through projects carried out jointly by and in developed countries (Joint Implementation).

The ensuing negotiations prepared the implementation of the Kyoto Protocol until it came into force in 2005. After its ratification by Russia, it comprised more than 55 per cent of 1990 emissions of developed countries. The summits now consisted of the Conference of the Parties to the Convention and the Conference of the Members to the Protocol.[1] Since then, parties have negotiated for the time after the first commitment period of the Kyoto Protocol in 2012. The Montreal summit therefore established a negotiation forum for the

---

1   For more convenient reading, this work will hereafter usually only refer to COP and not COP/CMP, or COP/MOP.

commitments of developed countries (Ad Hoc Working Group on Further Commitments for Annex I Parties under the Kyoto Protocol, or AWG-KP).

The next milestone marked the Bali Action Plan in 2007. This road map towards a post-Kyoto regime entailed two negotiation tracks for members of the Convention and of the Protocol. So an additional, second forum emerged next to the existing Kyoto Protocol Working Group, which included all countries (known as Ad Hoc Working Group on Long-term Cooperative Action under the Convention, or AWG-LCA). Bali was the promise to negotiate a new agreement with commitments for developed *and* developing countries within two years.

The positive momentum, however, got lost on the way towards Copenhagen. Parties adopted a passive negotiation attitude. At the Poznań COP in Poland, no one conceded ground before the summit in Denmark. Many negotiators commented on these two years as lost time without real negotiations. Copenhagen then became the highest profile summit in history, including 120 heads of state and government. However, parties could not find consensus within these intense two weeks and merely took note of the Copenhagen Accord, which had been crafted last minute by an exclusive circle of the US and emerging powers. Although countries eventually adopted the Cancún Agreements at COP-16, the latter were not legally binding as once envisioned in Bali. So, parties drafted the Durban Platform in 2011 to negotiate a binding agreement by 2015, taking effect by 2020. Since then, they have made very little progress, and most non-European countries did not join the second commitment period of the Kyoto Protocol in Doha in 2012. So, the world is now waiting for a global agreement which is currently envisioned to emerge from the Paris summit in 2015.

Understanding climate negotiations

Without doubt, climate talks are among the most complex global negotiations. They progress in multiple stages, take place in countless fora and are governed by rules that occasionally are not very straightforward (for a detailed account: Yamin and Depledge 2004). Throughout the year of one negotiation Presidency of a host country, preparatory consultations precede the summit. They are not considered official negotiations but begin to advance discussions on difficult areas and tremendously influence later developments, as they *inter alia* already engage in discussing draft texts. The Presidency can initiate consultations on contested issues that can be critical for later success given the only short two weeks of a COP. During 2010, for instance, the Presidency and the UNFCCC Secretariat organized 13 consultations among countries before Cancún, not even counting numerous bilateral meetings and talks between groups of countries.

The two-week summit of a COP entails a technical and political phase. The more technical expert negotiations last for seven to ten days. Delegates negotiate in several major groups. First, the plenary sessions of the COP and CMP are used for organizational matters and political statements, as well as for the final decision on a COP proposal. It is usually not the place for substantive negotiations due to its large size, openness to the public, and the rigidity of procedural rules (Yamin and Depledge 2004: 450). Next, several major groups broadly structure negotiations: for Copenhagen and Cancún, it was the two Ad Hoc Working Groups on Long-term Cooperative Action and on the Kyoto Protocol (AWG-LCA and AWG-KP). They largely addressed the issues of highest impact, such as emission reductions.[2]

These major groups meet regularly during a COP and are facilitated by selected delegates as chairs. They split up into dozens of informal working groups on myriad sub-issues (and often into yet another layer, known as informal consultations, or 'informal informals'). This is where the actual negotiations under these working groups are held closed to the public. Parties then make text proposals reflecting their positions. The chair finally compiles them in one document, highlights the differences between the positions and possibly issues a 'chair's text' as a compromise at some point.

The more political negotiations, known as the high-level segment, start with the arrival of ministers and occasionally heads of state and government in the second COP week. Less restricted in their negotiation mandate, they are better equipped to compromise in the final rounds. Ministers often even chair negotiations on crucial outstanding issues and negotiate for their countries bilaterally in varying circles. These salient political activities are not prescribed by fixed rules. The high-level segment culminates in the final night with a round-the-clock search for compromise, often in small exclusive circles chaired by lead organizers and politicians. Finally, the summit ends with a closing plenary session and the decision on an agreement.

The most crucial fora though are often beyond the official negotiation structure, such as negotiations in an exclusive small group (or Green Room, Friends of the Chair). They are usually set up by the organizers and key delegates. These selected representatives of the main coalitions negotiate few issues, but essential make-or-break ones, throughout the summit. The reduced complexity of less participants and issues significantly facilitates negotiations. Second, countless confidential bilateral negotiations are ongoing before and during a summit. Parties meet in conference offices of delegations, in corridors, and restaurants to resolve essential issues. Third, and entirely outside the UN process, parties negotiate in multiple other fora, such as the Major Economies Forum on Energy and Climate (MEF) and the G-8 or G-20.

Formal and informal rules guide UNFCCC negotiations. The key provision has proven to be the decision-making rule. As parties have never agreed on majority voting (Draft Rule 42), the current unwritten rule requires consensus for substantive decisions (Sabel 1997). This has repeatedly stirred turmoil in closing plenaries with diverging interpretations of the regulation. In Kyoto, Raúl Estrada reached consensus despite dissenting countries (e.g. Depledge 2005).

2   Besides, the Subsidiary Body for Implementation (SBI) and that for Scientific and Technological Advice (SBSTA) deal with implementation and technical advice.

Mexican COP President Patricia Espinosa gavelled consensus in Cancún despite the explicit objection of Bolivia. With this understanding of climate negotiations in mind, let us now dive deep into the thrilling events of their fall and rise during the successive Danish and Mexican Presidencies.

Negotiations on the brink during the Danish Presidency

The original idea of the UN climate summit in Copenhagen and preparations by the later Danish Climate and Energy Ministry date back to 2005, and so long before the summit in 2009 (Meilstrup 2010: 114).[3] In March 2007, parties gave the Presidency for COP-15 to Denmark: the government had reached its goal of hosting this possibly historic event. Denmark finally came under the spotlight with the take-over of the operational Presidency after COP-14 in Poznań on 13 December 2008.

The rollercoaster of ambitions during preparatory negotiations

Myriad preparatory negotiations within[4] and outside the UNFCCC process were held in 2009 in the run-up to the COP. After the Poland summit, delegates reconvened in Bonn in early April. Ambitions were high and the mood quite positive: 'The year started with high expectations that a deal would be sealed closing the next Kyoto period. Maybe this was naïve.'[5] For the first time, the more climate-friendly Obama administration represented the US. The central negotiations bodies (AWGs) were working towards a text to be ready for the next Bonn session in June. The group comprising developing and developed countries alike (AWG-LCA) was meant to identify elements for such a draft text for their commitments in a future global agreement. Yet, despite some progress in 'consolidating ideas... all delegates were quick to point out that not only is there a surplus of issues on the table, but also substantive disagreement...' (IISD 2009a: 13). The Kyoto Protocol group (AWG-KP) mostly discussed mitigation and related issues. Developing countries were largely dissatisfied with the very low mitigation ambition after 2012 by Kyoto parties (ibid.: 2). So the outlook seemed to be that 'everyone acknowledges that the AWG-KP is in for some rough times' (ibid.: 13).

In early June, parties returned to Bonn. The AWG-LCA expanded a 50 page draft by its Chair, released shortly before the conference, into a very comprehensive text of 200 pages.[6] A facilitator[7] commented that it turned into a 'compendium

---

3   Denmark(5)-12.08.2011.
4   For an account of UNFCCC meetings see the comprehensive IISD's *Earth Negotiations Bulletin* (www.iisd.ca/enbvol/enb-background.htm).
5   G-77(4)-22.07.2011.
6   FCCC/AWGLCA/2009/8 and then in the end: FCCC/AWGLCA/2009/INF.1
7   'Facilitators' are chairs of the negotiation working groups (e.g. the AWG-LCA or AWG-KP in the UNFCCC negotiations), key hosts (e.g. the COP President or a lead official), and senior treaty Secretariat officials (e.g. the UNFCCC Executive Secretary).

made of negotiation positions instead of a joint text'.[8] The antagonistic mood between parties became evident when 'they were all looking for *their* parts in later drafts [of the LCA text]. Even the attribution of the text parts to the authoring country was still included. It took three entire meetings to take them out.'[9] Among other issues, parties fought over the legal form of a future comprehensive agreement. While many developed and highly vulnerable developing countries favoured a legally binding form, larger developing countries were opposed. Analysts at the time increasingly saw the need for political vision and guidance and counted on upcoming non-UNFCCC summits like the G-8 and MEF for this (IISD 2009b: 24). Countries seemed too far apart for a legally binding outcome.[10]

The Kyoto Protocol group continued negotiations on mitigation without major progress at 'Bonn II'. One struggle was over whether to fix new individual and aggregate reduction targets or new quantification rules first. Parties could eventually not even agree on a mandate for their chair to prepare a text to amend the Kyoto Protocol in Copenhagen. So a concluding analysis echoed the result of the other working group: '[M]any suspect ... that significant political hurdles must be overcome to reach agreement under the AWG-KP in Copenhagen' (IISD 2009b: 24).

In between the official UNFCCC sessions, the Danish Presidency organized numerous informal meetings for a more candid dialogue between key parties. One such non-public gathering by 30 ministers and heads of delegations was the Greenland Dialogue in the Arctic town of Illulissat in early July. It was an important meeting for the Presidency as it 'got ministers started to really talk politics'.[11] The most tangible outcome was a confirmation of the goal to keep the temperature rise to a maximum of 2°C and a call for continued political consultation before the COP (Hedegaard 2009).

The US-sponsored Major Economies Forum on Energy and Climate (MEF) was another series of meetings between April and October. They met at leadership level for the first time at the G-8 Summit in L'Aquila, Italy, also in early July. It proved to be an important milestone on the way to Copenhagen. After very tough, line by line all-night negotiations in Rome just before the start[12] and hard negotiations between China and the US[13] the MEF confirmed the 2°C goal. The outcome received great public attention as this was the first time on a leadership level despite the previous resistance by China and India (MEF 2009: 2).[14] It was a breakthrough[15] and was one basis of the later Copenhagen Accord.[16] The US saw it as an important step to a new, bottom-up structure, which would replace

8   Mexico(3)-15.06.2011.
9   AWG/SB-Chair(4)-14.06.2011.
10   Umbrella Group(3)-14.06.2011.
11   Denmark(2)-16.06.2011.
12   EU/EU-country(10)-16.08.2011.
13   Denmark(3)-11.08.2011.
14   Umbrella Group(2)-02.06.2011.
15   EU/EU-country(10)-16.08.2011.
16   Denmark(3)-11.08.2011.

commitments for countries so far determined by a top-down process.[17] The G-8 had been the first meeting with newly appointed Danish Prime Minister Lars Løkke Rasmussen. He found 'his [G-8] colleagues...frustrated with the UNFCCC process...A common understanding emerged that a potential outcome, designed by the presidency, ought to be tested in bilateral meetings on the level of heads of state' (Meilstrup 2010: 124).

The next UNFCCC meeting in Bonn in mid-August revealed a sense of urgency. The AWG-LCA produced complementary material, such as reading guides to the rearranged 200 pages of negotiation text.[18] The latter stayed nearly unchanged, with 2,000 brackets (IISD 2009c: 1) resulting in its nickname 'the brick'. The AWG-KP made no concrete progress either, discussing 'top-down' versus 'bottom-up' approaches. Chair John Ashe stated that 'we will have to work twice as hard in Bangkok in six weeks' (IISD 2009c: 7). In a media briefing on the last day, UN climate chief Yvo de Boer warned that 'at this rate, we will not make it' (UNFCCC Secretariat 2009).

The meetings outside the UNFCCC process moved forward on their way towards a political agreement. In mid-September, the UN Secretary-General hosted a high-level event on climate change for more than 100 heads of state and government in New York. Many participants supported the 2°C goal and a 50 per cent emission reduction below the 1990 levels by 2050 (Ban 2009). On the fringes of the high-level event, Rasmussen received an informal mandate by UN Secretary-General Ban Ki-moon and several leaders to begin 'testing a compromise proposal with a number of leaders from both developing and developed countries' (Meilstrup 2010: 124). The emerging text was supposed to combine both AWG-outcomes as one final COP-15 document (*ibid.*: 125). In parallel, the ministerial Greenland Dialogue in New York advanced on key issues. Indian Environment Minister Jairam Ramesh presented constructive suggestions on the measurement, reporting and verification of commitments of parties (MRV), which later formed one core part of the Accord.[19] Overall however, tactics seemed to increase at the Greenland Dialogue with the approaching summit.[20]

In early October, negotiators got together in Bangkok again in the official UNFCCC process. The overall bones of contention in the AWG-LCA remained unchanged. Developing countries worried that the principle of 'common but differentiated responsibilities' was being watered down for emission reduction commitments. At the same time, some saw '"extremely positive" signals coming from key developing countries such as Brazil, China and India' given ambitious national mitigation plans (IISD 2009d: 19). Nevertheless, many countries still considered a low-carbon economy as a risk.[21] On finance, developed countries

17   Umbrella Group(2)-02.06.2011.
18   FCCC/AWGLCA/2009/INF.2.
19   EU/EU-country(10)-16.08.2011.
20   EU/EU-country(9)-26.05.2011.
21   EU/EU-country(8)-05.05.2011.

still put no specific numbers on the table. Eventually, the LCA text was hardly manageable after Bangkok. '[W]e had come back with a monster with 200 pages full of brackets.'[22] The Kyoto group did not advance either. They could neither agree on further mitigation steps nor on a framework of the new agreement. Would the Kyoto Protocol continue separately or be merged with new LCA obligations into a new overarching deal (IISD 2009d: 19)? Overall, the main coalitions seemed deeply divided,[23] and observers were concerned about the 'distrust and entrenched positions' at this point of negotiations (IISD 2009d: 19).

The resumed AWGs meeting in Barcelona in early November did not lead to any real progress either, despite the display of constructive openness by ministers in another Greenland Dialogue just one week earlier.[24] Analysts now observed the downplaying of expectations and that the 'meeting amplified... divergent interests, polarization, frustration and mistrust between developed and developing countries' (IISD 2009e: 17). Negotiators across the board were disappointed as a legally binding agreement seemed increasingly out of reach.[25] 'I even used points of order because the way of discussion was not conducive to getting to an outcome.'[26] The AWG-LCA did neither fully clarify the options for Copenhagen nor streamline the text (IISD 2009e: 15). The Green Fund on climate financing draft illustrates the antagonism. The same ideas were listed one after another just because they were from different parties.[27] LCA Chair Zammit Cutajar eventually acknowledged that Copenhagen would lead to several COP decisions but not a legally binding outcome. The AWG-KP kept the battle lines of the previous sessions.

Between the Bangkok and Barcelona meetings, simmering Danish power struggles now fully erupted among the teams of Prime Minister Rasmussen, headed by Bo Lidegaard, and of Climate and Energy Minister Connie Hedegaard, led by Thomas Becker. Allegations over mishandled travel expenses made Becker resign on 16 October. The Presidency lost the person who had the idea of hosting the COP in Denmark, convinced the Danish government in 2005, and briefly later got Brazil to transfer its hosting right as it had been in line for COP-15 (Meilstrup 2010: 115). The promise to Brazil and other developing countries was to conduct a Presidency unbiased to developed countries, to work towards a legally binding agreement, and to ensure strong financial assistance.[28] The Danish Presidency lost a well-known, trusted person with Becker's resignation.

After the exit of their principal rival, the preference of the Prime Minister's team for a political agreement was quickly followed. Rasmussen now downscaled

22   G-77(4)-22.07.2011.
23   BASIC(2)-16.06.2011.
24   Denmark(3)-11.08.2011.
25   Umbrella Group(4)-04.07.2011.
26   Mexico(3)-15.06.2011.
27   Mexico(3)-15.06.2011.
28   Denmark(5)-12.08.2011.

ambitions, publicly advertising the option of 'one agreement, two steps' at an international meeting of parliamentarians in Copenhagen on 26 October (Meilstrup 2010: 125), an idea that had been shared by the US and Rasmussen's team for a while. A political agreement of COP-15 would soon be followed by a legally binding one. Most parties thereby became aware that another kind of agreement was not possible at Copenhagen: 'It also helped to lower expectations. No one else had dared to say it before.'[29] This was a blow against the Climate and Energy Ministry and Hedegaard, who was supposedly furious about the announcement.[30] It aggravated the internal Danish strife, which reflected the general deep divisions over the goal of the negotiation: 'At that point there was no way to get consensus on what parties want: a full completion of the Bali Roadmap, or a reduced scope with work left over after Copenhagen.'[31]

Officials from the Climate and Energy Ministry recall that '[telephone] calls from all over the world...asking "what the hell is this?"' came after Rasmussen's announcement: parties were disappointed that the Danish promise to work towards a legally binding deal was no longer kept.[32] In the following weeks, Rasmussen spread this approach, such as at an ASEAN-US summit in Singapore in mid-November in the presence of Obama and other leaders (New York Times 2009a). The two-step approach left developing countries nervous (Meilstrup 2010: 127). They had been unsatisfied since the COP in Bali that their commitments in the overarching LCA track should be pinned down simultaneously to, and not later than, those of developed countries in a second Kyoto Protocol period.[33] They considered this treatment extremely unfair.

The preparatory summit meeting in Copenhagen with 40 ministers tried to give a last push to the dynamic of the negotiations in mid-November. Hedegaard and de Boer applauded the 'very good spirit' in the final press conference and reported the affirmation of the 2°C goal (Hedegaard and De Boer 2009). The day before, the US and Chinese Presidents had even declared at a bilateral to aim for a COP-15 result with immediate operational effects. At the same time, the Hedegaard team remained nervous due to the two-step strategy and bilateral Danish talks about a compromise proposal by the Presidency (Meilstrup 2010: 127). Selected countries saw a draft version of such a 'Danish text' at this pre-COP (IISD 2009f: 28).

One week before COP-15, an even smaller group of 20 to 30 countries met informally in Copenhagen to assess the potential Presidency compromise. At the demand of the US, China and Russia – and despite Hedegaard's objection for fear of leakage – the suggested compromise text was sent out to participants before

29   Mexico(3)-15.06.2011.
30   Denmark(5)-12.08.2011.
31   BASIC(3)-08.07.2011.
32   Denmark(5)-12.08.2011.
33   EU/EU-country(10)-16.08.2011.

the meeting (Meilstrup 2010: 127). Rasmussen's team was very positive about the reaction of countries to the draft recalling that the 'spirit was great'.[34]

The turbulent start of the Copenhagen summit

Finally, after one year of preparatory negotiations COP-15/MOP-5 opened in Copenhagen on Monday 7 December, to last until Saturday 19 December. It was originally meant as an endpoint to the negotiations guided by the Bali Roadmap towards a comprehensive, new climate deal. Yet, the preceding behaviour already shed bad light on its prospects: these 'were two years without any sense of urgency between the parties.'[35] Many found that negotiations 'only really started in Copenhagen itself'[36] and characterized negotiations before as 'superficial' and 'philosophical'.[37] At this point, hopes for the 'big bang' of a comprehensive deal were only dim. Public interest in the summit was bigger than ever. Forty thousand representatives of countries, civil society, and media had applied for registration. As the venue of the Bella Center held only 15,000 people, thousands waited long hours in the cold outside to register with many eventually left outside (IISD 2009f: 28).

Inside the Bella Center, countries started negotiating in the principal subsidiary bodies outlined above, with the AWGs dealing with the key political issues. From 8 December onwards, the AWG-LCA negotiated on all elements of the Bali Action Plan, such as mitigation, finance, and technology transfer. The one contact group split into multiple informal drafting groups. Starting the same day, AWG-KP Chair Ashe stressed to focus on the amendments to the Kyoto Protocol and especially post-2012 emission reduction targets and flexibility mechanisms (IISD 2009f: 19).

Also on Tuesday, mistrust was aggravated by the publication of a 'Danish text' in the British newspaper *The Guardian*. It had probably been leaked by one of the few countries asked for feedback by the Presidency beforehand. China[38] or even a larger 'G-77 conspiracy'[39] was suspected. Major developed countries assumed that some parties thereby wanted to undermine agreement.[40] At the time of publication, the text was an outdated version from 29 November (*Guardian* 2009a), and its origins were from much earlier that year. The Danish Climate and Energy Ministry had to agree to write a text for the Danish government as a working document for the negotiations that took the entire administration on board.[41]

34   Denmark(4)-12.08.2011; similar: EU/EU-country(2)-20.11.2010.
35   EU/EU-country(3)-03.12.2010.
36   AWG/SB-Chair(4)-14.06.2011.
37   EU/EU-country(10)-16.08.2011.
38   E.g. EU/EU-country(6)-16.03.2011, EU/EU-country(3)-03.12.2010.
39   Denmark(2)-16.06.2011.
40   Umbrella Group(3)-14.06.2011, EU/EU-country(10)-16.08.2011.
41   Denmark(2)-16.06.2011.

The leaked text drastically deepened suspicion that the Presidency was holding negotiations parallel to the UNFCCC tracks to prepare a final compromise. However, several fiercely protesting countries, such as Sudan, had seen the draft at the small group meeting in early December in Copenhagen (Meilstrup 2010: 128). Many developing countries were upset by what they considered a bias towards developed countries (*Guardian* 2009b). The leaked version though was only the LCA part of the 'Danish text' referring to a KP-decision in a separate document in its headline. Nonetheless, even UN officials and Danish Presidency members[42] saw a severe US bias in the LCA text itself. Rasmussen's team had prioritized getting the US on board. The accusation was made that they 'spoke early and lengthy to the Americans but went quite late to the developing countries'.[43] De Boer and many others attributed a major impact on the COP to this leakage: 'The Danish letter...destroyed two years of effort in one fell swoop' (Meilstrup 2010: 129).[44]

Negotiations stalled in the following days. Zammit Cutajar made another attempt to table a chair's text for the AWG-LCA on Thursday as a middle-ground between the leaked 'Danish text' and the former LCA text – yet it now seemed to favour developing countries.[45] Moreover, the text was not used well on its way up the levels.[46] Ministers were soon in a disorienting position between expert negotiators and the arriving heads of state, so the usually key ministerial process became 'a farce'.[47] Negotiations were in an 'abysmal state...It was catastrophic.'[48] A Danish official admitted that their original strategy did not materialize: 'After the first week was over, it was still "Monday"'.[49] At the beginning of the second week, there was still no sign of consensus with the same debates continuing.[50] Now, people 'progressively panicked that they would not get to an agreement, which made things worse.'[51]

The dynamics culminated in the middle of the second week. The delegates of the key negotiations working groups officially handed over their work to their arriving leaders. During the night to Wednesday the groups held their closing plenaries. The closing report of the group on the Kyoto Protocol revealed the prevailing disagreements on core issues.[52] According to Chair Ashe parties had made 'significant progress' but couldn't agree on new mitigation goals after the

---

42   UNFCCC Secretariat(1)-28.04.2010, Denmark(3)-11.08.2011.
43   UNFCCC Secretariat(2)-04.12.2010.
44   EU/EU-country(4)-27.01.2011, EU/EU-country(8)-05.05.2011, UNFCCC Secretariat(4)-17.05.2011.
45   UNFCCC Secretariat(2)-04.12.2010.
46   UNFCCC Secretariat(5)-14.06.2011.
47   UNFCCC Secretariat(5)-14.06.2011, UNFCCC Secretariat(1)-28.04.2010.
48   UNFCCC Secretariat(1)-28.04.2010.
49   Denmark(1)-02.12.2010.
50   EU/EU-country(8)-05.05.2011.
51   UNFCCC Secretariat(1)-28.04.2010.
52   FCCC/KP/AWG/2009/L.14 and 15.

Kyoto Protocol would run out in 2012 (IISD 2009f: 10). The group on long-term commitments for all parties held its closing plenary in the early morning, from 4.45am to 6.50am. After year-long negotiations, parties were still so divided that they could only agree to forward the entire textual package[53] as 'unfinished business' to their leaders (IISD 2009f: 18). Despite some progress on adaptation, technology, and REDD, the critical issues of mitigation and finance remained highly contested (ibid.: 27). The group's closing plenary was perceived as 'an awful mudslinging' and occasionally 'free of any respect': 'People fought like crazy... The expectation was that heads of states would rescue us.'[54]

The arrival of the leaders

On Wednesday morning, 16 December, the high-level segment opened with around 120 heads of state and government, turning 'Copenhagen' into the largest summit on one specific issue in history. Danish Prime Minister Rasmussen took over the Presidency from Climate Minister Hedegaard who became 'the COP President's Special Representative'. The change deepened the divide inside the Danish organizers. The official line was that the chairing by a head of government was more appropriate given the large presence of leaders. Yet, the team around Hedegaard feared a lack of support for the Prime Minister since many parties associated the leaked 'Danish text' with him (Meilstrup 2010: 130). Moreover, the Climate Minister 'hoped that there was more collaboration. Yet, there were more and more people from the Prime Minister's team invading space, people that had never done anything on climate change.' Many parties were puzzled by the switch,[55] 'not knowing what this meant'.[56] A G-77 negotiator doubted the official reason in harsh words ('this is bullshit') and suspected that Hedegaard was 'taken out' for political reasons.[57]

In the COP plenary, Hedegaard had still announced putting forward a compromise proposal later that day 'based substantially on the two texts forwarded by the AWGs' (IISD 2009f: 4). This had been the Danish 'Plan B' for a potential stalemate at the beginning of the high-level segment (Meilstrup 2010: 130). There was an 'explosion' by many countries as an immediate reaction.[58] They had not been able to see the texts beforehand and insisted that the work of both core negotiation bodies, produced over a long time and just now with an 'overnight marathon', was the only legitimate base for negotiations. Others welcomed the compromise proposal as the only way out given the short time left and the state of the current texts (IISD 2009f: 28). Rasmussen held

53   FCCC/AWGLCA/2009/L.7 and Adds.1-9.
54   EU/EU-country(9)-26.05.2011.
55   Mexico(3)-15.06.2011.
56   Denmark(2)-16.06.2011.
57   G-77(2)-13.06.2011.
58   UNFCCC Secretariat(5)-14.06.2011.

informal consultations throughout the day and night on how to proceed (*ibid.*: 4), with negotiations on substance essentially suspended. In the reconvened plenary that evening, many G-77 countries expressed their worry that the process was neither transparent nor inclusive. AWG-LCA Chair Zammit Cutajar then forwarded the LCA report and texts to the summit plenary (*ibid.*: 4). It was a far from completed and workable text for leaders to negotiate with.

In the Thursday noon summit plenaries on the next day, Rasmussen confirmed that remaining negotiations would be based on the documents produced by delegates in their working groups so far. The compromise texts, 'the jewel in the crown of the Danish strategy' (Meilstrup 2010: 131), prepared by the Danish Presidency and reiterated with key parties for months were never tabled. Instead, a contact group under Hedegaard was created that split into numerous drafting groups to address the critical, unresolved issues. Yet, the parallel negotiations on the expert and leader levels proved disadvantageous. After a productive start, the expert level lost momentum with the announcement that the Danish Prime Minister would conduct additional facilitation in a leaders' meeting on Thursday evening.[59] Tensions in expert working groups were high. One room even discussed whether to put another set of brackets from beginning to end in a text that was already fully bracketed – with brackets indicating areas of disagreement.[60] Delegates reported to the contact group on their progress on late Thursday evening (IISD 2009f: 5). After an intense discussion on the process forward, Hedegaard decided that the drafting groups would continue and that a 'friends of the Chair' group would be established (IISD 2009f: 6).

Parallel to this work of delegates, the Danish Queen hosted a dinner for heads of state and government on Thursday evening. There, Rasmussen organized support among leaders for negotiating a shorter, political agreement on the core issues in the final hours of Copenhagen (Meilstrup 2010: 131). So later that evening, a meeting of 28 heads of state and government, presided over by Rasmussen's adviser Lidegaard, began negotiating a final compromise. It broke down on a leader level around 2am. Ministers continued without success until 6.30am. Among others, representatives of all major economies, the heads of G-77 and the Alliance of Small Island States (AOSIS) were present. Yet, no delegate of the Latin American ALBA group participated, which had many non-mainstream positions.[61] The selection of this salient small group became highly contested. The Danes had nominated participants after consultations with UN Secretary-General Ban: 'If we had asked the Sudanese Chair of the G-77, for

59   UNFCCC Secretariat(5)-14.06.2011.
60   Umbrella Group(3)-14.06.2011.
61   Delegations in this small group (EU/EU-country(10)-16.08.2011): Algeria, Australia, Bangladesh, Brazil, China, Colombia, Ethiopia, Sweden, European Commission, Gabon, Germany, France, Grenada, India, Indonesia, Japan, Republic of Korea, Lesotho, Maldives, Mexico, Norway, Poland, Russian Federation, Saudi Arabia, South Africa, Spain, Sudan, UK, US.

instance, to nominate countries, it would not have happened.'[62] When the meeting started, all participating delegates supported the process, the group's composition, and the text as a working document, according to a Danish official.[63] Outside, the selection process was heavily criticized. Countries could for instance not nominate their regional representatives for this crucial meeting.[64] Another Dane described that the selection of people 'sent the whole Bella Center crazy'.[65] This was unfortunate as there had been some positive dynamic during the day through several major players that built up to 'one possible moment'. The EU had pushed its 30 per cent goal, US Secretary of State Hilary Clinton had declared to mobilize US$100 billion, and Brazil had said they would act domestically on mitigation.[66] The dynamic, however, vanished in the late hours of that night.

The textual starting base for the small group was also problematic as leaders found they 'could not work' with the 'substandard' text from expert negotiations.[67] The Danish Presidency had supposedly not detailed how to merge the outcomes of the key expert working groups and input from ministerial work so that 'it never happened'.[68] In this situation, leaders apparently told the Danish Prime Minister's team in bilateral talks at the end of the second week that 'they must present something now'.[69] In response, they began the Thursday night meeting with a draft of a short, political Accord rather than the comprehensive, legally binding alternative that had been negotiated for two years. A longer and more concrete version of the short draft (with the same political content) had been welcomed at the Copenhagen meeting one week before the COP.[70] The shorter text was mainly a product of the so-called 'writing team', which consisted of various Danish ministries led by the Prime Minister's team and Hedegaard's advisory group of eight international negotiators and experts.[71]

On this basis, heads of state and government were negotiating the text line by line, with the BASIC leaders mostly absent, however.[72] The setting created stellar stress for all: leaders 'were not used to negotiate an agreement all by themselves. They had done line-by-line negotiations last time at the 1945 post-war meeting in Potsdam.'[73] During this meeting, the UNFCCC Secretariat did not play any significant role: de Boer was present but largely abstained from

62   Denmark(4)-12.08.2011.
63   Denmark(4)-12.08.2011.
64   EU/EU-country(8)-05.05.2011.
65   Denmark(3)-11.08.2011.
66   EU/EU-country(7)-04.05.2011.
67   UNFCCC Secretariat(5)-14.06.2011.
68   Denmark(2)-16.06.2011.
69   Denmark(4)-12.08.2011.
70   Denmark(4)-12.08.2011.
71   Denmark(3)-11.08.2011.
72   Denmark(4)-12.08.2011.
73   EU/EU-country(10)-16.08.2011.

interfering in a negotiation of more than 20 heads of state and government.[74] With the takeover by Rasmussen, the Secretariat also lost much of its influence.

During the same night, at 3am on Friday 18 December, Hedegaard's contact group of expert negotiators reconvened parallel to the leader's level to hear back from the drafting groups. Several parties now called for political guidance on the numerous outstanding issues (IISD 2009f: 6). Delegates were confused and frustrated by these parallel negotiations led by Hedegaard on one side and by Rasmussen on the other. The Prime Minister worked on a compromise document behind the scenes that was scarcely linked to the large other part of the negotiations.[75]

The final collapse

Throughout Friday, negotiation levels remained disconnected with expert negotiations largely on hold. 'Many well-known negotiators were seen nervously waiting in the corridors with everyone else. Presidents and Prime Ministers, followed by their entourages and journalists, were seen rushing from one meeting to another' (IISD 2009f: 28), for instance to one high-level US–Chinese bilateral.[76] Many believed until Friday afternoon that something would happen to save the summit.[77]

Meanwhile, the high-level group of 28 had continued its work from the night before in the Jacobsen Room of the Bella Center. One key problem was a struggle between the US not to commit to more mitigation than 17 per cent below the 2005 level by 2020, and China not to allow for international controls of its emission reductions (Meilstrup 2010: 131). The mood inside the room was 'horrible'.[78] China was only represented by one lead negotiator, He Yafei, despite the Prime Minister's presence at the summit. Fellow heads of states in the group received this badly. French President Nicolas Sarkozy even accused the Chinese of hypocrisy at one point (Rapp *et al.* 2009). There seemed 'a lack of respect' between participants, and Rasmussen supposedly 'allowed for a mere ping-pong between China and the US... He didn't even give the floor to Merkel, Sarkozy or the Japanese Prime Minister when they wanted to speak.'[79] Apart from the small group, the sense of a 'G-2' negotiation between the US and China was widely shared.[80] Even the UN had been sidelined by that time. Ban and de Boer were both in the small group meeting. Rasmussen largely ignored the UNFCCC Secretariat and was, if anything, only relating to the UN Secretary-General.[81]

---

74 UNFCCC Secretariat(4)-17.05.2011.
75 UNFCCC Secretariat(2)-04.12.2010.
76 Umbrella Group(2)-02.06.2011.
77 EU/EU-country(9)-26.05.2011.
78 EU/EU-country(9)-26.05.2011.
79 Umbrella Group(4)-04.07.2011.
80 G-77(2)-13.06.2011.
81 UNFCCC Secretariat(4)-17.05.2011.

Furthermore, the 'New York UN' also seemed to be on the margins.[82] 'If 20 heads of states negotiate, you don't get in the way' commented a UN official.[83] So the key role among organizers was played by the Danish Prime Minister.

During a lunch break, Obama reached out in vain to fellow leaders to assess what they needed to forge a deal. His attempts for another bilateral with China, or one with India, South Africa or Brazil, were rejected.[84] The small group meeting was resumed in the afternoon until the Chinese head negotiator asked for an interruption to consult with his Prime Minister at around 4pm (Rapp et al. 2009). The circle never reconvened. Instead, the BASIC leaders Wen, Singh, Lula and Zuma had gathered to discuss the situation of the summit in a non-scheduled meeting, for which the Indian Prime Minister even returned from the airport. They debated whether to take on more commitments and how to ensure higher support for their implementation.[85]

Having heard of the meeting when searching for the Chinese Prime Minister, Obama forced his way into the BASIC room around 7pm to seek a possible compromise.[86] All other countries, including economic powers such as the EU or Japan, and all organizers from Denmark or the UN, were left outside.[87] They only gradually learnt about this last decisive negotiation. When Obama joined, the BASIC leaders were ending their meeting and about to release a press text, reported a US official.[88] Instead, US–BASIC negotiations started building on the draft Accord from the preceding small group negotiations of 28 except for two brackets on MRV.[89] Heads of state and government were drafting an agreement in a kind of emergency operation.[90] A Danish Presidency member judged from outside that 'the most important which happened was to link [the main body of] the text and the Annex'.[91] It implied the acceptance of this structure by China to also submit its targets equally with other countries in the Annex and subject them to a text that included language on MRV. Owing to the long Western infringement of Chinese sovereignty, he said that 'never before the last day of Copenhagen had the Chinese accepted that MRV would be done on their emissions…it took the active, dramatic intervention by Wen' for this.[92] China's difficulty to agree was also revealed afterwards by the lack of a clear line about interpreting the Accord.[93] The US in turn conceded on MRV. They accepted a

82   EU/EU-country(10)-16.08.2011.
83   UNFCCC Secretariat(4)-17.05.2011.
84   Umbrella Group(2)-02.06.2011, Denmark(4)-12.08.2011.
85   BASIC(2)-16.06.2011.
86   Umbrella Group(2)-02.06.2011.
87   Denmark(4)-12.08.2011.
88   Umbrella Group(2)-02.06.2011.
89   Denmark(4)-12.08.2011.
90   EU/EU-country(6)-16.03.2011.
91   Denmark(4)-12.08.2011.
92   Denmark(4)-12.08.2011.
93   EU/EU-country(10)-16.08.2011.

global MRV methodology leaving their original position of always implementing international agreements in their own way.[94] Another major US concession was to approve of different intensities of MRV for developing and developed countries.[95] Last but not least, developed countries' financing promises had fulfilled a non-negotiable need of developing countries.[96]

A leading Danish politician blamed the Presidency for a miserable preparation:

> There was no contingency plan for the unforeseen, chaotic developments of the last days, for example not even the availability of a productive meeting room when the final round of leaders met with Obama. They were cramped in a room of a few square meters only, with hardly any air left after some time had passed.[97]

A senior BASIC negotiator commended Obama for his facilitation:

> I was extremely impressed by Obama: how he saw the importance of having the largest emitters of tomorrow inside an agreement. Overall, he gave a masterly performance. He got the key concerns of the big leaders on board, [also to] bring in fast start and long-term financing which was needed and essential to get.[98]

Having finished the meeting around 10.30pm, Obama made a five-minute announcement to the press before returning to the US. He started by saying that '[t]oday, we have made a meaningful and unprecedented breakthrough here in Copenhagen' (*New York Times* 2009b). He then referred the breakthrough to the US–BASIC negotiation and acknowledged that he was 'leaving before the final vote but we feel confident that we are moving in the direction of a significant accord' (*ibid.*). Despite these caveats, most delegations were furious about the process as they had not even seen the compromise at the time of the announcement.

The proposal was forwarded to negotiations in the group of 28, while the word spread on its key elements. The Presidency also had to convince the Secretariat of the text, which was 'extremely hostile' and turned into a 'negotiation in itself',[99] according to a senior Danish official. Tensions between the Presidency and developing countries were also high. Leading G-77 representatives said they were supposed to meet with Rasmussen to discuss the proposal. According to

94 Denmark(4)-12.08.2011.
95 EU/EU-country(10)-16.08.2011.
96 ALBA(2)-09.12.2011.
97 Denmark(1)-02.12.2010.
98 BASIC(2)-16.06.2011.
99 Denmark(4)-12.08.2011.

them, they waited for him for an hour and when Sudanese negotiator Ibrahim Mohammed Izzeldin reached out to Rasmussen 'he did not want to speak to him'.[100] They described this incident as 'highly impolite and very uncourteous'. In the following plenary, Hedegaard noted that they 'consulted the G-77 but they didn't want it'. A senior negotiator and lead Danish officials shared the latter interpretation of the incident.[101]

Finally, at 3am on Saturday 19 December, the closing plenaries of the summit began. Rasmussen now officially introduced the 'Copenhagen Accord', suggesting to parties to consult on the text for one hour and then return to the plenary. Delegates severely criticized this 'take it or leave it' approach: 'You can't do that. In these kinds of negotiations this is normally a bad idea and has to be the last resort. In Copenhagen, it came too soon and was furthermore even badly handled.'[102] A heated debate followed (IISD 2009f: 7–9). In particular those countries excluded from negotiating the Accord in the group of 28 countries or in the US–BASIC group heavily criticized the process. In particular, Venezuela, Bolivia, Nicaragua and Cuba of the ALBA group raised strong objections. A developed country negotiator described how many were taken by surprise: 'All their flags were the first to go up ... [We] were shocked by the Bolivarians [sic] as how prepared and coordinated their attack was. We were surprised by it, and so were the Europeans.'[103] Most criticism focused on process, such as the lack of transparency and inclusiveness. One extreme example of the objection to substance and of the debate's intensity was Sudan's comparison of the disastrous consequences of a temperature rise of more than 1.5°C, as suggested by the Accord, to the Holocaust. Nonetheless, most countries supported the compromise, among them the 'spokespersons for AOSIS, LDCs and the African Group' (IISD 2009f: 28), who represent highly vulnerable countries. Yet the US and BASIC leaders could no longer use their political and rhetorical weight to advocate their compromise as they had left Copenhagen, like many of their colleagues. It could have made the decisive difference.[104]

During the debate, the Danish Prime Minister committed grave procedural mistakes and largely lacked control of the plenary. It was 'crazy and chaotic. Parties jumped on the stage when they tried to get the Accord accepted.'[105] At one point, Rasmussen called for a vote which UNFCCC rules exclude as they demand consensus. Next, he addressed the plenary stating he was 'not [to be] familiar with your procedures'.[106] Combined with the ill will generated earlier by *inter alia* the 'Danish text', the atmosphere turned hostile towards a visibly

100 On this incident: G-77(2)-13.06.2011.
101 Mexico(3)-15.06.2011, Denmark(6)-09.02.2012, Denmark(3)-11.08.2011.
102 Mexico(3)-15.06.2011.
103 Umbrella Group(2)-02.06.2011.
104 Umbrella Group(1)-20.04.2011.
105 AWG/SB-Chair(4)-14.06.2011.
106 Cf. UNFCCC-webcast: http://unfccc.int/press/multimedia/webcasts/items/5857.php.

exhausted Rasmussen. He 'was mishandled by the plenary' in a 'harsh and violent' way.[107] The COP President eventually left the podium without returning. 'He couldn't manage it anymore.'[108] Meanwhile, negotiators had also reached their physical limits, saying that 'during the last two days in Copenhagen, me and many others did not get any food or sleep from 9am on Friday to 4pm on Saturday'.[109]

After five hours of this nocturnal struggle, the plenary was suspended. UN Secretary-General Ban helped to facilitate informal consultations. After reconvening at around 10.30am, parties compromised by deciding to *take note* of the Copenhagen Accord with the option for countries to associate with the Accord after the summit and to submit reduction goals by 31 January 2010 (IISD 2009f: 9). Only a handful of parties had eventually maintained their objection, such as Venezuela, Bolivia, Nicaragua and Cuba. Nevertheless, the consensus rule prevented the adoption of the Accord. The original plan of the Prime Minister's office had failed. As envisioned, a small circle of leaders agreed on a text. Yet the team had underestimated the resistance to such a process, which eventually inhibited the 'gaveling through' in the final plenary.[110]

Taking note of the Copenhagen Accord

The turbulent Copenhagen summit came to a close just after 2pm on December 19. After long years of negotiations, parties only took note of the Accord and did not adopt any agreement.[111] On mitigation, the Accord shifted away from binding top-down emission reduction goals towards a voluntary bottom-up approach. While countries confirmed their aspiration to limit the temperature rise to 2°C, developed countries made only voluntary pledges for 2020. These will be monitored, reported, and verified. Developing countries put forward emission reductions with only domestic MRV accompanied by a limited sort of oversight through international consultation and analysis (ICA). International MRV only applies in case of foreign mitigation support. A new mechanism for REDD+ to benefit from cost-efficient mitigation through preserving forests would be installed. Overall however, no emission peak year or long-term global emissions goal was specified (IISD 2009f: 29). On finance, developed countries promised US\$30 billion for mitigation and adaptation aid to developing countries between 2010 and 2012 ('fast-start'), and the mobilization of US\$100 billion annually from public and private sources by 2020. Mechanisms were agreed for technology transfer and capacity building for developing countries to accelerate mitigation

---

107   Mexico(4)-16.06.2011.
108   UNFCCC Secretariat(7)-03.08.2011.
109   Mexico(2)-08.02.2011.
110   Denmark(3)-11.08.2011.
111   FCCC/CP/2009/11/Add.1.

and adaptation. Finally, the AWG-LCA's and AWG-KP's mandates were extended by one year.[112]

Media, observers, most negotiators and organizers reacted very negatively to the Copenhagen outcome and its negotiation management. Yvo de Boer 'called the Accord a "letter of intent" [while] Connie Hedegaard said it was "disappointing"' (Meilstrup 2010: 133). The big powers 'only agreed what they don't want, for example no legally binding outcome', conceded a senior Dane.[113] A leading Danish politician found that it 'was the biggest diplomatic effort and undertaking in recent modern Danish history with such little to no results'.[114] Another high-ranking Danish official commented that 'we had the biggest chance in the world to position ourselves so positively. We are now seen as provincial, xenophobic . . .'.[115] Many countries were disappointed that the Accord was only 'on paper' without being an official UNFCCC agreement.[116] A long-standing UN official described COP-15 as 'a traumatic experience' for many. 'It was a combination of physical fatigue and distress over the outcome. It took months to recover from this.'[117] Senior US officials 'felt terrible for Denmark. They had meant it so well. It was a colossal failure and so painful. They did not deserve this. It's going to be a long time until they get over it.'[118]

Some also identified positive elements lauding the political guidance provided by the Accord. One Danish official argued that only leaders could have achieved the 'great bargain' of Copenhagen, and Cancún showed that the deal was global consensus.[119] Acknowledging its weakness from a climate science perspective, he found it was the only attainable level: 'Despite the fuzz, the shouting, and the chaos, the last day in Copenhagen produced the greatest advance in climate history.' A UN official commented that 'we did get an agreement'[120] – regardless of the fact the COP took only note of the Accord. Some BASIC negotiators applauded the political 'agreement on the leadership level . . . and that an overall architecture came in.'[121] One observer highlighted the finance agreement and the compromise on MRV/ICA for developing countries as important steps.[122] He further noted the domestic impact of greatly raised public awareness of climate change through Copenhagen, such as in China.[123] Parts of the US administration were perceived as satisfied with the shift from a legally binding, top-down

112   FCCC/KP/CMP/2009/L.8.
113   Denmark(6)-09.02.2012.
114   Denmark(1)-02.12.2010.
115   Denmark(5)-12.08.2011.
116   Observer(3)-16.06.2011.
117   UNFCCC Secretariat(2)-04.12.2010.
118   Umbrella Group(3)-14.06.2011.
119   Denmark(4)-12.08.2011.
120   UNFCCC Secretariat(7)-03.08.2011.
121   BASIC(2)-16.06.2011, also: BASIC(4)-16.03.2012.
122   Observer(3)-16.06.2011.
123   Observer(3)-16.06.2011.

structure to a voluntary pledge-and-review system.[124] The continuity of this shift remains uncertain as debates at succeeding negotiations have shown. At the 2012 Doha summit, for instance, the top-down Kyoto framework was reconfirmed for a second period. After Copenhagen, 141 countries joined the Accord (UNFCCC Secretariat 2011), representing over 90 per cent of global emissions (Meilstrup 2010: 134).

The recovery of negotiations during the Mexican Presidency

Healing the wounds throughout 2010

With the closing of the Copenhagen summit, the incoming Mexican Presidency started to take over control of the process. The first salient endeavour was to heal the wounds from Copenhagen and to restore trust among the parties. 'Everybody was disappointed by the complete disaster in Copenhagen. It was terrible.'[125] Shock still prevailed in the first meetings in 2010: 'It was nearly like everybody was in the mood for a psychiatrist, explaining what had happened in Copenhagen.'[126]

Seeing the importance of diplomacy from COP-15, Mexican President Felipe Calderón soon decided to give the COP Presidency to the Mexican Foreign and not to the Environment Ministry, against usual practice so far. They saw the Presidency as an 'issue of chairing and negotiation skills'[127]. The designated COP President, Mexican Foreign Minister Patricia Espinosa, was a career diplomat with deep multilateral expertise. Luis Alfonso de Alba from the Foreign Office, with comparable diplomatic experience, became Mexican chief adviser. De Boer at the UN reacted with relief and the initial brief bureaucratic conflict between the Mexican Environment and Foreign Ministries was soon settled.[128] Calderón remained involved and attended Mexican stock-taking meetings on a monthly and from August onwards on a weekly basis. Externally, he reached out to fellow leaders on climate change at G-20, MEF and comparable meetings.[129]

The Mexican Presidency hosted a series of informal, topic-specific consultations throughout the year. The first meeting was in March in Mexico City on the methodology of work towards COP-16. Participants analysed COP-15 before discussing the approach for preparatory negotiations leading to Cancún.[130] Parties and organizers considered this openness on strategy and the successive meetings

124   EU/EU-country(7)-04.05.2011.
125   Umbrella Group(4)-04.07.2011.
126   Mexico(2)-08.02.2011.
127   Mexico(1)-02.02.2011.
128   Mexico(1)-02.02.2011.
129   Mexico(2)-08.02.2011.
130   Mexico(2)-08.02.2011.

as critical steps.[131] Yet, as Mexico only held the incoming Presidency, many countries also criticized the unusually proactive stance of a Presidency at the first Bonn meeting: 'the process was still in trouble . . . also the Mexicans faced problems'.[132] Afraid of a growing negative dynamic, the Presidency placated worries. One official described how Central American countries subsequently developed trust through Mexican visits: 'We know de Alba personally. He is so nice and has always played with open cards. We trust him.'[133] Dynamics improved by early summer when the informal, topic-specific consultations had become 'very popular',[134] and the Mexicans were widely trusted.[135]

A week after the first topic-specific consultation in Mexico, a group of developed and developing countries gathered for the first 'Cartagena Dialogue for Progressive Action' in Colombia. They bridged traditional dividing lines and strove for faster action than what was possible under the consensus rule. They met again in the Maldives in July and in Costa Rica in November. The dialogue continued during COP-16 and proved very helpful by feeding fresh ideas into negotiations. Also early in 2010, the UN Secretary-General's High-level Advisory Group on Climate Change Financing was initiated to develop recommendations for the summit.

The first official UNFCCC meeting of the Presidency was the AWGs' session in Bonn in early April. Bonn was intended to rally parties behind a methodological approach for the preparatory work towards COP-16 (IISD 2010a: 1). The start was rough as 'the first part of the year after Copenhagen was used for shock treatment'.[136] One even considered it 'a terrible meeting'.[137] The struggle of the LCA working group about the text mandate for their new Chair Margaret Mukahanana-Sangarwe reflected the heated final plenary of COP-15. Several developing countries rejected the Accord as an illegitimate base for her to draw upon. Among the critics were those excluded in Copenhagen, like Venezuela and Bolivia, but also some that had negotiated the text line by line, such as China and India (IISD 2010a: 11). Eventually, the Chair's draft for the June session could reference the Accord and the LCA report (ibid.: 1), and overall, parties were more conciliatory than expected after Copenhagen (ibid.: 11). As at COP-15, the Kyoto Protocol group still negotiated further mitigation commitments for developed countries and the relation to the LCA track. The Copenhagen Accord attempted to move developed and developing countries closer together in a new structure. Greater MRV notwithstanding, most developing countries defended the separate tracks.

131   BASIC(3)-08.07.2011, EU/EU-country(10)-16.08.2011, Mexico(1)-02.02.2011.
132   UNFCCC Secretariat(1)-28.04.2010.
133   Mexico(2)-08.02.2011.
134   Mexico(2)-08.02.2011.
135   UNFCCC Secretariat(1)-28.04.2010.
136   UNFCCC Secretariat(5)-14.06.2011.
137   Umbrella Group(3)-14.06.2011.

Countries increasingly worried about the future of the UNFCCC-process. One group doubted that it could deliver the required progress and considered acting through non-UNFCCC fora, such as the Norwegian–French REDD+ initiative. At the same time, many developing countries feared the loss of influence through smaller circles (IISD 2010a: 12). Countries hence softened their negotiation style, and Mexico discouraged heads of state from attending Cancún so the summit would provide expert negotiators maximum time for compromises (*ibid.*).

The smaller setting of the MEF convened several times also during 2010. Yet Mexico's lower emphasis on leaders reduced its significance for climate. Furthermore, Obama's high ambition had suffered blows from the failed climate bill in the spring and from the Republican takeover of the House of Representatives in mid-term elections in the autumn. For lack of domestic support, the US focused on MRV, which took pressure off the MEF.[138] Countering the MEF, Bolivia hosted a World's Peoples Conference in Cochabamba addressing multiple issues from the 'first world's climate debt' to additional mitigation by developed countries (IISD 2010a: 13). De Alba joined to build trust for the Mexican Presidency among more sceptical Latin American countries.[139] Mexico concentrated on countries where they felt 'attention was needed', such as Cuba, Bolivia, Venezuela or Nicaragua, but also on African Union meetings and Asian countries.[140] Connecting to the idea of an informal meeting of environmental ministers under the Greenland Dialogue, Germany and Mexico co-hosted the Petersberg Climate Dialogue in Bonn in May. Calderón expressed Mexico's strong commitment to the Presidency and supposedly reached participants with this signal.[141] Despite the meagre progress on content[142] the atmosphere was good and negotiations picked up speed.[143] Shortly afterwards, negotiators held informal consultations on climate change finance in Mexico City.

After this series of smaller, intermediate meetings, the large Bonn session convened in June. Delegates negotiated constructively with openness for dialogue and a sincere engagement with positions (IISD 2010b: 22). The LCA group discussed the newly introduced Chair's text and made some progress on finance, where the US suggested a fund accountable to the COP (*ibid.*: 23). Developing countries, however, rejected a draft with the session's revisions as unbalanced in the final plenary. The Kyoto Protocol group discussed further emission reductions and flexibility mechanisms, especially in light of the submitted pledges under the Accord that fell short of keeping the science-supported

138   EU/EU-country(10)-16.08.2011.
139   Mexico(2)-08.02.2011.
140   Mexico(3)-15.06.2011.
141   Mexico(5)-07.07.2011.
142   UNFCCC Secretariat(1)-28.04.2010.
143   EIG(1)-09.08.2011.

2°C goal. The impending expiry of the Protocol made parties address legal questions to ensure a seamless transition into a second commitment period (IISD 2010b: 1). At the end of the Bonn session, Christiana Figueres from Costa Rica took over as new UNFCCC Executive Secretary from de Boer, who left after a five-year-period, encompassing the Bali Roadmap and the Copenhagen Accord.

The G-20 dealt with climate change during the summits in Toronto in June and in Seoul in November. Seoul called for a balanced outcome in Cancún that would contain the key elements of the Bali Action Plan (IISD 2010d: 2). Yet, like the MEF, none of these summits reached the level of importance for climate negotiations seen in the previous year. In July, the Presidency hosted informal consultations in Mexico City on the contested issue of mitigation.

The last Bonn session took place in August. The LCA group discussed the new Chair's draft.[144] Similarly to the LCA text in advance of Copenhagen, the Chair criticized that parties again filled in their 'political positions' so that the draft expanded by half from 45 to 70 pages. Some even saw this expansion as a 'hostage taking' of the work (IISD 2010c: 12). The Kyoto Protocol group continued negotiations around mitigation, avoidance of a gap for the time after the period post-2012, and other mitigation-related issues including social and economic consequences of response measures (ibid.: 1). Both groups clarified options slightly so policymakers could eventually compromise in Cancún (ibid.: 12). Generally, expectations were now at a moderate level: no one 'expect[ed] a legally binding agreement in Cancún, but rather a package of implementing decisions' (ibid.).

The Geneva Dialogue on Climate Finance held by Mexico and Switzerland in September was helpful in advancing on a further essential issue for a Cancún agreement.[145] The idea of a Standing Committee for the Green Climate Fund was presented and countries confirmed the long-term finance pledges of Copenhagen.[146] Ministers met informally on climate change on the fringe of the annual UN General Assembly meeting in New York end of September. In contrast to the high-level meeting by Ban Ki-moon in 2009, heads of state and government were not involved, and there was less impact on the process.

China hosted the final meeting of working groups in Tianjin in early October. The LCA group built on the negotiation text produced after the last Bonn session[147] and generated draft material for Cancún. Parties mostly sought areas of convergence, such as REDD+ on forests and technology, and set aside issues that could not be resolved in the remaining time (IISD 2010c: 1, 12). The Kyoto Protocol group narrowed down some options within its well-known issues (ibid.: 1). Among others, the base year for calculating mitigation and the length of a

144   FCCC/AWGLCA/2010/8.
145   Mexico(2)-08.02.2011.
146   EIG(1)-09.08.2011.
147   FCCC/AWGLCA/2010/14.

potential second commitment period were highly contested, let alone the actual emission reduction numbers (*ibid.*: 15). The group's outcome resulted in a revised Chair's draft proposal for the summit.[148]

Overall, Tianjin made little progress, with some even judging it a 'total waste of time'[149] or simply 'a mess'.[150] For others, the meeting was crucial though as red lines became visible[151] with countries testing 'trial balloons' to see what would fly.[152] After Tianjin, the likeliest Cancún outcome appeared to be a set of decisions in a few issue-specific areas, which left some countries concerned that it would reduce chances of a legally binding agreement in the mid- to long term (IISD 2010c: 15, 16). Some senior Mexicans welcomed slow progress in Tianjin so countries would call for a stronger Presidency: '[We] could start right away with informal consultations in Cancún.'[153]

After Tianjin, two remaining core topics were covered in informal consultations by the Mexican Presidency. The talks on MRV and ICA in Mexico City in October were an important step for converging on this central question.[154] The Presidency had intentionally placed the most contested issues towards the end to rebuild trust first.[155] A new technology mechanism was finally discussed in an informal ministerial dialogue in New Delhi in mid-November.

Around 40 ministers and key negotiators attended the pre-COP ministerial meeting in Mexico City in early November to 'smoothen negotiations' at the upcoming summit.[156] A Mexican official found that all key players got on board there, showed great flexibility, and trusted the Presidency to conduct an open and inclusive process.[157] At this preparatory meeting, Mexico invited ministers to Cancún unusually early for the first weekend of COP-16 to facilitate negotiations in pairs of developing and developed countries. Countries crucially accepted this methodology.[158]

Just before Cancún, the MEF met on a ministerial and expert level in Crystal City, US. It asked for a 'package of decisions' on the core elements of the Bali Action Plan in Cancún (IISD 2010d: 2). India provided a refined outline for a MRV/ICA solution to enable consensus between the big players. As a US official noted: 'It was...critical as the US maintained that there would be no agreement without MRV, and China said there would be no agreement with

148   FCCC/KP/AWG/2010/CRP.3.
149   Mexico(3)-15.06.2011.
150   Umbrella Group(2)-02.06.2011.
151   UNFCCC Secretariat(7)-03.08.2011.
152   BASIC(2)-16.06.2011.
153   Mexico(3)-15.06.2011; similar: Umbrella Group(2)-02.06.2011.
154   Mexico(5)-07.07.2011.
155   Mexico(2)-08.02.2011.
156   AWG/SB-Chair(2)-04.12.2010.
157   Mexico(1)-02.02.2011.
158   UNFCCC Secretariat(7)-03.08.2011.

MRV for all.'[159] So the proposal was highly welcomed, also as a contribution from India as a major developing country making it easier for others to join.[160]

Growing confidence at the Cancún summit

After a year of intense preparations, the climate summit (or COP-16/MOP-6[161]) opened in the Moon Palace Hotel in Cancún on the Caribbean Sea on a warm and sunny Monday, 29 November, to last until Saturday 11 December. With 12,000 participants it was much smaller than Copenhagen. In the opening cere-mony, Mexican President Calderón stressed the 'open, inclusive, and transparent' process crafted by the COP Presidency to re-establish trust in the UNFCCC process.[162] Delegations welcomed this approach in the first plenary, especially those that had heavily criticized the Danish process before, such as Venezuela for the ALBA countries lauding the 'environment of trust and secu-rity'. The organizers called on parties to be pragmatic and leave out those areas that endangered reaching any outcome, repeating mantra-like that 'the perfect is the enemy of the good'. In an observer briefing, a US negotiator described the goal of COP-16 as the operationalization of issues on a concrete level, but not a comprehensive, final treaty. Despite timid optimism, there was also scepticism about reaching an agreement in the beginning.[163]

The main working groups started on Monday afternoon. The LCA Chair presented a structure of a possible outcome[164] leaving key parts such as mitigation open for parties to focus negotiations on.[165] The paper caused irritation in the run-up to the meeting as it had come without an explicit mandate by negotia-tors. Moreover, the omission of a few of their important positions produced major upheaval among G-77 countries: 'It did not even include them in brackets, and was hence very unbalanced.'[166] The LCA Chair stressed that the comprehensive Tianjin text remained valid with her new paper only meant to facilitate discus-sions (IISD 2010e: 9). In the following days, the LCA negotiators formed a contact group containing four drafting groups on shared vision, adaptation, miti-gation, as well as finance, technology, and capacity building.

Their negotiations were complemented from day one by daily informal consultations led by Mexican lead facilitator de Alba. They started with 25 participants and rose to 70 by the time COP-16 President Espinosa chaired the

159   Umbrella Group(2)-02.06.2011.
160   Umbrella Group(2)-02.06.2011.
161   16th Conference of the UNFCCC and the 6th Conference of the Parties serving as Meeting of the Parties to the Kyoto Protocol.
162   Where no sources are cited, the COP-16 account draws on the participant observation of the author.
163   UNFCCC Secretariat(1)-28.04.2010.
164   FCCC/AWGLCA/2010/CRP.1.
165   UNFCCC Secretariat(5)-14.06.2011.
166   G-77(1)-04.12.2010.

informal at the beginning of the second week.[167] A few core countries were always present while others varied depending on the questions tackled.[168] In contrast to Copenhagen, not the COP Presidency but regions themselves nominated participants.[169] Consultations were open to every country that wished to attend but had not received an email invitation. Mexicans dubbed them as 'open–closed meetings' and considered them one way to 'undermine obstructionists'.[170] Sceptical countries, such as Bolivia, also joined and even left the room in protest that 70 participants would be too many.[171] Consultations addressed essential areas, such as mitigation and finance, which the Presidency wanted to accompany. Unsurprisingly, it became 'very turbulent with heated discussions'[172] around concrete proposals but also more general ideas without a pre-defined agenda. They were facilitated by the Mexican Presidency and not only the main working group-Chairs as issues cut across many fields. The presence of the chairs ensured the linkage to the regular work-streams. A few parties questioned the mandate for this kind of Mexican facilitation, which revealed their ongoing worry that official negotiation groups would be sidelined.[173] Nevertheless, parties participated in these small group consultations.[174]

Besides, delegates soon tested common ground in bilaterals, such as the US and China on the first Thursday of the COP.[175] In addition 20 to 30 countries of the Cartagena Dialogue met daily for a frank exchange across 'coalitions'.[176] They funnelled solutions on various questions back into official working groups, so negotiations benefited tremendously from this input.[177] In addition, the Presidency held countless bilateral meetings to gather and distribute information between delegations,[178] and on balance many more informal consultations than the Danes.[179] Also contrary to Copenhagen, Calderón remained outside the public spotlight and worked his network on only very few key issues.[180]

The early – and deep – involvement of ministers

On Saturday 4 December the Presidency arranged an informal plenary to take stock after one week. The LCA Chair issued her second draft text capturing the

167   Mexico(3)-15.06.2011.
168   AWG/SB-Chair(2)-04.12.2010.
169   UNFCCC Secretariat(2)-04.12.2010.
170   UNFCCC Secretariat(2)-04.12.2010.
171   Mexico(3)-15.06.2011.
172   AWG/SB-Chair(2)-04.12.2010.
173   Denmark(1)-02.12.2010.
174   Mexico(3)-15.06.2011.
175   Umbrella Group(2)-02.06.2011.
176   EU/EU-country(4)-27.01.2011.
177   EU/EU-country(10)-16.08.2011.
178   Mexico(3)-15.06.2011.
179   UNFCCC Secretariat(4)-17.05.2011.
180   AWG/SB-Chair(4)-14.06.2011.

state of negotiations.[181] She saw some progress but also backward steps and urged parties to redouble their efforts. Espinosa underlined once more that no Mexican text was being prepared and negotiations would continue in a transparent and inclusive manner. This permanent reassurance was one key point of the Mexican strategy.[182] She also pointed out the need for political guidance and vaguely announced that ministers would be integrated in the negotiations, another elementary part of their strategy:[183] Mexico had therefore asked ministers to arrive unusually early on the weekend in the middle of the summit to facilitate negotiations throughout the entire second week. In the subsequent debate, many negotiation groups welcomed the new LCA text and the process so far. At the same time, several ALBA countries but also a few others criticized the process. They stressed the need for a 'party-driven process', parties' 'ownership of the text', and that 'ministers should only guide but not substantively engage in negotiations'.

In an unusual move, the COP Presidency invited parties to an informal plenary for Sunday. Apart from the new Chair's text of the Kyoto Protocol group, the Mexicans now laid out more concrete plans for the second week, also on the inclusion of ministers in the negotiations. So, pairs of ministers from a developed and a developing country eventually facilitated negotiations on one core issue of the Bali Action Plan each, such as mitigation and MRV. They complemented the work of the AWGs' drafting groups and became a key factor for building agreement.[184] The Mexicans continued to inform all countries and observers in regular informal stocktaking plenaries on the status of negotiations in all these groups to explicitly ensure transparency.

The high-level segment officially started on Tuesday 7 December. As planned, only a moderate number of 22 heads of state and government, and so around 100 less than in Copenhagen, attended the COP (IISD 2010e: 27). From UN headquarters, Ban Ki-moon was present. In contrast to COP-15, expert and ministerial negotiations continued to feed into the process including during the high-level segment. Their progress was reflected in the third LCA draft and a revised proposal by the Kyoto Protocol group's Chair on Wednesday.[185] In the morning stocktaking plenary, LCA Chair Mukahanana-Sangarwe underlined that significant progress was still needed on mitigation and MRV as the new text was still full of options and brackets. The enhanced trust generated by the Presidency should allow parties to concentrate on substance, and 'not too much on process'. Espinosa then reiterated her 'full commitment' that consultations 'remain open and inclusive ... No group, small or large, can take decisions on behalf of anyone else ... everyone is needed'.

181 FCCC/AWGLCA/2010/CRP.2.
182 Mexico(2)-08.02.2011.
183 Mexico(2)-08.02.2011.
184 UNFCCC Secretariat(7)-03.08.2011.
185 FCCC/AWGLCA/2010/CRP.3 and FCCC/KP/AWG/2010/CRP.4/Rev.2.

Negotiations continued in minister-facilitated circles and AWGs all day and during the night from Wednesday to Thursday. At this point, the Kyoto Protocol group agreed on a few issues for a second commitment period of the Protocol, such as 1990 as base year with an optional reference year, the maintenance of emissions trading and project-based mechanisms (IISD 2010e: 13). Essential aspects such as further mitigation commitments remained unresolved. In the Thursday evening stocktaking plenary at 9pm, ministerial consultations reported on their progress. Espinosa called for parties' flexibility, stressing that an outcome was 'in reach'. She underlined that the number of participants was never fixed but open to everyone who had attended the consultations of the past hours. After the plenary, numerous countries were largely satisfied with the process. At the same time, a leading African delegation expressed that many did not consider the process inclusive and transparent because Chairs produced texts, so it was not a party driven process.[186] 'Some parties were put off for not being invited to a smaller group session', found another delegate.[187]

On late Thursday evening, the Presidency invited 50 countries to address all remaining difficult issues, while others were free to also attend. The organizers had moved this decisive last round from Friday to Thursday, so time would not run out as in Copenhagen.[188] Many considered the continuation of this open-door policy decisive.[189] The session split into break-out groups, each facilitated by three to four ministers during another long night, *inter alia* on shared vision and mitigation moderated by ministers from Brazil and the United Kingdom, and on finance with ministers from Australia and Bangladesh. According to one participant, 'experienced people' went through 'the heart of the mitigation text' to assess whether it appeared acceptable for all parties.[190] The mitigation and MRV group was probably among the most important for a compromise in that final night:

> The US was brought in as they could say that all countries had MRV commitments, while developing countries could show that they received a differentiated treatment by another kind of MRV. The Japanese received their footnote on the Kyoto–LCA track relation.[191]

Importantly overall was that India agreed to the structure of the deal and that China accepted 'to have some obligations at all'.[192]

---

186   Informal conversation, Cancún, 09.12.10.
187   Informal conversation, Cancún, 09.12.10.
188   Mexico(3)-15.06.2011.
189   UNFCCC Secretariat(7)-03.08.2011, UNFCCC Secretariat(1)-28.04.2010.
190   EU/EU-country(6)-16.03.2011.
191   EU/EU-country(10)-16.08.2011.
192   Umbrella Group(1)-20.04.2011.

Showdown in the early hours

By Friday morning, the small minister-chaired groups delivered their drafts to the Presidency after a long night, which combined these inputs and the work of the AWGs to craft the final text of the Cancún Agreements. The multiple negotiation groups across levels had been largely coordinated, facilitators asserted.[193] The plenary to circulate the final text had originally been scheduled for 8.30am. Yet, the organizers announced more time was needed to resolve the last outstanding issues. The Mexicans insisted on eradicating all brackets around contested text elements before publishing the final text, widely seen as salient move.[194] It became a day of uncertainty and many still doubted reaching an agreement.[195] For most negotiators outside the handful of people engaged in finalizing the text, the process eventually became opaque: 'In the latest hours of Cancún, there was something blurry [about how the text was created].'[196]

The text was finally handed out at 4.30pm. Under intense time pressure, the COP President and UNFCCC Executive Secretary had cleaned the text in person supported by their lead staff, inter alia de Alba and LCA Chair's lead Secretariat support, Halldor Thorgeirsson.[197] The extensive preceding consultations by the Presidency during the year in finding options and developing a compromise formula now paid off.[198] The organizers built on the elements from the LCA Chair's paper and the ministerial consultations with minister pairs going in and out to contribute their input.[199] In the words of a Mexican official: 'We didn't need to draft but to put them together. So there was little Mexican ink in the end. It was more about finding balances.'[200] The Secretariat vitally assisted in clearing all brackets and options given its much greater content expertise than that of the Presidency: 'The last cleaning was done by us as the Secretariat.'[201] Some negotiators claimed that major powers, such as the US and China, saw the text before its printing: 'They took a high risk by showing it to only very few people beforehand.'[202] Post-summit discussions emerged about who had drafted the final compromise. Yet Mexican officials rejected detailing this process when approached by negotiators in subsequent months.[203]

Parties convened around 6pm for an informal plenary where the final draft decision text was officially tabled. At this opening, the plenary gave COP

193 AWG/SB-Chair(4)-14.06.2011.
194 UNFCCC Secretariat(7)-03.08.2011, EU/EU-country(6)-16.03.2011.
195 Informal conversations, Cancún, 10.12.10.
196 G-77(4)-22.07.2011.
197 Mexico(5)-07.07.2011, G-77(4)-22.07.2011, EU/EU-country(11)-10.12.2011, Denmark(2)-16.06.2011.
198 UNFCCC Secretariat(1)-28.04.2010.
199 Mexico(5)-07.07.2011.
200 Mexico(3)-15.06.2011.
201 UNFCCC Secretariat(7)-03.08.2011.
202 EU/EU-country(10)-16.08.2011; also: G-77(4)-22.07.2011, Denmark(3)-11.08.2011.
203 G-77(4)-22.07.2011.

President Espinosa a several-minute-long standing ovation. Multiple interpretations emerged. Many saw it as recognition of Mexican leadership: 'Even without
seeing the text, they were already clapping.'[204] Others perceived it more as a
cathartic process ('Let's get Copenhagen out of our system') and a relief about
nearing success.[205] Rare voices found that civil society organizations in the room
initiated the applause on behalf of the Mexicans to influence delegations.[206]
Whatever the motivation, though, the clapping led to an emotional atmosphere
and tears in the eyes of Espinosa. She underlined that it was not 'Mexican text'
but work produced by parties that had been compiled 'under her own responsibility' (IISD 2010e: 15). Parties now had 'limited time for a last push' (*ibid.*), so
negotiators were informally trying to reach last minute changes of the text
already during this informal plenary.[207]

After scrutinizing the draft agreements parties reconvened at 9.30pm for an
informal stocktaking. Right away, Espinosa and the Presidency received another
standing ovation from delegates who were now more familiar with the text. The
standing ovation revealed a mood that implied an agreement was in reach:
'When the clapping burst out of for the Mexican Presidency under Espinosa . . . I
knew we would get this outcome.'[208] The atmosphere suddenly turned very tense
as several negotiators were not let into the overcrowded room, among them
Bolivia's head negotiator. The UN security chief had directed the closure.
Sensing the diplomatic threat, Espinosa urged Figueres to find a way around, and
it was soon reopened.[209] In particular, ALBA delegations voiced their anger about
this incident and the text itself. They underlined its failure to seriously address
climate change, with an inadequate 2°C goal, and demanded a return to negotiations in the AWGs. Saudi Arabia supported their call. Contrary to that, the
great majority of countries, including those most vulnerable to climate change
(i.e. from AOSIS, Asia or Africa), spoke fervently in favour of an adoption, as
did all major powers. The Maldives underlined that it was a question of survival
for numerous countries, and not only about mere economic interests.
Appreciation of the negotiation management came from myriad and diverse
countries, such as Iran, Zimbabwe, Kenya and the US. They applauded its transparency and inclusiveness, and underlined that Cancún had restored 'confidence
in the multilateral system' (IISD 2010e: 16).

The key working group plenaries followed this informal plenary. After two
weeks of facilitation by Chair Mukahanana-Sangarwe, the ministerial pairs, and
numerous co-facilitators, the LCA group presented its compromise draft decision. COP President Espinosa commended that they had 'laid the ground for the

204 Mexico(5)-07.07.2011.
205 UNFCCC Secretariat(2)-04.12.2010.
206 G-77(2)-13.06.2011.
207 EU/EU-country(10)-16.08.2011.
208 EU/EU-country(7)-04.05.2011.
209 Mexico(1)-02.02.2011.

outcome' of COP-16[210] (IISD 2010e: 4). The Kyoto Protocol group had not reached agreement on the future of the Kyoto Protocol but had progressed on several sub-items. This resulted in a revised Chair's proposal and draft decisions on the clarification of Kyoto Protocol issues.[211] Presidency and Secretariat had then consolidated them into the summit's draft outcome. The reports of both groups were forwarded to the COP plenary by 2am.

Tension in the final plenary remained high as Bolivia claimed a grave violation of the UNFCCC rule of consensus were Espinosa to overrule its vocal objection to the draft Agreements. The plenary was 'at the edge of the cliff'.[212] At that point, Bolivia's ALBA allies, such as Venezuela, Cuba and Nicaragua, kept quiet, which negotiators explained was the result of 'a lot of conviction and talk behind the scenes. Mexico might have done it, as it is itself situated in Latin America and hence has a closer relation to these countries.'[213] At this delicate moment of the long night-time debate, Espinosa gave the COP Presidency's understanding of consensus:

> Consensus requires that everyone is given the right to be heard and have their views given due consideration and Bolivia has been given this opportunity. Consensus does not mean that one country has the right of veto, and can prevent 193 others from moving forward after years of negotiations on something that our societies and future generations expect.
>
> (IISD 2010e: 28)

Espinosa finally gavelled down the decisions at 4.30am on 11 December.[214] Relieved negotiators jumped from their chairs, clapped and shouted wildly. Bolivia protested heavily, pointing out that any other country could be overruled next. The delegate of another ALBA country expressed its anger in hindsight: 'They steamrolled Bolivia.'[215] Yet no other party publicly joined Bolivia's objection in that moment. The Cancún Agreements were officially adopted.

The Cancún Agreements

The Agreements combined decisions under the Convention and the Kyoto Protocol tracks on mitigation, finance, REDD+, adaptation and technology, among others (IISD 2010e: 29). Cancún finally brought much of the substance developed in Copenhagen under the UNFCCC roof, while adding substantial detail on several issues (ibid.: 17). On mitigation, the Agreements confirmed the

210   FCCC/AWGLCA/2010/L.7.
211   FCCC/KP/AWG/2010/CRP.4/Rev.4, FCCC/KP/AWG/2010/L.8/Add.1/.2.
212   EU/EU-country(7)-04.05.2011.
213   UNFCCC Secretariat(2)-04.12.2010.
214   Decision 1/CP.16 and 1/CMP.6; FCCC/CP/2010/7/Add.1.
215   ALBA(2)-09.12.2011.

Copenhagen Accord's 2°C goal as an official COP decision, but without new emission reduction commitments by countries. Technical rules detailed reduction quantifications, together with a registry for mitigation action by developing countries. The Copenhagen provision on MRV/ICA was refined to keep track of reductions. Pledges on fast-start and long-term financing were now stamped as official COP decisions, with more precise regulations for the Green Climate Fund. Forest-related mitigation (REDD+) had long been ripe for a decision and was adopted. Technology transfer would be enhanced by adding specifics to the Technology Mechanism. Developing countries welcomed the Cancún Adaptation Framework as progress on adaptation support.

Mexican President Calderón lauded the Agreements in the plenary for saving multilateralism and being a next big step against climate change. Parties showed great relief with their final standing ovation: 'It was an outcome that no one had expected: a comprehensive agreement with 145 paragraphs.'[216] They proved that the process could deliver and so many negotiators 'saw restoring faith in the process and laying to rest the ghosts of Copenhagen as the most important achievement' (IISD 2010e: 29).

So the Cancún Agreements were not an empty shell. At the same time, there was widespread acknowledgement that the Agreements were not sufficient (IISD 2010e: 1). The lack of progress on mitigation was a central weakness since the existing pledges of the Copenhagen Accord fell far short of scientific recommendations to combat climate change (*ibid.*: 20). Moreover, no decision was taken on a second commitment of the Kyoto Protocol, or on a legal form of mitigation commitments by non-Kyoto members, such as the US and the big emerging BASIC economies. Bolivian head negotiator Solón compared this voluntary bottom-up approach on mitigation with building a dyke where everyone contributes voluntarily hoping to reach an appropriate level by pure coincidence, with the great risk of being wrong. Others complained about vagueness and a lack of concrete ideas on finance, such as on the Green Climate Fund.[217] Its mere creation, though, was a key point for many G-77 negotiators: 'We had looked for [this] since a long time.'[218] So negotiations would continue under the South African Presidency, but for now Espinosa closed COP-16 at 6.22am on 11 December 2010, after delegates had successfully reached the Cancún Agreements.

Conclusion

The Danish and Mexican Presidencies significantly differed in their negotiation management and final outcomes. Looking at just a few examples, the Danes struggled with extreme internal clashes, while the Mexicans established clear

216   Umbrella Group(3)-14.06.2011.
217   Umbrella Group(4)-04.07.2011.
218   G-77(2)-13.06.2011.

responsibilities early on. Further, the crucial negotiation in Copenhagen occurred in a very small circle of the US and BASIC countries, while decisive negotiations in Cancún were held in multiple small, but open-ended, groups. The summits took very different courses, and parties eventually rejected adopting the suggested final proposal in Copenhagen, while they reached the Cancún Agreements one year later.

Equipped with this solid background on the history of the two years, it will be now be of interest to find the key drivers behind the course of these events.

References

Ban Ki-moon. (2009) *Summit on Climate Change – Summary by the UN Secretary-General*. New York: United Nations.

Depledge, Joanna. (2005) *The Organization of Global Negotiations: Constructing the Climate Change Regime*. London: Earthscan.

Guardian. (2009a) Draft Copenhagen Climate Change Agreement – the 'Danish Text'. *The Guardian* 8 December: www.theguardian.com/environment/2009/dec/08/copenhagen-climate-change.

Guardian. (2009b) Copenhagen Climate Summit in Disarray after 'Danish Text' Leak. *The Guardian* 8 December: www.theguardian.com/environment/2009/dec/08/copenhagen-climate-summit-disarray-danish-text.

Hedegaard, Connie. (2009) *The Greenland Ministerial Dialogue on Climate Change, Ilulissat, Greenland, 30 June–3 July 2009, Chair's Summary*. Copenhagen: Danish Ministry of Climate and Energy.

Hedegaard, Connie, and Yvo De Boer. (2009) Press Conference after Pre-COP – with Connie Hedegaard and Yvo De Boer – Part 1 Copenhagen. www.youtube.com/watch?v=42c1wBJOup4&feature=related (accessed 20 July 2011).

IISD. (2009a) Summary of the 5th Session of the AWG-LCA and the 7th Session of the AWG-KP. *Earth Negotiations Bulletin* 12.

IISD. (2009b) Summary of the Bonn Climate Talks 1–12 June. *Earth Negotiations Bulletin* 12.

IISD. (2009c) Summary of the Bonn Climate Talks: 10–14 August 2009. *Earth Negotiations Bulletin* 12.

IISD. (2009d) Summary of the Bangkok Climate Talks: 28 September–9 October 2009. *Earth Negotiations Bulletin* 12.

IISD. (2009e) Summary of the Barcelona Climate Talks: 2–6 November 2009. *Earth Negotiations Bulletin* 12.

IISD. (2009f) Summary of the Copenhagen Climate Change Conference. *Earth Negotiations Bulletin* 12.

IISD. (2010a) Summary of the Bonn Climate Talks: 9–11 April 2010. *Earth Negotiations Bulletin* 12.

IISD. (2010b) Summary of the Bonn Climate Talks: 31 May–11 June 2010. *Earth Negotiations Bulletin* 12.

IISD. (2010c) Summary of the Bonn Climate Talks: 2–6 August 2010. *Earth Negotiations Bulletin* 12.

IISD. (2010d) UN Climate Change Conference in Cancun: 29 November–10 December 2010. *Earth Negotiations Bulletin* 12.

IISD. (2010e) Summary of the Cancun Climate Change Conference. *Earth Negotiations Bulletin* 12.

MEF. (2009) *Declaration of the Leaders – the Major Economies Forum on Energy and Climate.* L'Aquila: Major Economies Forum.

Meilstrup, Per. (2010) The Runaway Summit: The Background Story of the Danish Presidency of COP15, the UN Climate Change Conference. In *Danish Foreign Policy Yearbook 2010*, edited by Nanna Hvidt and Hans Mouritzen. Copenhagen: Danish Institute for International Studies.

New York Times. (2009a) Leaders Will Delay Deal on Climate Change. *New York Times* 14 November: www.nytimes.com/2009/11/15/world/asia/15prexy.html?_r=0.

New York Times. (2009b) President Obama on a Climate Agreement. *New York Times* 18 December: http://video.nytimes.com/video/2009/12/18/multimedia/1247466194031/president-obama-on-a-climate-agreement.html (accessed 9 August 2011).

Rapp, Tobias, Christian Schwägerl, and Gerald Traufetter. (2009) *Das Kopenhagen-Protokoll.* Hamburg: Der Spiegel.

Sabel, Robbie. (1997) *Procedure at International Conferences: A Study of the Rules of Procedure of International Inter-Governmental Conferences.* Cambridge: Cambridge University Press.

UNFCCC Secretariat. (2009) *Bonn Climate Change Talks – August 2009.* Bonn: UNFCCC Secretariat.

UNFCCC Secretariat. (2011) *Copenhagen Accord.* Bonn: UNFCCC Secretariat.

Yamin, Farhana, and Joanna Depledge. (2004) *The International Climate Change Regime: A Guide to Rules, Institutions and Procedures.* Cambridge, MA: Cambridge University Press.

Chapter 3

Negotiation management during the Danish and Mexican Presidencies

Let us now turn to the issue at the heart of this book, and ask whether and how the differences in negotiation management influenced the outcomes of the Danish and Mexican Presidencies. What do the interviews around the world and the observation of several summits reveal about the various elements of negotiation management (transparency and inclusiveness, capability of the organizers, authority of the lead organizer, and negotiation mode)? The goal is to see *whether* one management factor was given, or not, when a particular negotiation outcome occurred (a 'correlation'). In a second step, I then examine *how* a management factor was causally connected to the outcome of the Copenhagen and Cancún summits by a careful tracing of the decision-making process. The rich detail on these connections may hopefully serve future organizers to avoid past mistakes and to benefit from best practices.

Before diving deep into the analysis, it is worth noting that negotiation management has its greatest effect when conditions are especially adverse. This is often the case for multilateral talks. Negotiations under the UNFCCC are consensus-based when adopting a new agreement as they do not allow for majority voting. Moreover, the constellation of parties' interests was such that they neither fully overlapped nor entirely collided at the outset of the Presidencies in the beginning of 2009 and 2010 respectively. To begin with the Danish Presidency, the lack of a complete overlap of interests became obvious at the adversarial Bonn negotiation in April 2009. At the same time, interests did not entirely lack any common ground. The convergence appeared sufficient for at least a moderate agreement after ambitions had been downscaled in the autumn: 'The fundamentals were possible but the process was not good.'[1] So, there was overall hope for an outcome at COP-15. It is fair to broadly conceive that interests at least partially overlapped at the outset so a zone of possible agreement between the parties existed. Conditions for an influence of negotiations management were met.

The overlap of interests had only slightly altered by early 2010 when the

---

1   UNFCCC Secretariat(3)-08.12.2010; similar: G-77(4)-22.07.2011, Observer(2)-08.12.2010.

Mexican Presidency started. Only one year had passed since the beginning of the Danish Presidency in 2009, so the fundamental interests of parties were still very similar, such as the hesitation by most countries to commit to further emission reductions and diverging interests on financing. The bitter fights of 2009 had also revealed their differences in positions. In the first meeting in 2010 '[p]eople were still shocked. They first had to digest what had happened in Copenhagen.'[2] At the same time, the interest of the large majority to prevent the worst conse-quences from climate change by acting on mitigation and adaptation remained unchanged. Hence, it was not a complete clash without any shared interests, and some parties had even moved a bit closer in their positions after one year of intense negotiations under the Danish Presidency. One additional interest for negotiations under the Mexican Presidency arose from COP-15: that of saving negotiations within the UNFCCC framework. Many parties feared that if climate negotiations moved their core activity to other fora like the G-20, they would lose any influence over the process. This became a joint interest for most countries and its impact is elaborated under structural explanations. Overall, parties' interests were only slightly more overlapping in early 2010 than in 2009. Thus, an efficient negotiation management, comprising the following four driv-ers, was still much needed.

Transparency and inclusiveness

I begin with one core lever of negotiation management in the hands of the organizers: transparency and inclusiveness during preparatory and summit nego-tiations. Practitioners of international politics have repeatedly stressed its importance across regimes in interviews for this book: 'The fact that we knew what was on the table [in the final plenary] contributed to our agreement to the proposal.'[3] Similarly, scholars from disciplines including International Relations, management theory and social psychology have increasingly studied the role transparency and inclusiveness play in group dynamics. Let us now examine the levels of transparency and inclusiveness of the negotiations during the Danish and Mexican Presidencies (and their correlation with agreement), before tracing the paths of their influence on negotiations.

The Danish Presidency: from the 'Danish text' to the 'US–BASIC' conclave

The negotiation process during the Danish Presidency was not very transparent or inclusive, from the 'Danish text' to the small 'US–BASIC' conclave on Friday. Overall, 'Many delegations in Copenhagen didn't know what went on and had

2   Mexico(2)-08.02.2011.
3   BASIC(3)-08.07.2011.

no role whatsoever.'[4] The assessment of very low transparency was nearly unanimous with respondents spread across coalitions and organizers (Table 3.1). Parties perceived negotiations also as not very inclusive. Only a few core country delegations were always included. One BASIC negotiator stated that he 'would rather call it inclusive [for his country] as we were actually part also of the small group negotiations... So we knew what was going on, others did not though and were excluded.'[5] Danish Presidency officials themselves shared this non-inclusive characterization.

I will now detail this 'big picture' by applying the indicators outlined in Chapter 1. Let us first assess *transparency* regarding small group negotiations, the negotiation text, and the negotiation schedule and progress. Small group negotiations caused tremendous havoc in 2009. Two small group settings in particular inhibited transparency in the crucial second week of COP-15: the ministerial small group meeting of 28 delegates from Thursday to Friday; and the US–BASIC round on Friday afternoon. It is internationally accepted for a small group to enter into separate negotiations.[6] However, information for non-participating countries at COP-15 was very scarce about either of the two small groups, despite their drafting of compromises on the crucial issues: 'The final meeting of [28] parties had been closed and was run by the Danes... The other parties did not even know what was going on. The final negotiations in the small room [BASIC and US] were not even known to parties at all.'[7]

The presence of heads of states and government, which the Danish Presidency had pushed for, had created a dynamic that resulted in an exclusive and secretive US–BASIC negotiation. It was 'probably the most unusual "small room" ever given heads of states of the most powerful countries in the world were drafting negotiation text themselves to reach an outcome',[8] with over one hundred

Table 3.1 Responses to the questions 'Did all parties know the crucial moves and steps before and at COP negotiations? How were parties included in the negotiations?' with respect to the Danish Presidency

Response	Transparent n (%)	Inclusive n (%)
Yes	0 (0%)	1 (2.8%)
No	39 (97.5%)	34 (94.4%)
Undecided	1 (2.5%)	1 (2.8%)
Total	40	36

4   Mexico(4)-16.06.2011; similar: EU/EU-country(9)-26.05.2011, BASIC(2)-16.06.2011.
5   BASIC(2)-16.06.2011.
6   EU/EU-country(10)-16.08.2011, BASIC(1)-04.12.2010.
7   UNFCCC Secretariat(6)-16.06.2011.
8   AWG/SB-Chair(1)-30.11.2010.

excluded leaders. A BASIC negotiator conceded that this was 'the worst'.[9] 'People were very angry... You don't let dozens of ministers wait for hours without knowing what is happening.'[10] They did not have any information on the small group's progress.[11] US President Barack Obama's compromise announcement immediately after the small group meeting aggravated the perception of lacking transparency.[12] Excluded leaders were now confronted with a finalized 'deal'. Prime Minister Rasmussen then 'basically presented it to just be approved'.[13] The Presidency tried to bring some transparency back by last minute information sessions, but it was insufficient and too late. The details of the small group compromise were thus largely unknown to negotiators at the closing plenary on Friday night. A BASIC negotiator admitted that 'several delegations said in the final plenary and afterwards that they didn't know about the whole substance until the final decision'.[14]

Second, the organizers undermined transparency by how they handled the origin, evolution, and conclusion of a compromise text. The Danish Presidency had started preparing a text early on during 2009. It was coordinated with several influential countries, as in a meeting in Copenhagen just before COP-15. Some participating delegations therefore emphasized that all major powers and groups had been included, among them China and the G-77 with its Sudanese Chair. Hence, they claimed that one could barely speak of a 'Danish' text.[15] However, the document had been developed by the Danes throughout the course of a year and didn't emerge from the majority of parties. Even from inside the Danish Presidency came the observation that the Danes 'spent so much time writing the text over and over again. It was a complete crazy approach. We were going to facilitate the negotiations not write a text ourselves.'[16] Information to all countries about this final coordination meeting in Copenhagen and the text was not wide enough: on the second COP day its leakage caused an outcry among all countries not involved in preparing it. They accused the Danes of producing a secret text. It 'came out of the blue'[17] for many, especially smaller nations that felt excluded: 'In the year leading to COP-15, no one knew where the process was heading. When you then go to Copenhagen and see that there is a secret text, there is something fishy about what is being cooked.'[18] The COP preparation was thus widely considered a 'disaster from the point of view of legitimacy and transparency.'[19] It was the downside of the Danish strategy of focusing on major powers.

9   BASIC(5)-15.06.2011.
10   Umbrella Group(5)-27.07.2011.
11   AWG/SB-Chair(1)-30.11.2010, Umbrella Group(5)-27.07.2011.
12   UNFCCC Secretariat(7)-03.08.2011.
13   Umbrella Group(5)-27.07.2011.
14   BASIC(3)-08.07.2011.
15   Umbrella Group(2)-02.06.2011.
16   Denmark(2)-16.06.2011.
17   Mexico(4)-16.06.2011.
18   G-77(4)-22.07.2011.
19   UNFCCC Secretariat(2)-04.12.2010.

Third, the Danish Presidency informed delegates insufficiently about the schedule and progress of negotiations: 'The Danes ... were planning actions but did not tell you what they were going to do.'[20] Even experienced diplomats found there was a lack of clarity on the process of consultations during the conference.[21] Many delegates didn't know when and where informal meetings were held. 'We had no choice whether we would go to a meeting, or not.'[22] These informal consultations are central though to resolve crucial issues. In sum, the process under the Danish Presidency was non-transparent given the scarce information on small groups, negotiation text, schedule and progress.

In addition to the lack of transparency, evidence suggests a low level of *inclusion* in the negotiation process, indicated by small group meetings, negotiation levels and organizers' outreach for deliberation: 'The perception that people needed to be included in the process was gravely ignored.'[23] First, small group negotiations at COP-15 were not very inclusive. As these meetings could not encompass all delegations, it became crucial for countries and negotiation blocs to be able to decide who would represent them. Yet, given the delay in COP-15 negotiations, the Danish Presidency wanted to circumvent any stalling tactics when forming the group, for instance by that year's G-77 Chair, as one official conceded.[24] So they consulted with the UN Secretary-General and then invited countries to the small group. Negotiation blocs could thus not select their representatives for this decisive meeting. While members of the small group seemed satisfied about the group's composition on Thursday night,[25] many outside felt unrepresented. This small group exclusion was regarded as a key mistake.[26]

Furthermore, the exclusion of non-mainstream delegations from the small group undermined its inclusiveness as it did not reflect the diversity of interests at the negotiations.[7] In particular the politically sensitive Latin American ALBA group was left out, or was even 'forgotten'[28] as a renowned facilitator claimed. Instead, they focused on building coalitions of states friendly to the process rather than integrating diverging countries. To be sure, inclusion requires a country's openness to cooperate. For COP-15, a lead negotiator recalled that the Danish Presidency sometimes tried to integrate non-mainstream voices more, such as the G-77 Chair, but the latter apparently rejected the invitation.[29] Nevertheless, more 'radical' voices were eventually excluded from the small group, be it consciously (a 'strategic decision'[30]) or accidently.

20 EU/EU-country(4)-27.01.2011.
21 Mexico(3)-15.06.2011.
22 G-77(3)-19.07.2011.
23 EU/EU-country (6), 16.03.2011.
24 Denmark(4)-12.08.2011.
25 Denmark(4)-12.08.2011.
26 EU/EU-country(8)-05.05.2011.
27 BASIC(1)-04.12.2010.
28 Mexico(3)-15.06.2011.
29 EU/EU-country(10)-16.08.2011.
30 EIG(1)-09.08.2011.

Second, the evidence shows a low degree of integration of negotiation levels during the Danish Presidency. Early in 2009, the Danes focused more on the participation of ministers than expert negotiators in the informal negotiations of the Greenland Dialogue.[31] The conviction around the Danish Prime Minister seemed to have grown by the G-8 meeting in July that the leader level was the only common denominator as the technical levels were in deep disagreement.[32] As a consequence, the Danish Presidency pushed for a conscious shift of levels that resulted in three isolated negotiation tracks of expert negotiators, ministers, and heads of state and government. The three tracks spoke in parallel with little mutual feedback.[33] The vast majority of expert negotiators were excluded from the ministerial and leader levels. Sidelining key chairs of working groups further aggravated the situation.[34] It became an 'upstairs-downstairs problem' and the Danish Presidency assumed that any result from the leaders' level would be accepted anyway.[35] Finally, a BASIC negotiator, a participant of the last-minute US–BASIC small group meeting, conceded that 'there was no connection between the high and the low level'.[36] The agreement from the small group leader level couldn't be brought back onto the other levels of the overall process.[37]

A third aspect of non-inclusion was the limited outreach by organizers for their compromise deliberation. Danish Climate and Energy Minister Hedegaard and her head of COP-15 team, Thomas Becker, had travelled extensively reaching out to numerous countries. Yet they were increasingly sidelined internally until Rasmussen and his COP-15 team head Lidegaard became the Presidency's most visible faces. They were considerably less known to most countries as both had joined the process much later. Moreover, Rasmussen showed little interest in broadly including countries' perspectives into the deliberation: 'He thought he would not have to consult, but tell people which direction to take.'[38] The focus on the US would eventually bring all others along.[39] Yet, many countries felt betrayed for not being included in the organizers' deliberation, contrary to earlier promises by the Climate and Energy Ministry.[40] Interviewees from all backgrounds reported this US focus and limited outreach.[41]

Communication about transparency and inclusiveness could not change the picture. The organizers were unable to convey the subjective notion of a transparent and inclusive process. It was an 'atmosphere of lacking transparency'

31   UNFCCC Secretariat(1)-28.04.2010.
32   Denmark(4)-12.08.2011.
33   Mexico(3)-15.06.2011, Mexico(4)-16.06.2011.
34   AWG/SB-Chair(4)-14.06.2011.
35   Umbrella Group(3)-14.06.2011.
36   BASIC(2)-16.06.2011.
37   G-77(3)-19.07.2011.
38   EU/EU-country(11)-10.12.2011.
39   Denmark(5)-12.08.2011.
40   Denmark(5)-12.08.2011.
41   Observer(3)-16.06.2011, ALBA(2)-09.12.2011, UNFCCC Secretariat(3)-08.12.2010.

where 'people overall felt excluded which was in sum a combination of myth and reality.'[42] The defensive response by the Presidency to the text leakage added to its perception as 'terrible'.[43] Eventually, the Danes had the reputation of having a closed door policy[44] and lost the communication battle.

In conclusion, information on small group negotiations, the negotiation text, and schedule and progress was insufficient during the Danish Presidency. Moreover, inclusion was low in small group negotiations, across negotiation levels, and in the outreach of organizers. Finally, the Danish and UNFCCC Secretariat organizers failed to at least establish the perception of a transparent or inclusive process through appropriate communication. A Danish official speculated as to a reason for the approach on the Danish side of the organizers: the Presidency had a bold conviction to steer the process in a self-determined way, originating in the confidence that 'Denmark is the smallest superpower in the world', as former EU politician Jacques Santer had said.[45] Low transparency and inclusiveness correlated with not reaching a COP agreement during the Danish Presidency.

The Mexican Presidency: from global outreach to the mantra of 'no Mexican text'

The analysis of negotiations during the Mexican Presidency paints another picture. The large majority of negotiators, UN officials and observers stressed the difference in transparency and inclusiveness (Table 3.2). Learning from the 'Danish mistakes', it was a conscious break with the previous process design.[46] Three-quarters of respondents found the Cancún negotiations adequately transparent, while 25 per cent were undecided or even said negotiations were not much more transparent than during the Danish Presidency. The eight respondents who did not find COP-16 transparent form a heterogeneous group comprising 'traditional' process sceptics from developing countries as well as BASIC and European negotiators, a UNFCCC official, and a Danish Presidency member. Nevertheless, the three-quarters majority also shows these diverse characteristics with numerous long-term delegates. The picture is even clearer on inclusiveness. Eighty-seven per cent of interviewees found it inclusive in 2010. Two deviating opinions come from countries that have always been critical of process handling. Given the diversity among the larger group cutting across all negotiation coalitions, it is reasonable to conclude that it was on the whole a transparent and inclusive process.

Verbal analysis of interviews corroborates the numerical findings. Small group negotiations were more transparent in 2010. During the preparatory year, several

42 UNFCCC Secretariat(1)-28.04.2010.
43 Umbrella Group(4)-04.07.2011.
44 Umbrella Group(2)-02.06.2011.
45 Denmark(5)-12.08.2011.
46 EU/EU-country(6)-16.03.2011.

Table 3.2 Responses to the questions 'Did all parties know the crucial moves and steps before and at COP negotiations? How were parties included in the negotiations?' with respect to the Mexican Presidency

Response	Transparent n (%)	Inclusive n (%)
Yes	26 (76.5%)	20 (87%)
No	5 (14.7%)	2 (8.7%)
Undecided	3 (8.8%)	1 (4.3%)
Total	34	23

informal meetings were held on expert negotiator and ministerial levels. The Presidency consciously reported back every time so all countries would know about the key steps taken.[47] A similar pattern was true for the COP. Not all parties could attend every informal meeting, yet they were always informed about the principal elements afterwards.[48] This regular reporting to all delegations about small group negotiations made it more transparent.[49]

The organizers also better informed delegates about the origin, evolution, and conclusion of the negotiation text. Before COP-16's last day, the Mexican Presidency never introduced text solely on their behalf, in striking contrast to the 'Danish text'. Any text would originate from delegations: 'There were no hidden papers.'[50] Of course, the organizers were closely involved in its development. Contrary to 2009, the text was more broadly coordinated to include all necessary elements for an agreement,[51] and organizers continuously informed about the textual evolution. Expert negotiations of the first week were broken up into smaller groups on core issues, chaired by ministerial pairs from a developed and a developing country. Towards the end, essential textual elements emerged from all these groups that were transparent to negotiators.[52] Finally, the UNFCCC Secretariat and the Presidency merged the final elements of the Cancún Agreements on the last day of the COP. Upon its release in the afternoon, all parties were largely familiar with the outcome.[53] This was in marked contrast to the previous year when the final text had arisen from the US–BASIC negotiations on the last day, so upon its release late on Friday night most parties had never seen it before.

Cancún was not fully transparent either. Some G-77 negotiators criticized the unclear process of finalizing the text on the last COP day. One went as far as to

47   Mexico(3)-15.06.2011.
48   EIG(1)-09.08.2011.
49   UNFCCC Secretariat(4)-17.05.2011.
50   AWG/SB-Chair(4)-14.06.2011.
51   Denmark(2)-16.06.2011.
52   BASIC(3)-08.07.2011.
53   BASIC(3)-08.07.2011.

judge that the 'text of Cancún did not have any ownership either as there were changes made to it after negotiators had produced its elements'.[54] As a consequence, countries negotiated the agenda for the subsequent year for a week at the first post-Cancún session, since 'subtleties were missing that could eventually mean a lot'.[55] However, it is nearly impossible to achieve complete transparency in any negotiation. 'How do you do it in the end? Someone has to eventually do it [finalize the text] and find the middle ground. But then, people complain.'[56] Providing a transparent origin and evolution of the text offers some leeway to conclude the drafting in the very end in a smaller circle.[57] In this sense, Cancún had a higher level of transparency than Copenhagen, despite not being fully transparent.

There was significantly more information about the negotiation schedule and progress in Cancún than in Copenhagen. Especially in COP-16's final days, the organizers repeatedly held 'informal stocktaking plenaries' where COP President Espinosa informed delegates about negotiation progress and the schedule ahead. Seasoned UN officials underlined that this had previously only been used for subgroups and provided a sense of wholeness about the state of negotiations.[58] 'In Cancún, we knew exactly where and when things were happening.'[59] Again, some uncertainty remained: at the end of Cancún's first week, delegations were unsure about the high-level segment's schedule, as the Mexicans wished to retain flexibility.[60] Their announcement at the weekend to create issue-dedicated small groups chaired by minister pairs without any further specifications deepened parties' confusion.[61] Next, a well-connected negotiator acknowledged that even she had not known on Thursday night of week two about the recent start of several small groups crafting the final compromises.[62] Nevertheless, she stressed that the Presidency frequently reported back on progress of these multiple 'informals' to the core small group of 50 to 60 negotiators. So, the constant usage of the informal stocktaking plenaries and the regular update of the small group still qualify it as transparent.

Inclusiveness during the Mexican Presidency was also higher. The starting point for the openness of small group negotiations in 2010 was the legacy of COP-15. As the Mexicans had learnt that 'small secret groups didn't work',[63] parties got plenty of opportunity to contribute with meetings open to

54   G-77(2)-13.06.2011.
55   G-77(4)-22.07.2011.
56   G-77(4)-22.07.2011.
57   UNFCCC Secretariat(2)-04.12.2010.
58   UNFCCC Secretariat(1)-28.04.2010, UNFCCC Secretariat(5)-14.06.2011.
59   G-77(3)-19.07.2011.
60   EU/EU-country(3)-03.12.2010.
61   UNFCCC Secretariat(3)-08.12.2010.
62   EU/EU-country(9)-26.05.2011.
63   UNFCCC Secretariat(7)-03.08.2011.

everybody.[64] The Mexico meeting in April hosted by the incoming Presidency set the tone. Officials were 'very relaxed... about who would be in [a small negotiation group] or not. De Alba was much more flexible on this.'[65] Politically weaker countries confirmed this open-ended nature of consultations.[66] The small groups' inclusiveness remained mostly true for the COP. Parties recall it as an 'important moment' when the COP Presidency convened around 50 people for small group consultations early on but left the door open for others to join, including the more marginalized voices.[67] Later, no one was prevented from coming despite shrinking circles of meetings.[68] While this undermined pure inclusiveness the openness of the original small core group had established trust in a general inclusiveness.[69] The Mexicans emailed invitations for these 'open–closed meetings' to only a few people but the meeting remained open to anyone and thus grew to 70 later on.[70]

Nevertheless, as this system did not inform all parties it stirred some anger. Some delegations didn't even know the time and place of several meetings. One G-77 negotiator commented that there is nothing like 'open consultations by invitation', and accused the Presidency of hypocrisy for the explanation that they lacked the negotiator's email address to send an invitation: 'They could have had it... even from Google.'[71] Another negotiator found little difference in the number of informal meetings at COP-15 and 16, so that 'both COPs were equally not transparent' for those countries that were not inside the smallest groups, especially towards the end of the COP.[72] The text eventually came from a 'hand-picked group... chosen by the Mexicans.'[73] It was a switch from the open-ended phase to the final text crafting on Thursday and Friday by a very small group, criticized by ALBA delegates and some European interviewees.[74] Was the 'Mexican system' for small groups not inclusive either?

It was certainly not fully so. Yet, there were some subtle, crucial differences to 2009. First, 'marginalized' delegations were consciously excluded in Copenhagen in contrast to their intentional small group inclusion in Cancún.[75] The Mexicans had engaged with the ALBA countries from the onset as the most vocal critics of the process. A top Danish Presidency official commended Mexico for the 'diplomatic masterpiece that all key figures were always on board.'[76] Second, the

64   EU/EU-country(4)-27.01.2011.
65   Denmark(3)-11.08.2011.
66   G-77(4)-22.07.2011.
67   UNFCCC Secretariat(2)-04.12.2010, UNFCCC Secretariat(7)-03.08.2011.
68   G-77(3)-19.07.2011.
69   EU/EU-country(7)-04.05.2011, UNFCCC Secretariat(1)-28.04.2010.
70   Mexico(3)-15.06.2011.
71   G-77(2)-13.06.2011.
72   EU/EU-country(10)-16.08.2011.
73   ALBA(2)-09.12.2011.
74   Denmark(2)-16.06.2011, EIG(1)-09.08.2011.
75   EU/EU-country(10)-16.08.2011, EIG(1)-09.08.2011.
76   Denmark(2)-16.06.2011.

door was 'wide open'[77] and certainly not locked. One could, in principle, always join any small group session. Psychologically, this made a very important difference, as UN officials, a key working group chair, and experienced negotiators underlined.[78] De Alba even physically opened the door so other parties could join in the first small group meeting in Cancún: 'This was quite a symbol.'[79] Overall, even a very critical ALBA negotiator granted that the 'Mexicans were more transparent and inclusive than the Danes'.[80] Compared to the Danes, the Mexican Presidency had reached a higher, albeit not full, small group inclusiveness.

Regarding the second criteria of inclusion, the organizers integrated negotiation levels more thoroughly than in 2009. Top UN and Presidency officials considered this integration as vital for the outcome,[81] warning against 'overstating'[82] politicians' role for reaching an agreement. The organizers avoided creating another summit of leaders. By not having a third, political leader level above the other two, they enabled a greater inclusiveness than in Copenhagen.[83] Ministers were closely involved in operational negotiations avoiding non-connected parallel structures. Integration began early in 2010 with several negotiator-level sessions while the Danes had started predominantly at the ministerial level. At the COP, expert negotiations had traditionally preceded those of ministers. Cancún instead integrated negotiations as developing and developed country minister pairs chaired selected expert negotiations during the high-level segment. Their mixed membership of experts and ministers ensured a strong linkage, while 'pure' expert negotiations could continue contributing despite the ministerial takeover of some issues.[84] Further, text that had been negotiated on expert levels was treated carefully by ministers: 'Facilitators made sure that the text was used that had always been used.'[85] The input of minister-chaired groups was returned to 'pure' expert negotiations by the end of the second week so AWG-chairs could bundle packages.[86] This integration was praised by the chairs and Secretariat, contrasting it with the Danes: it 'empowered' the chairs and allowed the Secretariat to better support them.[87] No issues were ever transferred from the AWGs to the ministerial consultations without the chair's consent.[88]

77   Umbrella Group(4)-04.07.2011.
78   UNFCCC Secretariat(5)-14.06.2011, AWG/SB-Chair(4)-14.06.2011, Umbrella Group(4)-04.07.2011.
79   UNFCCC Secretariat(1)-28.04.2010.
80   ALBA(2)-09.12.2011.
81   Mexico(3)-15.06.2011, UNFCCC Secretariat(7)-03.08.2011.
82   UNFCCC Secretariat(1)-28.04.2010.
83   EU/EU-country(8)-05.05.2011.
84   EU/EU-country(11)-10.12.2011.
85   Mexico(5)-07.07.2011.
86   UNFCCC Secretariat(5)-14.06.2011.
87   UNFCCC Secretariat(5)-14.06.2011, also: AWG/SB-Chair(4)-14.06.2011, UNFCCC Secretariat(4)-17.05.2011.
88   AWG/SB-Chair(4)-14.06.2011.

Overall, the substantial exchange between levels was widely lauded as an 'organic' process where everything built on itself.[89] 'At the end of the second week we had [AWG-LCA Chair] Margaret's papers elements from the negotiators' level plus the input from the ministerial level' so that Presidency and Secretariat only needed to compile them without writing their own text.[90] A chief ALBA negotiator contradicted this, arguing that the break up into small groups meant that the final document did not come from all parties.[91] Yet, negotiation levels were much more integrated in Cancún than in Copenhagen, and inclusion is not only given with full participation.

The Mexicans reached out to myriad countries to include them in their deliberation of key negotiation issues.[92] 'They created an atmosphere of inclusion where every voice would be heard.'[93] Mexican lead facilitator de Alba travelled around 260 days in 2010 leading up to COP-16.[94] The outreach was wider than usual[95] with Mexico going far beyond the big players, in contrast to Denmark, which had aimed for the US and other major economies. Mexico concentrated on those countries where 'attention was needed', inter alia countries that had obstructed the process in Copenhagen, like Cuba, Bolivia, Venezuela, or Nicaragua.[96] A big power negotiator praised this approach: 'We were baffled by how much time they were spending with them. They did so much to outreach to parties. I doubt that the Danes went to La Paz or Caracas. Everyone had a voice.'[97] Moreover, they addressed further countries that had slowed the process, such as members of the Organization of Petroleum Exporting Countries (OPEC). According to one insider President Calderón met with the Saudi Oil Minister on Thursday of COP's second week to advocate for a final agreement.[98] This was positively noted by these traditionally more sceptical delegations.[99] In the final days, when it is essential to have everyone on board, Mexico tried to speak to 'absolutely all countries'.[100]

Despite its outreach, the Presidency met with people in small circles. A G-77 negotiator, for instance, was upset that the Presidency had spoken with delegations of the Cartagena Dialogue separately from the G-77.[101] The negotiator had

89   UNFCCC Secretariat(2)-04.12.2010, UNFCCC Secretariat(4)-17.05.2011, UNFCCC Secretariat(5)-14.06.2011, BASIC(2)-16.06.2011.
90   Mexico(3)-15.06.2011.
91   ALBA(2)-09.12.2011.
92   Mexico(3)-15.06.2011.
93   EU/EU-country(7)-04.05.2011.
94   Mexico(3)-15.06.2011.
95   UNFCCC Secretariat(2)-04.12.2010, EU/EU-country(11)-10.12.2011, Observer(3)-16.06.2011.
96   Mexico(3)-15.06.2011.
97   Umbrella Group(2)-02.06.2011.
98   Umbrella Group(2)-02.06.2011.
99   G-77(5)-08.12.2011.
100 EU/EU-country(11)-10.12.2011.
101 G-77(2)-13.06.2011.

not been invited and complained about secrecy. The organizers' outreach for their deliberation did thus not reach complete inclusiveness. However, having all parties always present would not have allowed for frank exchange with facilitators. The general level of inclusion during the Mexican Presidency was therefore as high as it could be while maintaining effectiveness.

The communication on transparency and inclusiveness also differed from that of the UNFCCC Secretariat and the Danish Presidency one year before. During 2010, the organizers used 'transparency and inclusiveness' and the assurance of 'no Mexican text' so early and continuously that participants spoke of a 'mantra' and a 'deep injection into people's minds'.[102] According to Presidency officials, it was part of a deliberate, strategic communication,[103] of 'sending the message of inclusion in Cancún'.[104] This communication strategy achieved the desired effect. Initially criticized concepts such as the 'open–closed' meetings were eventually perceived more positively by participants.[105] So while not everything was fully transparent and inclusive, the appearance was well established.[106] It made even some of the fiercest critics approve of the process: 'The meetings in Cancún were supposed to be open and transparent. Maybe they really wanted to know about countries' positions. They should have the benefit of the doubt. But the Danes didn't even want to know.'[107] In summary, the Mexicans applied a more subtle, if manipulative, strategy in contrast to the straightforward but partially offensive Danish way.[108] They generated a subjective sense of transparency and inclusion.

The evidence along all criteria shows that negotiations during the Mexican Presidency were objectively more transparent and inclusive than in the previous year. Moreover, through their communication strategy, organizers achieved a perception of transparency and inclusiveness above and beyond the objective reality. In short, transparency and inclusiveness during the Mexican Presidency correlated with reaching the Cancún Agreements.

How transparency and inclusiveness influenced the summit outcomes

As correlation does not equal causation a detailed tracing of the process during both Presidencies will now show *whether and how* an agreement depends on transparency and inclusiveness. We turn to the 'big picture' first. Around 90 per cent of the 46 interviewees asserted that transparency and inclusiveness affected the agreement (Table 3.3). Respondents include senior current and former

102   UNFCCC Secretariat(1)-28.04.2010, Denmark(3)-11.08.2011.
103   Mexico(2)-08.02.2011.
104   Mexico(3)-15.06.2011.
105   EU/EU-country(10)-16.08.2011.
106   EIG(1)-09.08.2011.
107   G-77(2)-13.06.2011.
108   G-77(2)-13.06.2011.

Table 3.3 Responses to the question 'Did this kind of transparency and inclusion have an influence on whether they agreed to the proposal?'

Response	n (%)
Transparency and inclusiveness *influenced* the outcome	41 (89%)
Transparency and inclusiveness influenced the outcome *somewhat*	3 (7%)
Transparency and inclusiveness *did not* influence the outcome	2 (4%)
Total	46

UNFCCC officials, observers, and negotiators of all major coalitions, such as BASIC, Umbrella Group, G-77 and the EU, and members of the Mexican and Danish Presidencies. One delegate summarized the dynamics of transparency *and* inclusiveness for COP-15's last day: 'Not just the lack of knowledge about the process but also the lack of involvement of parties was a factor in the final night in Copenhagen.' Three interviewees from Western countries argued that content was more decisive than transparency and inclusiveness. Two highly process-crit- ical G-77 negotiators denied *any* such influence. They said that their approval of the Cancún Agreements was solely based on content. I will discuss these critiques below.

Four paths emerge from the evidence that show *how* a transparent and inclu- sive process influenced the probability of reaching an agreement:

1   process and content knowledge;
2   contribution ability;
3   obstruction ability; and
4   feeling of respect.

I will now examine this connection between transparency and inclusiveness and reaching an agreement. It details the first negotiation management element of the framework laid out above (Figures 3.1 and 3.2).

Transparency and inclusiveness influence the degree of *knowledge among nego- tiators about the process and content of the negotiations* (path 1). There are varying information levels about the various elements of a negotiation text and the key steps taken in such complex negotiations, such as in small groups and bilateral negotiations. Who was deciding or compromising, on which elements, under what circumstances? 'You also want to understand why other concerns are included...This makes for a deeper understanding why the final agreement looks like this, which reasons and considerations are behind it. It "makes you a part of it".'[109] This knowledge influenced the reaching of an agreement during the Danish and Mexican Presidencies in several ways.

109   UNFCCC Secretariat(6)-16.06.2011.

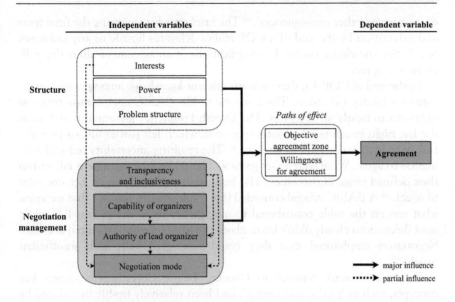

Figure 3.1 Negotiation management framework

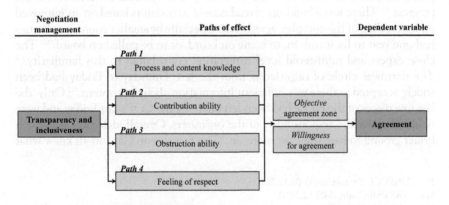

Figure 3.2 Process-tracing between transparency and inclusiveness and agreement

First, process and content knowledge determine a delegation's awareness of what it is actually supposed to decide on in the COP's final days. If delegates are not sure whether the proposal is above their reservation point, they aren't able to determine whether they are in the zone of a possible agreement. From a rational decision-making perspective, they would be unable to agree. The high uncertainty may cause stalemate given a 'big fear of countries to lose with serious economic and other consequences'.[110] The brief time for reviewing the final texts and exhaustion by the end of a COP makes delegates hostile to any unknown text.[111] So, knowledge on the key implications of an agreement alters the willingness to agree.

By the end of COP-15, there was insufficient knowledge among most participants for taking a decision. The last minute US–BASIC compromise text was unknown to nearly all delegates. The Danish Presidency presented it at 1am in the last night granting 60 minutes to read it, which left parties furious over the lack of time to understand its content.[112] The resulting uncertainty reduced willingness to agree. What were exact gains and costs? Did the agreement fall within their defined range of outcomes? The time was too short,[113] and it became safer to reject.[114] A BASIC official conceded that 'undoubtedly, the fact that we knew what was on the table contributed to our agreement to the proposal',[115] while most delegations clearly didn't know about the substance until the final decision. Negotiators emphasized that they could not agree with such insufficient insight.[116]

This was in stark contrast to Cancún. Before Copenhagen, several key concepts, such as 'pledge and review', had been relatively freshly introduced by the US and like-minded countries,[117] and talks were fast-paced throughout 2009. Many countries hesitated to quickly follow this fundamental shift, making an agreement in Copenhagen difficult.[118] On the other side, negotiations were proceeding more slowly at COP-16. This allowed delegations to better follow the progress.[119] There was a build-up of readiness of negotiators based on an improved understanding of the complex agreement, especially by smaller countries: 'Parties had one year to let it sink in, to come on board, or to be pulled on board.'[120] The close expert and ministerial level integration contributed to this familiarity.[121] The narrower circle of negotiators from the last Thursday to Friday had been widely accepted as there was sufficient information about its content.[122] Only 'the last five pieces of the puzzle had been left out'[123] by the COP's last Friday and were finalized under the responsibility of the organizers. Overall, delegates had much firmer ground to base their decisions on: 'The fact that in Cancún all knew what

110 UNFCCC Secretariat(3)-08.12.2010.
111 AWG/SB-Chair(3)-07.12.2010.
112 ALBA(1)-17.06.2011.
113 Observer(3)-16.06.2011.
114 EU/EU-country(5)-17.02.2011.
115 BASIC(3)-08.07.2011.
116 Umbrella Group(4)-04.07.2011.
117 Umbrella Group(1)-20.04.2011.
118 Umbrella Group(4)-04.07.2011.
119 Denmark(3)-11.08.2011.
120 BASIC(2)-16.06.2011.
121 BASIC(3)-08.07.2011.
122 G-77(3)-19.07.2011.
123 UNFCCC Secretariat(5)-14.06.2011.

the President was doing and that she invited them all into the small room created confidence. People knew what happened and went along with it.'[124] To imagine the counterfactual, higher transparency and inclusiveness before and during COP-15 could have provided much more background and information on the newly introduced suggestions. Copenhagen revealed much of parties' preferences for Cancún.[125] The enhanced level of information helped parties to find a compromise acceptable to all. But why should it not have been possible to accelerate this process? Learning could have been enabled much earlier than only in 2010 and allowed parties to agree in Copenhagen. Acknowledging the need to get familiar with new ideas, an 'incredibly skilful' negotiation management may still have made an agreement possible.[126]

A second consequence of lacking knowledge is the delegation's inability to fulfil its obligation as 'agent' to comprehensively report to its 'principal', the government. COP-15 infringed upon this vital delegate's duty. For lack of information, a delegation could not have truly reported back what it had agreed to. In the same vein, delegations frequently must consult their principals for permission to agree to proposals outside their mandate. This became very difficult in Copenhagen because of scarce information on the new texts. At COP-16, it was much easier for parties to report back to decision makers thanks to a significantly higher level of information.

Finally, the process's legitimacy added to the acceptance of the final ruling on consensus by COP-16 President Espinosa. Legitimacy increased at COP-16 as the decision was reached through a process that ensured certain rule-based transparency and inclusiveness: parties saw and participated in the text's evolution. Espinosa considered this crucial: '[W]hat gives credibility to a decision where you do not have a unanimous opinion is the process behind that decision...that you can at the end say...this is really consensus' (Espinosa 2011: 8). COP-15 produced the reverse dynamic. A rule-neglecting process was deprived of legitimacy which finally turned against the Accord.[127] Parties lacked the most substantial knowledge such as where certain texts came from.[128] Delegates found that a fair process would have given legitimacy to the outcome, which the US–BASIC small group negotiations had achieved.[129] This way, an agreement may have been possible in Copenhagen. The overall perception of legitimacy increased from COP-15 to 16 in such a way that countries did no longer block the agreement on process grounds.

Path 2 traces how transparency and inclusiveness determine delegates' *ability to contribute* to developing a proposal that lies within the zone of possible

124   UNFCCC Secretariat(2)-04.12.2010.
125   EU/EU-country(8)-05.05.2011.
126   Umbrella Group(2)-02.06.2011.
127   UNFCCC Secretariat(2)-04.12.2010.
128   G-77(2)-13.06.2011.
129   G-77(3)-19.07.2011.

agreement between parties, and how this impacts agreement chances. Inclusion allows delegations to contribute directly while transparency at least leaves the ability to understand the negotiation progress and contribute indirectly by inter- vening through delegations that participate in smaller groups. Overall, parties want at least some idea about and influence on the negotiations.[130] This ability to contribute to the negotiations worked through several mechanisms.

First, it maximized parties' inputs during the Mexican Presidency, which helped to create a proposal inside the objective agreement zone. With wide participation and information the 'willingness to engage came back soon during the year'.[131] The close integration of expert and ministerial levels and the coop- eration between the Presidency and the subsidiary body chairs ensured that all input was considered for the final proposal.[132] The output was a comprehensive text reflecting the totality of the 2010 negotiations. This was in stark contrast to COP-15. On the final Thursday, expert negotiators had stopped their work of over one year in despair after when they learnt that leaders were meeting in a small group. The ability and willingness to contribute was 'down to zero',[133] and so too the opportunity to find broadly acceptable solutions.

Second, the inclusion of diverging, more 'radical' parties in the deliberations enabled a comprehensive final proposal acceptable for all in Cancún. Mexico held countless 'bilaterals' to include as many countries as possible, and did not focus solely on big powers.[134] Non-mainstream voices had been included in the final small group negotiations so that at least some of their views could be reflected in the text.[135] They had ensured that all 'opinion leaders' were inte- grated avoiding their risky isolation as during the Danish Presidency.[136] Eventually, ALBA delegations no longer rejected an agreement as in 2009, except for Bolivia. 'There must have been a lot of conviction and talk behind the scenes for this to happen.'[137] The approach generated a comprehensive agreement and a subjective willingness to agree. In contrast, the Danish Presidency had focused on selected developed countries. According to an Asian observer, this exclusion triggered the final objection: 'That's why China and the G-77 opposed.'[138] There was also a sound rational side to this objection.[139] The secre- tive process posed a risk for the excluded parties. Approval of the outcome would have set a precedent to neglect process rules and to further exclude non-main- stream views in subsequent negotiations.

130 UNFCCC Secretariat(5)-14.06.2011.
131 BASIC(3)-08.07.2011.
132 UNFCCC Secretariat(5)-14.06.2011.
133 UNFCCC Secretariat(5)-14.06.2011.
134 Mexico(3)-15.06.2011.
135 UNFCCC Secretariat(6)-16.06.2011.
136 UNFCCC Secretariat(3)-08.12.2010.
137 UNFCCC Secretariat(2)-04.12.2010.
138 Observer(3)-16.06.2011.
139 UNFCCC Secretariat(4)-17.05.2011.

Third, the ability to contribute increases the identification by negotiators with the output. This enhanced buy-in raises the willingness to agree while they see the agreement as representing their joint will. At COP-15, not many parties eventually identified with the text. It had not been everybody's effort[140] and was thus found seriously unsatisfactory.[141] The selection of the salient small group on the last Thursday night was a case in point as it undermined true representation: 'You need those that are outside to feel represented by those inside.'[142] Next, the US–BASIC meeting had resolved weighty political issues, yet it lacked the buy-in from all parties.[143] The 'G-2 focus' on the US and China within the US–BASIC group aggravated this further.[144] The process had a detrimental effect on many excluded countries: 'Many countries do not just go along with what major powers are suggesting.'[145] One failure of Copenhagen seemed that a small group of countries tried to decide for the rest, echoed one ALBA negotiator.[146] As many delegations supported the proposal's substance, the objective agreement zone was probably reached – yet, crucially, there was insufficient identification with the result, and no willingness to agree.

During the Mexican Presidency in turn, transparency and inclusiveness lent negotiators the feeling of being part of the process.[147] Parties identified more with the suggested text since they were able to contribute. They had worked intensely on the text involving everyone. 'They knew that they have had a chance before to make their input.'[148] A sense of ownership[149] and responsibility emerged as parties were continuously engaged by the Mexicans to make them feel part of the process.[150] The active participation by minister pairs as in the small groups built further commitment by key parties whose minister facilitated.[151] This identification with the process may have also allowed for compromises that could have been difficult otherwise. The organizers developed an image to embody the common will of the international community which allowed for an agreement.[152] The higher willingness to agree may have contributed to a repositioning of countries on an objective level.

Path 3 describes how transparency and inclusiveness influence countries' *ability to obstruct* negotiations. Unsatisfied with the suggested outcome at COP-15,

140 Mexico(5)-07.07.2011.
141 G-77(3)-19.07.2011.
142 UNFCCC Secretariat(7)-03.08.2011.
143 AWG/SB-Chair(1)-30.11.2010.
144 UNFCCC Secretariat(6)-16.06.2011.
145 BASIC(1)-04.12.2010.
146 ALBA(1)-17.06.2011.
147 EU/EU-country(9)-26.05.2011.
148 Mexico(5)-07.07.2011.
149 Mexico(4)-16.06.2011.
150 Mexico(3)-15.06.2011.
151 Umbrella Group(4)-04.07.2011.
152 Mexico(3)-15.06.2011.

delegates partially used process as an instrument.[153] They tried to undercut the organizers' efforts[154] and leveraged the notion of lacking transparency and inclusiveness. A Danish official accused parties of deliberately wasting time to delay the entire process.[155] Numerous parties used process to counter the shift to a pledge-and-review emission reduction system.[156] A prominent G-77 negotiator frankly stated that '[p]arties use the argument of legitimacy often as pretext for rejection if they don't like a text – if they do however, the point of legitimacy is never raised.'[157] A Danish politician even spoke of a 'procedural weapon to torpedo negotiations',[158] and a negotiator that 'We need to keep people from throwing bombs at the process.'[159] Finally, several participants suggested that the 'Danish text' had been deliberately leaked by China or India to undermine the process, which was eventually 'successful'.[160] The procedural complaint on the lack of transparency and inclusiveness to draft this text was also used as a means of obstruction.

In contrast, the widespread conviction of a fair process at COP-16 took away the credibility for 'spoilers' to 'play the process card'.[161] For the Mexican Presidency, the transparent and inclusive process was one way to 'undermine the obstructionists' and to 'disarm the enemy'[162] (e.g. the ALBA countries wouldn't be able to blame the Mexicans for excluding them).[163] Also, Saudi Arabia no longer objected to the agreement in the final plenary in Cancún: 'The Saudis felt that they wouldn't, couldn't, and shouldn't block the agreement in Cancún...It was not possible to attack it as a result of a flawed process.'[164] The political price for blocking became too high with only Bolivia willing to pay.[165]

Path 4 works mostly on a subjective level. Being a delegate in a transparent and inclusive process increases the *sense of respectful treatment*. Subjective opinion is central in the crucial decision moment when it depends on the willingness of the individual negotiator to agree. Being treated fairly increases the sense of respect and thereby the willingness to agree. 'Several UN rules are silly...But if you ignore them you also disrespect developing countries. It is their only

153 EU/EU-country(5)-17.02.2011, AWG/SB-Chair(1)-30.11.2010, Umbrella Group(1)-20.04.2011.
154 Umbrella Group(3)-14.06.2011.
155 Denmark(1)-02.12.2010.
156 Umbrella Group(1)-20.04.2011.
157 G-77(1)-04.12.2010.
158 Denmark(1)-02.12.2010.
159 Umbrella Group(2)-02.06.2011.
160 Denmark(1)-02.12.2010, Denmark(6)-09.02.2012, Umbrella Group(3)-14.06.2011, EU/EU-country(6)-16.03.2011.
161 Denmark(3)-11.08.2011, also: G-77(4)-22.07.2011, G-77(3)-19.07.2011, Mexico(5)-07.07.2011.
162 Mexico(3)-15.06.2011.
163 Umbrella Group(5)-27.07.2011.
164 UNFCCC Secretariat(2)-04.12.2010.
165 G-77(3)-19.07.2011.

common venue for multilateral diplomacy',[166] noted a Danish official. Most negotiators are permanent UN representatives and highly accustomed to this
rulebook.[167] A former COP President emphasized the importance of this individual level: 'People should never go to bed feeling excluded'.[168]

The Danish Presidency conveyed a lack of respect: 'People felt left out.'[169] The
Copenhagen Accord was 'impos[ed] ... on us ... creating a sour taste in their
mouth ... We didn't matter anymore.'[170] A BASIC negotiator of the small group
showed understanding for this perception as the Accord 'had only been tossed
onto them'.[171] This illustrates the discontent voiced in interviews. Many negotiators therefore lost trust in the organizers,[172] which by the end of COP-15
diminished their willingness to agree. The missing respect caused extreme
emotions among people in Copenhagen, noted a veteran of 20 years of climate
negotiations.[173] It altered delegates' view on a deal, rendering an agreement less
likely. Rasmussen for instance triggered an outburst of anger when he took over
as COP-15 President and announced that he would table a Danish compromise
proposal, after delegates had just finished an overnight marathon on an expert-
level negotiation text.[174] Negotiators protested massively, and the Danes
withdrew the text. The willingness to agree reached its nadir when the text
finally came out on Friday night: 'Even though [the] substance was agreeable ...
Everybody was just really pissed and angry.'[175]

In a consensus system, non-mainstream groups in particular need respect. In
Copenhagen, the lack of small group transparency and inclusion created anger
among the vocal ALBA countries: 'Convening people without legitimacy, keeping Venezuela and Bolivia out drove them very angry.'[176] At COP-15, even their
heads of state were excluded. Venezuelan President Hugo Chávez underlined in
the Friday morning plenary that he would reject any agreement from such a small
group. After this public statement, there was hardly any face-saving way to
retreat.[177] They signalled to the global public that they would not simply follow
US–BASIC leaders without consultation.[178] The presence of high political leaders in Copenhagen had given ALBA leaders an unforeseen opportunity to
publicly shame the US. This had created an unanticipated coalition among

166   Denmark(5)-12.08.2011.
167   Denmark(2)-16.06.2011.
168   EU/EU-country(5)-17.02.2011.
169   AWG/SB-Chair(4)-14.06.2011.
170   G-77(4)-22.07.2011.
171   BASIC(2)-16.06.2011.
172   G-77(4)-22.07.2011.
173   EU/EU-country(11)-10.12.2011.
174   UNFCCC Secretariat(5)-14.06.2011.
175   UNFCCC Secretariat(1)-28.04.2010.
176   UNFCCC Secretariat(2)-04.12.2010; similar: Denmark(3)-11.08.2011.
177   EU/EU-country(10)-16.08.2011.
178   Mexico(3)-15.06.2011.

them.[179] The absence of most leaders at COP-16 then limited its geopolitical use again. A Danish official conceded that this bold and unified ALBA stance had surprised the Presidency.[180] 'I asked Bo [Lidegaard] what they were planning to do with heads of state like Chávez, Ahmadinejad, and others. He could not give a response.'[181] This lack of geopolitical sensitivity obstructed the agreement.

Besides, leaders in general felt that they were treated without sufficient respect. Usually courted respectfully, politicians are even more sensitive than experts if they do not 'feel themselves heard.'[182] COP-15's last two days were especially harmful. Ninety heads of state and government were excluded from the small group from Thursday to Friday. Dozens of ministers waited without word for hours, which made them very angry.[183] A BASIC participant of the smaller US–BASIC negotiation conceded that countries where the 'Prime Minister' was not in the room had essentially not negotiated the agreement: 'For [us] it made a big difference having been part of the small group … We would have rejected it otherwise.'[184] The same was true for other countries who told the interviewed BASIC negotiator explicitly that they rejected the agreement for this reason – such as Saudi Arabia, Sudan as the G-77 Chair, Colombia and Kenya. An OPEC member country negotiator confirmed: 'Imagine my President is here, and he is not invited. What do you think he does?'[185] The impact was enormous as only 30 out of 120 heads of state and government were invited to the small group. Ninety were 'slapped in their face'.[186] The organizers had underestimated this question which further reduced COP wide consensus. Finally, experienced negotiators, facilitators, and UN officials all considered Obama's press statement that a deal was achieved detrimental as it showed little respect for those excluded.[187] While it reduced delegates' willingness further, some core opponents had already prepared their 10–15 minutes plenary interventions, so it probably didn't make much difference for them.[188]

In contrast, the Mexican Presidency conveyed a much higher sense of respect, where parties felt represented, consulted, and generally taken much more seriously.[189] This was probably also true for most ALBA delegations, which no longer objected to the agreement. 'The change in stance of ALBA countries came because de Alba treated them so carefully…'.[190] Yet one ALBA negotiator

179   EU/EU-country(11)-10.12.2011.
180   Denmark(3)-11.08.2011.
181   EU/EU-country(10)-16.08.2011.
182   EU/EU-country(6)-16.03.2011.
183   Umbrella Group(5)-27.07.2011.
184   BASIC(2)-16.06.2011.
185   G-77(5)-08.12.2011.
186   EU/EU-country(10)-16.08.2011.
187   Mexico(3)-15.06.2011, EU/EU-country(8)-05.05.2011, UNFCCC Secretariat(7)-03.08.2011.
188   Umbrella Group(2)-02.06.2011.
189   Denmark(3)-11.08.2011, UNFCCC Secretariat(7)-03.08.2011, EU/EU-country(11)-10.12.2011.
190   Denmark(3)-11.08.2011.

suggested both COPs were unfair. He pointed to a difference in content, not in transparency and inclusiveness: 'We were steamrolled in both COPs but with more style in Mexico.'[191] Yet, the claim that substance made the difference is not convincing: the core provisions were largely similar between COP-15 and 16, so they could have already agreed in Copenhagen. Contrary to this one view, a standing ovation expressed the appreciation of the respectful treatment by the organizers when Espinosa presented the final text in the Friday afternoon plenary.[192] Most negotiators had not even fully read the final text then but accepted the organizers' approach and thereby also bought into its result.[193] A sense of respect for the leaders and of being respected can thus crucially influence the subjective willingness to agree.

Overall, the subjective sense of a transparent and inclusive process suffices for paths 3 and 4. The ability to use process as an argument to obstruct negotiations decreases if the subjective notion of a fair process is widespread. Or, a negotiator feels respected if the process is perceived as transparent and inclusive. So for those who disagree that negotiations during the Danish Presidency were objectively less transparent and inclusive than during the Mexican Presidency, paths 3 and 4 still hold. It is unchallenged that at least the perception was one of transparency and inclusiveness during negotiations in 2010.

Conclusion

The Danish and Mexican Presidencies and their UNFCCC Secretariat counterparts applied the tool of transparency and inclusiveness very differently. This contributed to the respective outcomes through four paths: process and content knowledge, contribution ability, obstruction ability, and feeling of respect. Transparency and inclusiveness played out both on an objective and a subjective level leading countries to reject the Copenhagen Accord and to approve the Cancún Agreements. This finding supports and refines research on transparency and inclusiveness group dynamics across disciplines, and observations made by myriad practitioners on this issue. Future organizers of negotiations may thus want to consider the core elements of transparency and inclusiveness to increase the chance of agreement. Let us now move to the next factor, which reveals similar striking differences between both years: the capability of the organizers.

Capability of organizers

Recent research has shown how important bureaucracies and individuals can be in international relations, as we have seen in Chapter 1. The capability of the Danish and Mexican Presidencies and their respective UNFCCC Secretariat

191   ALBA(2)-09.12.2011.
192   EU/EU-country(4)-27.01.2011.
193   UNFCCC Secretariat(5)-14.06.2011.

counterparts had a large impact on the course of the climate negotiations. Shakespearean strife inside both the Danish administration and the UN system was followed by the work of the diplomatic masters of the Mexican Presidency in 2010. I will first paint the big picture using a numerical interpretation of interview responses and then substantiate it in more detail by applying the indicators of capability (Figure 1.4, page 12).

The Danish Presidency: a tale of Shakespearean strife

We begin with the Danish Presidency on an *institutional level*. Respondents nearly unanimously saw it as low in its overall capability (Table 3.4). The only deviation was one interviewee from the Danish Presidency with a possible self-interest. 'There was mistake after mistake.'[194] This view was taken by negotiators across the board, observers, and UN officials but most importantly also by lead Danish Presidency members. The capability indicators for organizers of (1) organizational and cultural fit, (2) process, and (3) content expertise now provide more detail.[195]

The Presidency had a very low organizational fit for the negotiations as it was internally divided by 'significant differences'[196]. It was split into a more inclusiveness-minded UNFCCC group, and a group oriented more at key powers and UN headquarters.[197] One side defended 'the Bonn line', the other side 'the New

Table 3.4 Responses to the question 'In hindsight, what was done well or not so well by the organizers (e.g. on process and content matters at the COP)?' with respect to the Danish Presidency

Response	Danish Presidency n (%)	Rasmussen n (%)	Hedegaard n (%)	Lidegaard n (%)	Becker n (%)	De Boer n (%)
Perceived high capability	1 (5%)	0 (0%)	5 (38.4%)	1 (5.3%)	10 (62.5%)	2 (8.7%)
Perceived low capability	19 (95%)	29	6 (46.2%)	11 (57.9%)	4 (25%)	21 (91.3%)
Undecided/ don't know person	0 (0%)	0 (0%)	2 (15.4%)	7 (36.8%)	2 (12.5%)	0 (0%)
Total	20	29	13	19	16	23

194   EU/EU-country(8)-05.05.2011.
195   There is no numerical indication for the capability of the UNFCCC Secretariat on an institutional level as this aspect only arose in the interviews and is thus analysed only verbally.
196   EU/EU-country(10)-16.08.2011.
197   Denmark(2)-16.06.2011; similar: EU/EU-country(1)-20.01.2010, Umbrella Group(4)-04.07.2011, EU/EU-country(8)-05.05.2011, UNFCCC Secretariat(4)-17.05.2011.

York line'.[198] Myriad responses echoed this cleavage (e.g. 'internal disagreements',[199] 'two heads of the Danish delegation',[200] 'relationship within the Danes was dreadful',[201] 'two-power centres'[202]). There were massive negative emotions between them as they were 'literally not talking to each other, slamming the door in front of each other'.[203] A long-time negotiator described the relations between Hedegaard and Rasmussen in these terms: 'Your boss is constantly bullying you. She had an unhappy role in relation to Rasmussen.'[204] An interviewee of Hedegaard's team asserted that most Danish ministries backed their approach so that 'the whole administration was against the Prime Minister's office.'[205] A more neutral Danish official finds this too harsh but conceded that the Climate and Foreign Ministries were more concerned with the 'balance of the proposal' and the 'inclusion of developing countries' whereas the Prime Minister's and Finance Ministry's teams emphasized a pure economic view.[206]

The differences are spelt out in multiple aspects of negotiation management. For example, the 'Rasmussen team' around Lidegaard deemed the early creation of a Presidency's compromise text important. In contrast, the 'Hedegaard team' around Becker saw this more critically ('completely crazy approach') and considered this a way for the Prime Minister to 'control' the Climate Ministry and streamline the Danish government.[207] Media attention was at first on the bigger Hedegaard team owing to their higher expertise and longer involvement. The sixty officials in the ministry stood against around ten in Rasmussen's team.[208] The Prime Minister had only come into office in spring 2009 and his adviser Lidegaard joined in 2007.[209] Being new to the process they also didn't know many of the key leaders.[210] Rasmussen and Hedegaard were also domestic competitors from two different parties: the liberal Venstre party and the Conservative People's Party.[211] The rivalry for public attention ignited jealousies further.[212] Finally, while both Danish camps saw the problems of the strict UN rulebook, only the Prime Minister's side opted to circumvent it by moving negotiation fora to the political level in summer 2009: Not used to the UN process, they saw it 'as a madhouse'.[213]

198   Denmark(4)-12.08.2011.
199   Denmark(6)-09.02.2012.
200   Umbrella Group(4)-04.07.2011.
201   EU/EU-country(8)-05.05.2011.
202   EU/EU-country(7)-04.05.2011.
203   UNFCCC Secretariat(7)-03.08.2011.
204   EU/EU-country(11)-10.12.2011.
205   Denmark(5)-12.08.2011.
206   Denmark(7)-16.02.2012.
207   Denmark(2)-16.06.2011.
208   Denmark(5)-12.08.2011.
209   EU/EU-country(9)-26.05.2011.
210   Umbrella Group(2)-02.06.2011, Mexico(5)-07.07.2011.
211   Denmark(7)-16.02.2012.
212   Denmark(5)-12.08.2011.
213   Denmark(3)-11.08.2011.

The divide culminated in two shifts in the Presidency's power distribution. The removal of Hedegaard's team leader Becker came first. Most interviewees perceived this change as political given their clashing ideas about the Presidency.[214] Further, Becker was 'more of a Social Democrat but within a conservative government.'[215] He had originally continued in this key position as the Danish administrative system has no ministerial cabinets, which change with each new government. Then however, '[t]hey drove him out'.[216] UN officials spoke of a 'sacking' of Becker[217] and a 'sort of coup d'état',[218] and negotiators saw 'rivalry and hatred'[219] between Lidegaard and Becker. The few voices that contested this political reasoning stem from the Prime Ministerial side. They saw Becker's violations of administrative rules as the only reason, and found 'a lot of hype about a political assassination . . . The Danish system doesn't work this way'; the differences between the ministries have 'nothing to do with this'. Accordingly, Becker gave his spin to it when the administrative violation was leaked. 'The Environment committee of the Danish Parliament heard the case. He has had warnings before.'[220] This account though seems hard to sustain given the abundant evidence of their power-based and strategic clashes. Leading Danish media also indicated these power struggles when Becker stepped down (e.g. Politiken 2009).

The second power shift was Rasmussen's takeover as COP President at the start of the high-level segment. Few people trusted the official Danish line that this change had long been planned[221] as the chairing by so many heads of state and government through a minister may have been diplomatically difficult.[222] Most found that Hedegaard 'did rather not go voluntarily'[223] and was 'taken out'.[224] Either way, delegations received the change very badly. The extreme internal divergences were tangible for everyone, and without clear responsibilities on how to resolve them.[225]

Next to this lack of organizational fit, there appeared to be a low cultural fit for these kinds of multilateral negotiations. Numerous interviewees perceived the Danish way of interaction as straightforward and very outspoken, compared with many other cultures. One Danish official commented that the Danes are 'often very blunt'.[226] A delegate complained about this direct way. When he made

214   Denmark(2)-16.06.2011.
215   Denmark(2)-16.06.2011.
216   Denmark(2)-16.06.2011.
217   UNFCCC Secretariat(4)-17.05.2011.
218   UNFCCC Secretariat(2)-04.12.2010.
219   Umbrella Group(4)-04.07.2011.
220   Denmark(4)-12.08.2011.
221   Denmark(6)-09.02.2012.
222   AWG/SB-Chair(4)-14.06.2011.
223   EU/EU-country(9)-26.05.2011.
224   G-77(2)-13.06.2011; similar: G-77(3)-19.07.2011.
225   Denmark(3)-11.08.2011.
226   Denmark(2)-16.06.2011.

suggestions about the text in a Danish meeting with G-77 representatives, Danish officials only rolled their eyes.[227] A Denmark-friendly negotiator described it as a 'rigid, un-empathic approach'.[228] A delegate from a similar cultural background sensed that the 'Danes have a straight manner which was not helpful then. It is not their fault as it is part of the culture. They were not native speakers either to express issues in the most appropriate way.'[229] This inter-cultural difference in communication created an unhelpful packaging of their approaches.[230] Overall, the slow, inclusive, and emotionally sensitive UN process was unfamiliar to the Danish culture.[231]

This cultural dynamic also fostered a very activist Danish approach, for which they received much blame. For instance, the creation of a 'Danish text' was seen by many as 'too intrusive'.[232] The very early drafting had increased the chances of its leakage.[233] The Mexicans in turn 'handed it over to the parties to tell [them] where to go. We did the opposite. We dragged everyone.'[234] The Danes were more content than process managers 'pushing particular outcomes'.[235] One Danish offi-cial saw this positively though: it was the proactive approach that enabled at least the note-taking of a political agreement saving the COP from a complete failure:

> It would have been so much easier for us to also say on the last day that this is not enough and blame it on the countries' lack of willingness. Instead, we chose the opposite by coming forward with a text and pushing for a political agreement nevertheless. With this of course, we got all the bashing.[236]

Yet according to the vast majority of interviewees, it had been the exclusive, high-level focus and intrusive activism of the Danish Presidency that had contributed to this malign state of the negotiations by the final COP days with the Danes no longer perceived as neutral and trusted facilitators.

Process expertise was low as the Presidency misinterpreted the negotiation situation in their planning and did not envision extreme scenarios. A Presidency

227 G-77(2)-13.06.2011.
228 EU/EU-country(7)-04.05.2011.
229 EU/EU-country(11)-10.12.2011.
230 UNFCCC Secretariat(1)-28.04.2010.
231 Denmark(2)-16.06.2011. This may be compared to the failure of COP-6 in The Hague in 2000. The Dutch Presidency under COP President Jan Pronk was similar in its style, 'very much pushing forward … They were so eager to get there that they ignored the process too much.' The success of the follow-up COP-6 bis in Bonn could be partially attributed to a change of process with the 'diplomatic skills of the Belgians. The then-Belgian minister and EU President Jacque Delors had a big influence in the success.'
232 Denmark(1)-02.12.2010.
233 EU/EU-country(8)-05.05.2011.
234 Denmark(3)-11.08.2011.
235 UNFCCC Secretariat(4)-17.05.2011.
236 Denmark(4)-12.08.2011.

member attributed the failure 'mainly...to the way the meeting was prepared': while they focused on creating a political level they underestimated the intense steering requirements of two parallel negotiation levels.[237] The Prime Minister's office supposedly mistook the complexity of a UN climate negotiation with a 'simpler' EU summit it had successfully hosted before, like on EU enlargement.[238] Moreover, EU member states grant the Commission and Presidency a stronger role as an active moderator,[239] which the Danes repeated here. Another such planning mismatch was the COP President's change. With rumours and suspicion abounding 'an actually non-dramatic event as the takeover of a COP Presidency became an important factor...We had not announced it properly in advance.'[240] Similarly, BASIC negotiators suggested to the Danes in vain that they needed fall-back options for the high-level segment:

> They were very incompetent on this. During the whole year we knew about all these problems and told them about it. Yet, they never listened. Plan B then was the worst. Some heads of states were in the small room, others were not. It was a power gamble that could have worked, or not.[241]

Several Danish interviewees acknowledged this lack of planning for the unforeseen, chaotic developments of the last days.[242] The Prime Minister's team 'thought it is only about cashing in a deal. They had not prepared at all for the case that no deal would be done.'[243] The Prime Minister and his team misread summit politics and the strategies of salient countries. For example, they underestimated the global dynamics of the emancipation of the BASIC countries.[244]

Numerous interviewees emphasized the poor physical negotiating conditions at the Bella Center. There was not enough space for the thousands of participants so that eventually even key delegates, such as the Chinese chief negotiator were not allowed back into. Thousands waited outside in heavy snowfall and very cold temperatures.[245] Danes and participants describe many meeting rooms, including the US–BASIC small room, as appalling: 'They were cramped in a room of only a few square meters with hardly any air left after some time had passed.'[246] The food at the site was often brought up as terrible.[247] As one COP veteran summarized: 'The logistics were horrible...It was about the worst I have ever seen.'[248]

237   Denmark(2)-16.06.2011.
238   Denmark(6)-09.02.2012.
239   Denmark(7)-16.02.2012.
240   Denmark(6)-09.02.2012.
241   BASIC(5)-15.06.2011.
242   Denmark(1)-02.12.2010.
243   Denmark(6)-09.02.2012.
244   Denmark(2)-16.06.2011.
245   UNFCCC Secretariat(6)-16.06.2011.
246   Denmark(1)-02.12.2010.
247   For example: Umbrella Group(3)-14.06.2011.
248   Umbrella Group(3)-14.06.2011.

The organizers' expectation management also implies low process expertise.[249] Initially, Copenhagen stood for the place where a grand new climate agreement should be sealed, which would include top-down commitment by major countries. It raised hopes too high, many suggested.[250] With COP-15 approaching and disagreement still widespread, the Presidency lowered expectations, which massively disappointed those that had trusted the high-flying vision. It pleased the few delegations that favoured a stepwise approach, rather than one 'big bang' that would resolve all questions.[251] The drastic lowering of ambitions infuriated 'large parts of the public'.[252] When Rasmussen announced this shift to the media in October 2009, Hedegaard was taken by surprise while travelling in Africa.[253] This lack of coordination and continuity in expectation management confused participants.

In sum, the Danish Presidency was of low capability in their organizational–cultural fit and their process expertise. It was split into two contending camps, faced intercultural difficulties, proceeded as too activist, fell short of coherent planning, and failed to manage expectations stringently. While it invested abundant human and material resources, and even established a 'mini-UNFCCC Secretariat' with shadow positions in Hedegaard's team, apparently only one diplomat was in charge.[254] This helps to explain its good content expertise, and the neglect of process. Content expertise though could not balance out the other significant capability issues.

Regarding individual Danish Presidency members, the two successive COP-15 Presidents are seen differently. Around 60 per cent of interviewees saw the capability of Danish Climate and Energy Minister Connie Hedegaard sceptically while others were more positive (Table 3.4). Results are randomly distributed and cannot be attributed to countries with sympathy for or highly critical of Denmark. Let us first turn to the personal-cultural fit with respect to the situation. Needless to say this is a partially subjective category but may change people's attitude to the process nonetheless. 'She is very talented, committed, stubborn and patient. She knew how to do it,'[255] acknowledged one negotiator. Another praised the sincere attitude that earned her respect from parties.[256] Multiple delegates, however, complained about aspects that may be culturally driven by the straightforward Danish way of communicating. They lacked sufficient empathy to take all parties on board, describing a kind of 'roughness'.[257] A

249 BASIC(3)-08.07.2011.
250 EU/EU-country(10)-16.08.2011, Umbrella Group(4)-04.07.2011, Umbrella Group(5)-27.07.2011, AWG/SB-Chair(4)-14.06.2011.
251 Umbrella Group(3)-14.06.2011.
252 Denmark(4)-12.08.2011.
253 Denmark(5)-12.08.2011.
254 UNFCCC Secretariat(5)-14.06.2011.
255 Umbrella Group(4)-04.07.2011.
256 UNFCCC Secretariat(5)-14.06.2011.
257 Mexico(3)-15.06.2011.

delegate with comparable cultural background commented that 'she is very analytic, but does not spread warmth to take people with her.'[258] Similarly, a Denmark-friendly negotiator did not find her 'terribly open'.[259] The tendency of a dominant facilitation style did not help. It coupled aspiration on content with a tight grip on the process: 'She tried to do too much herself. Plus, she had too strong ideas of what needed to happen. Yet, parties did not always agree how she wanted it.'[260] Regarding content, her proximity to EU positions endangered her neutrality as COP President.[261]

Process and content expertise also yielded a mixed picture. Negotiators underlined her abundant time investment and much better understanding of parties' constraints when compared to Rasmussen.[262] Her commitment and knowledge were lauded.[263] 'Connie travelled a great deal to meet with many of us. She understood our concerns.'[264] Her awareness of sensitivities also grew: 'Starting off very outspoken and straightforward, she learnt a lot over two years on how cautious one has to be, and how much rules had to be obeyed. She usually is much more proactive.'[265] The Danish administration had prepared Hedegaard for five years from smaller to ever bigger meetings,[266] until she had a good expertise of the process.[267] Nevertheless, former journalist Hedegaard had less experience of UN processes than long-time diplomat and Mexican Foreign Minister Espinosa. That contributed to a series of process shortcomings.[268] For instance, she relied on an overly small group of confidants for getting input, instead of the breadth with which the Mexican Presidency had collected parties' views.[269] The emphasis on the political–ministerial level triggered dialogue among ministers but neglected the informal space for expert negotiators and chairs.[270] Concluding, the overly activist and outspoken manner, and several process mistakes undermined the high personal talent and content expertise.

In contrast, no single negotiator, UN official, or observer approved of Rasmussen's capability as COP-15 President, including close allies of Denmark (Table 3.4). They saw him as a 'disaster',[271] 'having a hard time'[272] and 'crucial for

258 EU/EU-country(9)-26.05.2011.
259 Umbrella Group(3)-14.06.2011.
260 UNFCCC Secretariat(5)-14.06.2011.
261 UNFCCC Secretariat(1)-28.04.2010.
262 EU/EU-country(3)-03.12.2010.
263 UNFCCC Secretariat(1)-28.04.2010.
264 BASIC(2)-16.06.2011; similar: Denmark(6)-09.02.2012.
265 EU/EU-country(10)-16.08.2011.
266 Denmark(3)-11.08.2011.
267 EU/EU-country(9)-26.05.2011.
268 UNFCCC Secretariat(1)-28.04.2010, UNFCCC Secretariat(5)-14.06.2011, EU/EU-country(11)-10.12.2011.
269 Mexico(3)-15.06.2011.
270 UNFCCC Secretariat(5)-14.06.2011.
271 UNFCCC Secretariat(1)-28.04.2010.
272 Umbrella Group(1)-20.04.2011.

the failure',[273] committing 'massive mistakes'.[274] His cultural–personal traits did not seem to fit the international context. Negotiators blamed Rasmussen for a poor sense of people and for being very undiplomatic:[275] 'He did not get the people together to get to an outcome. A friendlier personality might have been needed.'[276] Rasmussen did not sufficiently consider countries' sensibilities ('bull-dozer'[277]), and seemed not very approachable with the door usually closed.[278] All this did probably not help to unite his own administration.[279] The low cultural–personal fit significantly reduced his capability as organizer.

Rasmussen's process and content expertise was not any better. He possessed scant international experience: 'he has never been even near a multilateral nego-tiation'.[280] Essential know-how to navigate these negotiations seemed absent. This ignorance was a major mistake.[281] For instance, he was still unaware of core UN provisions by the end of the COP, like consensus-based decision-making. Instead, he suggested voting on the compromise proposal during the last night. Negotiators and UN officials were highly irritated: 'It is unbelievable that he did not know this';[282] 'that did really hurt', 'one was afraid of what would happen next... everyone watched him struggle';[283] 'Rasmussen had no clue at all about the UN process';[284] he was 'absolutely lost'[285] and 'very amateurish'.[286] Parties sensed that Rasmussen had underestimated the complexity of multilateral nego-tiations: 'Rasmussen had thought... he could just pop in from his office and do it.'[287] Various comments illustrate how they saw him unfit to manage this chal-lenging task: 'Rasmussen thought he... had only local mayors in front of him'.[288] Many interviewees expressed their anger about the – from their point of view – provincial approach of Rasmussen's negotiation management in such harsh words in confidential interviews for this research, that the author preferred to abstain from printing these quotes in verbatim. Overall, the Prime Minister had low capability for managing this multilateral negotiation.

The Danes had two subsequent lead facilitators and advisers to Hedegaard and

273   EU/EU-country(6)-16.03.2011.
274   UNFCCC Secretariat(2)-04.12.2010.
275   EU/EU-country(11)-10.12.2011.
276   BASIC(2)-16.06.2011.
277   EU/EU-country(3)-03.12.2010.
278   G-77(5)-08.12.2011, UNFCCC Secretariat(2)-04.12.2010.
279   BASIC(2)-16.06.2011.
280   G-77(2)-13.06.2011; similar: AWG/SB-Chair(4)-14.06.2011.
281   UNFCCC Secretariat(5)-14.06.2011.
282   EU/EU-country(4)-27.01.2011.
283   UNFCCC Secretariat(4)-17.05.2011.
284   EU/EU-country(10)-16.08.2011, or in similar terms: Umbrella Group(4)-04.07.2011.
285   Mexico(5)-07.07.2011; similar: EU/EU-country(8)-05.05.2011, Umbrella Group(3)-14.06.2011.
286   ALBA(2)-09.12.2011.
287   EU/EU-country(10)-16.08.2011.
288   EU/EU-country(10)-16.08.2011.

Rasmussen, which reflected the internal divide. Thomas Becker on the side of the Climate and Energy Ministry came first. Among the 2009 organizers, he received by far the highest share of positive capability assessments, with 62.5 per cent (Table 3.4). Despite the small sample size the equal distribution of respondents by origin provides a representative indication. Let us begin with the cultural–personal level. Becker had strong convictions about the right substance, which many saw negatively.[289] 'We know which direction we are going … [hence] I simply do this now'[290] seemed his attitude, which many considered 'a little bit tough'.[291] While his negotiating skills and creativity to successfully manage delegates[292] were partially praised, he was also described as 'blunt'.[293] This fits the overall picture of an activist and pushy Danish Presidency with a clear view about the right outcome: Becker and Lidegaard were both perceived as 'pushy characters'.[294] Another sensed the same 'roughness' from Becker and Hedegaard.[295] Others saw Becker as 'big personality' that conflicted with that of Lidegaard.[296] So, there is an overall ambiguous cultural–personal fit.

In contrast, interviewees across the board lauded Becker's deep understanding of process and content nurtured by his long climate experience. Involved in early discussions on the bid in the Climate and Energy Ministry in 2005,[297] Becker had long been in touch with negotiators as one of the 'fathers' behind a COP in Denmark.[298] He became the Danish lead facilitator and administrative focal point.[299] He had already gathered process and content expertise in the UN system before[300] and was a 'skilled and a classic "Kyoto-negotiator"'.[301] As the only Dane to fully understand the process,[302] Becker was hard to substitute.[303] He had also gained trust over all these years from developing countries, in contrast to the Danish Prime Minister's team. 'He had the trust of the Africans',[304] assured one lead African negotiator. 'We understood each other even though we fought a lot',[305] appreciated a very critical G-77 delegate. 'He had an ear for the developing countries that was missed in Copenhagen. He had a sense of what went on

289   UNFCCC Secretariat(4)-17.05.2011.
290   EU/EU-country(11)-10.12.2011.
291   G-77(5)-08.12.2011.
292   EU/EU-country(9)-26.05.2011.
293   Denmark(2)-16.06.2011.
294   EU/EU-country(10)-16.08.2011.
295   Mexico(3)-15.06.2011.
296   Denmark(2)-16.06.2011.
297   Denmark(5)-12.08.2011.
298   EU/EU-country(9)-26.05.2011.
299   EU/EU-country(9)-26.05.2011.
300   Denmark(2)-16.06.2011, Denmark(4)-12.08.2011.
301   Denmark(4)-12.08.2011.
302   EU/EU-country(8)-05.05.2011.
303   UNFCCC Secretariat(4)-17.05.2011.
304   G-77(4)-22.07.2011.
305   G-77(2)-13.06.2011.

on the ground, and what was needed there.'[306] Despite questionable cultural–personal fit his process expertise and dense network of all relevant players rendered him capable as lead facilitator.

The official successor for Becker was Foreign Office diplomat Steffen Smidt. His good process expertise notwithstanding, Smidt arrived too late to the process and could not play any major role,[307] remaining unknown to most delegates. Instead, Bo Lidegaard became the de facto sole Danish lead facilitator after Becker's removal in October 2009. He was seen largely sceptically by respondents with only one granting high capability (Table 3.4). Many considered him 'poor on process' and even as 'crucial for the failure.'[308] An unusually large number of 36.8 per cent were undecided or didn't even know Lidegaard. The undecided saw his capability as at least partially positive, stemming mainly from the US and BASIC countries. Lidegaard had focused on them at the expense of smaller countries. How was the assessment in more detail?

In some cultural–personal aspects, Lidegaard received positive feedback: 'very intelligent',[309] 'very charismatic, likeable person',[310] of high rhetorical skill.[311] He was very committed to reach an outcome.[312] One saw him as effective in his work with 'the larger problem [being] his Prime Minister'.[313] At the same time, Danish officials and negotiators (who all knew him well) criticized a big personality[314] and pushiness,[315] and some even cited arrogance.[316] He was very convinced of his views, including on content:[317] 'He has a strong mind and idea where to go and how to do it.'[318] He would steer meetings proactively in his preferred direction, yet without achieving parties' sustainable buy-in, sensed an accompanying Dane.[319] Further, the determination undermined creative flexibility.[320] The attempt of a tight grip also materialized in the drafting of the Danish text to maintain control over the outcome *vis-à-vis* the other parts of the Danish government and negotiating countries.[321] Lidegaard failed in his attempt to present the text to Prime Ministers in the high-level segment, 'who would accept it

---

306 Umbrella Group(3)-14.06.2011.
307 EU/EU-country(9)-26.05.2011, Umbrella Group(4)-04.07.2011, Denmark(2)-16.06.2011, Mexico(3)-15.06.2011.
308 EU/EU-country(6)-16.03.2011.
309 Mexico(3)-15.06.2011.
310 EU/EU-country(8)-05.05.2011.
311 Denmark(3)-11.08.2011.
312 Mexico(5)-07.07.2011.
313 BASIC(2)-16.06.2011.
314 Denmark(2)-16.06.2011.
315 EU/EU-country(10)-16.08.2011.
316 Denmark(3)-11.08.2011.
317 UNFCCC Secretariat(5)-14.06.2011.
318 Denmark(3)-11.08.2011.
319 Denmark(2)-16.06.2011.
320 EU/EU-country(9)-26.05.2011.
321 Denmark(2)-16.06.2011.

and then it would be gavelled through.'[322] Such proactiveness combined with quick thinking led him to advance too fast, thereby often not reading the situation well[323] and leaving people behind.[324] All this substantially reduced his personal–cultural fit for the required facilitation, and mirrored the pattern of the Presidency, Hedegaard, and Becker: very smart minds combined with overly pushy and self-confident facilitation.

Second, Lidegaard's process expertise was low with only scant experience and connections in multilateral negotiations: he was 'not an expert on UN meetings'.[325] He led the Prime Minister's team but had come to the process only in 2007, two years later than Becker.[326] After joining, Lidegaard first played a minor role as most preparatory meetings were initially not held on the leaders' level. His clout started to grow with the shift towards heads of state and government by the Prime Minister's side in summer 2009, until he was 'fully in control' by the last weeks before COP-15.[327] He was more visible in fora outside the UNFCCC like the MEF, where the advisers of heads of states and government usually participated.[328] This explains why many well-connected expert negotiators did not know him.[329] His influence partially waned during the high-level segment where he 'became sidelined'[330] by the presence of the leader level. Yet, after the shifts in power away from the ministry, it was still the Prime Minister's team that had most of the control among the Danish Presidency's groups.

Besides, Lidegaard disdained the UN process[331] and adopted an overly simplistic focus on big powers neglecting process complexities.[332] He trusted that the approval by 'big players' brings all others on board. So Lidegaard turned to the US, embedded in the government's strong transatlantic vision.[333] He shared the 'Danish text' 'fully and early on with them',[334] which created its US bias. A BASIC negotiator noted an additional European bias as 'Bo pushed the Danish and EU agenda.'[335] It stood in stark contrast to Becker's comprehensive process understanding, network, and approach. Finally though, he mastered the negotiation substance:[336] 'He is a 'big thinker' and the outcome's framework also reflects

---

322 Denmark(3)-11.08.2011.
323 UNFCCC Secretariat(5)-14.06.2011.
324 Denmark(3)-11.08.2011.
325 Umbrella Group(4)-04.07.2011; similar: former BASIC negotiator in UNFCCC Secretariat(6)-16.06.2011, Mexico(3)-15.06.2011.
326 EU/EU-country(9)-26.05.2011.
327 Mexico(3)-15.06.2011.
328 Umbrella Group(3)-14.06.2011.
329 G-77(4)-22.07.2011, but also EU/EU-country(11)-10.12.2011, G-77(2)-13.06.2011.
330 BASIC(2)-16.06.2011.
331 UNFCCC Secretariat(5)-14.06.2011.
332 Denmark(3)-11.08.2011.
333 Denmark(3)-11.08.2011.
334 Denmark(3)-11.08.2011.
335 BASIC(2)-16.06.2011.
336 EU/EU-country(6)-16.03.2011, Umbrella Group(3)-14.06.2011.

some of his thinking.'[337] In sum, the sound substantive skills did not offset the mixed cultural–personal fit and the low process expertise.

Overall, the capability analysis of the individual Danish actors yields an ambiguous picture. The cultural–personal side raises doubts about a too direct and forceful communication style for this negotiation context. Process expertise was more nuanced. It was higher for Hedegaard and especially Becker from the Climate and Energy Ministry in charge for most of the preparation with decreasing control towards COP-15. In contrast, process expertise was much lower for Rasmussen but also Lidegaard on the Prime Ministerial side. What does this imply for the analysis? During the decisive final weeks of preparation and COP-15 itself,[338] we find a correlation between low capability (especially process expertise, and doubts about a cultural–personal fit) of the key Presidency organizers and no agreement, while content expertise was high for all of them nevertheless.

Let us now move to the UN co-organizers. Institutionally, the UN suffered from organizational shortcomings in 2009. It faced clashes over responsibilities and strategies between Ban Ki-moon's team in the UN headquarters and the UNFCCC Secretariat before and during COP-15.[339] They reflected the political–technical split inside the Danish administration. Within the UN system, headquarters were oriented at a high level, while the UNFCCC Secretariat focused more on expert negotiators.[340] Given their common strategic focus on the leader level, the Danish Prime Minister's team reached out more to New York. Moreover, the high-level involvement in UNFCCC negotiations was a novelty for the UN system. Although Ban had been active at the salient COP-13 in Bali,[341] negotiations had still been largely on the expert and ministerial level. The momentum created by its summit character made Copenhagen the first time with such a stellar interest by a UN Secretary-General, causing rivalry between Ban and de Boer: 'there was a lot of tension among egos'.[342] The headquarters envied de Boer's strong position in the struggle for media attention.[343] They eventually installed a Climate Change Support Team for Ban, a 'small climate secretariat' headed by Janos Pasztor to supposedly counterbalance Bonn's strategic preferences.[344] Finally, Ban was considered weak in his COP mediation and thus contributed significantly to the failure, according to a seasoned negotiator.[345] In sum, a divided UN was in bad organizational shape for this complex task.

337 Umbrella Group(1)-20.04.2011.
338 This phase was crucial for the outcome and is hence the focus for the correlation. A BASIC negotiator underlined that Hedegaard was 'no longer Conference President at the important moments of decision' (BASIC(2)-16.06.2011; similar: EU/EU-country(9)-26.05.2011).
339 EU/EU-country(10)-16.08.2011.
340 Denmark(4)-12.08.2011.
341 UNFCCC Secretariat(4)-17.05.2011.
342 UNFCCC Secretariat(2)-04.12.2010.
343 Denmark(5)-12.08.2011.
344 Denmark(5)-12.08.2011.
345 EU/EU-country(6)-16.03.2011.

The individual-level assessment of UNFCCC Executive Secretary Yvo de Boer by interviewees parallels that of the Danish Prime Minister. Only two out of 21 respondents granted de Boer unconstrained high capability in his role *during* the Danish Presidency (answers may of course differ for previous Presidencies). Respondents reflect the whole spectrum of UN officials, negotiators from all coalitions, and observers. Let us examine each indicator. Cultural–personal aspects were not ideal for the situation. De Boer was very straightforward and for some even harsh in his communication, sometimes lacking the necessary sense of diplomacy.[346] He could be 'very disrespectful' but certainly not hypocritical.[347] He was perceived as a very strong personality with abundant self-confidence,[348] and contrasted with the less vocal, long-time Executive Secretary Zammit Cutajar.[349] Similarly to the Danes, his direct form of communication may be rooted in Dutch culture. One lead negotiator, for instance, compared the style of de Boer to that of Dutch COP-6 President Jan Pronk.[350] For some, de Boer even seemed to feel superior,[351] taking a very directive approach of telling parties what to do.[352] A negotiator sympathetic to the UN, with experience of all COPs, found him 'totally arrogant', pretending 'to be the sole owner of the truth … He had lost the capability to listen and to see what is really going on.'[353] Overall, he was perceived as more distant and less approachable than his successor Figueres.[354]

Furthermore, many saw his activism sceptically, especially his attempts to steer the process and his numerous public suggestions.[355] Some delegates accused him of transgressing his role as Executive Secretary by negotiating with parties himself, becoming detrimental to the process:[356] 'Yvo was trying to influence your decision.'[357] De Boer was perceived as aiming to be too much in the foreground[358] and headlines:[359] 'Yvo was all about the press and the media.'[360] The Executive Secretary's influence waned with the start of the high-level segment.[361] For example, even though he was present in the salient small group meeting of 28 on the last Thursday night at COP-15, de Boer hardly intervened in the debate

346   EU/EU-country(1)-20.01.2010.
347   Denmark(5)-12.08.2011.
348   EU/EU-country(9)-26.05.2011.
349   Observer(2)-08.12.2010.
350   Umbrella Group(3)-14.06.2011.
351   Mexico(3)-15.06.2011.
352   UNFCCC Secretariat(7)-03.08.2011.
353   EU/EU-country(11)-10.12.2011.
354   Mexico(5)-07.07.2011.
355   EU/EU-country(10)-16.08.2011.
356   Umbrella Group(4)-04.07.2011.
357   Mexico(3)-15.06.2011.
358   EU/EU-country(9)-26.05.2011.
359   EU/EU-country(7)-04.05.2011.
360   Umbrella Group(3)-14.06.2011.
361   G-77(5)-08.12.2011.

dominated by the political leaders.[362] In sum, his straightforward, direct and activist style did not fit the situation.

Second, de Boer had long built up process and content expertise, for instance as special adviser to COP-6 President Pronk. He had accumulated rich process experience as UNFCCC Executive Secretary since 2006.[363] He was considered to be 'one of the smartest heads' that were ever part of this process.[364] Similarly, a Danish Climate and Energy Ministry's official lauded de Boer as 'the best UN guy we have ever had', who is 'not just bullshitting'.[365] One insider claimed that de Boer 'knew everything and predicted everything that could have happened'.[366] Yet this praise of process and content expertise came alongside accusations of a bias for developed countries and European positions in particular.[367] His origin and appearance as a European might have added to this.[368] A BASIC negotiator, befriended by de Boer, confirmed: 'Some among ... the G-77 felt that Yvo tended to push the EU agenda', and by the COP 'everyone' believed this.[369] Many accused him of advocacy for private-sector solutions, like carbon trading.[370] Regarding the internal Danish clash, he openly sided with Hedegaard's group, which some perceived as another blow to his neutrality.[371]

Overall, his capability as Executive Secretary proves highly ambiguous. De Boer is 'a very complex person. He is extremely capable but more so on content. He was very and maybe too outspoken. Everyone respected his intellect.'[372] So, a very high content and long process experience was dimmed by doubts about his neutrality as facilitator and a problematic cultural–personal fit for the situation.

Having discussed the capabilities for the Presidency and the UN, a final indicator is their *alignment as organizing bureaucracies*. None of the interviewees found them well aligned (Table 3.5). Besides negotiators, respondents include key officials from the Danish and Mexican Presidencies, and the UNFCCC Secretariat. The internal Danish divide was reflected in their diverging relations with the UNFCCC Secretariat. While Hedegaard's ministry was strategically better aligned with the UNFCCC Secretariat, Rasmussen's office was in outright conflict with them by the end of COP-15. As the Prime Minister's team was largely in control inside the Danish administration by COP-15, one must conclude that the Presidency was no longer aligned with the treaty Secretariat during the crucial negotiation phase.

362 UNFCCC Secretariat(4)-17.05.2011.
363 AWG/SB-Chair(4)-14.06.2011.
364 EU/EU-country(9)-26.05.2011.
365 Denmark(5)-12.08.2011.
366 Umbrella Group(4)-04.07.2011.
367 Denmark(2)-16.06.2011; similar: EU/EU-country(6)-16.03.2011.
368 Denmark(5)-12.08.2011; similar: UNFCCC Secretariat(4)-17.05.2011.
369 BASIC(2)-16.06.2011.
370 G-77(2)-13.06.2011.
371 Mexico(3)-15.06.2011.
372 UNFCCC Secretariat(1)-28.04.2010.

Table 3.5 Responses to the question 'How well aligned was the interaction between host country and UNFCCC Secretariat during 2009?' with respect to the Danish Presidency

Response	n (%)
Host country[a] and UNFCCC Secretariat well aligned	0 (0%)
Host country and UNFCCC Secretariat less aligned	21 (91.3%)
Undecided	2 (8.7%)
Total	23

Note: a. Nearly all respondents referred to the team of the Danish Prime Minister (and not of the Climate and Energy Minister) when answering this question.

Let us now scrutinize these alignments in detail. The Climate and Energy Ministry had a close relationship with the UNFCCC Secretariat, as both sides asserted ('We had a good relationship with Connie and her team';[373] 'Very good relationship with Yvo de Boer throughout the year'[374]). The Prime Minister's office confirmed this alignment noting the preference of Ministry and Secretariat for only a ceremonial role of leaders.[375] This even reached an individual level. 'Connie was very linked' to the UNFCCC Secretariat and, vice versa, de Boer 'openly supported Connie, and opposed Rasmussen'.[376] Becker also got along well with de Boer having long known each other from environmental diplomacy.[377]

Nevertheless, the relationship was not without tensions. De Boer's insistence on his tight involvement in preparations caused conflicts with Hedegaard's team. Apparently, documents often reached Hedegaard with a delay due to the clearing demand from the Secretariat, so that both sides clashed before the pre-COP.[378] Possibly, de Boer had become used to recent weaker Presidencies by Poland and Kenya, which contrasted with the self-confident Danes. An 'old hand' of the negotiations even stated that neither of the two Danish groups got along with Yvo de Boer, who was 'marginalized and unhappy'.[379] This seems too extreme in the overall light of responses, yet echoes that there were some tensions also with the Ministry.

The relations between the Prime Minister's office and the UNFCCC Secretariat were widely described as 'an extremely bad relationship',[380] with de Boer's constant warnings of failure should the Prime Ministerial team proceed on its envisioned way. Disagreeing with the Secretariat, the Prime Minister's office

373   UNFCCC Secretariat(5)-14.06.2011.
374   Denmark(6)-09.02.2012.
375   Denmark(4)-12.08.2011.
376   Mexico(3)-15.06.2011; similar: EU/EU-country(10)-16.08.2011.
377   Denmark(3)-11.08.2011.
378   Denmark(3)-11.08.2011.
379   EU/EU-country(8)-05.05.2011.
380   Denmark(5)-12.08.2011.

expressed little interest in cooperation or in de Boer's advice.[381] In Copenhagen, the Executive Secretary was eventually 'put aside'[382] and 'everything...taken from him through the Danish Presidency'.[383] Rasmussen solely focused on Ban and the heads of states and sidelined de Boer.[384] In contrast to previous Presidencies, Copenhagen was politically so important that the Secretariat had lost the ability to manage the process.[385] By COP-15, the Secretariat didn't even feel responsible any more, sensed one Dane.[386] While some working relationship was maintained until the first week, it turned into 'a fight' towards the end of Copenhagen.[387] A UN official summarized that it 'ranged from antagonism to no relationship whatsoever'.[388] How did it get that far?

There were myriad bones of contention. One was the level of Danish activism. About five months before the COP, it became very clear that the Danes wanted to put forward their own text, which the Secretariat rejected strongly.[389] Next, the Secretariat had advised against the handover to Rasmussen during COP-15, yet again in vain.[390] In turn, Rasmussen's team opposed the Secretariat's emphasis on the technical level arguing that leaders were much needed in case negotiations stalled. According to a Prime Minister's official, leaders during the high-level segment increasingly requested a document they could negotiate with. So the Danes called for the small group meeting of 28 on the last Thursday of COP-15 to provide such a text: 'The UNFCCC Secretariat was furious about it.'[391] A Secretariat member underlined that the meeting was run by the Danes and was not even supported by UN staff.[392] The Secretariat blamed Prime Ministerial advisers for thinking agreement would come 'out of the sky' from heads of states and not from expert or ministerial negotiations.[393] Vice versa, officials from the Prime Minister's team found de Boer to be representative of the ineffective party-driven process.[394]

In summary, the Climate and Energy Ministry and the UNFCCC Secretariat were comparatively well aligned. The Danish Prime Minister's office as lead host institution, though, and the UNFCCC Secretariat were fully opposed during the critical phases of the negotiations. With their very directive leadership styles,

381 Denmark(2)-16.06.2011, Umbrella Group(4)-04.07.2011.
382 G-77(2)-13.06.2011.
383 G-77(5)-08.12.2011.
384 UNFCCC Secretariat(4)-17.05.2011; similar: UNFCCC Secretariat(5)-14.06.2011.
385 UNFCCC Secretariat(4)-17.05.2011.
386 Denmark(7)-16.02.2012.
387 Mexico(5)-07.07.2011.
388 UNFCCC Secretariat(7)-03.08.2011.
389 Denmark(7)-16.02.2012.
390 Denmark(6)-09.02.2012.
391 Denmark(4)-12.08.2011.
392 UNFCCC Secretariat(6)-16.06.2011.
393 UNFCCC Secretariat(5)-14.06.2011.
394 Denmark(6)-09.02.2012.

both competed for influence over the right approach of negotiation management. A Prime Ministerial official conceded a clash of administrations on all levels: 'a fight between the leaders and the UN headquarter versus the negotiators and the UNFCCC Secretariat'.[395] Hence, low alignment correlated with no agreement.

To conclude on the capability of organizers during the Danish Presidency, the evidence indicates low capability of the Presidency as a whole given their internal divide, directive style, and excessive activity. We find a similar picture for those in charge of the decisive phase of the Danish Presidency: COP President Rasmussen and his lead adviser Lidegaard. They were of questionable cultural–personal fit for these complex UN negotiations and of low to moderate process expertise.[396] The UN system showed serious deficits with an internal split between New York and Bonn. The evidence on UNFCCC Executive Secretary de Boer for his time during the Danish Presidency yields high content and moderate process expertise, but only low cultural–personal fit for the negotiation circumstances. Finally, the Danish Prime Minister's team and the Secretariat ended up in fierce opposition by COP-15. In short, salient capability deficits of the organizing institutions and individuals in charge during the crucial phases, as well as their non-alignment correlated with no agreement in Copenhagen.

The Mexican Presidency: masters of diplomacy at work

The set-up of the organizers was very different during the Mexican Presidency. On the host side, it had clear-cut institutional responsibilities and continuity of leadership personnel. The Foreign Ministry stayed in the lead, with Espinosa as COP President and de Alba as principal facilitator. On the UN side, Figueres succeeded de Boer as UNFCCC Executive Secretary, while headquarters in New York showed greater restraint. Accordingly, the interviews paint a strikingly brighter picture of the organizers' capability with a unanimously positive view of the Mexican Presidency (Table 3.6). Espinosa and de Alba received a similarly uncontested judgment of high capability. The data is also largely positive for Figueres. Only one interviewee saw her with low capability in her new role, which is the same, highly process-sceptical G-77 negotiator who saw Espinosa and de Alba critically. Those undecided found Figueres had only negligible influence.

How did respondents see capabilities in detail along the indicators of (1) organizational–personal and cultural fit, (2) process, (3) content expertise, and finally (4) the organizers' alignment? The capability of the Mexican Presidency was praised across all groups: comments included 'Some very smart people in

395 Denmark(4)-12.08.2011.
396 The first COP-15 President Hedegaard and her lead adviser Becker fared better in process terms, yet with mixed evidence on cultural–personal fit. However, the Climate and Energy Ministry were no longer in control during the critical phase.

Table 3.6 Responses to the question 'In hindsight, what was done well or not so well by the organizers (e.g. on process and content matters at the COP)?' with respect to the Mexican Presidency

Response	Mexican Presidency n (%)	Espinosa n (%)	De Alba n (%)	Figueres n (%)
Perceived high capability	21 (100%)	23 (95.8%)	24 (95%)	20 (83.3%)
Perceived low capability	0 (0%)	1 (4.2%)	1 (5%)	1 (4.2%)
Undecided	0 (0%)	0 (0%)	0 (0%)	3 (12.5%)
Total	21	24	25	24

Mexico...they used their talents very well';[397] 'excellent job';[398] 'very smart individuals';[399] 'very competent';[400] 'a great job'.[401] What led to this positive assessment? Above all, the Presidency had a better organizational fit than the Danish Presidency as the Mexican administration acted much more united.[402] Learning from the Danish experience, President Calderón had soon resolved initial power struggles in the government by giving the lead to the Foreign instead of the Environment Ministry.[403] Environment ministries had been traditionally in charge of climate Presidencies, yet Mexico considered diplomatic and negotiation skills more important than technical expertise for the success of the Presidency.[404] Officials viewed it as a geopolitical problem for which the rich multilateral experience of Mexico would be useful.[405] UN officials and negotiators alike confirmed the importance of the diplomatically skilful lead by the Mexican Foreign Ministry;[406] it was 'the strongest COP support team we have ever had'.[407] Learning another lesson from Copenhagen, Calderón fully backed his officials[408] but restricted himself to an internal role, except for selected support on key outstanding issues.[409] Even these actions remained 'behind the scenes' to uphold clear responsibilities externally, and he let Espinosa and her

397 BASIC(5)-15.06.2011.
398 Denmark(6)-09.02.2012.
399 G-77(3)-19.07.2011.
400 EU/EU-country(8)-05.05.2011.
401 Umbrella Group(3)-14.06.2011.
402 UNFCCC Secretariat(4)-17.05.2011.
403 Denmark(2)-16.06.2011, UNFCCC Secretariat(5)-14.06.2011.
404 Mexico(1)-02.02.2011 Mexico(3)-15.06.2011, Mexico(4)-16.06.2011.
405 Mexico(4)-16.06.2011.
406 UNFCCC Secretariat(4)-17.05.2011, UNFCCC Secretariat(5)-14.06.2011, UNFCCC Secretariat(7)-03.08.2011, Umbrella Group(1)-20.04.2011.
407 UNFCCC Secretariat(1)-28.04.2010.
408 Mexico(3)-15.06.2011, Denmark(3)-11.08.2011, Denmark(5)-12.08.2011.
409 AWG/SB-Chair(4)-14.06.2011.

team under de Alba facilitate during the entire Presidency.[410] Finally, good political and personal relations smoothed cooperation in the Presidency: Espinosa
and Calderón were in the same political party, and key personnel had known and
appreciated each other for a long time, such as Espinosa and de Alba.[411] In sum,
the Mexicans were much more a team than the Danes.[412] This had been one
central piece of advice from the Danes when handing over: 'Get the house in
order.'[413]

Second, Mexico had a higher cultural fit for the specific situation. The country traditionally bridged developing and developed countries,[414] and especially
understood both North and Latin America in cultural, economic, political, and
even linguistic terms. Mexicans were better able to embrace among others the
sceptical Latin American ALBA coalition. After the experience of Copenhagen,
they put extreme efforts into this relationship.[415] Espinosa switched repeatedly
from English to Spanish in plenaries and addressed Latin American delegates as
'mis hermanos' (my brothers). Interviewees from developed and developing countries found this attention vital.[416] The bridge-building was complemented by the
breadth of the outreach of extensive travelling and myriad informal consultations (see 'Transparency and inclusiveness' section earlier in this chapter).[417]

Mexican culture possibly also influenced their facilitation style in its level of
activism. The Danes were very present, highly activist and known as pioneers
and advocates of quick emission cuts. Compared to that, the Mexicans worked
more behind the scenes, pushed content less and emphasized process instead.[418]
For example, the text was not prepared by Mexico but was developed in constant
interaction between working and ministerial levels. Only at the very end, the
Presidency and Secretariat compiled the final version. Most parties considered
this to be the right balance between activism and restraint. Initially though,
numerous countries had accused Mexico of acting without explicit mandate,
such as the informal consultations in Bonn in the spring when African
delegations denied Mexico the mandate to hold any further informal consultations. As parties successively saw the transparent and inclusive Mexican
approach, the criticism soon vanished.[419] It occasionally resurged as when Mexico
began early informal consultations at the COP. Again, Mexican openness and

410   Denmark(2)-16.06.2011.
411   UNFCCC Secretariat(5)-14.06.2011, EU/EU-country(11)-10.12.2011.
412   G-77(3)-19.07.2011, BASIC(2)-16.06.2011, Denmark(5)-12.08.2011.
413   Denmark(3)-11.08.2011.
414   Mexico(3)-15.06.2011.
415   Umbrella Group(3)-14.06.2011.
416   G-77(4)-22.07.2011, Umbrella Group(3)-14.06.2011, Umbrella Group(2)-02.06.2011,
      Umbrella Group(4)-04.07.2011.
417   Denmark(6)-09.02.2012, EU/EU-country(10)-16.08.2011.
418   EU/EU-country(10)-16.08.2011.
419   Mexico(2)-08.02.2011.

'unthreatening' style helped negotiators to accept at least some activism:[420] 'They had no own agenda, created a good atmosphere, and got everyone together in an open process.'[421] The Mexicans also kept themselves back as persons: 'De Alba and Espinosa were very modest and really listened to people.'[422] So while the Mexicans were perceived as less activist from the outside their own strategy was not to 'sit back' as host but to 'have a strong facilitation...like Raúl Estrada in Kyoto'.[423]

Regarding process expertise, there was a better match between Mexican strategic planning and reality.[424] This stands in contrast to the 'under-planning' of the high-level segment by the Danish Prime Minister's team. Besides, Mexico remained flexible to adapt to new situations as original ideas were often quickly outdated by the dynamics of the process.[425] The emphasis on process over specific substance left manoeuvring room to change paths.[426] Regarding physical negotiation conditions, the Cancún COP was in a spacious and quiet Caribbean resort. After 47,000 pre-registrations and 28,000 issued badges in Copenhagen, the organizers had limited participation. Around 13,000 people eventually attended, including 7,400 observers and journalists.[427] The separation of side events from negotiations and the abundance of meeting rooms further smoothed the navigation of negotiations. Pleasant weather and food reminded many delegates of COP-13 in Bali. The diplomatic expertise of the Foreign Ministry enabled such proficient strategic planning and logistics. In sum, the Mexican Presidency possessed high organizational and cultural fit as well as outstanding process expertise, while content expertise appeared to be average.

On the individual level, respondents attributed high capability to Foreign Minister Patricia Espinosa as COP-16 President (Table 3.6). Espinosa's high cultural–personal fit was based on multiple facets. High emotional intelligence[428] was combined with a very calm character.[429] Even in the heated plenary debate of the final night with Bolivia opposing an agreement and at the point of exhaustion, she seemed in nearly full control of herself.[430] Another element was a warm,[431] modest[432] and very approachable personality.[433] Even a very critical

420   Mexico(3)-15.06.2011.
421   UNFCCC Secretariat(5)-14.06.2011, also: BASIC(2)-16.06.2011.
422   EU/EU-country(11)-10.12.2011.
423   Mexico(4)-16.06.2011, Mexico(3)-15.06.2011: 'There is a huge difference to be passive or to still act within the will of the parties but be more active.'
424   G-77(3)-19.07.2011, Denmark(1)-02.12.2010.
425   G-77(3)-19.07.2011.
426   UNFCCC Secretariat(4)-17.05.2011.
427   Mexico(1)-02.02.2011.
428   EU/EU-country(9)-26.05.2011.
429   Denmark(2)-16.06.2011.
430   Participant observation.
431   EU/EU-country(9)-26.05.2011.
432   EU/EU-country(11)-10.12.2011.
433   UNFCCC Secretariat(2)-04.12.2010.

negotiator expressed that 'there was a closer personal relationship so one could talk to them',[434] and a sceptical G-77 delegate conceived of her similarly.[435] She emphasized communicating frankly to delegates[436] and to really take time for this: Espinosa 'listened and listened to the parties.'[437] Nevertheless, she found a balance between open-minded listening and confident steering.[438] While she did not explicitly follow her own substantive agenda, she could be persistent and even stubborn.[439] Yet, she facilitated very politely and skilfully so it was not perceived as dominating but respecting negotiators' pride.[440] Finally, her cultural proximity to Latin America helped to relate to more marginalized countries, such as the ALBA group. In short, her cultural–personal background was highly appropriate for these negotiations.[441]

Turning to process and content expertise, Espinosa has worked as a diplomat mostly on global issues, chairing multilateral negotiations for decades:[442] 'She spent her life in this world.'[443] It provided her with a rich diplomatic toolkit, understanding of the process and of situations.[444] Espinosa travelled intensively in preparation of the COP, reaching out to a broad range of countries to get as many of them on board as possible.[445] Eventually, she knew many ministers well by COP-16,[446] in contrast to Rasmussen in 2009. While her climate change knowledge was not extensive,[447] she was described as a 'quick learner'.[448] So her growing expertise on substance[449] and excellent briefings by her team[450] ensured sufficient knowhow. In sum, Espinosa showed such high expertise in process and substance, combined with a personal fit to the situation that process 'veterans' dubbed her a 'calm, serious, and heavyweight figure',[451] or simply a 'gem'.[452]

434   ALBA(2)-09.12.2011.
435   G-77(5)-08.12.2011.
436   BASIC(3)-08.07.2011.
437   Umbrella Group(4)-04.07.2011; similar: BASIC(2)-16.06.2011, EU/EU-country(11)-10.12.2011.
438   UNFCCC Secretariat(1)-28.04.2010.
439   Umbrella Group(4)-04.07.2011.
440   UNFCCC Secretariat(5)-14.06.2011.
441   AWG/SB-Chair(4)-14.06.2011.
442   UNFCCC Secretariat(1)-28.04.2010.
443   UNFCCC Secretariat(2)-04.12.2010.
444   EU/EU-country(10)-16.08.2011, UNFCCC Secretariat(5)-14.06.2011.
445   Umbrella Group(4)-04.07.2011, Mexico(1)-02.02.2011,EU/EU-country(8)-05.05.2011.
446   Mexico(5)-07.07.2011.
447   UNFCCC Secretariat(5)-14.06.2011.
448   UNFCCC Secretariat(7)-03.08.2011.
449   EU/EU-country(6)-16.03.2011.
450   EU/EU-country(9)-26.05.2011.
451   EU/EU-country(8)-05.05.2011.
452   UNFCCC Secretariat(1)-28.04.2010.

On the administrative level, the widely praised Luis Alfonso de Alba led Mexican facilitation (Table 3.6).[453] De Alba shares many cultural–personal traits with Espinosa. He was also attributed tremendous empathy,[454] the balancing of a firm but polite approach,[455] and the fostering of compromises, such as between a bottom-up and top-down approach.[456] A modest attitude and an eagerness to listen to people complemented this well.[457] De Alba kept himself back, did not openly push a personal agenda, and rather handed it over to parties to tell him where to go.[458] For example, a process-critical negotiator mentioned with relief that in a meeting early in 2010, de Alba had expressed he would be fine with any COP outcome independent of whether an agreement was reached.[459] So overall he followed a cautious strategy in a low key way.[460] He held an unusually high number of informals to gather information on parties' preferences and to test the feasibility of suggestions[461] through which he could 'guide' parties a bit.[462] Several interviewees found him 'fluid... making people relax'[463] and 'never in conflict' with any of the parties.[464] Some saw this smoothness as manipulation. It made people 'feel nice' and thereby perceive negotiations as transparent, when 'in fact [they] were not'.[465] 'Capability' here though is not judged on an ethical level but by a cultural–personal fit for an effective facilitation.

De Alba's process expertise was also on par with Espinosa's. He had been a diplomat for 25 years, serving exclusively in multilateral positions so he knew UN processes inside out. Mexicans speak of him as their 'best multilateral negotiator'.[466] Only the resigned Becker had comparable intimate multilateral process knowledge on the Danish side. Accordingly, fellow negotiators described de Alba's mastery of all procedural tricks: 'as cunning as a fox'.[467] For instance, he occasionally insisted on bilaterals without the UNFCCC Secretariat, if this seemed more promising.[468] His wide outreach created connections to all negotiators and made him 'the face of the Mexican Presidency' on the expert level.[469] De

453   UNFCCC Secretariat(4)-17.05.2011 and EU/EU-country(1)-20.01.2010 compared him to Argentine diplomat Raúl Estrada, who had been a major driver behind the Kyoto Protocol negotiations in 1997.
454   EU/EU-country(7)-04.05.2011.
455   Denmark(3)-11.08.2011.
456   UNFCCC Secretariat(2)-04.12.2010.
457   EU/EU-country(11)-10.12.2011.
458   EU/EU-country(9)-26.05.2011, EU/EU-country(11)-10.12.2011.
459   G-77(5)-08.12.2011.
460   Umbrella Group(4)-04.07.2011.
461   UNFCCC Secretariat(5)-14.06.2011.
462   Mexico(3)-15.06.2011.
463   Umbrella Group(3)-14.06.2011.
464   UNFCCC Secretariat(5)-14.06.2011; similar: EU/EU-country(11)-10.12.2011.
465   G-77(2)-13.06.2011.
466   Mexico(5)-07.07.2011.
467   EU/EU-country(10)-16.08.2011; also: EU/EU-country(9)-26.05.2011.
468   EU/EU-country(8)-05.05.2011.
469   Denmark(2)-16.06.2011.

Alba's knowledge on the negotiation substance was similarly general like that of Espinosa, since he had not been a climate change expert before.[470] Yet, the level of expertise was sufficient to navigate the complex process, and might have even been advantageous as de Alba brought an unconstrained, fresh perspective.[471] In sum, he was highly capable with a good cultural–personal fit, tremendous process and moderate content expertise.

Turning to the UN, its capability as a whole was higher in 2010. The organizational fit had improved remarkably as it was far less divided. With the leader level less present, the UN headquarters kept a lower profile during the Mexican Presidency and encountered no serious clashes with the UNFCCC Secretariat. The change of leadership in Bonn may have decreased tensions. In May 2010, de Boer resigned after several years and Christiana Figueres from Costa Rica succeeded as Executive Secretary (Table 3.6). She started with abundant goodwill and support from parties.[472] Regarding indicators of her capability, respondents noted she had scarcely been tested during her short time in office.[473] Several characteristics though resemble those of the widely lauded lead Mexicans, such as her high cultural–personal fit. Her origin from Costa Rica gave her a better political, cultural, and linguistic understanding of developing countries and Latin America in particular, that also enhanced the relations with the ALBA group.[474] Besides, it allowed her to better build bridges between the developed and developing world.[475] She was a Spanish native speaker, interacted in an open, personal, modest, down-to-earth, and warm-hearted way with a broad array of delegations:[476] 'Christiana walks into the room and hugs you...She grabs her telephone and calls you directly.'[477] She then listened carefully,[478] kept herself back, and mostly managed quietly behind the scenes.[479] Being new to the position, she gave the Presidency and experienced Secretariat officials the leeway to take appropriate steps,[480] and acted more as supporting administrator.[481] She also did not openly advocate a specific substantive shape of the agreement.[482] Instead of being directive, she would provide parties with several possibilities to choose

470   Umbrella Group(4)-04.07.2011, Denmark(2)-16.06.2011, Mexico(5)-07.07.2011.
471   Mexico(4)-16.06.2011.
472   BASIC(3)-08.07.2011.
473   EU/EU-country(7)-04.05.2011.
474   Danish Presidency (2) 16.06.2011.
475   EU/EU-country(11)-10.12.2011, BASIC(2)-16.06.2011, G-77(5)-08.12.2011, Observer(3)-16.06.2011.
476   Mexico(3)-15.06.2011, Mexico(5)-07.07.2011, EU/EU-country(11)-10.12.2011, G-77 (5)-08.12.2011.
477   Mexico(5)-07.07.2011.
478   EU/EU-country(9)-26.05.2011.
479   Umbrella Group (1) 20.04.2011, EU/EU-country(6)-16.03.2011, EU/EU-country(9)-26.05.2011, UNFCCC Secretariat(5)-14.06.2011.
480   AWG/SB-Chair(4)-14.06.2011.
481   EU/EU-country(9)-26.05.2011.
482   EU/EU-country(11)-10.12.2011.

from.[483] All this stood in remarkable contrast to Figueres's more directive predecessor de Boer, who had pushed very actively towards his envisioned outcome and strove for public attention.[484] Her greater restraint was widely welcomed.[485] 'She was everything that Yvo wasn't'.[486]

Second, Figueres had gained abundant expertise on process and content as Costa Rican delegate since 1995, holding various positions in UNFCCC negotiations, among others member of the COP Bureau in 2008 and 2009.[487] Probably owing to her work on the Executive Board of the Clean Development Mechanism, a sceptic of carbon markets accused her of bias and of not being an 'advocate for developing countries and for the integrity of the Convention'.[488] Yet, this was only scattered criticism. Instead, her positioning in the background with scarce advocacy for specific substance resulted in her overall perception as a neutral facilitator. In sum, Figueres's Central American origin and the behind-the-scenes support meant a good cultural–personal fit for the negotiation situation. The rich process and content expertise added to her high capability.

Regarding the principal organizers jointly, Mexico and the Secretariat were better aligned than in the previous year as many interviewees asserted (Table 3.7), yet as always not entirely free of conflict.[489] The random variation of views across these respondent groups indicates a very low bias.

The more nuanced analysis of responses shows that the relationship between the Mexicans and the UNFCCC Secretariat developed over time. Early in 2010, de Alba and de Boer clashed over the best process approach, aggravated by their

Table 3.7 Responses to the question 'How well aligned was the interaction between host country and UNFCCC Secretariat during 2010?' with respect to the Mexican Presidency

Response	n (%)
Host country and UNFCCC Secretariat well aligned	7 (43.75%)
Host country and UNFCCC Secretariat less aligned	3 (18.75%)
Undecided	6 (37.5%)
Total	16[a]

Note: a. UNFCCC and Mexican officials with good insight into this relation primarily answered this question, hence the small *n*.

483   UNFCCC Secretariat(7)-03.08.2011.
484   Umbrella Group(4)-04.07.2011, Mexico(3)-15.06.2011, EU/EU-country(11)-10.12.2011.
485   Umbrella Group (1) 20.04.2011, Umbrella Group(4)-04.07.2011, Mexico(3)-15.06.2011, EU/EU-country(11)-10.12.2011, EU/EU-country(7)-04.05.2011.
486   Umbrella Group(3)-14.06.2011.
487   EU/EU-country(9)-26.05.2011.
488   G-77(2)-13.06.2011.
489   UNFCCC Secretariat(7)-03.08.2011.

personalities with de Boer's forceful and self-confident attitude after years in climate negotiations and de Alba's decades-long experience in multilateralism and his scepticism towards the Secretariat.[490] De Boer was convinced of his process and content views, while the Mexicans doubted that the UN had diplomatic expertise superior to theirs. A UN official complained that the Mexicans initially saw the role of the Secretariat as simply to 'provide a room, switch on the light, and serve coffee'.[491] The situation improved with Figueres's takeover in May.[492] Suddenly, the cultural constellation of organizers was one of Latin American homogeneity.[493] Mexicans noted the ease of sharing one language and of her understanding for the more creative and 'chaotic' Mexican working mode.[494] As a supporter of Figueres's UNFCCC application, Mexico now benefitted from these similarities[495] and from a Secretariat that gave them sufficient leeway. This managing behind the scenes avoided rivalry and added to a good relationship with Espinosa.[496] Moreover, Figueres and Espinosa got along very well personally.[497] Contrary to the Danes, the Mexicans sent a liaison diplomat to work with Figueres and her deputy Richard Kinley. It fostered the information exchange and ensured the instant detection of differences.[498] The Secretariat also appreciated dealing with only 'one' Mexican government.[499] Finally, Mexico crucially proved open to using the deep knowledge of sensitivities of countries by the Secretariat for finalizing the text in Cancún.[500] They were much more willing to cooperate than the Danes.[501]

Nevertheless, while the relationship improved during 2010, tensions between Presidency and Secretariat kept fluctuating. After a nearly 'cordial' start with Figueres, it transformed into a good 'working relationship' without ever being antagonistic.[502] The Mexicans repeatedly suggested process innovations in the coordination meetings, which the Secretariat met with regular scepticism or objection.[503] Bonn conceived of itself as 'steward of the process'.[504] Its long institutional memory made it 'fearful' of deviations from the process parties expect and are familiar with.[505] The Mexicans often insisted anyway, and the UN

490 UNFCCC Secretariat(4)-17.05.2011, Mexico(3)-15.06.2011, Denmark(3)-11.08.2011.
491 UNFCCC Secretariat(4)-17.05.2011.
492 Mexico(4)-16.06.2011.
493 UNFCCC Secretariat(2)-04.12.2010.
494 Mexico(5)-07.07.2011.
495 Mexico(4)-16.06.2011.
496 EU/EU-country(9)-26.05.2011.
497 Mexico(5)-07.07.2011, UNFCCC Secretariat(1)-28.04.2010.
498 Mexico(5)-07.07.2011.
499 UNFCCC Secretariat(5)-14.06.2011.
500 ALBA(2)-09.12.2011, UNFCCC Secretariat(5)-14.06.2011.
501 EU/EU-country(11)-10.12.2011.
502 UNFCCC Secretariat(7)-03.08.2011.
503 Mexico(2)-08.02.2011, Mexico(4)-16.06.2011, Mexico(5)-07.07.2011.
504 UNFCCC Secretariat(7)-03.08.2011.
505 Mexico(4)-16.06.2011.

attitude strengthened de Alba's preference to act with Espinosa, and to exclude the Secretariat, if necessary.[506] So despite oral approval of cooperation, Mexico occasionally proceeded on its own and had 'no collaborative relationship' with the Secretariat.[507] Even if all this slightly soured the atmosphere, the Secretariat overall trusted the Mexicans. They had long process experience and Figueres knew de Alba well from before.[508]

Presidency officials illustrated this ambiguous relation with two examples. The Mexicans proposed a plenary on Sunday between the first and second week of COP-16.[509] Despite the Secretariat's objection for lack of money, translation capacity, and the fear of upsetting people with a meeting on Sunday, the Mexicans proceeded anyway and all parties attended. The Presidency informed delegates about the plans for the second COP week, thereby saving valuable time and increasing transparency and inclusiveness. Negotiators appreciated the meeting.[510] Another example was the final Friday of COP-16. UN–Mexican tension on process had risen again towards the end of the conference. Changing strategy, the Mexicans had pushed to already tackle all crucial, unresolved issues on Thursday, and not on the last COP day. Four groups with ministers, key negotiators, and organizers addressed mitigation, MRV, and other core areas before splitting up further. According to Presidency officials, Mexicans were confronted with serious doubts about their approach by the Secretariat on early Friday morning, which had also been somewhat excluded.[511] De Alba's explanation of the strategy appeared convincing to Figueres however, so the Mexicans moved on, and later finalized the text jointly with the Secretariat.

In summary, the Mexicans remained largely in control of negotiation management,[512] with modest cooperation with the Secretariat.[513] The relationship was closer on the substance of the agreement. The UN with Figueres took on a more 'auxiliary' role as a supporting institution for the Presidency,[514] without openly fighting over the right approach or for public attention. This still provided for a better alignment than in 2009.

In conclusion, the Mexican Presidency as a whole was highly capable. It spoke with one voice and acted with high cultural sensitivity, moderate activism, and an appropriate combination of comprehensive planning and flexibility. Their lead individuals Espinosa and de Alba had a high cultural–personal fit for the situation, outstanding process and decent content expertise. The UNFCCC Secretariat was much more united under new Executive Secretary Figueres, who

506   EU/EU-country(10)-16.08.2011,EU/EU-country(8)-05.05.2011, Denmark(6)-09.02.2012.
507   UNFCCC Secretariat(1)-28.04.2010.
508   Mexico(2)-08.02.2011.
509   Mexico(5)-07.07.2011.
510   Mexico(2)-08.02.2011.
511   Mexico(3)-15.06.2011.
512   UNFCCC Secretariat(5)-14.06.2011.
513   Denmark(6)-09.02.2012.
514   EU/EU-country(10)-16.08.2011.

supported the Presidency with her high cultural–personal fit and good process expertise, without rivalling for the lead. Finally, the Presidency had process disagreements with the Secretariat but was still better aligned than the Danes. In short, a strong cultural–personal and organizational fit, excellent process and average content expertise, and a decent alignment between the organizers correlated with the reaching of an agreement in 2010. To what extent did this high capability contribute to the Cancún Agreements?

How capability influenced the summit outcomes

While a correlation between capability and agreement became evident for both Presidencies, their causal influence will now be traced in detail. Nearly 90 per cent of interviewees fully (or at least partially) assert such an impact on reaching an agreement (Table 3.8). They find, for instance, that 'the existence of strategic steering is highly dependent on the capacity of the Secretariat and the individual COP Presidency to do so'.[515] On the individual dimension, they highlighted that for 'big agreements like the WTO, climate change…personalities are running 90%' of the negotiations.[516] This view is equally distributed between the different country groups, organizers, and observers.

A more nuanced analysis reveals the paths of influence from capability (cultural and personal-organizational fit, process and content expertise, and organizers' alignment) to outcome, which work through (1) institutional effectiveness, (2) process navigation and (3) access of the organizers to people (Figure 3.3). The three mechanisms play out on an objective level by enabling a proposal inside the zone of agreement, but also on a subjective level by creating the emotional willingness to agree: 'international agreements need skilful facilitation. It's not just about substance but also about emotions…It's not mechanical.'[517]

The capability of organizers influences their institutional effectiveness in several ways (path 1). The animosities within the Danish government and the

Table 3.8 Responses to the question 'How did capability influence the reaching of an agreement?'

Response	n (%)
Capability of organizers influenced the outcome	30 (76.9%)
Capability of organizers influenced the outcome somewhat	5 (12.8%)
Capability of organizers did not influence the outcome	4 (10.3%)
Total	39

515 Observer(2)-08.12.2010.
516 Denmark(5)-12.08.2011; similar: G-77(2)-13.06.2011, Observer(2)-08.12.2010.
517 UNFCCC Secretariat(5)-14.06.2011.

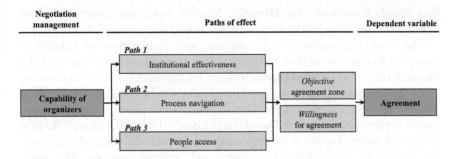

Negotiation management	Paths of effect	Dependent variable

Figure 3.3 Process-tracing between organizers' capability and agreement

UN cost organizers valuable time in 2009. Danish officials told of how long the resolution of their internal differences lasted, including during the endgame where every hour counted.[518] Large parts of the Danish administration were unfamiliar with the process and disregarded it, so the Climate Ministry 'spent many meetings explaining them that you have to do "x, y, z", but they said "no, we don't want to"'.[519] Furthermore, the restructuring of the organization after Becker's resignation meant another loss of time.[520] The working level contacts with the Secretariat had to be newly coordinated as well: efficiency was diminished as 'The previously built relationship with the Hedegaard team was no longer useful.'[521] The growing differences between Secretariat and the new power centre of the Presidency required additional efforts.[522] Further friction costs resulted from the internal divide between the UN in Bonn and the Secretary-General's team in New York. All this stood in contrast to 2010, where greater internal and external alignment of the Mexican Presidency and the UN saved valuable time not needed to resolve differences. As for its impact, let us imagine the counterfactual of less delay by greater institutional alignment (and by fewer other process errors). It would have allowed delegates to sufficiently consider the last-minute compromise and not upset them further in the crucial final hours. Or, most key leaders would not have left Copenhagen when the final plenary started on Friday night. The presence of Obama and his colleagues may have created the necessary dynamics in the decisive debate to close the deal among everyone, conceded a lead Danish official.[523] Having reached this agreement one day earlier

518   Denmark(6)-09.02.2012, EU/EU-country(7)-04.05.2011.
519   Denmark(3)-11.08.2011.
520   EU/EU-country(9)-26.05.2011.
521   UNFCCC Secretariat(5)-14.06.2011.
522   Observer(2)-08.12.2010, Denmark(2)-16.06.2011.
523   Denmark(4)-12.08.2011.

may already have made the difference. Veteran negotiators assert that 'there would have been possibilities to turn things around for a success'.[524]

The clear distribution of responsibilities and mutual trust of institutions empowered organizers in their facilitation. Parties could count on the word of a Mexican official as he would speak with an uncontested mandate. In contrast, given the uncertain Danish responsibilities delegates hesitated to rely on their suggestions, which weakened the Danish ability to facilitate.[525] This also gave parties opportunity to exploit Danish (and internal UN) differences,[526] 'to play games with us [the Danes]'.[527] By supporting one Danish side or the other at sensitive points in time, delegations aggravated internal tensions. The more unanimous Mexican Presidency protected it better against outside interference. Further, the deep suspicion of the Danish Prime Minister's team against the Secretariat inhibited the information flow between key organizers,[528] and their use of UN expertise. Instead, the UNFCCC Executive Secretary played only a minor role in 2009 and was 'put aside'.[529] Key negotiators hold that some of the gravest mistakes may have been avoided had Rasmussen relied more on de Boer's advice.[530] The sidelining of the Secretariat weakened its standing among developing countries, which doubted that it could ensure a balanced compromise.[531] While Mexico also stayed at arm's length with the Secretariat over its scepticism towards any process innovation, there was still a good working relationship that allowed the flow of essential information. Espinosa's empowerment in the final plenary is a case in point. The diplomatic experience and unity of her team in cooperation with the UN provided strong backing and excellent instructions, which proved essential:[532] for the make-or-break moment to rule on consensus she was thoroughly briefed on all her options.[533] It allowed navigating those hours in a calm and determined way. Finally, Figueres empowered Espinosa towards the outside by giving her the clear lead and supporting from behind the scenes.[534] While some therefore attributed only little impact to the Executive Secretary,[535] her positive influence was exactly in this approach to her role.

Finally, the deep internal strife in 2009 reduced the motivation of organizing officials. The departure of Becker left large parts of the Danish organization in

524   EU/EU-country(9)-26.05.2011.
525   Denmark(5)-12.08.2011, UNFCCC Secretariat(3)-08.12.2010, UNFCCC Secretariat(4)-17.05.2011.
526   Denmark(2)-16.06.2011.
527   Denmark(3)-11.08.2011.
528   Umbrella Group(4)-04.07.2011.
529   G-77(2)-13.06.2011.
530   EU/EU-country(10)-16.08.2011.
531   UNFCCC Secretariat(4)-17.05.2011.
532   Denmark(2)-16.06.2011,EU/EU-country(8)-05.05.2011, Umbrella Group(3)-14.06.2011.
533   EU/EU-country(6)-16.03.2011.
534   UNFCCC Secretariat(5)-14.06.2011.
535   ALBA(2)-09.12.2011.

'shock':[536] shortly before the summit they had worked towards for years, their central pillar with his profound process expertise and wide network was removed. Anxiety about a possible collapse was rising. The near hostility inside the administration soured working relations and spirit between the Danish teams. Besides, the new emphasis on the leader level led to a neglect of expert negotiators causing 'violent and bitter fights in bureaucracies', not just in Denmark but 'everywhere' between the responsible ministries and the leaders' cabinets.[537] It decreased their eagerness to work hard for an agreement. In 2010, the opposite dynamic from greater cooperation maintained the spirits of organizers (and delegates). In sum, capability affected the agreement through time availability, the empowerment of organizers and their motivation level.

Capability also impacts on whether organizers can navigate the process of these complex and fragile negotiations in a sophisticated way (path 2). First, process expertise and cultural–personal fit enable them to find the most appropriate measures for a given situation. Let us start with the Mexican and Danish lead facilitators. Knowledge of the dynamics of multilateral negotiations is the daily bread and butter of diplomats like de Alba. Some even spoke of the Mexican Presidency as a 'diplomat-driven process'[538] and many saw de Alba as 'absolutely essential to get a deal.'[539] His high empathy allowed him a good reading of situations and the most appropriate reaction.[540] He would use all possible tricks, and sometimes even be 'ruthless', some said.[541] He continuously questioned hitherto accepted approaches to find the best handling of a situation, irrespective of the conventions to date.[542] In consequence, the Presidency occasionally pulled delegates out of their comfort zone to reach positional changes, including through 'phone calls by Calderón to get key countries on board.[543] The counterfactual for 2009 is that Becker and not Lidegaard would have continued as Danish chief adviser. Given his long-standing expertise, negotiators across all regions argued that Becker would have taken more appropriate actions.[544] He had a good sense of the situation and needs on the ground.[545] In a slightly pointed way, the Danes had 'no one...left who understood the process'.[546] When G-77 Chair Lumumba accused the Presidency of not meeting with him, officials did not sufficiently master the diplomatic stratagems to respond to this allegedly false

536 EU/EU-country(9)-26.05.2011.
537 Denmark(4)-12.08.2011.
538 Denmark(2)-16.06.2011.
539 Umbrella Group(1)-20.04.2011; similar: UNFCCC Secretariat(2)-04.12.2010.
540 EU/EU-country(7)-04.05.2011.
541 EU/EU-country(8)-05.05.2011.
542 Mexico(5)-07.07.2011.
543 EU/EU-country(8)-05.05.2011.
544 G-77(4)-22.07.2011, EU/EU-country(10)-16.08.2011, Umbrella Group(3)-14.06.2011, Umbrella Group(4)-04.07.2011, more doubtful: AWG/SB-Chair(4)-14.06.2011, G-77(5)-08.12.2011.
545 Umbrella Group(3)-14.06.2011.
546 EU/EU-country(8)-05.05.2011.

but powerful claim. Hedegaard had been too far from the Bella Center to meet up at the time of the alleged request,[547] yet 'without [Becker] we didn't have the competence to use dirty tricks, or to defend against those.'[548] These instances aggravated the perception of a Danish bias against developing countries, and so reduced their willingness to agree. Some cautioned that de Alba had simply learnt the lessons from Copenhagen.[549] While this is one factor, the extensive interview evidence on the cultural–personal side and his multilateral track record attribute a distinctive role to his higher capability.

On situation-appropriate measures of the Conference Presidents, the scarce process expertise and low cultural–personal fit of Rasmussen led to grave mistakes. Before the COP, the very late lowering of the overall goal of Copenhagen, which had followed Becker's sacking, turned out to be poor expectation management. In late October, Rasmussen abandoned the long-time promise to work towards a binding agreement. Some had initially seen these high expectations as a problem,[550] yet it offended the vast majority of countries, including the powerful BASIC group. The commitment had been part of the deal with Brazil in exchange for letting Denmark host COP-15. Some said that the BASIC countries decided to answer this move by implacably sticking to the rules and rejecting any text by the Presidency.[551] The change from stellar to low expectations confused negotiators and the public, and undermined trust in the Presidency.[552] Moreover, delegates now lacked any sense of a common negotiation goal, and thus lost much time and energy.[553] In contrast, they were more open-minded again in Cancún due to more constant expectations during 2010 and the lack of what some even described as Danish 'betrayal' of developing countries.[554]

During the 2009 summit, the Conference President's low capability contributed to his fatal mishandling of the last night.[555] Rasmussen lacked the will and knowledge to adhere to the most basic rules, and his recurring mistakes had undermined the willingness of delegates to finally agree to a compromise.[556] After all, the rules protected the interests of weaker countries. His call for a vote on the final text in the closing plenary (against the fundamental consensus provision) highly 'irritated' parties.[557] Or, as only a few delegations opposed the Accord, Rasmussen pondered aloud whether they may simply be ignored. 'Then

547 Denmark(6)-09.02.2012.
548 Denmark(3)-11.08.2011.
549 BASIC(3)-08.07.2011.
550 G-77(5)-08.12.2011.
551 Denmark(5)-12.08.2011.
552 Denmark(3)-11.08.2011.
553 UNFCCC Secretariat(4)-17.05.2011.
554 Denmark(5)-12.08.2011.
555 Mexico(3)-15.06.2011.
556 Denmark(3)-11.08.2011.
557 EU/EU-country(4)-27.01.2011.

you can forget it. That's it,' commented a delegate.[558] Delegates now started panicking, for fear of failure, which further spoilt the atmosphere.[559] This way of running a plenary 'full of sharks'[560] was considered 'a disaster'.[561] Rumour had it that Rasmussen eventually had a nervous breakdown[562] and needed to quit the plenary.[563] All this significantly decreased chances for an agreement and turned the willingness negative until no consensus was reached.[564] Even worse, Rasmussen lacked advisers with sufficient multilateral experience to compensate for this deficit of his predominantly domestic expertise: 'In the end, he also was not well advised',[565] and 'with better advice it would have been different'.[566] A Danish official conceded that he was simply very badly prepared.[567]

In contrast, Espinosa's diplomatic expertise was a 'large reason for their success'.[568] Her cultural–personal fit and her long experience as ambassador let her master the process, easing moments of suspense with the right tonality throughout the COP.[569] One illustration was Cancún's last day. The storming applause for her by the overwhelming majority made delegates feel that they did 'not want to ruin the party'.[570] To the extent that the applause was partially stage-managed, it was an effective trick to use such group dynamics, making it hard to object: 'The management of the meeting was the reason why we got an agreement in Cancún.'[571] Her effective balancing of restraint and leadership culminated in the decision to state consensus despite Bolivia's objection in the final plenary, which led to the Cancún Agreements.[572] It was a fine line between a violation of UN rules and a legitimate interpretation of consensus. Such a move is of 'highest diplomatic art',[573] and comparable to Raúl Estrada's consensus decision in the Kyoto plenary.[574] Her diplomatic way of phrasing decisions and the correct wording of messages were of additional help,[575] and so she received only marginal, although very fierce, criticism. One delegate complained that Copenhagen's final plenary had at least respected the rules of procedure, while

558 Umbrella Group (4) 04.07.2011.
559 UNFCCC Secretariat(1)-28.04.2010.
560 UNFCCC Secretariat(2)-04.12.2010.
561 UNFCCC Secretariat(1)-28.04.2010.
562 EU/EU-country(7)-04.05.2011.
563 UNFCCC Secretariat(7)-03.08.2011.
564 Umbrella Group(1)-20.04.2011.
565 EU/EU-country(8)-05.05.2011.
566 Umbrella Group(3)-14.06.2011.
567 Denmark(3)-11.08.2011.
568 Denmark(3)-11.08.2011.
569 BASIC(2)-16.06.2011, EU/EU-country(9)-26.05.2011.
570 BASIC(2)-16.06.2011.
571 BASIC(2)-16.06.2011; similar: Umbrella Group(4)-04.07.2011.
572 Mexico(5)-07.07.2011.
573 EU/EU-country(6)-16.03.2011.
574 Observer(2)-08.12.2010.
575 BASIC(3)-08.07.2011.

Cancún was the first UNFCCC decision against an explicit objection.[576] This is not the place to assess the legality of the ruling though but its acceptance by parties. Delegates widely welcomed her decision, as Espinosa explicitly attempted to adhere to UN rules following the accepted notion that consensus does not require unanimity, and as she chaired in a firm but very tactful way. This was contrary to Rasmussen who had proposed a vote clearly against UN rules, earning a storm of criticism.

Closing the circle back to the Rasmussen analysis, we can imagine the counterfactual of a Chair like Espinosa presiding during Copenhagen's last night. The accumulated evidence suggests that she may have been able to 'grab . . . the whole room'.[577] A continuation of Hedegaard as COP President, for instance, may already have been sufficient.[578] These hypothetical chairs may have chosen more appropriate measures for this delicate situation, as Espinosa did when stating consensus despite Bolivia's objection while not offending everyone else. Rare voices question whether Espinosa or Hedegaard would have made a difference given the different dynamics of Copenhagen and Cancún.[579] Yet the overwhelming record of grave mistakes by Rasmussen suggests such impact by a more capable COP President.

Last but not least, the capability of organizers influences the creation of supportive physical negotiation conditions, which are a critical element of situation-appropriate process design. The differences between Copenhagen and Cancún weighed heavily on the constructive spirit of delegates, who are exhausted after weeks of intense preparation and summit negotiations: 'These are people. They often haven't slept, their eyes are burning, and they have had horrible food over several days.'[580] It had been an explicit emphasis of the Mexicans to satisfy everyone with their overall excellent logistics.[581] A seasoned and unsentimental negotiator underlined that 'this matters'.[582] While organizational proficiency doesn't guarantee an agreement it can substantially add to stalemate.[583] In sum, the variance in capability affected the appropriate response by organizers in very complex situations, and thereby the reaching of an agreement zone and the willingness of parties to agree.

Second, the match of original strategy with negotiation reality and the flexibility to respond to deviations influence the ability to navigate the process. One example of mismatch was how the Danes were overwhelmed by the united and forceful stance of the ALBA countries.[584] This surprise may have been avoided

576   ALBA(1)-17.06.2011.
577   Denmark(2)-16.06.2011, similar for many others: UNFCCC Secretariat(2)-04.12.2010.
578   AWG/SB-Chair(4)-14.06.2011.
579   UNFCCC Secretariat(4)-17.05.2011.
580   EU/EU-country(9)-26.05.2011.
581   Mexico(5)-07.07.2011.
582   Umbrella Group(1)-20.04.2011; similar: Observer(2)-08.12.2010.
583   UNFCCC Secretariat(1)-28.04.2010.
584   EU/EU-country(11)-10.12.2011.

through a more intimate knowledge of negotiating factions. Worse though, the Prime Minister's office then lacked multilateral experience to master the situation on an ad hoc basis. Moreover, Presidency and Secretariat had created massive pressure on delegates with their originally stellar expectations for a binding, comprehensive agreement with far-reaching economic ramifications. Yet it turned out, that this view did not properly reflect the position of several key countries at the time, making the original Danish strategy redundant. The lowering of pressure then came several months too late.[585] In contrast, the moderate ambition in Cancún with the mantra that 'the perfect is the enemy of the good' better matched the preferences of most delegates and allowed for a smoother process. In addition, organizers in 2009 originally restrained their flexibility to adapt to evolving negotiation circumstances by their narrow definition of success as a comprehensive agreement.[586] So the mismatch of strategy and reality, and low flexibility rendered the Presidency's facilitation much more difficult. This was in contrast to the Mexicans whose strategy better matched countries' preferences and remained flexible on process and outcome.

Finally, varying facilitation styles affected how neutral organizers were perceived to be by delegates. The high Danish level of activism and the pushing of a particular outcome proved detrimental.[587] The early preparation of a 'Danish text' for example made parties believe in a strong US bias, which severely diminished their trust.[588] This was aggravated in the final meeting of the 28 negotiators on Thursday night, where Rasmussen allowed a nearly exclusive exchange between China and the US, ignoring anyone else.[589] Their strategy to focus on a select group of the highest leaders though failed, underlined even a former senior BASIC negotiator: 'An agreement by world leaders is not enough. Legally it has to be a UN agreement.'[590] At the same time, de Boer tried to actively steer the process in a dominant manner many delegations disliked.[591] It aggravated his collision with the Prime Minister's team and undermined parties' confidence in his neutrality. It came in addition to parties' already existing perception of his European bias.[592]

Organizers in 2010 avoided offending parties and cautiously balanced passiveness and activeness.[593] Delegations had reacted extremely sensitively to any infringement of their role as 'drivers of the process' before. Organizers were not meant to negotiate with but to neutrally facilitate between parties.[594] Some

585 EU/EU-country(9)-26.05.2011, EU/EU-country(10)-16.08.2011.
586 UNFCCC Secretariat(4)-17.05.2011.
587 UNFCCC Secretariat(4)-17.05.2011.
588 EU/EU-country(1)-20.01.2010; similar: UNFCCC Secretariat(1)-28.04.2010.
589 Umbrella Group(4)-04.07.2011.
590 UNFCCC Secretariat(6)-16.06.2011.
591 EU/EU-country(10)-16.08.2011.
592 Denmark(2)-16.06.2011.
593 Mexico(3)-15.06.2011.
594 BASIC(1)-04.12.2010.

delegations still criticized the more restrained approach during the Mexican Presidency, which had inter alia organized several issue-specific consultations. Bolivia, for instance, protested against facilitation by the organizers in an email to parties on 30 November.[595] They contested the release of a mere option paper by the LCA Chair on COP-16's first day, which had left the original negotiation text untouched. The critique was not widely shared but reflected the issue's general sensitivity. Others in turn worried that pure party-driven negotiations risked that the multiple text parts would eventually not be compatible in their degree of detail. Overall, parties appreciated the middle way of organizers between these varying expectations of activism in 2010 and largely perceived them as neutral. This trust could eventually even trump content.[596] In Cancún, the African Group had reservations about the outcome but accepted it out of respect for the hard diplomatic efforts by the Mexicans.[597] Interviewees repeatedly stated that 'at the end of the day it is people that represent countries. So the trust between these people is a key.'[598] I discuss the effect of authority of the COP President more specifically in the following chapter.

In sum, capability affected the ability to navigate the process through situation-appropriate measures, the reality-match of strategy and flexible adaptation, and the perception of neutrality. The three mechanisms added to a better facilitation for a text inside the objective agreement zone and increased parties' willingness to agree on a subjective level.

Finally, a high cultural–personal fit widens the access of organizers to delegates (path 3). It opens up negotiators for conversation and thus to sharing of information with organizers, which is essential for facilitation. The opposite occurred in 2009. Many were alienated by the Presidency's actions perceiving them as disrespectful, instead of a cultural–personal misfit: 'Eventually, there was a lot of ill feeling towards the Danes by lots of countries.'[599] One behavioural norm of multilateral negotiations prescribes a middle way between pushiness and restraint for interaction. It not only impacts on the Presidency's neutrality, but also on how delegates feel respected as individuals. The Danes and de Boer were often seen as too pushy, while the Mexicans and Figueres showed more restraint. Lidegaard's fast-paced and tough way was occasionally even described as arrogant.[600] This feeling of disrespect prevented the Danes from accessing people to the extent the Mexicans did in 2010. De Alba's low-key style created trust among people.[601] His charisma and charm[602] made delegates feel respected. Even very process-sceptical negotiators conceded that this laid-back and open-hearted

595   Denmark(1)-02.12.2010.
596   EU/EU-country(5)-17.02.2011.
597   AWG/SB-Chair(4)-14.06.2011.
598   G-77(3)-19.07.2011.
599   EU/EU-country(8)-05.05.2011.
600   Denmark(3)-11.08.2011.
601   EU/EU-country(9)-26.05.2011.
602   Observer(1)-06.12.2010.

approach widened his access including to more closed-up delegations, and often built personal relationships.[603] Similarly, Espinosa's style respected the pride of negotiators.[604] Together with her calm and open character, she unlocked delegations getting wide access:[605] 'People related better to Espinosa',[606] in striking contrast to Rasmussen. Keeping back and attentively listening to delegates also gave Figueres wide access.[607] A process-critical delegate noted that 'even if you don't get anything, you feel good about it at least'.[608] In contrast, de Boer's pushiness and media focus lowered parties' readiness to reveal their preferences to him.[609] 'It may well be' that his personal style contributed to COP-15's outcome.[610]

Second, wide access to delegations allows lead organizers to build bridges and bring people together that may otherwise not constructively exchange their views to find a compromise.[611] In 2009, the Danes and the Dutch de Boer had been seen as representing Europe and the developed world.[612] Their restricted access made it very difficult to organize informal consultations with all groups to discuss key procedural matters, for instance. Regularly, the G-77 and BASIC countries would not participate prohibiting any meaningful progress.[613] Instead, the cultural proximity granted the 2010 organizers better access to their Latin American neighbours, and disabled those that had used the organisers' origin as an excuse to obstruct negotiations.[614] The Presidency built bridges to include a broad range of views, especially of the ALBA countries that had actively fought the agreement one year earlier. De Alba leveraged his access and multilateral experience to convene hitherto unseen combinations of parties, creating fresh dynamics.[615] In sum, the cultural–personal fit influenced the access organizers had to delegates through greater conveyed respect. This access eased the vital sharing of information and bridge-building between parties.

Conclusion

Climate negotiations during 2009 and 2010 suggest that the capability of the organizers of the Danish and Mexican Presidencies, and of their UNFCCC Secretariat counterparts, affected negotiations. To be sure, the capability of an

603   ALBA(2)-09.12.2011.
604   UNFCCC Secretariat(5)-14.06.2011.
605   EU/EU-country(9)-26.05.2011.
606   G-77(4)-22.07.2011.
607   EU/EU-country(9)-26.05.2011.
608   G-77(5)-08.12.2011.
609   EU/EU-country(7)-04.05.2011.
610   BASIC(2)-16.06.2011.
611   EU/EU-country(6)-16.03.2011.
612   Observer(1)-06.12.2010.
613   Mexico(3)-15.06.2011.
614   UNFCCC Secretariat(4)-17.05.2011.
615   Mexico(5)-07.07.2011.

institution alone does not determine the decision of a delegation,[616] and some deem factors, such as power and interests, to be much more important.[617] Yet, abundant evidence has shown that the higher institutional capability of both the Presidency and Secretariat in 2010 led to more effective institutional processes saving the organizers critical time and energy. This supports and complements recent scholarship on the autonomous role of institutions on an international level. As for individual organizers, there is, of course, no certainty that Espinosa, de Alba, and Figueres would have facilitated a comprehensive deal in Copenhagen.[618] Yet, their better cultural–personal fit and greater process expertise than Rasmussen, Lidegaard, and de Boer suggest a higher probability under their leadership. They could better navigate the process and benefit from wider access to delegates. This finding echoes the widely held salience of individuals such as Raúl Estrada for reaching the Kyoto Protocol and of Mustafa Tolba for enabling the Montreal Protocol. Capability thus is a second, critical lever for organizers.

Authority of the Conference Presidents

This chapter touches upon the fundamental question, addressed by scholars for decades and longer: to what extent can individuals alone make at least a short- to mid-term difference in international politics? It zooms in further by focusing on the lead organizer only, and so on the Conference President in the case of climate negotiations. I build on the analysis of the capability of the lead organizer in the preceding chapter, and address what authority delegates granted COP Presidents Rasmussen (and Hedegaard) in Copenhagen and Espinosa in Cancún. This is naturally affected by the capability they showed in their roles as negotiation chairs. The assessment of authority of the Conference Presidents precedes the analysis, in the final section of this chapter, of whether and how varying degrees of authority obstructed agreement in Copenhagen, and enabled it in Cancún.

Rasmussen's loss of authority

The Copenhagen summit suffered from a tremendous loss of authority of the Conference Presidents, especially of Prime Minister Rasmussen, with authority defined as overall trust in his or her role by the large majority of key negotiators. Beginning the analysis with the *first COP President, Hedegaard*, thirty per cent of respondents trusted her in her role, while senior negotiators from various regional backgrounds and leading UN officials saw a lack of authority (Table

---

616   Umbrella Group(4)-04.07.2011.
617   EU/EU-country(7)-04.05.2011.
618   UNFCCC Secretariat(4)-17.05.2011.

3.9). However, only 10 respondents answered the authority question on Hedegaard, so it can only serve as a rough indication.

The following analysis of interview evidence along the indicator of the trust continuum outlined above (Figure 1.6) offers more insight than the scant numerical overview. When Denmark started reaching out widely to countries early in 2009, Hedegaard began extensive travelling. She collected the myriad perspectives of countries, built trust, and was gaining authority among parties: she 'established relationships with everyone'.[619] Yet dynamics changed in the weeks before COP-15. The loss of her lead facilitator, Becker, was a blow to her authority: 'Connie did have trust. But she did the mistake to fire Thomas Becker. She then tried to save her image,' noted one negotiator close to her.[620] Irrespective of the exact circumstances of his exit, the departure of the principal thinker behind Copenhagen and alleged guarantor of a fair deal between developed and developing countries so shortly before the COP highly irritated parties.

At the COP, the leakage of the 'Danish text' undercut Hedegaard's authority further. A former COP Presidency member described that you 'never come with your own ideas as a Chair…The Danish violated this rule. Yet then, you lose as a Chair and you never recover.'[621] Becker's resignation and the leaked text undermined the trust in Hedegaard's neutrality. Would she act in the interest of all countries, many developing countries wondered?[622] Finally, her only temporary position as COP President did not allow her to restore her authority among most delegates: 'Connie achieved this authority as far as she could, but she was a President on call back.'[623] So overall, Hedegaard enjoyed a moderate degree of trust, but certainly not high levels by the majority of key negotiators.

Table 3.9 Responses to the question 'Did you have full trust in their authority for their negotiation role as Conference President?' with respect to the Danish Presidency

Response[a]	Hedegaard n (%)	Rasmussen n (%)
Conference President with authority	3 (13.6%)	0 (0%)
Conference President without authority	7 (31.8%)	22 (100%)
No answer on one of them	12 (54.6%)	0 (0%)
Total	22	22

Note: a. 22 interviewees covered the question on at least one of the Danish COP Presidents.

619 Mexico(5)-07.07.2011.
620 Umbrella Group(4)-04.07.2011.
621 EU/EU-country(5)-17.02.2011.
622 UNFCCC Secretariat(1)-28.04.2010.
623 EU/EU-country(9)-26.05.2011.

More importantly, though, what does the data show on then-Danish Prime Minister Rasmussen? He was Conference President during the high-level segment of the final days and the closing plenary, when authority could have exerted crucial influence on reaching agreement. The interviews yield a clear picture. 'Rasmussen didn't have any [trust of the parties]', commented a top UN official.[624] This was the unanimous view by all interviewees, including Denmark-friendly negotiators and Danish officials (Table 3.9).

The early notion that Rasmussen was overly close to the US ('an executor for the US'[625]) cost tremendous trust. Apparently, US officials had even written briefing papers for the Danish Prime Minister in spring 2009.[626] Suspicion further grew among developing countries due to the Prime Minister's negative view of the Secretariat.[627] Would Denmark as a European country circumvent the more neutral Secretariat to push through a 'Western' agenda? Parties gradually did no longer believe in an honest, open-ended brokerage but the 'selling [of] a product, the Copenhagen Accord', or worse: 'swallow what I got'.[628] The earlier noted frequent neglect of process further undermined his authority. While Rasmussen perceived UN rules as 'ridiculous', Espinosa 'knew the game and the procedures straight away'.[629] Many negotiators conceived of him as 'a bully who tried to push issues, violating basic UN principles'.[630]

Delegates pitifully watched Rasmussen's obvious inability to fulfil a core task as head of government: to unite his own administration behind one goal. Parties often wondered '[f]or whom within the Danish Presidency [an official] would they speak?'[631] This did not foster trust, and throughout the year, 'things went from bad to worse'.[632] The exit of Becker and later Hedegaard as COP President cost additional credibility.[633] Once the COP President's change was communicated at the beginning of Copenhagen, Rasmussen 'had a bad name from day one'.[634] Parties had built relations with Hedegaard for over a year, yet 'no one knew Rasmussen. He had left all to his underlings. He was disconnected.'[635] So in the second week of COP-15, when facilitation for agreement would have been direly needed, the actual change of COP Presidents dealt another mighty blow to Rasmussen's authority.[636] Authority reached a low point in the final plenary. Parties reacted harshly to his dismal presiding performance, so even a balanced

624   UNFCCC Secretariat(7)-03.08.2011.
625   G-77(4)-22.07.2011.
626   Umbrella Group(2)-02.06.2011.
627   UNFCCC Secretariat(4)-17.05.2011.
628   Mexico(3)-15.06.2011.
629   Denmark(2)-16.06.2011.
630   G-77(4)-22.07.2011.
631   EU/EU-country(8)-05.05.2011.
632   UNFCCC Secretariat(1)-28.04.2010.
633   Mexico(5)-07.07.2011, EU/EU-country(8)-05.05.2011.
634   UNFCCC Secretariat(5)-14.06.2011.
635   Umbrella Group(3)-14.06.2011.
636   BASIC(3)-08.07.2011.

official described that Rasmussen was eventually 'mishandled' there: 'There was an unnecessary roughness between the delegates and the Prime Minister. It was harsh and violent towards him. He even had to leave the Plenary.'[637]

Overall, lack of authority of the lead organizer correlated with not reaching agreement during the Danish Presidency. In the case of Hedegaard, at least a good part of negotiators trusted her in her role. During the most crucial days of the high-level segment however, Danish Prime Minister Rasmussen enjoyed hardly any authority as new COP President. Let us now compare this finding to the Mexican Presidency.

The wealth of Espinosa's political capital

Foreign Minister Patricia Espinosa, who continuously led the Mexican Presidency, enjoyed significantly more authority as Conference President than Rasmussen. She was able to accumulate a wealth of political capital. All but one interviewee respected her authority as COP President (Table 3.10). Most respondents instantly replied with an 'absolutely yes',[638] including delegates from all coalitions and Danish officials.

How can we explain her authority, and how did capability and fair process add to this? The Presidency started building authority early on. 'Patricia had long been involved in the process. You have to build this authority as it's not there by itself. The success of Cancún started in January 2010.'[639] It was an enormous challenge after the shattered trust of Copenhagen, and it took several months to bring it back to high levels. In April 2010, for instance, 'the process was still in trouble' when several delegations complained about overly active Mexican facilitation, and only subsequently built up trust.[640] Espinosa's long multilateral experience served her well for this, and Mexico 'invested heavily into transparency and trust during the whole year'[641] (see 'Transparency and inclusiveness'

Table 3.10 Responses to the question 'Did you have full trust in her authority for her negotiation role as Conference President?' with respect to the Mexican Presidency

Response	Espinosa
Conference President with authority	21 (95.5%)
Conference President without authority	1 (4.5%)
Total	22

637 Mexico(4)-16.06.2011.
638 EU/EU-country(9)-26.05.2011.
639 Mexico(4)-16.06.2011.
640 UNFCCC Secretariat(1)-28.04.2010.
641 BASIC(3)-08.07.2011.

section earlier in this chapter). Espinosa visited many countries herself, and personally held consultations. She thereby developed personal relations with myriad negotiators.[642]

By COP-16, Espinosa was 'well known to everyone', in contrast to Rasmussen one year before.[643] She had built up 'good political capital' and knew 'all key negotiators by name, and parties' positions'.[644] Her widely praised mastering of multilateral procedures became most evident during the heated days of a summit (see 'Capability of organizers' section earlier in this chapter), when it further raised her image.[645] Perceived by many as 'referee' without pushing one particular outcome, her neutrality enhanced credibility,[646] to which a constant open-door policy contributed.[647] On the last Friday of COP-16, Espinosa's popularity reached its highest levels. She received standing ovations when giving the text to parties after one day of hectic finalizing. Delegates were already clapping even before seeing the text and its two-hour review though.[648] In the closing plenary, she was seen by many as 'a very strong chair'.[649] The acceptance of the overruling of Bolivia by delegations and the storm of applause after the consensus decision indicated her 'moral authority'.[650] Most countries supported Espinosa widely, including several ALBA countries.[651] In short: 'No single COP President has ever seen so many standing ovations that reflected that we show our full respect for what has happened so far.'[652]

A few negotiators still regarded her with scepticism until the end. One doubtful voice affirmed that she was 'open towards Espinosa until the end. Yet, she would tell us one thing, but then she would do something else.'[653] For example, Espinosa did not invite all developing countries to her meetings with the Cartagena Group, which undermined this negotiator's confidence in her neutrality given the diverging positions within the G-77. Yet, it is uncontested as standard for a lead organizer to have confident bilaterals with all different groups. Regarding the standing ovations at the end of COP-16, the negotiator denied that they did express support for Espinosa: 'the applause... came from behind, from civil society organizations. The Mexicans told these organizations to put pressure on Asian governments' to approve the proposal.[654] Yet, civil society organizations were a minority in the back, and it is hardly conceivable that

642 G-77(3)-19.07.2011.
643 Umbrella Group(3)-14.06.2011.
644 Mexico(5)-07.07.2011.
645 Denmark(2)-16.06.2011.
646 UNFCCC Secretariat(4)-17.05.2011.
647 Umbrella Group(2)-02.06.2011.
648 Mexico(5)-07.07.2011.
649 Umbrella Group(2)-02.06.2011.
650 UNFCCC Secretariat(5)-14.06.2011.
651 EU/EU-country(6)-16.03.2011.
652 EU/EU-country(9)-26.05.2011.
653 G-77(2)-13.06.2011.
654 G-77(2)-13.06.2011.

delegates gave standing ovations because of them. One negotiator acknowledged that Espinosa enjoyed more trust than the Danes, while this allegedly decreased with less transparency towards the end.[655] Nevertheless, interviews yield a clear picture of broad acceptance by the majority of key negotiators, across negotiation groups and cultures. A high level of authority of Mexican lead organizer Espinosa as COP President correlated with the reaching of an agreement during the Mexican Presidency.

How authority influenced the summit outcomes

So, did the varying levels of authority of Rasmussen and Espinosa affect consensus? The first cut analysis shows a clear tendency, with two-thirds of responses attributing influence of trust-based authority on outcome (Table 3.11): 'The lack of trust eventually killed Copenhagen.'[656] Individuals have long affected multilateral negotiations: 'Any major achievement in the UN always depended on a few people or a few countries.'[657] Counterfactually, respondents claim that had the Danes presided over Cancún's final plenary, 'they would not have achieved the same outcome' due to their lack of authority.[658] Another quarter of interviewees granted some effect to authority (consensus was 'partly Espinosa's authority, and partly due to the goodwill of others'[659]), or underlined the equal importance of structural factors, such as interests ('had an influence, but was not decisive'[660]). Only 12 per cent doubted that authority had any effect on outcome: 'Governments don't work this way. Governments want to work with you such that they can achieve their position and interests. They want to see whether that is possible and don't care about authority.'[661] The impact of these structural factors will be considered later on. Results were equally distributed among respondents by negotiation coalition and by different organizing entities.

Table 3.11 Responses to the question 'Did that influence your rejection or acceptance of the proposal, e.g. in the final nights when accepting the overruling of Bolivia at COP-16?'

Response	n (%)
Authority influenced the outcome	16 (64%)
Authority influenced the outcome somewhat	6 (24%)
Authority did not influence the outcome	3 (12%)
Total	25

655 ALBA(2)-09.12.2011.
656 Observer(1)-06.12.2010.
657 Mexico(3)-15.06.2011.
658 EU/EU-country(7)-04.05.2011.
659 Umbrella Group(1)-20.04.2011.
660 EU/EU-country(10)-16.08.2011; similar: EU/EU-country(6)-16.03.2011.
661 Umbrella Group(1)-20.04.2011.

Closer analysis uncovers three paths, which connect authority and agreement: (1) parties' goodwill, (2) the Conference President's leeway, and (3) parties' blockade potential (Figure 3.4). They work through on an objective and subjective level. For instance, greater goodwill based on trust may move hitherto 'red lines' and thereby enable agreement. Let us now examine the causal chain between authority and agreement in more detail.

Authority produces *goodwill among parties* towards an agreement, which increases the chances of compromise (path 1). Ultimately, it is delegates who take the decision: 'There is no such thing as countries. There is "people".'[662] Their behaviour can be traced along several steps during a negotiation. Goodwill affects the scrutiny of the proposal. In negotiation terms, parties controlled their target and reservation points more or less strictly. Delegations may have rejected the proposal in Copenhagen even though it was within their range of acceptable outcomes. Rasmussen's lack of authority and the exclusive small group negotiations destroyed the willingness to agree: 'had we not been in the [small group] negotiation room [of the last Friday] in Copenhagen, we had been put off by Mr Rasmussen as well and would have rejected the deal'.[663] Yet the exclusion of countries from small group negotiations does not mean that the proposal was automatically outside their desired range of outcomes: they signed on to a very similar proposal only one year later. The rejection was based on being 'put off by Mr Rasmussen', a clear lack of authority and goodwill for an agreement. Vice versa, negotiators may also have accepted proposals grounded in trust and despite uncertainty about its consequences: 'You have personal relationships. If a person you trust proposes something, how do you take it? Or, if there is no trust, how do you take it then? This personal side is just natural.'[664] This shows how trust-based authority of a COP President altered the openness towards a proposal in the

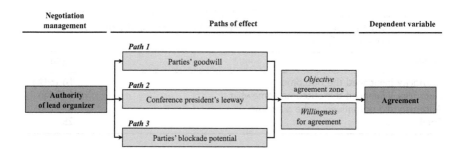

Figure 3.4 Process-tracing between authority of lead organizer and agreement

662   Umbrella Group(3)-14.06.2011.
663   BASIC(2)-16.06.2011.
664   G-77(2)-13.06.2011.

turbulence of the last COP hours. If parties feel they can trust a Conference President, they are confident that their interests are at least seriously considered, and not overlooked: 'Patricia [Espinosa] was trusted to recognize all interests.'[665]

Parties did not only show varying scrutiny of proposals. At COP-16, trust even led to the lowering of reservation points to enable agreement (i.e. to consciously giving in on issues against their interests). Authority can therefore sideline some of the country's rejections on substance: 'Patricia was wonderful. Even though we didn't like some parts we said "yes" due to the trust and authority she had enjoyed amongst us.'[666] This dynamic seemed also partially true for those countries that switched from 'no' to 'yes' between COP-15 and 16. 'Colombia is a great example for this. They became admirers of Espinosa.'[667] She radiated an 'environment of competence'[668] in which countries cooperated more constructively. The right personality might change positions as '80% of governments don't even have a final position on issues. Even the 20% might change this in the light of pressure and due to the process.'[669]

Next, authority affects how delegates treat procedural mistakes or contested decisions by the lead organizer. This much depends on the President's attitude towards negotiation rules. Rasmussen had demonstrated his low appreciation for them in words and deeds, and so he received no indulgence by exhausted delegates: 'At COP-15, no one helped Rasmussen. He tore down every bridge that one built. At some point, you just don't want any more.'[670] It peaked in his grave violation of rules calling for a vote on the agreement on the last night. Such mistakes are fatal in a central position, assured a former COP President: 'As soon as [the COP President] makes some mistakes, he is out.'[671] With a different prior behaviour and greater authority, parties might have allowed Rasmussen to take bolder decisions in the final hours of COP-15 and establish consensus given only a handful of moderately powerful countries opposed the deal, such as Bolivia, Cuba, Nicaragua or Venezuela. But the atmosphere had long turned against him.

In contrast, Espinosa's chairing adhered carefully to the essential rules, and her rare deviations were mostly forgiven. The Sunday meeting between the first and second week of COP-16 illustrates this well. Espinosa ruled on a concern raised by one party, which was a procedural fault as it was not an official meeting. She corrected her mistake immediately, receiving no complaints: 'People were willing to work with her... and no one said anything.'[672] Or, when organizers drafted the final text on the last Friday, the relative lack of transparency and inclusiveness was received mildly due to the accumulated goodwill. 'Everyone was

665 Mexico(3)-15.06.2011.
666 BASIC(2)-16.06.2011.
667 BASIC(2)-16.06.2011.
668 UNFCCC Secretariat(1)-28.04.2010.
669 Mexico(3)-15.06.2011.
670 EU/EU-country(9)-26.05.2011.
671 EU/EU-country(5)-17.02.2011.
672 Mexico(5)-07.07.2011; similar: EU/EU-country(1)-20.01.2010.

completely left in the dark on the last Friday afternoon of COP-16. But they trusted the Mexicans.'[673] The effect of this goodwill culminated in the make-or-break moment of Cancún's closing plenary: 'it influenced their approval to overrule Bolivia [at COP-16] because she had until then exactly stuck to the rules'.[674] Bolivia had been protesting vocally against the agreement and negotiation management, yet the united front against the deal in Copenhagen was now split:

> The ALBA group was divided in Cancún. Pablo [Solón, Bolivia] felt he was betrayed. When he spoke up against the agreement in the final plenary he thought Claudia [Salerno, Venezuela] and Cuba would do the same. Yet, the Latin American countries kept silent for their higher level of trust which they had into Espinosa.[675]

Veteran negotiators mirror this assessment that ALBA countries granted 'exactly this authority [to overrule Bolivia]' to her.[676] Espinosa had the backing of close to all parties to overrule Bolivia, even of Venezuela, mostly due to the accumulated goodwill.[677] Trusting the COP President, delegates accepted her decision on the final night.[678]

This leads to a second route between authority and agreement: perceived sufficient leeway empowers the COP President to dare to take difficult decisions (path 2). It stems from the conviction of broad support by parties. In Cancún for example, the repeated standing ovation for Espinosa conveyed this notion and offered sufficient emotional backing:

> The more I talk about it, the more I see emotions underneath...The last night was at the edge of the cliff. When the clapping burst out of for the Mexican Presidency under Espinosa at the opening of the final plenary, I knew we would get this outcome.[679]

The atmosphere turned very emotional for many: 'The feeling of the last night was absolute euphoria. Espinosa was like a rock-star.'[680] Such broad, emotional support empowers the lead organizer to take difficult decisions: '[The rebuilding of trust] was much needed...That was one reason why they [the Mexican Presidency] could do and did in Cancún what they did, as they had created the

673   Denmark(3)-11.08.2011.
674   Denmark(2)-16.06.2011.
675   G-77(4)-22.07.2011.
676   EU/EU-country(6)-16.03.2011.
677   EU/EU-country(4)-27.01.2011.
678   Mexico(5)-07.07.2011.
679   EU/EU-country(7)-04.05.2011.
680   UNFCCC Secretariat(1)-28.04.2010.

capital and goodwill needed to gavel a decision.'[681] At COP-15, the hostile treatment of Rasmussen reduced his perception of leeway to take bold decisions. A
Denmark-allied negotiator concedes that 'a stronger chair could have possibly
achieved an agreement in the last night of COP-15. Rasmussen was unable to
close the deal. He had a lack of authority.'[682] He was too weakened to seize the
moment when he received standing ovations by the majority of the room, started
by the then British Secretary of State for Energy and Climate Change Ed
Miliband: 'Rasmussen did not take it. Espinosa took it.'[683] Ultimately, fair process,
trust, and resulting authority are the prerequisites for such empowerment: 'An
'investment' through the Presidency is needed to be allowed to lead in key
moments as Presidency.'[684]

Finally, the level of authority influences parties' blockade potential and hence
the likelihood of agreement (path 3). Interviews suggest that authority affects
the respect and caution with which negotiators interact with the Conference
President. For example, parties are less likely to openly block the process if a
COP President has, so far, competently dealt with procedural interventions:

> Espinosa was able to give meaningful answers to questions from the floor.
> Everyone was able to try her, and then she would get back tough on them.
> This was different to Rasmussen who could only say stupid things, like 'I
> don't understand your process'.[685]

Espinosa's authority went so far that some negotiators were even said to be
'afraid' of her: 'She was so good that she could not be pushed around by countries
but would put them back into their place if they tried.'[686] The Saudi Arabian
intervention against Espinosa, for instance, would have meant attacking an
honest broker and damaging the country's reputation.[687] Taking process objections off the table in Cancún (and only leaving substantive points) therefore
significantly strengthened Espinosa, compared to Rasmussen, who had to deal
with both in Copenhagen.[688] Rasmussen's poor track record invited the few
opposing countries to jeopardize the agreement on procedural grounds in the
already chaotic and heated atmosphere of the final night. It allowed them to act
as guardians of process, and not saboteurs of substance.

Only a few interviewees found that trust in the COP President was not a factor
for parties' ultimate decision. The rejection in Copenhagen allegedly only affected

681 G-77(3)-19.07.2011, Umbrella Group(2)-02.06.2011.
682 Umbrella Group(1)-20.04.2011.
683 Umbrella Group(1)-20.04.2011.
684 EU/EU-country(6)-16.03.2011.
685 Denmark(3)-11.08.2011.
686 UNFCCC Secretariat(1)-28.04.2010.
687 EU/EU-country(6)-16.03.2011.
688 Umbrella Group(2)-02.06.2011.

the style of their reaction to the text.[689] Yet, this very style of opposing a deal influences how the COP President can counter their objections. Another held that personalities influenced only the process set up. Once the 'sound process' by the Mexicans had been in place, authority did not matter too much.[690] Yet, the greater empathy which leads to a better process may also impact on their acceptance by delegates. Finally, some stated that interests outweighed considerations of authority,[691] which will be discussed in the chapter on alternative explanations.

Conclusion

So did single individuals influence climate negotiations? This result supports those that argue that the analysis of international relations should be complemented with a micro-level view. The evidence suggests that the degree of authority perceived by delegates of the lead organizer, Rasmussen and Espinosa respectively, impacted on reaching an agreement. The influence can be traced through various paths for preparatory negotiations and the summits of Copenhagen and Cancún: authority affected agreement likelihood through the goodwill of parties, the perceived leeway of the lead organizer, and the blockade potential of parties. The final assessment is only made after analysing alternative explanations. Yet for now, low authority of Conference President Rasmussen seems to have contributed to the collapse of Copenhagen. Vice versa, Espinosa's high authority possibly helped to reach the Cancún Agreements. Let us now proceed to the final element of negotiation management: the role of the negotiation mode of parties.

Negotiation mode

The way in which delegates negotiate with each other significantly influences the course of events. Are they arguing more in an open-minded and constructive manner revealing their underlying interests, or do they bargain in a hard-headed fashion by sticking to their positions? Arguing often creates ideas and room for compromise, whereas bargaining frequently leads to deadlock, or at least suboptimal outcomes. As we found in Chapter 1, organizers affect this 'negotiation mode' of parties. Influencing this choice is hence a further facilitation tool for organizers. Regarding this element, this book combines constructivist thinking on discourse with International Relations and management negotiation theory on arguing and bargaining. Moving from positions to underlying interests is also a key phase in any mediation process. So which negotiation mode did eventually prevail during the Danish and Mexican Presidencies, and did it have any impact on the outcome of the summits?

---

689   BASIC(3)-08.07.2011.
690   UNFCCC Secretariat(7)-03.08.2011.
691   UNFCCC Secretariat(6)-16.06.2011.

Hard-headed bargaining 'taking over' as the Copenhagen summit nears

After a constructive start parties eventually moved towards hard-headed bargaining during the Danish Presidency. The numeric interpretation of interview responses shows this shift from the preparatory talks in 2009 towards COP-15 (Table 3.12), at least when looking at all parties *jointly*. Specific subgroups, which were not only confined to major powers, such as the Greenland Dialogue, maintained an arguing mode throughout preparatory negotiations, but did not play any major role in Copenhagen. At COP-15, major powers tended to argue especially during the high-level segment, when leaders tried to craft a compromise. As for the interview sample size, the small number for the preparation period provides only indicative evidence, while many respondents covered COP-15.

Let us now examine these results in more detail. Preparatory negotiations saw attempts by all parties for an open-ended search for a solution.[692] The preceding years brought an extensive exchange of information and of ideas for solutions leading to 'very informed negotiations'.[693] One indication for this was the abundance of negotiation documents, such as on technology or adaptation.[694] Yet,

Table 3.12 Responses to the question 'Did you see open-ended arguing and problem-solving about content?' with respect to COP-15. Here 'open-ended arguing and problem-solving' was defined as 'Constructive discourse which is open to a change of minds based on facts and logical insights in order to find a joint solution', and was contrasted with 'bargaining', defined as 'the distribution of an assumed fixed set of gains and burdens, based on merely stating countries' positions'

Response	All parties n (%)[a]	Major powers n (%)	Other subgroups n (%)
Preparatory negotiations in 2009			
Arguing	4 (80%)	0 (0%)	4 (80%)
Bargaining	1 (20%)	0 (0%)	1 (20%)
Both/ambiguous	0 (0%)	0 (0%)	0 (0%)
Total	5	0	5
COP-15			
Arguing	1 (4.2%)	7 (78%)	0 (0%)
Bargaining	21 (87.5%)	0 (0%)	0 (0%)
Both/ambiguous	2 (8.3%)	2 (22%)	0 (0%)
Total	24	9	0

Note: a. n is the number of responses (not the interviewees). It could be the same interviewee commenting on the negotiation mode of all parties and major powers.

692 EU/EU-country(8)-05.05.2011, similar but not fully convinced: UNFCCC Secretariat(2)-04.12.2010.
693 Denmark(3)-11.08.2011.
694 BASIC(2)-16.06.2011.

parties argued mostly about politically less sensitive issues resulting in myriad proposals on technical items. Towards COP-15, delegations increasingly only stated *their* positions instead of looking for joint solutions, like in the Green Climate Fund negotiations in Barcelona, which created a compendium of proposals without an overarching framework.[695]

No data were available on the negotiation mode among major powers alone during the preparatory year. Major powers however gathered with other countries in subgroups, whose participants reported that arguing dominated. For instance, the Danish Presidency hosted various Greenland Dialogue meetings, one with around 30 countries in summer 2009. It created the space and atmosphere for an open dialogue outside the normal process and resulted in myriad good ideas.[696] Participants perceived these discussions on a ministerial level as 'really good' to find solutions[697] and to build convergence around issues.[698] Nevertheless, some ministers and lead negotiators read out pre-formulated statements, inhibiting a veritable dialogue.[699] Candid discussions also occurred at MEF meetings during 2009, where major economies gathered to find solutions to the problem of emissions.[700] In sum, arguing was present among all parties in the first half of preparatory negotiations in 2009, as well as in subgroups like the Greenland Dialogue and the MEF. In all of these cases though, delegates increasingly bargained.

Let us now turn to COP-15. The Presidency's behaviour did not foster a frank dialogue. Their preference and active push for a particular negotiation outcome let irritated parties close up.[701] The Danish choice to develop the outcome with very few major powers did not entice arguing among all.[702] Isolated negotiations on expert and political levels inhibited arguing, which would have integrated all levels.[703] So the mood turned adversarial through Danish negotiation management and the mode of negotiations between all parties swung towards bargaining in Copenhagen. Any open discussion on substance[704] and a profound exchange about underlying interests[705] was missing, judged UN officials with a very good COP-15 overview. It became 'a recitation of positions, pride, and focus on each one's red lines'.[706] Options were put back in and the formal negotiation text went

695   Mexico(3)-15.06.2011.
696   Denmark(2)-16.06.2011, UNFCCC Secretariat(5)-14.06.2011.
697   EU/EU-country(9)-26.05.2011.
698   G-77(3)-19.07.2011.
699   Denmark(1)-02.12.2010.
700   Denmark(1)-02.12.2010, UNFCCC Secretariat(5)-14.06.2011.
701   Denmark(2)-16.06.2011.
702   ALBA(2)-09.12.2011: 'The document was written by the US.'
703   G-77(5)-08.12.2011, G-77(3)-19.07.2011.
704   UNFCCC Secretariat(4)-17.05.2011.
705   UNFCCC Secretariat(1)-28.04.2010.
706   UNFCCC Secretariat(1)-28.04.2010; similar: AWG/SB-Chair(4)-14.06.2011, Observer(3)-16.06.2011.

backwards.[707] One working group discussed the possibility of adding brackets to an already entirely bracketed text.[708] On Tuesday night of the second week, just before the high-level segment, delegates 'fought like crazy until 7 am' without any significant changes.[709] Countries showed little willingness to consider other proposals,[710] and the hostile atmosphere made it difficult for chairs to suggest compromises. Obstruction, the most extreme form of bargaining, became not unusual.[711] As a major agreement was potentially up for decision, delegates were anxious about suffering losses. They were not ready to move[712] and started to hold back tactically for a later joint package.[713] The US bargained by not announcing the US$100 billion long-term financing until the second-to-last COP day, instead of creating a constructive atmosphere much earlier.[714] Chinese delegates held firm to their tight orders from Beijing until major powers gathered in the US–BASIC small group.[715] That the EU had its cards open only owed to its internal set up. Experts and ministers each waited for the next higher level to arrive and take the decisions, until it was too late when heads of state and government came to Copenhagen.[716] Arguing in negotiations among all parties only continued in some groups on technical issues at COP-15. With more time to familiarize with issues and proposals, and greater openness, negotiators found more commonalities than they expected, for instance in the 'informal informal' technology contact group.[717] Arguing mostly prevailed.[718] Negotiators expressed how helpful it was to actually hear an explanation first instead of just stating a position. The arguing came too late however, to still reach agreement. This stood in contrast to the pure bargaining of 'the basic political questions'.[719] Overall, negotiations among all parties had shifted to bargaining mode.

Negotiations among major powers shifted to arguing at the end of COP-15 (in the sense of *integrative*, but not *positional* bargaining[720]), especially in the decisive US–BASIC meeting. It was seen as 'maybe the only place' in Copenhagen with

707   EU/EU-country(8)-05.05.2011; similar: EU/EU-country(7)-04.05.2011.
708   Umbrella Group(2)-02.06.2011.
709   EU/EU-country(9)-26.05.2011.
710   UNFCCC Secretariat(3)-08.12.2010.
711   EIG(1)-09.08.2011. For instance, some countries insisted on equal time for all topics irrespective of their importance.
712   EU/EU-country(10)-16.08.2011, EU/EU-country(6)-16.03.2011, Umbrella Group(4)-04.07.2011, Mexico(5)-07.07.2011, UNFCCC Secretariat(1)-28.04.2010.
713   EU/EU-country(9)-26.05.2011.
714   Umbrella Group(2)-02.06.2011.
715   Umbrella Group(2)-02.06.2011.
716   UNFCCC Secretariat(4)-17.05.2011.
717   Umbrella Group(3)-14.06.2011.
718   EU/EU-country(3)-03.12.2010.
719   Umbrella Group(1)-20.04.2011.
720   Some respondents spoke of *bargaining*, yet their description indicated more *integrative* than *positional* bargaining, and hence *arguing*.

arguing on core political issues.[721] The underlying interests of all major powers were understood and integrated to reach the Copenhagen Accord. All sides gained from the proposal beyond a mere zero-sum deal, which is another indicator that major powers had argued and partially revealed their differing interests, instead of simply bargaining. On the other hand, US–BASIC leaders did not resolve the most crucial and contested issue of how to distribute obligations to reduce emissions for a 2°C goal. They had eventually omitted issues they would not be able to agree on in this negotiation round, which is no evidence for bargaining or arguing. Negotiation modes of major powers also varied. The description of the Chinese lead negotiator's mode appears to be defensive and closed, indicating bargaining. The Indian Environment Minister seemed more open to engaging in a true dialogue, hence arguing.[722] Overall, the US–BASIC small group meeting probably was the forum that came closest to arguing in Copenhagen.

In sum, bargaining dominated negotiations among all parties at COP-15, while arguing only continued in a few technical areas (Figure 3.5). Moreover, specific subgroups such as the Greenland Dialogue and MEF, which had shown arguing during 2009, discontinued it at COP-15. Arguing prevailed only at the US–BASIC meeting leading to its compromise draft for the final plenary. Arguing hence correlated with the agreement of the major powers. At the same time, bargaining among all parties correlated with no agreement of the COP. Besides the COP, the tendency of arguing among all countries in the beginning of preparatory negotiations in 2009 and in the subgroups of the Greenland Dialogue and the MEF did not correlate with a Copenhagen agreement by all parties. The ideas developed in the subgroups during preparation were not sufficient for an agreement in the overall COP, but may have at least contributed to the compromise among major powers, which became the Copenhagen Accord.

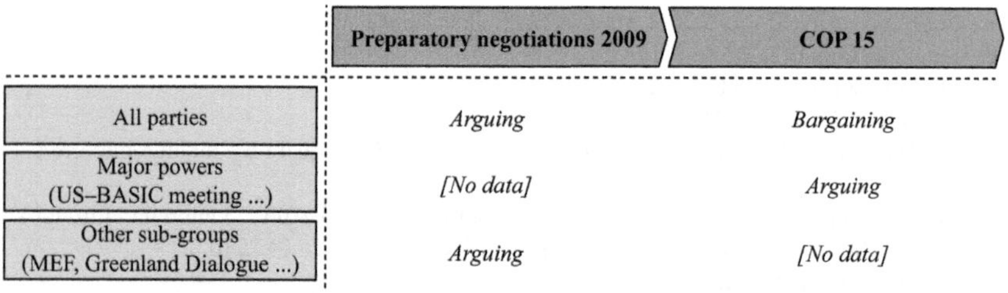

	Preparatory negotiations 2009	COP 15
All parties	*Arguing*	*Bargaining*
Major powers (US–BASIC meeting ...)	*[No data]*	*Arguing*
Other sub-groups (MEF, Greenland Dialogue ...)	*Arguing*	*[No data]*

Figure 3.5 Negotiation modes during the Danish Presidency

721　UNFCCC Secretariat(1)-28.04.2010; similar: AWG/SB-Chair(4)-14.06.2011.
722　EU/EU-country(3)-03.12.2010.

The return to arguing during the Mexican Presidency

Looking at the big picture of the Mexican Presidency, parties argued more than they bargained during 2010 (Table 3.13). The few direct comments on the negotiation mode for preparatory negotiations are clear cut. Subgroups, such as the Petersberg Dialogue, are emphasized for their high share of arguing, resembling the Greenland Dialogue as its precursor. Needless to say, the few respondents for the preparatory negotiations only allow using them as approximations. In 2010, delegates kept their arguing spirit during negotiations among *all* parties at the summit, found over two thirds of interviewees close to or participating in the negotiations, with a solid number of respondents (*n* = 27). The remaining third felt that neither mode dominated, or even a prevalence of bargaining. This third was a heterogeneous group with good negotiation insight, so only the more detailed verbal analysis can resolve the contradictory evidence. For lack of small group negotiations by exclusively major powers in Cancún, there are no data on this subgroup. Other subgroups, such as the Cartagena Dialogue between several developing and developed countries, negotiated in an arguing mode, as its participants pointed out. In short, the dominance of arguing over bargaining correlated with an agreement in 2010.

The following analysis scrutinizes this numeric interpretation. Preparatory negotiations in 2010 saw more arguing than bargaining among all parties. Only a few, but unanimous, comments were available. While the COP is often hectic and adversarial, the longer time of pre-COP negotiations allows for more arguing.[723] In the reverse order of 2009, parties shifted away from bargaining to more arguing, especially in the numerous informal issue-specific consultations by

Table 3.13 Responses to the question 'Did you see open-ended arguing and problem-solving about content?' with respect to COP-16. (Terms defined as in Table 3.12.)

Response	All parties n (%)[a]	Major powers n (%)	Other subgroups n (%)
Preparatory negotiations in 2010			
Arguing	4 (80%)	0 (0%)	3 (75%)
Bargaining	0 (0%)	0 (0%)	1 (25%)
Both/ambiguous	1 (20%)	0 (0%)	0 (0%)
Total	5	0	4
COP-16			
Arguing	19 (70.4%)	1 (100%)	4 (100%)
Bargaining	5 (18.5%)	0 (0%)	0 (0%)
Both/ambiguous	3 (11.1%)	0 (0%)	0 (0%)
Total	27	1	4

723   UNFCCC Secretariat(2)-04.12.2010.

Mexico,[724] which were much more frequent than in 2009.[725] Their goal was to make the concerns of parties on selected issues fully understood and detect potential problems before Cancún.[726] The consultations proved important for developing better concepts and for re-establishing trust.[727] By the final official preparatory round in Tianjin in October, parties bargained significantly less despite some retaining their bargaining mode throughout. Salient countries in all key coalitions opened up by the beginning of COP-16:[728] within the BASIC group, highly engaged Indian Environment Minister Ramesh contributed to the MRV solution through an open-minded search for compromise,[729] and Brazil also adopted a constructive role. The G-77 was chaired by well-meaning Ambassador Alsaidi, the African Group by similarly open negotiator Mpanu Mpanu, and also the ALBA group became more conciliatory, including vocal negotiator Salerno of Venezuela. Developed countries added to the arguing mode, such as New Zealand, Germany, and the United Kingdom acting as intermediaries towards developing countries.

Arguing during preparatory negotiations became even more prevalent in subgroups like the MEF and the Petersberg Dialogue. While the MEF played a lesser role than in 2009, the salient Indian MRV proposal was originally introduced and discussed at an MEF meeting before it diffused into the larger negotiations.[730] The smaller number of issues and its more frequent meetings allowed for a candid and constructive atmosphere at the MEF.[731] A further step for MRV was the Petersberg Dialogue in Bonn, organized by Mexico and Germany, where arguing prevailed. Conversations were 'offline' as in the preceding Greenland Dialogue, so ministers spoke very openly[732] in a constructive atmosphere.[733] A few parties continued bargaining by simply restating their positions through pre-formulated statements.[734] Overall, arguing among all parties increasingly dominated towards the end of the preparatory negotiations in 2010, especially with regard to issue-specific consultations by the Mexican Presidency and negotiations of the MEF and the Petersberg Dialogue.

Arguing continued at the Cancún summit, even among all parties. There was a greater willingness to explore options, consider each other's proposals, and find common ground.[735] The LCA Chair's text, introduced at COP-16's first day,

724   AWG/SB-Chair(2)-04.12.2010, AWG/SB-Chair(4)-14.06.2011.
725   UNFCCC Secretariat(4)-17.05.2011.
726   AWG/SB-Chair(4)-14.06.2011.
727   EIG(1)-09.08.2011.
728   For the following: participant observation, Mexico(5)-07.07.2011.
729   AWG/SB-Chair(2)-04.12.2010, EU/EU-country(8)-05.05.2011.
730   AWG/SB-Chair(2)-04.12.2010.
731   AWG/SB-Chair(2)-04.12.2010.
732   AWG/SB-Chair(3)-07.12.2010.
733   EIG(1)-09.08.2011.
734   Denmark(1)-02.12.2010.
735   UNFCCC Secretariat(3)-08.12.2010, EU/EU-country(9)-26.05.2011, EU/EU-country(8)-05.05.2011.

illustrated this.[736] It no longer only recited national positions, but aggregated them into an integrative proposal. After the initial rejection of this proactive step by the Chair, parties constructively negotiated on this basis. Further, delegations were ready to break through the established walls between developed and developing countries, finding partners on the other side, and thereby better understanding their respective interests.[737] For example, negotiators creatively endeavoured to define NAMAs, the mitigation goals for developing countries, in such a way that they didn't overly infringe on sovereignty. This creative search was also true for the main emitters US and China, which were cautious to avoid another 'Copenhagen',[738] but of course still debated livelily in mitigation negotiations during 2010.[739] Furthermore, negotiators reported a lot of bargaining in their sessions with parties pushing for their own position without compromise: 'Some parties also don't want a real agreement', using domestic pretexts to not accept any proposal.[740] Moreover, cleavages were sometimes not resolved but only hidden by ambiguous language.[741] To some then, the negotiation style was not so different from Copenhagen.[742] Looking at responses overall though, we have seen a greater willingness to compromise and accept 'nationally sub-optimal outcomes'.[743]

Another element of arguing as integrative bargaining was the openness to integrate and balance issues. The lower pressure on parties by the organizers of not having to reach an all-encompassing agreement allowed them to address only those fields where they felt ready. The dictum 'nothing is agreed until everything is agreed' had stalled progress before.[744] The atmosphere that 'every voice would be heard' then motivated parties to actively participate in open-minded arguing,[745] instead of defending the status quo.[746] This was especially true for negotiations on further mitigation ambition. Instead of another stalemate, countries rather argued on numerous issues of mitigation implementation.[747] Parties carefully balanced the different 'building blocks' and their varying interests to eventually reach a balanced text, which left everyone equally (un-)satisfied.[748] This wide inclusion of negotiation elements indicates integrative bargaining (and hence arguing), versus positional bargaining.[749] The lack of written

736   Mexico(3)-15.06.2011.
737   Observer(3)-16.06.2011.
738   EU/EU-country(6)-16.03.2011.
739   EU/EU-country(3)-03.12.2010.
740   Umbrella Group(4)-04.07.2011.
741   UNFCCC Secretariat(2)-04.12.2010.
742   Mexico(3)-15.06.2011.
743   UNFCCC Secretariat(1)-28.04.2010, Observer(3)-16.06.2011.
744   EU/EU-country(10)-16.08.2011.
745   EU/EU-country(7)-04.05.2011.
746   Danish Presidency (3) 11.08.2011.
747   UNFCCC Secretariat(5)-14.06.2011.
748   Denmark(2)-16.06.2011, Mexico(5)-07.07.2011.
749   BASIC(3)-08.07.2011.

documentation makes it difficult to assess whether this balancing of elements was done more by arguing or bargaining. Some hold it was a 'give-and-take' without discussing underlying interests to maximize joint gains.[750] Yet, the dominance of arguing was widely reported at least for a large part of negotiations.[751]

Arguing dominated also in the smaller concentric circles of negotiators in the second COP week, where a high level of trust allowed a frank exchange.[752] Ministers and expert negotiators jointly resolved the final issues.[753] The outcomes of arguing on the expert level and of the later smaller minister-led concentric circles were periodically collected by the organizers. The latter then considered the issues in arguing sessions before returning their results to expert negotiators. There were two such iterations in Cancún, which participants characterized as arguing. The decision-oriented mind-set of arriving ministers helped further, and stood in contrast to expert negotiators who are often 'more bargainers than anything else',[754] as an experienced Chair described. Eventually, some key compromises were struck, such as on MRV, financing, and technology mechanism. Those that had criticized the Mexican finalizing of the text as intransparent and exclusive did not consider this open-minded arguing but a take-it-or-leave-it strategy.[755] Yet as discussed earlier, the Mexican Presidency was among the most transparent and inclusive processes possible. So, arguing was the slightly dominating negotiation mode regarding all parties in 2010.

No exclusive negotiations among major powers were reported for Cancún, such as the US–BASIC meeting in Copenhagen, and there is no data on any potential smaller bilateral meetings. In contrast, negotiations in other subgroups were much more important at COP-16, like the Cartagena Dialogue. Initiated in March 2010, the forum fostered a dialogue between developed and developing countries, which were more ambitious to move the process forward. It should break up traditional negotiation blocs without dissolving them altogether.[756] Around 30 small and medium powers attended, such as the United Kingdom and Switzerland, or Mexico and the Maldives, but not China and the US (Lynas 2011).[757] The absence of slower-moving countries allowed for a candid and forward looking discussion of ideas. At the same time, this absence inhibited their transfer back into normal negotiations with all other countries, which had not participated in these discussions. Its constructive spirit nevertheless helped

---

750   UNFCCC Secretariat(4)-17.05.2011.
751   Denmark(2)-16.06.2011, G-77(4)-22.07.2011.
752   G-77(3)-19.07.2011.
753   For the following: BASIC(2)-16.06.2011.
754   AWG/SB-Chair(4)-14.06.2011.
755   ALBA(2)-09.12.2011.
756   EU/EU-country(6)-16.03.2011.
757   Members were (March 2010): Australia, Bangladesh, Chile, Costa Rica, Democratic Republic of Congo, Denmark, EU, France, Gambia, Germany, Ghana, Grenada, Indonesia, Kenya, Lesotho, Malawi, Maldives, Marshall Islands, Mexico, Netherlands, New Zealand, Norway, Panama, Peru, Samoa, South Africa, Spain, Sweden, UK, United Arab Emirates.

moving overall negotiations towards arguing.[758] The group continued meeting in Cancún daily, sometimes even with several subgroups, to funnel fresh ideas into overall negotiations: 'Getting the negotiations and a real dialogue going is central, not just by making public statements such as in the open plenary',[759] explained a participant. Countries frankly discussed their underlying interests, such as small island states about their survival, or others about their economic development. It helped to understand 'what certain ideas actually meant'.[760] In sum, the Cartagena Dialogue enabled arguing, which also affected COP-16's general negotiation mode.

Concluding, arguing slightly dominated over bargaining in negotiations among all parties, especially in the informal issue-specific consultations during the year, but also generally at COP-16 (Figure 3.6). The same is true for the subgroups of the Petersberg Dialogue and the MEF during preparatory negotiations, and the Cartagena Dialogue before and during COP-16. This is not to forget that there is never purely one single mode. In sum, arguing correlated with agreement during the Mexican Presidency. Let us now trace whether and how it influenced the outcome.

How negotiation modes influenced the summit outcomes

Beyond mere correlation, we can find an influence of negotiation mode on the summit outcomes. Of the large number of 32 overall responses, three-quarters support such a link (Table 3.14). They cover nearly all negotiation groups, as well as AWG and subsidiary body Chairs, and UNFCCC officials. The few doubting this effect cannot be attributed to one specific group, and are from three developed and one developing country. The clear majority, though, provides solid first evidence for such a connection.

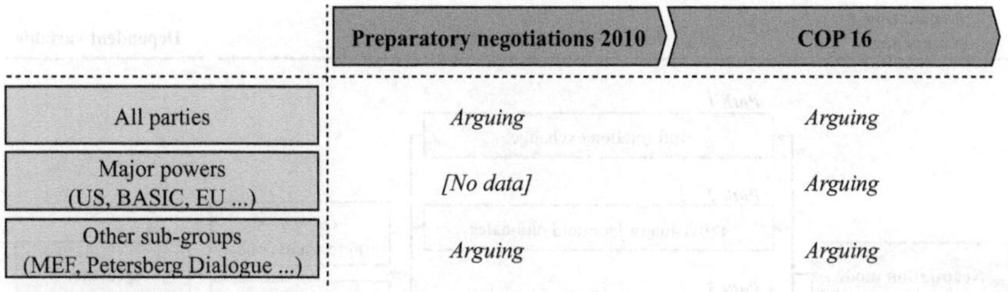

	Preparatory negotiations 2010	COP 16
All parties	*Arguing*	*Arguing*
Major powers (US, BASIC, EU ...)	*[No data]*	*Arguing*
Other sub-groups (MEF, Petersberg Dialogue ...)	*Arguing*	*Arguing*

Figure 3.6 Negotiation modes during the Mexican Presidency

758 EU/EU-country(8)-05.05.2011.
759 EU/EU-country(4)-27.01.2011.
760 EU/EU-country(11)-10.12.2011.

Table 3.14 Responses to the question 'Did the negotiation mode get parties closer to or further away from agreement?'

Response	n (%)
Negotiation mode influenced the outcome	25 (78.1%)
Negotiation mode influenced the outcome somewhat	3 (9.4%)
Negotiation mode did not influence the outcome	4 (12.5%)
Total	32

Negotiation mode seemed to have impacted on agreement through several paths (Figure 3.7):

1   the open exchange of information;
2   the provision of facts and rationales;
3   the comprehensive consideration of issues; and
4   the openness to new solutions and compromise beyond one's mandate.

When parties argue, negotiators are mutually revealing information about the motivations, which underlie their positions (path 1). This leads to a better understanding of positions *and* interests, including the reservation points of parties. It helps to go beyond mere positions and to use the differences in interests to create outcomes where all sides benefit most. This enables agreements that are inside objectively agreeable zones. The enhanced trust from information sharing enhances the willingness to agree with each other. In short, greater information and the resulting trust render agreement likelier. This dynamic of increased understanding and trust during preparatory negotiations became evident at the MEF

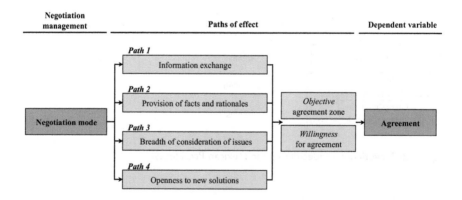

Figure 3.7 Process-tracing between negotiation mode and agreement

and the Greenland Dialogue during the Danish Presidency,[761] and the Petersberg Dialogue and the informal topic-specific consultations during the Mexican Presidency.[762] The stepwise release of information gradually created familiarity between participants that eventually contributed to smooth negotiations. Even though these preparatory dialogues might not yet be conceived of as 'official' negotiations, they provide the information and trust necessary later. Contrary to this, bargaining moves delegates sooner to a text-based discussion, which induces parties to focus on their respective written positions, without looking at the deeper reasoning behind them. It makes it more difficult to find the other side's motivation behind the text and then craft solutions that trade on these differences in interests. Accordingly, countries wanting to slow the process often request such a text-based negotiation, such as Saudi Arabia among others.[763]

This greater understanding of interest, often created in small groups, must then be transferred to the overall negotiations. In 2009, parties did not keep the level of information exchange and trust building between participants of the Greenland Dialogue and the MEF during the COP, and could thus not advance overall negotiations. During 2010, such a dynamic was fostered by the topic-specific consultations from spring onwards and the Petersberg Dialogue in May. They created the necessary atmosphere of trust to enable true dialogue, which reinforced their trust.[764] The pre-COP meeting of around 40 ministers, core negotiators, and chairs in November 2010 had a similar dynamic. Not meant to take any decision,[765] it successfully generated an open arguing atmosphere. In 2010, the 'real'[766] and 'constructive'[767] dialogue became central for the agreement by the end of the year. Delegations provided better information on their own ideas, truly listened to and considered those of others, and engaged in a back and forth on various proposals.

Such an open information exchange is vital for reaching a mutually beneficial agreement: 'People first would have to really say what they want and need', which is often not done.[768] It is based on the notion of mutual respect for each other's interests, and not just a mere search of one's profit even at the cost of the others.[769] 'You try to understand each other', expressed one lead chairperson while 'when bargaining, it is just a clash'.[770] This understanding of interests is crucial to identify solutions acceptable to all,[771] and to increase the overall willingness for an agreement. A frank exchange also allows identifying key

761   Denmark(3)-11.08.2011.
762   EIG(1)-09.08.2011.
763   EIG(1)-09.08.2011.
764   EIG(1)-09.08.2011 for the Petersberg Dialogue.
765   AWG/SB-Chair(2)-04.12.2010.
766   EU/EU-country(4)-27.01.2011.
767   UNFCCC Secretariat(1)-28.04.2010.
768   Umbrella Group(4)-04.07.2011.
769   EU/EU-country(9)-26.05.2011.
770   AWG/SB-Chair(4)-14.06.2011.
771   EU/EU-country(1)-20.01.2010.

political questions that are then taken to ministers to resolve the last but crucial outstanding issues to move the proposal into the objective agreement zone.[772]

This dynamic played out at COP-16, for example in the negotiation about the demand of Kyoto Protocol members that other developed countries and also the big emerging economies should join the Protocol. Negotiators told how it was 'a key to unpack their [developing countries'] concerns to find what is behind their positions' not to join the Kyoto Protocol.[773] In particular this arguing in bilateral meetings moved the discussion forward, facilitated by the Brazilian and UK ministers, the AWG-KP Chair and a UNFCCC official. Talks then entered informal negotiations of the small groups dedicated to these specific issues.[774] Arguing had formed the basis for constructing a middle ground for emission reductions, which satisfied the varying mutual expectations through multiple mitigation mechanisms. These small, non-public fora had generated the necessary initial trust to argue openly.[775] The US–BASIC small group arguing at COP-15 is another case in point. Through arguing, they had integrated all their main interests and reached their 'grand bargain':[776] the US joined because of the shift to a pledge-and-review (instead of a binding top-down) emission reduction system. Developing countries promised their own moderate mitigation pledges and granted restricted emissions' tracking under MRV/ICA, an essential US–EU demand, while maintaining the principle of common but differentiated responsibilities. They also ensured support on finance and technology. Negotiating leaders, and especially the US and China in that small group,[777] had thus set priorities within the 'amorphous and unclear' list of issues of the Bali Roadmap.[778] In sum, a frank exchange of information on underlying interests increased the chances for an agreement between those involved: be it the major powers' small group in Copenhagen, or all parties in Cancún.

Such understanding is also influenced by the method of advocating and considering proposals. Concretely, arguing provides more rationales and factual information behind possible solutions in negotiations than mere bargaining (path 2). The Danish and Mexican Presidencies showed this mechanism. Participants of the Cartagena Dialogue described that its frank and thorough discussion allowed 'sorting out how certain ideas [were] actually meant'.[779] It

---

772 AWG/SB-Chair(2)-04.12.2010.
773 EU/EU-country(8)-05.05.2011.
774 UNFCCC Secretariat(3)-08.12.2010.
775 G-77(3)-19.07.2011.
776 For the following: BASIC(2)-16.06.2011, similar BASIC(3)-08.07.2011: The agreement on implementation measures was exchanged for further mitigation commitments, also: UNFCCC Secretariat(2)-04.12.2010, G-77(3)-19.07.2011, Umbrella Group(2)-02.06.2011: '[G]rand bargain between financial support in exchange for emission mitigation action.'
777 Observer(3)-16.06.2011.
778 UNFCCC Secretariat(5)-14.06.2011.
779 EU/EU-country(11)-10.12.2011, EU/EU-country(3)-03.12.2010: For a similar forum: the 'actual explanation of positions to other parties … was indeed very helpful'; similar: Mexico(3)-15.06.2011.

disclosed how negotiators often do not fully understand each other's suggestions, which inhibits finding a joint solution. Or, the issue-specific consultations by the Mexican Presidency helped to develop better concepts, according to participants of the mitigation meeting for example.[780] Negotiators really discussed issues with much greater openness in extended conversations, enhancing the understanding of the complex challenges and solutions on all sides.[781] At COP-16, for example, the EU used logic and facts extensively. They introduced abundant calculation logics and new information into the AWG-KP discussions, as emission reductions are strongly influenced by their calculation rationale. While China kept pushing to how much mitigation the EU would commit (positional bargaining), the EU continued showing graphs and tables to increase the understanding that the effective size of the pledges depended on the accounting rules, and thus needed to be decided first. According to EU sources, AOSIS and some other countries then began thinking in this direction once the suggested logic had come across.[782] The rationale had assimilated negotiators' language of emission quantifications and increased agreement chances.

The effect of these insights from logic and facts was reduced by several factors. First, negotiators often switched back to bargaining by reciting their well-known positions once they had moved back into official UNFCCC fora. For instance, while the informal exchange in the Greenland Dialogue had enhanced the mutual understanding of ministers and delegation heads, it did not fully translate back to move the process decisively forward before Copenhagen.[783] The atmosphere back at the UNFCCC negotiations in Barcelona in November only one week after the last meeting of the Greenland Dialogue was nearly hostile and characterized by bargaining mode. There were similar accounts even for the Tianjin negotiations just before Cancún, despite the overall increase in arguing during 2010.[784] With only a few expert negotiators present in these Dialogues (next to the ministers), the progress made was not properly transmitted to the expert level.[785] Seemingly not all ministers instructed their negotiators of changes in thinking after the Dialogue, or official mandates simply differed from their informal statements in the Dialogue.[786] Of course, arguing alone cannot overcome lack of political will.[787] So, one problem during both Presidencies was to integrate the productive atmosphere and ideas into the often adversarial, formal process.[788] The transfer seemed easier when discussions focused on a clear question with a concrete output,[789] which is obviously very hard to achieve for the

780   EIG(1)-09.08.2011.
781   UNFCCC Secretariat(5)-14.06.2011.
782   EU/EU-country(10)-16.08.2011.
783   G-77(3)-19.07.2011, Mexico(4)-16.06.2011.
784   EU/EU-country(3)-03.12.2010.
785   EU/EU-country(3)-03.12.2010.
786   Denmark(3)-11.08.2011.
787   G-77(1)-04.12.2010.
788   Denmark(1)-02.12.2010.
789   AWG/SB-Chair(2)-04.12.2010.

myriad salient, complex issues. Moreover, new facts and rationales from arguing often emerged only late in the process. Positions had largely been formed and expressed, and time was very short to craft joint proposals based on the newly acquired understanding. These caveats notwithstanding, the provision of facts and rationales at least adds to the likelihood of an agreement.

The comprehensive consideration of interests underlying the positions of parties increased the willingness to agree across the board, and thereby made consensus likelier (path 3). While this first cost valuable time, such as in Cancún, it later improved efficiency and effectiveness. Facilitators in Cancún also added to this. The AWG-LCA Chair integrated the numerous submitted proposals into one draft instead of successively listing many ideas on the same topic. This integration moved negotiations forward towards an objective agreement zone as parties better understood the congruence between their suggestions. The comprehensive consideration of issues allowed parties to trade concessions, such as leaders did on the more political questions in the US–BASIC group in Copenhagen. The US 'got' the switch to a pledge-and-review system, and developing countries received substantial financing commitments.[790] Such a selection and weighing of issues in a more integrative approach consider divergent interests and make agreement with maximum benefits likelier (Pareto optimal solution).[791]

Of course, exaggerated comprehensiveness can also be used to obstruct the process. Including abundant issues risks their linkage to an otherwise agreeable proposal for another issue. The issue is 'taken hostage'. This proved detrimental in Copenhagen with its originally all-encompassing approach.[792] The opportunity to obstruct further arose from aiming at one deal out of two separate negotiation tracks (the LCA and Kyoto Protocol Working Groups) of the Bali Roadmap. The separation made the trade-off between issues much more difficult, which was in the interest of those who aimed at retarding negotiations.[793] In contrast, when a salient issue like REDD+ was ripe for decision in Cancún only very few countries linked it to other, less accepted issues, such as 'response measures' (which compensate future foregone income from oil resources).[794] In sum, the breadth of consideration of issues influenced the acceptance of a proposal, the possibility to trade on differences, and the opportunity to obstruct.

Finally, negotiation mode influences the openness to new solutions (path 4). First, arguing often entails the readiness to deviate from national negotiation mandates. This determines the breadth of the zone of possible agreement, or simply speaking the room for compromise. 'These are my instructions, and that's

790   BASIC(2)-16.06.2011.
791   BASIC(3)-08.07.2011, also: UNFCCC Secretariat(4)-17.05.2011, and Umbrella Group(1)-20.04.2011, yet stressing that also overall bargaining led to a Copenhagen Accord.
792   UNFCCC Secretariat(1)-28.04.2010.
793   EIG(1)-09.08.2011.
794   G-77(4)-22.07.2011.

it' is commonly heard prohibiting any substantive negotiations, which would refer to underlying interests, actual costs and benefits. In consequence, the recitation of positions and mandates in Copenhagen undermined the exchange of information for a constructive solution finding, and cost scarce time at COP-15. Expert negotiators waited for the ministers and then leaders to arrive to take decisions. This positional bargaining had the effect that 'no single point' was changed before the high-level segment.[795] In contrast to that, the openness to new solutions by deviating from a mandate and lowering reservation points widened the overlap between parties and thus the objective zone of potential agreement at COP-16.[796]

Second, the risk perception of negotiators also influences their openness, and their subjective ability to creatively search for solutions. In a bargaining mode, they conceive of the situation as zero-sum. In this case, there is a fixed amount of benefits and costs that is distributed among parties. The risk to lose through a compromise is high because whichever gain is made on one side is lost on the other side.[797] This raises tensions and decreases the creativity of negotiators to develop new solutions. It all limits the chances of a widely acceptable proposal. Disturbingly, climate and many other multilateral negotiations are not even zero-sum situations, but are treated as such.[798] Contrary to this, the positive dynamics of a win-win notion by an arguing mode foster the finding of common ground as parties see a lower risk in compromising. In sum, the openness for new solutions widens the zone of agreement. The lower risk perception makes it easier for parties to creatively craft compromises.

Conclusion

These findings support, refine and complement current strands of constructivism and negotiation theory, which acknowledge an influence of discourse and negotiation modes on the emergence of cooperation. The evidence has shown that negotiators frequently varied between the negotiation modes of arguing (or, problem-solving / integrative bargaining) and bargaining (or, positional bargaining) during the Danish and Mexican Presidencies. This was naturally their own choice, but was also affected by the negotiation management of the organizers and by the exogenous factors of negotiation phase and issue. During both Presidencies, arguing dominated at least for some time in various negotiation groups during preparatory negotiations. Yet, as COP-15 did not reach agreement, there is no overall correlation between arguing during preparation time and

---

795 EU/EU-country(9)-26.05.2011.
796 Respondents occasionally referred to this as 'goodwill' and 'constructive attitude', and not 'negotiation mode' (Mexico(3)-15.06.2011).
797 EU/EU-country(7)-04.05.2011.
798 The notion of limited carbon space indicates a zero-sum assumption. Yet, the potential *benefits* of reduced emissions (such as disaster risk reduction and 'green growth') make it a global win–win situation.

eventual outcome. This was different for the COPs where the dominance of one or the other mode correlated with reaching an agreement. At COP-15, arguing among the major powers led to an agreement among *them*, but not all parties. Generally, bargaining had prevailed in Copenhagen when considering *all* parties and no official agreement was reached. At COP-16, arguing dominated among all parties overall (with occasional exceptions, of course), and in subgroups like the Cartagena Dialogue, so arguing correlated with reaching an agreement. Process-tracing finally revealed strong evidence that negotiation modes influenced the outcome through (1) the open exchange of information, (2) the provision of rationales and facts, (3) the comprehensive consideration of issues, and (4) the openness to new solutions. This assessment of the negotiation mode of parties concludes the analysis of the four elements of negotiation management.

Preliminary findings

We have seen a strikingly different approach along all four elements of the management of climate negotiations between the Danish and Mexican organizers and their UNFCCC Secretariat counterparts in 2009 and 2010. To reiterate, negotiations in 2010 were much more transparent and inclusive than in the previous year. Organizers of the Mexican Presidency and UNFCCC Secretariat had a better organizational and cultural–personal fit for the situation. They possessed higher process and content expertise, and were also better aligned than in 2009. Furthermore, Conference President Espinosa reached a higher acceptance among parties in Cancún than Rasmussen in Copenhagen allowing her a better facilitation. Last but not least, organizers contributed to a negotiation atmosphere during 2010 that was more conducive to arguing, and thus better supported the converging of positions. Taken together, this kind of negotiation management facilitated an acceptable compromise and increased the willingness of delegates to agree on a subjective level, sometimes even beyond rational interests. Meticulous process tracing documented the myriad paths of *how* negotiation management affected the probability of an agreement. So, negotiation management may partially explain the variance in summit outcomes. To maximize the internal validity of this preliminary finding, let us now evaluate how alternative factors explain the outcomes of the Danish and Mexican Presidencies, and thereby complete the analysis of the comprehensive negotiation framework.

References

Espinosa, Patricia. (2011) *From Cancun to Durban: Implications for Climate and Multilateral Diplomacy*. Speech transcript. London: Chatham House.

Lynas, Mark. (2011) Thirty 'Cartagena Dialogue' Countries Work to Bridge Kyoto Gap. *Mark Lynas* 10 March: www.marklynas.org/2011/03/thirty-cartagena-dialogue-countries-work-to-bridge-kyoto-gap.

Politiken. (2009) Magtkampe Fælder Hedegaards Højre Hånd [Power Struggles Cause the Loss of Hedegaard's Right Hand]. *Politiken* 9 October: http://politiken.dk/klima/ECE807190/magtkampe-faelder-hedegaards-hoejre-haand.

Chapter 4

Explanations of climate outcomes beyond negotiation management

Without doubt, several additional aspects contributed to the results of these climate negotiations. I first turn to interest and power, which neoliberalism and neorealism regard as principal factors of international cooperation. They are the most prominent approaches, which put the 'international structure' at the heart of their argument. Interest and power complement the analysis of this book, which started by looking at process and people first. Moreover, the collapse of the Copenhagen summit and the existence of the 'blueprint' of the Copenhagen Accord may have further increased chances of agreement in Cancún.[1] What role these factors played in 2009 and 2010, and to what extent they undermined the importance of negotiation management, are the intriguing questions of this chapter.

Similar political substance of proposed outcomes

Let us begin with the overall puzzle of the explanations based on interest and power. The political substance of the proposals for agreement in Copenhagen and Cancún was very similar.[2] Further, temporal proximity between Copenhagen and Cancún suggests that interests and power distribution also remained largely constant. Yet parties rejected the Copenhagen proposal and accepted the compromise only one year later in Cancún. To be sure, organizers in 2009 had first aimed at a comprehensive agreement with far-reaching economic commitments.[3] However, ambitions had been extremely downscaled towards COP-15 so that the agreement became acceptable to most. That did not change by Cancún.

---

1 What I exclude early on is regime theory's variable of the structure of the problem of climate change (cf. Figure 1.1). This factor seems hardly able to explain the variance in negotiation outcomes of 2009 and 2010. If anything, the structure of the challenge of climate change with its high complexity of issues and affected parties, and its tremendous negative ramifications has worsened during that time, making an agreement in Cancún even unlikelier, according to regime theory (cf. Chapter 1).

2 Denmark(7)-16.02.2012, Mexico(5)-07.07.2011, BASIC(1)-04.12.2010, BASIC(2)-16.06.2011, G-77(2)-13.06.2011, G-77(5)-08.12.2011.

3 EU/EU-country(7)-04.05.2011.

Organizers of COP-16 also postponed harder political questions (e.g. precise emission targets, legal form) and solved more technical issues instead (e.g. the governance of the Green Climate Fund).[4] Besides, Cancún differed in its higher level of detail and operationalization, such as on finance.[5] Yet overall, if the political substance of the final proposals was so similar between both years *constant* interest and power can hardly explain why parties first rejected it in 2009 and then accepted nearly identical terms in 2010. While big powers and many other countries continued backing the proposal in Cancún (as predicted), a series of parties behaved contrary to these neoliberal and neorealist expectations: after their rejection in 2009, they supported agreement in 2010. Let us therefore examine whether the pay-offs from the suggested final agreements, interests and power really remained constant, before looking at further explanations.

I start with a comparison of the suggested agreements of Copenhagen and Cancún regarding their general principle and key issues of mitigation, monitoring, reporting and verification, finance, and technology transfer, to name just a few (cf. chronologies in Chapter 2 and Appendix I). The cross-cutting principle of 'common but differentiated responsibilities' of the Framework Convention had been a cornerstone of negotiations: all climate actions should be fair, from emission reductions to cost distribution. Many countries cautiously observed that their efforts are 'fair' regarding their historic emissions so far, but also relative to other countries' obligations,[6] no matter whether they gain greater environmental benefits in absolute terms when they maximize their own mitigation. This general principal was keenly upheld in both years, especially by developing countries.

Regarding concrete action, the mitigation of greenhouse gas emissions was the most salient issue for effectively tackling climate change. Countries' relative gain concerns drove the fierce struggle over the distribution of mitigation obligations, especially by developed countries from the Umbrella Group with the US on one side and large developing countries (such as the BASIC group) with China on the other. Similarly, some of the Kyoto Protocol members (mainly from the Umbrella Group, like Japan or Australia), worried that non-member states, like the US or fast-growing China, would gain significant economic advantages if they had no comparable mitigation obligations.[7] New economic realities clashed with outdated conditions of the 15-year-old Kyoto Protocol, while 'common but differentiated responsibilities' was still held highly.[8] By Copenhagen, the Protocol only covered one quarter of emissions any more (US Energy Information Administration 2012). Furthermore, reductions in their advanced

4   UNFCCC Secretariat(1)-28.04.2010.
5   Denmark(2)-16.06.2011, Denmark(5)-12.08.2011. After only three pages in the Copenhagen Accord, the Cancún Agreements provided much more detail in 24 pages on Long-Term Cooperative Action, two pages on the Kyoto Protocol, and one page on LULUCF.
6   BASIC(4)-16.03.2012.
7   Umbrella Group(4)-04.07.2011, Umbrella Group(5)-27.07.2011.
8   BASIC(4)-16.03.2012.

economies were incurring very high marginal abatement costs, which led countries like Japan to reject any one-sided continuation of the Protocol.[9] In the same vain its Umbrella Group allies asked for mitigation in all major economies, independent of their current Protocol membership. Among large developed economies, only the EU was ready to commit for a second period.

The BASIC group and other developing countries in turn insisted on a Protocol continuation for developed countries, while striving to avoid constraints on their own economies. They highlighted the 'carbon space' concept (Winkler *et al.* 2009): accordingly, the goal of a maximum temperature rise of 2°C limits the amount of emissions that the atmosphere can absorb. Higher allowances for one would reduce those of others.[10] Historically, the developed world had already used much more than their 'fair share' of this space. So, emerging developing countries would only accept moderate mitigation responsibilities with some form of monitoring, with economic growth and poverty alleviation as dominating their policy choices.

Overall then, positions of most developed and developing countries on mitigation embodied a short-term economic perception of their interests. The majority objected to committing to reduction goals recommended by science, such as by the IPCC, and the suggested agreement moved away from legally binding, top-down obligations and towards a pledge-and-review system, both in Copenhagen and Cancún.

A similar continuity of debate and final proposal was true for the external control of emissions. Especially large developed economies, such as the US, found it crucial that rapidly developing nations, such as China, would subject their emission reductions to multilateral monitoring, reporting and verification (MRV).[11] This way they would ensure that they at least knew the mitigation burden other economies were actually shouldering.[12] The underlying interest was to avoid an exaggerated disadvantage and relative loss in economic power. In the end, the BASIC countries conceded to a compromise. For the first time ever, they would accept proposals with outside monitoring of their emission developments, yet at a lighter level of scrutiny at least for internationally unsupported mitigation with international consultations and analysis (ICA). This result was mirrored in both the Copenhagen and Cancún proposals, besides further implementation details in 2010.

Financing and technology transfer from developed countries was of crucial interest for the developing world. They were lacking the financial resources and technical expertise for their own mitigation contribution and the direly needed adaptation.[13] The minimum level of support in these areas was therefore a 'red

9   Umbrella Group(4)-04.07.2011.
10   Denmark(1)-02.12.2010.
11   Umbrella Group(1)-20.04.2011.
12   AWG/SB-Chair(2)-04.12.2010.
13   G-77(2)-13.06.2011.

line' for the G-77, with BASIC countries strongly advocating on their behalf.[14] AOSIS negotiators, for instance, would only accept regular emission reporting if financial and technical support for urgently needed adaptation would be granted.[15] This illustrates the contrasting interests to those of most developed countries. Adaptation is usually not a vital issue but primarily a cost issue for developed countries. They hence perceive less pressure, in spite of the economic losses from delayed action.[16] As a result, the 'rich world' in Copenhagen offered fast-start financing of US$30 billion to developed countries between 2010 and 2012, and long-term pledges that would grow to US$100 billion by 2020. This proposal of the Accord was turned into an official UNFCCC obligation by the adoption of the Cancún Agreements, without any significant changes in substance. The important novelty in 2010 was the development of implementation mechanisms, such as the Green Climate Fund and structures to facilitate the technology transfer. Once more, the proposals essentially remained unchanged.

It is conceivable though that proposed agreements in Cancún varied from Copenhagen through non-climate related side agreements between some parties, which could make a substantial difference for the involved countries. Stakeholders with a high interest in reaching an agreement in 2010, such as Mexico, may have created incentives for those that had still objected in Copenhagen, such as Venezuela and Nicaragua among others. They would have sufficiently increased the pay-offs of these rejecting countries so that the latter would at least abstain in Cancún. As the official proposals for agreement were nearly identical in their core substance, side-agreements could have made the difference.

While the argument is generally conceivable, it is tremendously difficult to unearth empirical evidence. Side-deals are struck outside the official fora and closed to public scrutiny. To keep confidentiality documentary evidence does usually not exist (and even if it does, close to impossible to access, especially for recent negotiations). Also interviewees of those potentially involved in the side-deal are inclined to retain its secrecy. Excluded participants again are less likely to have obtained this information. These methodological dilemmas notwithstanding, two avenues allowed at least approximating an answer.

The first approach was interviews with potential participants of side-deals and non-involved negotiators with intimate knowledge of the negotiations. These interviews found only very scant indications for side deals. According to one rumour Mexico promised Venezuela investments in cement plants, which was credibly rejected by one Mexican interviewee close to Conference President Espinosa, as was any notion of a side-deal in general.[17] Another suspicion is about

14   UNFCCC Secretariat(6)-16.06.2011.
15   Mexico(5)-07.07.2011.
16   Umbrella Group(4)-04.07.2011.
17   Mexican Presidency anonymous. For this reference and several others below (indicated here by labelling those references 'anonymous'), beyond the anonymity provided for the vast majority of interviews, some statements were politically of greater sensitivity so that date and location were also removed in these special cases, indicated here by labelling those references.

regional security arrangements struck with ALBA members. Yet even those rare rumours are not widely supported. When explicitly asked, one ALBA negotiator hinted at non-climate considerations, such as bilateral relations, regional issues, and behaviour regarding other conventions.[18] However, the respondent did not describe a side-deal in Cancún but rather the breadth of interests that are generally considered for finding the country's position. They influence the country's position but are not a tacit outside agreement. Next, a G-77 negotiator hinted at the use of pressure on governments through bilateral relations and personal relationships. Yet again, the respondent did not claim this specifically for COP-15 or 16, and pressure on non-climate issues is not automatically equivalent to a side-deal.[19] Numerous other senior organizers and lead negotiators – potential participants of side-deals or negotiation insiders – unanimously said they had not heard of side-deals or even rejected any such notion.[20]

Apart from these interviews, we can ask whether a side-deal is theoretically likely under the given circumstances of COP-16. Latin America is politically very heterogeneous with differing geopolitical interests, including even within the ALBA coalition. The latter contains oil-rich countries such as Venezuela on one side and Bolivia on the other, which has considerably less energy resources. This heterogeneity makes a coherent approach for an 'ALBA side-deal' fairly inconceivable. Furthermore, individual economic aid for poorer countries, such as Cuba or Nicaragua, could theoretically be imagined at COP-16. Yet, the nature of such complex multiparty and multi-issue negotiations, such as on climate change, renders such side-agreements very difficult. After all, it is nearly inconceivable to predict the precise terms of the eventual overall agreement of the summit. It depends on numerous factors outside the control of only a few countries. Yet, without knowing the shape of final proposal, how can one determine the necessary pay-off for the bilateral side-deal, and for which exact countries of the 194 delegations it would be needed?[21] Regarding OPEC members, it is true that Espinosa conceded to take the further exploration of 'carbon capture and storage' and the compensation from advanced action on climate change on to the negotiation agenda. Yet, this was a move *inside* the climate negotiations. Apart from that, this 'concession' was not much different from what had earlier been discussed in Copenhagen. Finally, most interviewees underlined the exceptional relation of the key 2010 organizers to countries that had switched their position. Moreover, with transparency and inclusion of the process during 2010 these countries had received what they had demanded in Copenhagen, as elaborated in the negotiation management chapters.

18   ALBA(1)-17.06.2011.
19   G-77(2)-13.06.2011.
20   G-77(2)-13.06.2011, Umbrella Group(5)-27.07.2011, BASIC(3)-08.07.2011, EU/EU-country(10)-16.08.2011, UNFCCC Secretariat(2)-04.12.2010, UNFCCC Secretariat(7)-03.08.2011, Mexico(5)-07.07.2011, Denmark(3)-11.08.2011, AWG/SB-Chair(4)-14.06.2011.
21   G-77(3)-19.07.2011.

In sum, it is methodologically close to impossible to prove that an event has *not* occurred (i.e. that no side-deal was struck). Nevertheless, neither empirical evidence nor logical argument support the notion of a side-deal in Cancún, which would have changed the pay-offs of those countries that no longer objected to an agreement. So unless shown otherwise, we can uphold the assumption that the principal substance of the proposals remained largely constant, and no side-deals changed the pay-off structure of those that objected in 2009. To conclude, the pay-offs from the proposed final agreements remained largely unaltered in their political substance between the Presidencies. Had interests and power distribution then changed to explain the rejection of the proposal in 2009 and its adoption in 2010?

Constant or 'not-so-constant' interests?

Large-scale environmental, economic, societal, and security ramifications from climate change are fundamentally affecting the interests of all countries.[22] This holds for big powers such as the US, China, and the EU, or smaller nations such as small island states and the Latin American ALBA coalition. These interests contribute to determining the positions of delegations on a global climate regime. Their specific interests differ of course, even within coalitions. Within the G-77, for instance, small island states are fighting for survival, fast developing countries like China or India care about economic growth, and OPEC countries worry about oil sales as their main revenue source.[23] In addition, abundant domestic political considerations by individual groups come into play and make it far from only a national environmental and economic issue: democratic governments want to be re-elected and autocratic regimes aim at safeguarding power, for example. Specific interests are so plentiful that negotiators 'sometimes [did] not even know their counterparts' domestic...contingencies'.[24] The reaction of an OPEC country delegate illustrated the high sensitivity of these constraints: 'I don't talk about this question. It is too political. We get some "red lines" from home, of course.'[25] Taken together, this mesh of interests makes their analysis (and the search for compromise) not easy.

I will examine the continuity of interests of several key countries and negotiation groups, starting with China as the world's largest emitter, with a 26 per cent

---

22   Interests of countries strongly influence negotiations and form the political foundation of an agreement. When interests are largely aligned, or fully opposed, interest-based theories can explain success or failure, and organizers make little difference. Yet, when they only narrowly overlap, process management may widen this small agreement zone, such as by creating new options and by helping parties redefine their preferences (cf. Chapter 1).

23   AWG/SB-Chair(2)-04.12.2010.

24   EU/EU-country(5)-17.02.2011.

25   G-77 anonymous.

share[26] in 2010 (Oliver *et al.* 2012; US Energy Information Administration 2012). China is preoccupied with preserving its steep economic growth. Furthermore, the Communist Party has a special interest to maintain the one-party system so that domestic stability becomes a central concern (Conrad 2012). The Communist Party cautiously monitors the country's rapid economic and social changes, and prioritizes its short-term power preservation over the mid-term consequences of climate change.[27] This preference lets the country shy away from far-reaching international commitments to limit its massive emissions. At the same time, China has begun to recognize the business potential of low-carbon technology for 'greening' its economy and for exporting high-tech products. China now aims for the lead in renewable energy in its 10-year plan until 2020, for instance.[28] This thinking starts to spread on all levels of government, and across business and the public, especially after the media attention for COP-15.[29]

In Copenhagen, an overly tight negotiation mandate resulted from the prevailing internal debates. The delegation thus lacked sufficient manoeuvring room for compromising.[30] The dilemma further materialized in serious internal delegation disagreements with senior delegates publicly seen shouting at each other. In the end, Chinese Prime Minster Wen could not be properly briefed upon his arrival, according to insiders.[31] High-level COP-15 organizers and experienced negotiators affirmed that the Chinese administration as a whole had not been fully willing for a far-reaching, ambitious agreement.[32] This did obviously not exclude the possibility of striking a less ambitious compromise, as in the US–BASIC meeting. In addition, China had become more aware of its position relative to other countries.[33] Internal disagreement and new self-consciousness resulted in a demonstration of strength in Copenhagen that alienated numerous other delegations, and for which China later received much international blame.[34] Either way, Chinese interests and positions did not change substantially between both years: it opposed an ambitious comprehensive deal but supported the moderate final proposals at the COP-15 and 16 final plenaries.

A similar internal tension applied to most countries. Regarding the remaining BASIC countries, their emphasis on an agreement with common but differentiated responsibilities reflected their moderate ambition. They were mainly

26   For lack of up-to-date 2010 UNFCCC data for developing countries, all following emission data are as share of global CO_2 emissions from energy consumption. The same database enables comparison between Annex I and non-Annex I countries.
27   BASIC anonymous (A), AWG/SB-Chair(2)-04.12.2010.
28   G-77(1)-04.12.2010.
29   BASIC anonymous-(A), EU/EU-country(8)-05.05.2011: it is similar for all BASIC-countries.
30   EU/EU-country(8)-05.05.2011.
31   Denmark(6)-09.02.2012.
32   UNFCCC Secretariat(4)-17.05.2011, Denmark(6)-09.02.2012, EU/EU-country(10)-16.08.2011.
33   Observer(3)-16.06.2011.
34   Observer(2)-08.12.2010, Denmark(1)-02.12.2010.

concerned to maintain their economic development, as they also faced less pressure for their emissions than their BASIC partner China, with an 8 per cent share in 2010 (compared with India at 5%; Oliver *et al.* 2012; US Energy Information Administration 2012). Examining them individually, internal clashes of interests were critical in India. Extreme poverty levels leave little option but economic (and thereby emissions growth), yet possibly disastrous climate effects for highly vulnerable India could undermine development gains.[35] So far, scarce financial resources limit the decoupling of economic from emission growth. On a political level, the adverse effects of climate change are slowly entering the public discourse as in the 2009 parliamentary elections, but they have not yet created pressure on parties.[36] On the contrary, Indian Environment Minister Jairam Ramesh faced criticism at home for its open-minded facilitation on MRV/ICA.[37] The economically much smaller South Africa is positioned between the developing and developed world, yet also partially speaks for Africa as one of its most powerful countries.[38] It also struggles to reconcile much-needed economic development (and its growing emissions) with the fight against climate change, as the country is highly vulnerable to its effects.[39] This endangers improvements from economic development. Brazil mirrors this schism between growth and emission reduction. With the world's largest rainforests, Brazil claims to protect and use this resource at the same time, without caring too much about other countries' obligations.[40] So, has this conflict of the remaining BASIC countries between economic development and poverty alleviation on one side, and high vulnerability to climate change on the other changed between Copenhagen and Cancún? The clear answer is 'no'. These political-economic interests were so deep-rooted that they remained unaltered. Their delegations rejected ambitious agreements in 2009 and 2010, but they all supported the moderate final proposals in Copenhagen and Cancún.

Most developed countries also traded off short-term economic growth (being of course much more affluent already), domestic politics, and climate change. Their emissions make a few of them central for any agreement, especially the United States as the world's second largest emitter, with 17 per cent in 2010 (Oliver *et al.* 2012; US Energy Information Administration 2012). Economic competitiveness has been a vital concern for the US and its Umbrella Group partners. The US, for instance, could hardly 'sell' any deal domestically that would not have comparable obligations for other major economies,[41] as this would disadvantage parts of US industry in the short term. The relocation of

35   BASIC anonymous-(B).
36   BASIC anonymous-(B).
37   EU/EU-country(8)-05.05.2011.
38   BASIC anonymous-(C).
39   BASIC anonymous-(C).
40   BASIC anonymous-(D).
41   Umbrella Group(1)-20.04.2011.

business to China, for instance, was one much-feared consequence.[42] The US worry over the BASIC countries was fuelled by the release of lower than expected Chinese and Indian energy intensity goals, and faster growing energy consumption than forecasted.[43] The US delegation wanted 'parity in the nature of the commitment',[44] reflecting its concerns about relative gains in power of rival countries.[45] There are no indications that this economic concern diminished after Copenhagen.

The US also had a tremendous domestic political constraint on emission cuts, which did not even get close to the European ambitions.[46] Already the moderate goal of 17 per cent mitigation below 2005 levels by 2020 had been 'a very tortured sentence' in the US climate bill.[47] The polarized discourse on climate change in the US made it very hard for the Obama administration to advance its originally more ambitious climate plans. Political tradition aggravated this situation: engrained scepticism of the US (and several other major powers) towards outside influence let them insist that they would domestically determine their ways of reaching mitigation goals: 'The world would not tell nation states what to do.'[48] This rationale also drove its fight for a loose bottom-up agreement.[49] So, the US President would have had only very modest chances of getting any deal from Copenhagen through Congress. Constraints even tightened during 2010 after the defeat of Obama's climate bill in Congress in the spring and the Republican victory in Congressional mid-term elections in the autumn. The US delegation was unable to commit to any further mitigation targets,[50] let alone a legally binding agreement:[51] 'The US can't deliver Congress.'[52] The US was strongly backed by its Umbrella Group allies, two of which had the highest stakes in continuing oil sales. In 2010, Russia and Canada were the world's first and third largest oil exporters to the OECD with 19 per cent and 7 per cent of the market respectively[53] (International Energy Agency 2012). Overall then, the US was constrained by a domestic political blockade and concerns about economic relative gains (as were its Umbrella Group allies) throughout 2009 and 2010. The position against an ambitious agreement, and in favour of a moderate agreement, was thus constant between Copenhagen and Cancún.

Very few countries underlined their willingness for emission reductions, even irrespective of other nations, including the European Union and the

42   Umbrella Group(2)-02.06.2011.
43   Umbrella Group(2)-02.06.2011.
44   UNFCCC Secretariat(4)-17.05.2011.
45   Umbrella Group(3)-14.06.2011.
46   EU/EU-country(4)-27.01.2011.
47   Umbrella Group(2)-02.06.2011.
48   Umbrella Group(1)-20.04.2011.
49   Denmark(3)-11.08.2011.
50   EU/EU-country(4)-27.01.2011, similar: AWG/SB-Chair(2)-04.12.2010.
51   Umbrella Group(5)-27.07.2011.
52   EU/EU-country(8)-05.05.2011.
53   Share of OECD imports of crude oil, natural gas liquids, and refinery feedstocks.

Environmental Integrity Group.[54] After years of reductions, the EU was now the third largest emitter with a 13 per cent share in 2010 (Oliver *et al.* 2012; US Energy Information Administration 2012). As the head negotiator of a major European economy put it: 'We did not look for equal pain...The 30% stood.'[55] Yet, even in this case, national businesses increasingly constrained the country's delegation by pointing at rising competition from the developing world. They lobbied treasuries and economic ministries in their countries:[56] 'The enemy [of the environment minister] was back home.'[57] Within the EU, for instance, Poland, with its high dependency on coal, had strong economic stakes against quick mitigation commitments, rendering internal EU coordination frequently very difficult. Nevertheless, a solid majority of European countries still favoured ambitious mitigation targets, such as Germany with Europe's largest economy.[58] As many voters have become environmentally ever more conscious, governments could domestically benefit from negotiation progress.[59] This disregard for 'relative' gains was in marked contrast to the Umbrella Group, which insisted on equal obligations for fast-developing economies. In sum, EU and EIG supported an ambitious agreement in 2009 and 2010.

Similarly to the EU, extremely vulnerable developing countries, such the AOSIS group and various African countries were driven less by relative and more by absolute concerns. Their goal is to ensure their physical survival as island states or countries exposed to extreme droughts and deserts: 'You have to understand their perspective: people are currently dying from this',[60] emphasized a G-77 negotiator. This is in contrast to environmentally vulnerable, but affluent developed countries, which can invest in adaptation, such as the dyke-building of the low-lying Netherlands. Another G-77 delegate accused developed countries of insufficient mitigation, stressing that current ambitions do not 'make me safe as an African. I would then rather have less [adaptation] money but more safety.'[61] Yet, there was also an internal G-77-countries schism, which became very evident during the Danish and Mexican Presidencies.[62] The interests of these very vulnerable developing countries differed from the rapidly emerging BASIC economies: 'Inside G-77, the attitude towards mitigation heavily depends on the state of economic development...maybe "mother nature"

54 EIG(1)-09.08.2011.
55 EU/EU-country anonymous.
56 Denmark(4)-12.08.2011.
57 EU/EU-country(5)-17.02.2011.
58 EU/EU-country anonymous.
59 EU/EU-country(6)-16.03.2011.
60 G-77(2)-13.06.2011.
61 G-77(4)-22.07.2011.
62 They showed greatest unity in their call for maximum financing of climate action by developed countries. By Cancún, it had become clear that there would not be more support than the US$ 100 billion by 2020, already proposed in Copenhagen. This understanding contributed to the agreement by the G-77 in 2010 (EU/EU-country(8)-05.05.2011).

will sober up'.[63] So, the most vulnerable countries continued advocating for more ambitious goals in 2009 and 2010, yet their mere moral leverage proved insufficient to convince other delegations.

Similar to AOSIS, the vocal ALBA coalition demanded far-reaching action at both summits and accused that current proposals would 'burn the planet'.[64] The group, however, had a mix of partially contradictory interests. Some of its members were environmentally and economically highly vulnerable with an interest in bold climate action. This rational interest for entire countries was complemented and partially contradicted by ideological concerns to please particular domestic constituencies.[65] Some ALBA delegations and politicians would benefit at home from a resistance to those that they generally opposed in world politics. One ALBA delegate stated that his country did not have any individual interest, but acted as part of a struggle between the developed and the developing world.[66] This ideological ALBA statement (neatly dividing the world irrespective of the myriad differences in interests inside these two camps) concurs with numerous interviewees who suspected that some delegations used the negotiations as a forum against global capitalism.[67] This may explain part of the ALBA resistance to the US at COP-15:[68] 'ALBA leaders like Chávez and Morales did not want Obama to get a success out of here'[69] was the reading of many participants.[70] As the White House had largely influenced the 'Danish text' creation, the 'defeat' of the Danish Presidency would also hit the US as its close ally.[71] Cancún was different due to process changes: state leaders had intentionally not been invited. Due to the reduced media attention in this lower-profile summit, delegations had less to gain from using political ideology and 'defeating Mexico'. This improved the atmosphere for compromise. Finally, ALBA countries had better realized their own high vulnerability from climate change by Cancún, so that 'pragmatism had taken over ideology',[72] reckoned a UN official. Taken together, less ideology supported the switch of the ALBA group (but for Bolivia) from rejection to support of a moderate agreement in 2010.

63   G-77(1)-04.12.2010, similar: Denmark(5)-12.08.2011, UNFCCC Secretariat(6)-16.06.2011.
64   ALBA(1)-17.06.2011.
65   UNFCCC Secretariat(5)-14.06.2011.
66   ALBA(2)-09.12.2011.
67   UNFCCC Secretariat(5)-14.06.2011, Denmark(3)-11.08.2011.
68   UNFCCC Secretariat(4)-17.05.2011.
69   Umbrella Group(2)-02.06.2011, similar: EU/EU-country(11)-10.12.2011, UNFCCC Secretariat(4)-17.05.2011.
70   G-77-anonymous. One reported incident may further illustrate this dynamic. Accordingly, Britain's Energy and Climate Minister Ed Miliband had tried to pressure Venezuelan delegation head Claudia Salerno at COP-15's final plenary through contacting her President Chávez. Salerno arguably got back to Miliband and promised him to become even harsher now, stating that she would thereby receive a promotion upon her return.
71   Denmark(3)-11.08.2011, similar Denmark(5)-12.08.2011.
72   UNFCCC Secretariat(7)-03.08.2011.

The most powerful of ALBA countries though had substantial interests in only slow negotiation progress, despite its rhetoric: Venezuela is a major oil producer and ranked second among OPEC exporters, only surpassed by Saudi Arabia (International Energy Agency 2012), selling 69 million metric tons of oil and gas[73] to OECD countries in 2010. Similarly, OPEC's largest exporter Saudi Arabia has frequently blocked climate negotiation progress. Ambitious mitigation through lower energy consumption would endanger the main income sources of many OPEC countries. To hedge against these economic risks, they pushed for carbon capture and storage, and for financial compensation.[74] Recently, occasional voices have hinted at opportunities from low-carbon growth even within OPEC,[75] yet overall, its members were still largely opposed to the other G-77 alliances, such as AOSIS, African Group and ALBA. OPEC countries worked against too ambitious agreements in 2009 and 2010, yet they did accept the moderate proposal in Cancún. So also in this case, underlying economic interests remained unchanged.

Beyond individual countries, has an emerging change in discourse transformed preferences on key negotiation issues between the Danish and Mexican Presidency, which were not reflected in these fundamental national interests yet? Countries have recently begun to see mitigation less as a short-term economic risk but a long-term opportunity for a low-carbon economy. Moreover, their concerns about losses from climate change kept rising.[76] One indication of a change in thinking is that during 2010, 80 countries followed the Copenhagen Accord's call for submitting national plans to the UNFCCC Secretariat, including China, India and Brazil.[77] It expressed the openness of numerous countries for action and added to an agreement-friendly atmosphere. Yet, the conviction behind the submissions did hardly emerge during the few weeks after Copenhagen, but had most likely developed over a longer time period. Hence, they did not mark a fundamental change to the pre-COP-15 interests and positions of most countries. The understanding among those that submitted (and even less among those that did not) was only slowly emerging that climate change was not a zero-sum game of emission reductions. Yet, the win-win notion was still not broadly supported, that all could benefit from avoiding the worst consequences, and from creating 'green growth'.[78] A disillusioned senior facilitator described even after Cancún: 'Negotiations are not on climate change . . . No one is really interested in it. It is only economic and power battles.'[79] The changing discourses had not altered preferences yet.

---

73 Crude oil, natural gas liquids, and refinery feedstocks.
74 G-77(5)-08.12.2011.
75 UNFCCC Secretariat(5)-14.06.2011.
76 EU/EU-country(7)-04.05.2011.
77 Umbrella Group(1)-20.04.2011.
78 UNFCCC Secretariat(5)-14.06.2011.
79 AWG/SB-Chair(4)-14.06.2011.

There was only one novel area of interests relevant to *all* parties, which changed their positions on reaching agreement: the diplomatic and personal interest to save the negotiation process. It was of stellar importance after no outcome had been reached in Copenhagen, which was perceived as a 'grand failure' by the public.[80] Most delegations wanted to avoid the process 'dying' in case of a second failure and so Cancún had to deliver: 'No one wanted another disaster.'[81] Many countries feared that negotiations would otherwise move entirely to smaller fora beyond their influence. Worse, it could set a precedent for other blocked multilateral negotiations, which negotiated in comparably comprehensive settings.[82] The stalled Doha trade round and the increasing fragmentation of the trade regime loomed large. Others feared that in case of a smaller 'club' of countries, emission-heavy industries might relocate to countries without any obligations. Last but not least, many delegates also personally worried about their life of travelling to conferences and earning significant per diems, as numerous interviewees asserted: 'The business class tickets, the daily UN allowances of US$200 are all very nice to them.'[83]

The Mexican Presidency repeatedly played this card of a second failure, so that the 'shock from Copenhagen'[84] augmented the willingness of parties for an agreement in 2010. It allowed the Presidency to offer a 'take-it-or-leave-it' proposal to delegations on Cancún's last day, as most direly wanted a success.[85] Given these high political stakes, some key delegations got orders from their capitals not to be blamed for a failure, such as China after Copenhagen: Chinese negotiators 'tried to keep the interaction smooth and moving forward', and India's Environment Minister Ramesh acted very constructively.[86] The 'confidence factor' of Copenhagen, which had caused a 'very strong tone', mostly vanished.[87] Likewise, ALBA delegations in Cancún appeared concerned about their political image (not to forget that Venezuela had now participated in the small room), and acted more conciliatorily, except for Bolivia. An ALBA negotiator conceded that some countries changed their decision to not block in Cancún as 'they couldn't afford a new failure…Many said "we don't agree but didn't want to spoil [it]".'[88] After initial attempts to block an agreement in Cancún's final plenary, resistance was soon abandoned by all but Bolivia. It was a known dynamic from another crucial moment in the history of the climate regime: an image concern had also been one driver behind the drawback of Saudi Arabia in Kyoto's last night in 1997 to let the Protocol pass.[89]

80   Cf. Chapter 2.
81   UNFCCC Secretariat(7)-03.08.2011.
82   BASIC(3)-08.07.2011.
83   E.g. Umbrella Group anonymous.
84   EU/EU-country(9)-26.05.2011, also: Umbrella Group(1)-20.04.2011.
85   BASIC(4)-16.03.2012.
86   EU/EU-country(8)-05.05.2011.
87   BASIC(3)-08.07.2011.
88   ALBA(1)-17.06.2011.
89   Observer(2)-08.12.2010.

In sum, the analysis of interests of individual countries and domestic stakeholders illuminated their underlying motivations.[90] They did not fundamentally change from 2009 to 2010, and can therefore not explain the variance in decisions on the highly comparable proposed outcomes in Copenhagen and Cancún. However, the diplomatic and personal interest in saving the process created 'considerable flexibility' regarding the final text.[91] This motivation did not affect the underlying interests but the indulgence with which parties kept 'red lines'. There is widespread conviction by interviewees across all coalitions that this was one major success factor.[92] The standing ovation by delegates for the organizers on the final day in Cancún indicated, inter alia, this existential wish to succeed:[93] many felt a 'desire for success' and a 'great need for catharsis'.[94]

To conclude, climate negotiations cast doubt about the usefulness of interests to fully explain recent regime evolution. Fundamental interests remained constant between the two negotiation years. Had they been the decisive factor, we would have expected a change in interests between both years to explain rejection in Copenhagen and acceptance in Cancún, given the steady pay-off structure of the suggested outcomes. The one interest that did change for nearly all countries was to avoid another failure and to thereby save the multilateral negotiation process. This weighed in addition to the changes in the negotiation management. So overall, the evidence weakens the explanatory power of the structural international relations approach of interests. This is not to forget that structural theory on interests more generally also takes a long-term perspective. Many scholars in this field may therefore not even attempt to explain the processes and difference in outcomes of such a negotiation series. Hence, this work serves to clarify that those developments at core summits are better explained by negotiation management theory, which complements the broader, long-term perspective of neoliberalism.

---

90   Interview data from the 2009 and 2010 negotiations indicates that most countries were uncertain about the interests for their supposed 'rational choice' when (dis-)agreeing at the end of COP-15 and 16. 79 per cent of interviewees (n = 24) conceded that delegations did not know the approximate cost-benefit impact of the different options on their respective countries (question: 'What was at stake for your (their) country, e.g. what size was the financial impact?'). At COP-15, many parties had decided to reject the outcome before even seeing the final text on the last evening (let alone analyse its impact on their countries), merely for the kind of process it was drafted with. This shows the empirical fragility of rational choice theory.

91   BASIC(3)-08.07.2011, Mexico(3)-15.06.2011, G-77(4)-22.07.2011.

92   For instance: Mexico(3)-15.06.2011, Denmark(6)-09.02.2012, UNFCCC Secretariat(4)-17.05.2011, UNFCCC Secretariat(7)-03.08.2011, Umbrella Group(5)-27.07.2011, Umbrella Group(2)-02.06.2011, EU/EU-country(4)-27.01.2011, EU/EU-country(9)-26.05.2011, BASIC(2)-16.06.2011, BASIC(4)-16.03.2012, G-77(1)-04.12.2010, G-77(4)-22.07.2011, ALBA(1)-17.06.2011, ALBA(2)-09.12.2011, EIG(1)-09.08.2011.

93   EU/EU-country(10)-16.08.2011.

94   UNFCCC Secretariat(2)-04.12.2010.

Hegemonic demise in a consensus-based system

Let us move to another strand of structural theories, and see whether neorealist thinking on the distribution of power, and hegemonic theory more specifically, better explain the varying behaviour of negotiating parties. It holds that progress on regime evolution cannot be achieved without the support of a hegemon, or of several big powers. Accordingly, we would have to observe:

1   a changed power distribution, where the countries supporting the agreement grew significantly stronger during 2010; or
2   a changed position of the large powers between 2009 and 2010 to support an agreement in the second year.

In the case that the preferences of major powers remained constant, hegemonic stability theory could not explain the rejection in Copenhagen and adoption in Cancún.

With respect to the first criteria, we now examine the development of power distribution between major players, such as the US, BASIC countries, and the EU. Significant power shifts had occurred over a longer period of over a decade with the rise of the BASIC countries. China for instance grew hugely along all economic dimensions, such as Gross Domestic Product, foreign currency reserves, and trade surplus, and so did its emissions. China roughly doubled its global share of 13 per cent in the Kyoto Protocol year of 1997 to 26 per cent in 2010 (US Energy Information Administration 2012). Yet, this has been a steady development with only moderate marginal change during 2010. Its BASIC partners India, Brazil and South Africa also grew gradually, without any particular leap in 2010. The US and the EU continued to suffer from the economic crisis, which slowly eroded their power base. Nevertheless, this one-sided weakening had started with the outbreak of the financial crisis in 2008 (or even earlier), and influenced their standing already in late 2009. Further, the slow decline of the EU as a vocal supporter of an agreement would have made an agreement in Cancún even less likely, i.e. predicting the opposite outcome. In sum, the constellation of major powers did not fundamentally change between 2009 and 2010.

Regarding the second theoretical implication of a change in the preferences of big powers between both years, the US, BASIC countries and the EU as the major parties started at different positions. As described in the interest analysis, the US and China were sceptical towards a comprehensive, ambitious agreement in Copenhagen at the outset of 2009,[95] in contrast to the EU as its advocate. Towards the end of the Danish Presidency however, expectations of most parties, including the big powers, slowly converged towards a moderate outcome. By the

95   EU/EU-country(8)-05.05.2011: the delegate suspected that China and India may have initially tried to undermine the reaching of an agreement at COP-15.

last day of COP-15, all big powers eventually supported at least a low-ambition agreement. Large parts of the US–BASIC small group meeting were said to have been a 'G-2' conversation between China and the US.[96] The superpowers concurred in the end, and the EU reluctantly supported the low-ambition proposal after the US–BASIC meeting on Friday. The big powers continued this support for a *moderate* agreement in Cancún. Interviewees' frequent comment that countries 'are waiting for China and the US'[97] instead refers to a push for an *ambitious* comprehensive deal, similar to the initial support by the US as hegemon in drafting the Kyoto Protocol's flexibility mechanisms.[98] As a small power delegate described, the US, the big emerging economies, and the EU are holding the key with one waiting for the other to turn it first.[99] An ambitious agreement however was against the will of big powers, and they countered any movement in this direction.[100]

Nevertheless, even this cooperation between major powers[101] turned out to be insufficient to ensure an agreement. The resistance of small-to-middle powers brought the proposal down in 2009, despite pressure from the US on Latin American countries.[102] So it was the allegedly weaker countries that had a significant impact on the failure to reach an agreement in Copenhagen. In Cancún in contrast, the resisting countries changed their behaviour and decided in favour. During two decades of climate talks, Saudi Arabia had already demonstrated how smaller countries can significantly undermine negotiations.[103] In these two years, small to middle powers exerted crucial influence against a hegemonic constellation.[104] So the unchanged support by big powers for the moderate proposals towards the end of both COPs did not explain the different outcomes by itself. It does not mean that power differences are irrelevant though. Had the US – and not Bolivia – protested vehemently against the proposal in Cancún's last night, the Mexican Presidency would hardly have overruled them, or other countries would have come to help the US.

96   Observer(3)-16.06.2011.
97   Denmark(2)-16.06.2011, similar: Umbrella Group(1)-20.04.2011, Umbrella Group(3)-14.06.2011.
98   UNFCCC Secretariat(5)-14.06.2011.
99   G-77(4)-22.07.2011.
100 G-77(4)-22.07.2011.
101 BASIC(3)-08.07.2011.
102 G-77(2)-13.06.2011.
103 Observer(2)-08.12.2010.
104 Moreover, small-to-middle powers can also create important dynamics through constructive engagement. They thereby exert a form of collective pressure through convincing discourse, which can bring opposed or neutrally minded countries on board (cf. ' Copenhagen as a "stepping stone" towards Cancún' section of this chapter on negotiation mode). One example was the Cartagena Dialogue, which unveiled important middle ground during 2010 and helped to shape the agreement at COP-16. While this is not sufficient by itself, the ideas the discourse generated added to the agreement's likelihood. (UNFCCC Secretariat(2)-04.12.2010, G-77(3)-19.07.2011).

Summarizing, climate negotiations in these two years have given evidence more to the impact of small than large powers, at least in consensus-based multilateral negotiations, where the extreme ends can influence progress.[105] Hegemonic support turned out to be insufficient: despite a variance in outcome, the approval by major parties, such as the US and BASIC countries, of a moderate agreement remained constant between Cancún and Copenhagen. As with theories focusing on interest, power-based and negotiation management theory may complement each other. In the core area of their application, neorealist approaches aim at longer time horizons and look less at a specific negotiation sequence and its dynamics. Thus, negotiation management approaches can explain the difference between several summits, while power illuminates the reasons behind the slow progress of the climate regime over two decades now, for instance by pointing at the scarce hegemonic support by the US or China. After interest and power as most prominent structural factors, I now turn to other alternative explanations.

Copenhagen as a 'stepping stone' towards Cancún

The most promising alternative explanation beyond interests and power is the 'stepping stone' effect of the Danish Presidency on the Cancún Agreements. In other words, the Mexican Presidency may have benefited from both the passage of time between the summits and the work accomplished in Copenhagen. This effect stretches over at least two rounds of negotiations (Presidencies): the outcome of one round serves as a stepping stone for a successive one, which can build on the previous work, such as on a blueprint of a rejected proposal like the Copenhagen Accord. The dynamic is different from 'learning'. The latter was dealt with under the aspect of transparency and inclusiveness. Learning is enabled through information gathering on negotiation proposals and the preferences of parties. Depending on the process, this information exchange occurs at varying speed levels. Low transparency and inclusiveness inhibited a quick diffusion of information (or learning) among parties during the Danish Presidency. In the case of a different negotiation management, a sufficient degree of information could have been attained within the year of the Danish Presidency to give a better understanding of the available options and the 'red lines' of parties.

A 'stepping stone' in turn requires preparatory work and a new round to bear the fruits which follow. During the Danish Presidency technical solutions and difficult political compromises had been struck on numerous issues. The most powerful countries, such as the US and BASIC countries, were politically largely bound in 2010 by the agreement that their leaders had crafted in Copenhagen. This preceding work (the 'great bargain',[106] as some called it) prepared the basis,

---

105   AWG/SB-Chair(1)-30.11.2010.
106   Denmark(4)-12.08.2011.

which COP-16 could successfully build on, as numerous interviewees across countries and organizations unanimously asserted.[107] The Accord thus served as a 'backbone'[108] and orienting framework for Cancún. Its content had to be carried over into an agreement accepted by all parties.[109] One even found that Copenhagen 'was essentially adopted one year later'.[110] This does not mean that several areas, such as MRV and finance, still needed to be detailed when COP-15 was meant to come to a close.[111] Yet, several crucial bargains had been made by the heads of states in Copenhagen, for which the Danes had shown 'lots of stamina': 'The Cancún agreements would otherwise not have been there',[112] acknowledged one Mexican official. A veteran negotiator echoed the significance of this preparation through COP-15 in asserting that 'anyone would have struggled to pull off such a deal right away'.[113] It provided a salient political framework for the 2010 negotiations.

Is this stepping stone effect mutually exclusive with the influence of negotiation management? Abundant evidence indicates that it contributed to the likelihood of success in Cancún. Yet, we cannot infer that such an effect is logically required, and hence necessary. Otherwise, we would never see an agreement emerging directly from one major negotiation round. An agreement would only be possible in case of one or several previous summits. The 'stepping stone' effect does also not suffice to ensure an agreement. This would have meant that the existence of the Copenhagen Accord alone guaranteed an agreement in 2010. Several insiders asserted that success in Cancún, however, was 'not a given' either.[114] We only need to imagine that the Mexicans had repeated the organizers' approach of 2009 in all its dimensions, such as a COP President without authority, a process without transparency and inclusiveness, and internally divided and internationally inexperienced organizers. Countries may well have parted again without result. Instead, the organizers transformed the process and used all available levers to bring those on board in Cancún that had rejected the Copenhagen Accord.[115] The outcome of 2009 hence made an agreement likelier in Cancún in addition to negotiation management, but it was neither necessary nor sufficient.

Moreover, varying negotiation strategies of delegations could also have affected the outcome from one year to another. Usually though, countries chose their strategy depending on their interests, or as a reaction to the negotiation

107   Mexico(3)-15.06.2011, Denmark(6)-09.02.2012, EU/EU-country(9)-26.05.2011, Umbrella Group(1)-20.04.2011, Umbrella Group(4)-04.07.2011, UNFCCC Secretariat(5)-14.06.2011.
108   UNFCCC Secretariat(7)-03.08.2011: They only needed to 'put flesh onto the backbone'.
109   EU/EU-country(8)-05.05.2011.
110   EIG(1)-09.08.2011.
111   EU/EU-country(10)-16.08.2011.
112   Mexico(4)-16.06.2011.
113   EU/EU-country(8)-05.05.2011.
114   For example: UNFCCC Secretariat(5)-14.06.2011.
115   EU/EU-country(9)-26.05.2011.

management they encounter. For instance, delegations chose the negotiation mode of arguing with a greater willingness to compromise in Cancún, also out of the interest to save the process. Further, different negotiation management did no longer allow blocking an agreement due to process mistakes. So, strategy changes of countries often depend on other factors.

The altered strategy of the EU in Cancún seemed to be more independent from interest and process however: it continuously wanted an ambitious deal and never used process to undermine agreement. Some say, its strategy changed nonetheless. After Copenhagen, Europeans became more active in coalition building by reaching out to those G-77 countries that were interested in enhanced action.[116] One result was the Cartagena Dialogue. So while the EU was relatively unsuccessful at COP-15, their tactics played out better in Cancún, and increased the agreement's likelihood. Nevertheless, 55 interviews with insiders of both climate Presidencies did not yield further indications of a major influence of negotiation strategies that changed independently of interest and process. This is despite explicitly open-ended interview questions about any observed success factors. In short, delegation strategies were usually dependent on countries' interests and the kind of process countries find themselves in.

Another factor is the capability of individual negotiators. Similarly to the analysis of lead organizers, capability is indicated by personal–cultural fit and process and content expertise. The personal fit of negotiators influences how delegations get along with each other. This fit varies and can enable or obstruct a fruitful atmosphere. Several interviewees described this with regard to some vocal negotiators: 'If you keep having people like [negotiator's name], you won't see a different approach.'[117] Regarding expertise, Commonwealth countries in particular have traditionally well-trained negotiators, such as the United Kingdom, Australia and Canada. Delegates of small countries can also exert influence. This usually depends on the individual negotiator's mastering of the process (e.g. the Colombian chief negotiator at COP-16).[118]

Several highly capable negotiators can thus enormously help to reach a breakthrough. They can detect room for compromise or are able to convince others of a proposal. The right chemistry between key negotiators can create the goodwill required to eventually make concessions. This dynamic is known from 'high politics'. The reported superb personal fit between then Soviet leader Mikhail Gorbachev and former German Chancellor Helmut Kohl was said to have facilitated negotiations on German reunification, for instance. Yet, while individual delegates certainly influenced negotiations, interview evidence did not single out particular negotiators during the Danish and Mexican Presidencies.

The same is true for the myriad other factors, such as the time allocation to issues, the daily end of sessions, the COP dynamic through constant format

116   Denmark(1)-02.12.2010.
117   Umbrella Group(5)-27.07.2011.
118   AWG/SB-Chair(1)-30.11.2010.

change in order for people to have expectations,[119] to name only a few.[120] Out of the countless possible drivers, scholarship, interviews, and participant observation have yielded as most influential those that are examined here. Future research may find evidence that other factors mattered to the same extent. For now, the 'stepping stone' effect remains the only additional alternative variable that contributed to the agreement in a meaningful way.

Conclusion

The final proposals of Copenhagen and Cancún were very similar in their core substance, yet parties rejected the compromise suggestion in 2009 and only adopted the agreement in 2010. Which alternative factors could explain this variance (Table 4.1), and do they complement or compete with negotiation management? The central structural variable of interest doesn't lead very far as the political and economic interests remained largely constant for the main coalitions and countries. Only the changed interest in reaching agreement in 2010 to save the process and the lesser use of negotiations as an ideological platform due to lower media attention raised Cancún's chances for success. The examination of power distribution could also not explain the difference. The big

Table 4.1 Alternative variables only partially explain outcome variance. The grey shading highlights those factors that changed between both years

UNFCCC Agreement	Moderate (for 2009)	Ambitious (for 2009)	Moderate (for 2010)	Ambitious (for 2010)
1. Perceived interests[a]				
Political	Yes	No	Yes	No
Economic	Yes	No	Yes	No
Ideological	No	No	Yes[b]	No
Diplomatic/personal	No	No	Yes	No
2. Hegemonic stability (big power support)	Yes	No	Yes	No
3. 'Stepping stone' effect	No	No	Yes	No
Actual agreement	No	No	Yes	No

Notes: a. 'Yes/No': No agreement of this kind if more than one country with clear preference against an agreement in the respective category of interest.

b. The absence of state leaders in Cancún with reduced media attention significantly lessened the ability to use the negotiations as a general ideological platform.

119   EU/EU-country(5)-17.02.2011.
120   EU/EU-country(1)-20.01.2010.

powers, such as the US, BASIC countries and the EU continuously supported at least a moderate proposal in Copenhagen and Cancún. The 'stepping stone' effect of the political agreement in Copenhagen turned out as the non-structural, alternative factor with most impact. Leaders had made difficult political compromises, so that the Accord served as a helpful preparation for Cancún.

Do these explanations undermine the preliminary findings on the role of negotiation management? Overall, negotiation management complements structural theories and thereby results in a comprehensive negotiation framework. Its greatest influence on reaching agreement depends on circumstances of narrowly overlapping interests and consensus rule. More generally, negotiation management can best explain a sequence of negotiation outcomes on short- to mid-term cooperation, while interest and power usually deal well with mid- to long-term changes. The diplomatic and personal interest to save the process after a failure and the 'stepping stone' effect of a preceding political agreement both additionally enhance agreement probability.

In sum, the analysis of interests, power, and other alternative explanations significantly strengthens the finding that negotiation management made a decisive difference ('internal validity'). While it is not sufficient for achieving cooperation by itself, it is a strongly enabling factor and so confirms the initial hypothesis. I will now scrutinize this framework in an analysis of two prominent sets of equally complicated global negotiations reaching beyond climate change. Let us see whether the same set of drivers holds for the complex areas of world trade and biodiversity negotiations ('external validity').

References

Conrad, Björn. (2012) China in Copenhagen – Reconciling the 'Beijing Climate Revolution' and the 'Copenhagen Climate Obstinacy'. *The China Quarterly* 210: 435–55.

International Energy Agency. (2012) *Monthly Oil Survey: April 2012*. Paris: International Energy Agency.

Oliver, Jos, Greet Janssens-Maenhout and Jeroen Peters. (2012) *Trends in Global CO_2 Emissions: 2012 Report*. The Hague: PBL Netherlands Environmental Assessment Agency.

US Energy Information Administration. (2012) International Energy Statistics. US Department of Energy. Available at www.eia.gov/cfapps/ipdbproject/iedindex3.cfm ?tid=90&pid=44&aid=8&cid=regions&syid=1997&eyid=2010&unit=MMTCD (accessed 18 July 2012).

Winkler, Harald, Shaun Vorster, and Andrew Marquard. (2009) Who Picks up the Remainder? Mitigation in Developed and Developing Countries. *Climate Policy* 9: 634–51.

Chapter 5

Trade negotiations

The bedevilled launch of the Doha Development Agenda

The two attempts to launch a new trade round in Seattle and Doha in 1999 and 2001 lend themselves as textbook cases of different approaches to the negotiation management of multilateral negotiations, just as their counterparts Copenhagen and Cancún did for climate negotiations. After a first breakdown in 1999, countries successfully reached agreement on a trade negotiation mandate two years later. A similar pattern of influence would strengthen the validity of the negotiation framework across regimes (Figure 5.1). The structure of this chapter thus mirrors the analysis of climate negotiations in order to enable comparison between the different cases. I will first outline the milestones from the besieged streets of Seattle to the calm of the Doha negotiations, before contrasting the differences in negotiation management. The assessment of the impact on summit outcomes and alternative explanations then serve as causal probing.

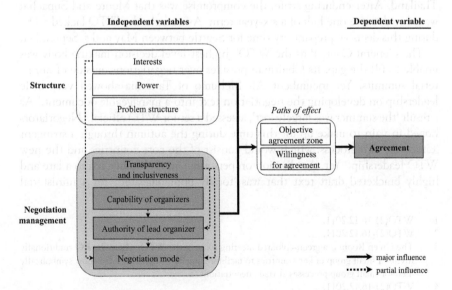

Figure 5.1 Applying the negotiation framework to trade negotiations

From the besieged streets of Seattle to the calm of Doha

The turmoil and collapse of Seattle in 1999

States have had a long tradition in negotiating terms of trade. The period since World War II has seen the pendulum swing back after the restrictive first half of the twentieth century towards a sweeping liberalization of the global exchange in goods. The last concluded year-long negotiation was the Uruguay Round under the GATT, which established the World Trade Organization in 1995 (Stiles 1996). After that, countries negotiated on the further evolution of the global trade system for nearly two decades (since 2001, officially within the context of the Doha Development Agenda), until reaching the 'Bali Package' in 2013. The trade talks have become highly complex multilateral negotiations with myriad issues to cover and 157 parties. Let us go back, though, to 1999, when countries negotiated about beginning new trade negotiations.

The launch of the Doha Round was a true roller coaster ride of trade negotiations. The first phase was the negotiation towards and at the summit in Seattle, from 30 November to 3 December 1999. Preparatory negotiations with ambassadors to the WTO started in Geneva months before the Seattle summit. Countries were deeply divided. Many developed countries favoured a new liberalization round, while numerous developing countries demanded a focus on the review and refinement of existing rules. Furthermore, they quarrelled over the succession of the outgoing Italian WTO Director-General (DG) Renato Ruggiero. Many industrialized countries supported Mike Moore of New Zealand, while most emerging economies advocated for Supachai Panitchpakdi of Thailand. After enduring strife, the compromise was that Moore and Supachai would each serve one half of a six-year term. As a result, the WTO lacked a DG during this decisive preparatory time for Seattle between May and 1 September.

The General Council as the WTO's highest-level decision-making body was unable to fill the gap. Its Chairman presides over negotiations outside of ministerial summits. Yet incumbent Ali Mchumo of Tanzania showed very little leadership on developing the negotiation text into a manageable document.[1] As a result 'the summer was largely lost', assessed a senior WTO official.[2] Negotiators hoped in vain to make up for this time during the autumn through a stringent 'Green Room'[3] process, which would consist of the core countries and the new WTO leadership.[4] Yet, the division on personnel and substance led to a late and highly bracketed draft text that was 'totally unmanageable'[5] for a ministerial

---

1   WTO(2)-16.12.2011.
2   WTO(2)-16.12.2011.
3   The Green Room is a green-coloured meeting room at the WTO, where the DG traditionally invites a small group of key countries to facilitate crucial compromises. It is now symbolically used for small group processes at trade negotiations.
4   WTO(2)-16.12.2011.
5   WTO(2)-16.12.2011.

meeting of only four days. Preparatory negotiations in Geneva, in short, had not resolved any issue (Odell 2009: 285).

The dynamics got worse at the Seattle summit. The opening ceremony on November 30 was meant to be addressed by the hosts and key organizers US Secretary of State Madeleine Albright, Conference Chair US Trade Representative Charlene Barshefsky, and WTO DG Moore (cf. the 'Authority of the lead organizers' section for details on these roles). Delegates of 135 countries, including many ministers, waited for over one and a half hours for Barshefsky and Albright, who never came as protesters blocked the way into the conference.[6] Of the 30,000 demonstrators a few thousand behaved obstructively or even destructively, according to a seasoned eyewitness (Bayne 2000: 136). Negotiations were nearly completely stalled on the first day (ICTSD 1999a), and the police were incapable of providing access to the venue for many delegates (Odell 2009: 273).

So Conference Chair Barshefsky only addressed the entire summit in the plenary[7] on the morning of 1 December, while the opening ceremony of the previous day had to be cancelled (Bayne 2000: 135). After an apology for the chaos, Barshefsky underlined that she would resort to Green Room consultations should negotiators not be open to concessions (WTO 1999a). While she emphasized her preference for an inclusive approach, the announcement heavily irritated delegations as most would be excluded from such small groups. On the same day, US President Bill Clinton visiting the summit infuriated developing countries further. In a newspaper interview, he demanded the inclusion of labour rights in future agreements, safeguarded by sanctions against non-abiding countries. Clinton was pleasing his labour union constituency among the angry protesters (Odell 2009: 286), yet the issue had been intensely negotiated before and had been finally not included in the agenda.

The conference established five negotiation working groups on agriculture, implementation, the Singapore (or, 'new') issues, market access, and systemic issues (e.g. institutional reform and transparency; ICTSD 1999a). Parallel to these groups, members started meeting in bilaterals and smaller circles (ICTSD 1999b). Agriculture stood out as one prominent dividing issue with the US-EU quarrelling over the level of ambition for the upcoming negotiation agenda:[8] how far should trade in agricultural goods be liberalized analogous to trade in other goods, how much should one-sided government support be reduced? Regarding the issue of implementation, developing countries demanded flexibility on existing WTO rules (e.g. for trade-related aspects of intellectual property rights) as they posed enormous difficulties for them, but also a renegotiation of agreements from the Uruguay Round that allegedly contained 'strong imbalances' (ICTSD 1999b). Launching negotiations on the Singapore issues, such as investment and

---

6   WTO(2)-16.12.2011.
7   Known as the Committee of the Whole (CoW) in trade negotiations.
8   G-10-country(1)-15.02.2012.

competition, was a third, highly contested field with developed countries push-ing for their inclusion. The list of differences could be continued.

The following day, 2 December, Barshefsky tried to alleviate grievances caused by the Clinton comment, yet with little effect (ICTSD 1999c). The mood was further soured by diverging expectations of transparency and inclusiveness. Latin American and African countries prepared statements to block any consensus should the negotiation process continue in its current manner. They expressed 'grave concern' about lacking transparency (ibid.). EU Trade Commissioner Pascal Lamy demanded a whole summit dedicated to making trade negotiations more transparent and inclusive. The Conference Chair's assertion that Seattle had the most transparent process in trade history with clearly defined, open-ended working groups did not calm the atmosphere (ibid.).

Regarding the negotiation substance, Barshefsky urged parties in the morning plenary to produce text without brackets (WTO 1999b). Delegates had already shifted gears to night-long negotiations. Meanwhile Barshefsky, Moore and working group chairs began compiling a draft declaration text for the last day. Due to at least moderate progress, the chairs of the agriculture and implementa-tion working group submitted first, yet still contested, syntheses to the organizers in the evening (ibid.). However, the two other salient working groups on new issues and market access were far from ready to follow suit (ICTSD 1999c).

Faced by the fast-approaching deadline, 20 to 40 ministers, working group chairs and WTO officials turned to informal Green Room negotiations from Thursday afternoon to the early hours of Friday morning, 3 December, the last day of the ministerial (WTO 1999c). By late afternoon, it became clear that despite good progress in some fields, such as agriculture or services (Bayne 2000: 135; Odell 2009: 287), an overall agreement was still not in reach. The 19-page draft ministerial declaration was still severely bracketed (ICTSD 1999e), and neither Conference Chair Barshefsky nor DG Moore dared suggesting a compromise text to parties. Organizers suspended negotiations in the final plenary session without launching a new trade round and without decisions in areas of consensus. Barshefsky appealed to parties to continue negotiations after Seattle in 'creative' ways and to improve process so it is 'both efficient and fully inclusive' (WTO 1999c), as it was no longer appropriate for today's higher complexity of negotiations (ICTSD 1999d).

Seattle did not meet its goal of an agreement on the launch of new trade talks. While numerous NGOs celebrated that no agreement had been achieved (Odell 2009: 273), the outcome was otherwise widely seen in a very negative light. Representative of many, a veteran WTO official characterized it as 'a shattering failure'.[9] A senior negotiator found Seattle achieved 'only trivial agreements'.[10] Many negotiators from developing and developed countries regretted a lost opportunity and the foregone benefits for their countries caused by the delay (ICTSD 1999d).

9   WTO(2)-16.12.2011.
10   EU-country(1)-29.11.2011.

Towards a successful launch in Doha in 2001

After the Seattle breakdown, talks on services and agriculture started only a little later in early 2000. They had already been scheduled by provisions in the Uruguay Round regardless of the launch of a new comprehensive agenda (WTO 1999c). With both sectors covering two-thirds of global output (WTO 1999d), it was a significant continuation of talks. The lack of trust after the events in Seattle was still deep-seated though (Odell 2009: 288). The organizers of negotiations reacted. WTO DG Moore and General Council Chairmen Kare Bryn of Norway, and later Stuart Harbinson of Hong Kong–China, were leading preparatory negotiations in Geneva throughout 2000 and 2001. They reached out explicitly to include as many countries as possible in deliberations (*ibid.*: 289). At the same time, negotiators of the two trade superpowers (the US and EU) travelled intensively to advocate for an agreement, made bilateral progress among themselves, and started softening their positions (e.g. Brussels's offer to largely abolish import tariffs for LDCs, and Washington's dropping of the labour rights issue under the new Bush administration; *ibid.*: 288).

Nevertheless, disagreement continued so that in July 2001 Harbinson and Moore announced the proposing of a compromise draft, which would use the bottom-up input they had collected since Seattle. They intended to avoid a Seattle-like situation, where the summit had opened with a long and highly contested text. In the meantime, smaller informal ministerial meetings in August and October in Mexico and Singapore helped move negotiations forward and provided additional space for negotiators to exchange openly before the summit (ICTSD 2001f). Eventually, the organizers issued draft proposals in late September and revised versions in late October,[11] which became the base for the summit. Some developing countries accused the drafts by Harbinson and Moore of a bias in favour of developed countries (Jawara and Kwa 2003: 67). India, for instance, vehemently complained about the textiles provisions (ICTSD 2001a). Overall though, preparatory negotiations were reported as rather 'uneventful' without any crisis comparable to the clash of the DG's succession in 1999.

Negotiations culminated in the 4th Ministerial Conference in Doha, Qatar, from 9 to 14 November 2001. Despite the shock and insecurity after the 9/11 terrorist attacks on the US, delegates of 142 countries gathered in Doha showing that countries can still cooperate under difficult circumstances. Regarding external conditions negotiations started smoothly on 9 November as the organizers largely inhibited any outside protests (Odell 2009: 291), in contrast to the over 30,000 activists reported in Seattle. As two years earlier in Seattle, the goal was still to negotiate the 'whether and how' of a new round of trade negotiations. Developed and many developing countries supported a further reduction of trade barriers, while several developing countries vehemently demanded to first resolve the severe problems associated with current rules (ICTSD 2001a).

11   JOB(01)/140/Rev.1, JOB(01)/155, JOB(01)/139/Rev.1.

On 10 November, negotiations made little progress in the six working groups with ministerial facilitators covering most issues already on the table in Seattle: agriculture, implementation (e.g. market access for textiles), the application of intellectual property rights to public health, the Singapore issues, environment and trade, and rule-making such as on anti-dumping. The US and the EU however, as two principal players, showed an extent of harmony, which one trade veteran had rarely seen before.[12] Parallel to this, informal consultations in smaller fora were started, yet Conference Chairman Sheikh Youssef Hussein Kamal, Qatari Minister of Finance, Economy and Commerce, emphasized that official working groups would remain at the heart of negotiations (ICTSD 2001b).

On 11 November, process concerns were voiced: LDCs complained about not having a single facilitator arising from their group, and too many non-inclusive meetings (ICTSD 2001c). Besides, delegates made hardly any progress on substance. The original US concession on textiles proved insufficient for developing countries, the EU raised its demands to include the environment in trade negotiations, the US reaffirmed its resistance to changing its anti-dumping rules, and several developing countries underlined their opposition to negotiating any new issues at all (ibid.).

Progress came one day later, when primarily Brazil and the US brokered a compromise on TRIPs on November 12 (ICTSD 2001d). This had been a salient issue for developing countries and was crafted mostly in their favour. Agriculture progressed with only the EU isolated in its opposition to the current draft. The US softened its anti-dumping stance, while it underlined it could not concede any further on textiles; no breakthrough was seen on new issues yet with continued opposition from the EU and developing countries (ibid.). Meanwhile, in the plenary developing countries welcomed the more transparent process than in Seattle and the creation of a working group facilitated by an LDC minister (ibid.). Nevertheless, some raised complaints about a lack of English translations for the working group meetings and on the missing indication of the location of informal meetings (ibid.).

On Tuesday 13 November, the final official day, Kamal issued a last version of the original Harbinson draft text. As the plenary could not reach agreement core negotiations moved into the Green Room in the evening. Twenty-three ministers from all major negotiation groups gathered, with six of them coming from developed countries (ICTSD 2001e; Moore 2003: 129).[13] To point out just a few stumbling blocks: as the EU had yielded some ground on its core issue of agriculture, the US and Japan now supported the EU to consider environment and the new issue of investment for the agenda of the upcoming round. India

12   WTO(2)-16.12.2011: 'The range of agreement between them [Zoellick for the US and Lamy for the EU] was striking.'
13   The 23 delegations comprised: Australia, Botswana, Brazil, Canada, Chile, Egypt, EU, Guatemala, Hong Kong, India, Japan, Kenya, Malaysia, Mexico, Nicaragua, Pakistan, Qatar, Singapore, South Africa, Switzerland, Tanzania, US and Zambia.

remained in stern opposition to negotiating any new issue (Jawara and Kwa 2003: 105–8; Odell 2009: 292). After a 12-hour all night marathon, the Green Room meeting was closed and the compromise presented in the morning as not open for changes, according to one source (Wolfe 2004: 581). The WTO DG and several key delegates, such as US Trade Representative Robert Zoellick and Kenyan trade minister Nicholas Biwott, eventually tried to convince Indian Commerce Minister Murasoli Maran in a separate small meeting in the afternoon, as the country was still opposing in the ongoing final plenary (Jawara and Kwa 2003: 110; Moore 2003: 134). The Solomonic decision was that Kamal would read out a statement that negotiation of the new issues would begin explicitly only by consensus, a caveat not included in the final text though.[14] Twenty hours after the original deadline parties finally reached agreement in the plenary on the evening of 14 November.

All countries had yielded positions important to them to concur on the work programme of the Doha Development Agenda (DDA)[15] to be completed by 1 January 2005. They settled very close to the compromise originally proposed by the organizers in October (Odell 2009: 293). A main declaration set the ground for a new round of liberalization with negotiations on agriculture (the EU granting a substantial reduction in subsidies), services, and potentially on the Singapore issues (developing countries accepting the option to negotiate after 2003). Furthermore, talks would be held on issues such as anti-dumping (despite fierce original opposition from the US) and the environment. Specific declarations addressed intellectual property and public health, as well as the alleviation of difficulties associated with the implementation of current WTO agreements. Another priority of the LDCs was also met with the waiver to allow a special treatment for poor countries of the ACP group. Taken together, these provisions were crucial for many developing countries (ICTSD 2001e) and eventually 'bought' their support (Jawara and Kwa 2003: 112; Wolfe 2004: 581).

Overall, countries eventually concurred on launching a new round of liberalization, on refining the implementation of existing WTO rules, and on respecting trade-related public health concerns in developing countries. To be sure, Doha did not have to pin down binding terms of liberalization or adjustments of current regulations. Yet, they achieved agreement on a mandate of a new round, which was difficult enough as demonstrated in Seattle. After the breakdown of Seattle, Doha had now successfully launched a new trade round. To what extent can negotiation management explain this difference in outcomes?

This book holds that negotiation management has its largest influence on negotiations in case of consensus-based decision making, which applies for trade negotiations under the WTO. Moreover, interests have to overlap narrowly at

14   WTO(2)-16.12.2011.
15   WT/MIN(01)/DEC/W/1, WT/MIN(01)/DEC/W/2, WT/MIN(01)/DEC/W/10.

the outset. 'A notary can't achieve anything if certain countries don't like to move', described a WTO official about the role of the organizers.[16] Such small convergences of interests were given for the beginning of the respective negotiation phases leading to Seattle, and later to Doha. Early in 1999, there was no complete clash as all main groups wanted at least some form of trade talks on either implementation *or* advanced liberalization. Although countries were generally open to discuss trade issues, a significant schism existed over whether implementation problems needed to be resolved first before any new liberalization, as many developing countries demanded. Hence, interests overlapped narrowly as countries intended to realize at least some of the benefits of their preferred choices. This zone of congruence slightly grew by 2000 when preparatory talks for Doha started, as the threat of a second breakdown added a common interest to parties' considerations. However, the still conflictive nature of the talks demonstrated that an agreement in Doha was also not a safe bet. In sum, there was room for negotiation management to make a difference given the narrow overlap of interests in both years. The following drivers show the astonishing contrast in negotiation management before and during both summits.

Transparency and inclusiveness

The gradual farewell to the Green Room tradition

The indicators of process transparency and inclusiveness for trade negotiations equal those of the climate regime, as the WTO trade negotiation structure is comparable to that of the UN climate negotiations. In the WTO trade realm, countries negotiate in many different fora with highly varying levels of transparency and inclusiveness. On one side are the open-ended General Council Room meetings during non-summit phases, mostly in Geneva at the WTO. They are accessible to all WTO members, and in this regard comparable to summit plenaries (or, Committee of the Whole). In these public settings with a high number of delegates and issues constructive discussion and discrete mediation are nearly impossible. Therefore, parties split in multiple working groups with specific mandates. Moreover, key organizers facilitate informal, small group negotiations with more efficiency but less transparency and inclusiveness, for instance the Green Room negotiations with the DG. Finally, bilaterals in completely informal settings are a primary setting for discretely exchanging information: 'Negotiations never take place in formal hall. It happens over dinner or drinks. That's where it is hammered out. Very informal meetings take place by the lake, over phone, etc. It is all based on personal relationships.'[17]

Overall, negotiations before and in Doha are widely conceived of as higher in transparency and inclusiveness than those in Geneva and Seattle (ICTSD

16   WTO(1)-16.12.2011.
17   ACP-country(1)-15.12.2011. For the decision-making process see also Odell (2005: 433, 446) and Wolfe (2004: 581).

1999e).[18] It symbolized a gradual farewell to the Green Room tradition. Let us turn to *transparency* first. Regarding small group transparency, organizers in both cases used Green Room diplomacy, however in varying ways. In the months before Seattle, newly appointed DG Moore tried to facilitate in smaller circles in the Green Room with the usual 20-plus participants. This excluded more than 100 delegations who were neither informed on participants nor on mandate, schedule and progress (Odell 2009: 285). It was the approach inherited from the old GATT days when the 'Quad' of the US, EU, Canada and Japan decided most rules. A Western negotiator conceded that 'transparency has always been difficult' in trade negotiations, with the self-critique that 'big countries wanted to come together and decide for others'.[19] In Seattle, Moore and Barshefsky held a series of small group meetings to facilitate a compromise, such as the one which was a last, unsuccessful attempt for agreement from Thursday to Friday, the last day of the summit. Given its importance, very little was known about this crucial final meeting, which hence stood for a non-transparent small group process.

The small group process before and in Doha was more transparent. In response to Seattle, General Council Chair Bryn increased transparency and inclusiveness by altering small group procedures: small group meetings would always be announced publicly and delegations invited to make their points. They usually would be open to all and the results be reported afterwards. It became the practice under Bryn and his successor Harbinson, without a formal adoption as it had been originally suggested by Bryn in July 2000 (Odell 2009: 289). This is not to say though that the Green Room meetings did not also retain their traditional importance during the ministerial,[20] but they were approached differently.

The negotiation text development also differed between the two years. In the run-up to Seattle, General Council Chair Mchumo was mostly preoccupied with the WTO DG successor search with little time to test the ground for compromise in bilaterals. The General Council therefore stayed at the centre of negotiations with long-lasting general discussions, according to a participant.[21] As a result, Mchumo brought forward a compilation of diverging positions of 32 pages full of brackets, which countries could eventually not resolve in the remaining time of the Seattle process. The General Council Chair was unable to provide at least a minimal focal point for parties (on the text evolution: Odell 2005: 438). Despite

18   To briefly reiterate, transparency of the negotiation process is indicated by the extent of information (1) on the mandate, schedule, and progress of the small group, (2) on the origin, evolution, and conclusion of the final compromise text, and (3) on the schedule and progress of overall negotiations. Regarding inclusiveness, salient indicators are (1) the direct participation (or at least appropriate representation) of countries in the small group, (2) the integration of levels of expert negotiators, ministers, and heads of state and government, and (3) the extent to which organizers reach out to parties during their facilitation efforts. The communication of organizers about transparency and inclusiveness is the final, overarching aspect.
19   EU-country(1)-29.11.2011.
20   WTO(2)-16.12.2011.
21   WTO(2)-16.12.2011.

a slightly higher transparency from the open-ended General Council discussions, even DG Moore did not consider pre-negotiations in Geneva as very transparent or inclusive (Moore 2003: 111).

From the beginning of the Doha preparations, General Council Chairs Bryn and later Harbinson reduced the number of formal council meetings to discuss key elements of a potential text. Instead, they saw delegations in smaller circles or even one by one to avoid a divisive debate, according to a senior WTO official: 'It was a very private process' with the text development in the hands of the General Council Chair with the support of WTO officials.[22] Nevertheless, the Geneva–Doha text development turned out to be a more transparent process than the Geneva–Seattle one. The single negotiation text eventually provided by the organizers before Doha did not appear 'out of the blue' for countries, as in the Copenhagen climate talks. Instead, organizers cautiously ensured that the key steps of the text evolution were always announced to all parties (e.g. the announcement in July 2001 that a chair's text would come forward in September). Further, organizers distributed as much text as possible early and widely among delegates, such as in the TRIPs negotiations. This was in contrast to Seattle, where 'the text went out only until it was too late'.[23] Eventually, the suggested compromise text reflected the inputs of a broad range of countries. A final major improvement on transparency compared to Seattle was the daily reporting of facilitators to all delegations on the *progress* made in their respective groups (Moore 2003: 124).

With respect to *inclusion* in small group meetings, Doha made great improvements over Seattle. One of the most striking examples was that Kenya, representing the 40-member-strong African Group, had not been invited to the Green Room in Seattle (Odell 2009: 286). In response to this mishap, two vocal African leaders, Gabon and Tanzania, participated in the 'mini-ministerial' meetings in Mexico and Singapore in the months leading up to Doha (ICTSD 2001f). They had also been excluded from the Seattle Green Room talks. One analysis finds though that participation in these 'mini-ministerials' was still skewed in favour of developed countries (Jawara and Kwa 2003: 59). Yet while not perfect, they were a step in the direction of more inclusiveness. After all, the Odell study reports for Doha that '[n]o minister denounced the WTO for excluding him or her from real decision making'. He quotes Nigeria's trade minister Mustafa Bello: 'Unlike in Seattle, Africa has been satisfied with all the stages in consultations and negotiation processes in Doha' (Odell 2009: 292). Increasingly, a system for small groups evolved that ensured all countries were at least represented by one member of their 'coalition', largely satisfying parties (Odell 2005: 435). In the final Doha Green Room negotiations during the night to 14 November, only six of the twenty-two participating ministers came from developed countries (Moore 2003: 129).

22   WTO(2)-16.12.2011.
23   WTO(2)-16.12.2011.

The integration of negotiation levels to include the input of both ministers and expert negotiators has also been conceived of as salient for trade negotiations. A strong focus on ministers disadvantages delegations with less professional support and thus inhibits the input of developing countries (Narlikar 2004). There is scarce data on this for Seattle. Early on at the ministerial though, Barshefsky had demanded that only ministers would be allowed to speak given the not very helpful preparatory work of expert negotiators.[24] The integration of levels in Doha gives a mixed picture. One negotiator reports that some major parties, such as the US, EU and Brazil, requested that only ministers and not ambassadors should be allowed to speak on core issues.[25] It is also said that ambassadors were only supposed to send notes to their ministers (Narlikar 2004: 422). Only ministers would have the political authority to step beyond originally defined 'red lines'. While such a restriction seemed not to have been the case for all meetings, it appears to be true for the final Green Room meeting in Doha (Jawara and Kwa 2003: 104). This posed a major problem for the poorer equipped developing countries with less informed ministers, and diminished their ability to participate. On balance though, the greater 'bottom-up approach' (WTO 2001) by General Council Chairs Bryn and later Harbinson during the Doha preparation, had ensured that ambassadors of all countries had been given the chance to provide their ideas, which enhanced the inclusion of the expert level. So overall, the integration was probably slightly deeper during 2000 and 2001.

A more clear-cut finding is that the leadership of the Geneva–Doha negotiations reached out explicitly wider than the Geneva-Seattle one. One study reports that Barshefsky spent too little time to 'ask and listen carefully' to parties to build consensus (Odell 2005: 432). In contrast, the two successive General Council Chairmen and the WTO DG travelled extensively to a wide range of countries when preparing the compromise text before Doha to deepen relationships beforehand (Odell 2009: 289). As a conscious strategic trust-building measure, Moore for instance visited Africa six times before Doha to include so far much neglected members. He found it 'perhaps the...crucial element in launching the round' (Moore 2003: 113). A WTO official sums up that all countries had been included in the process of consultations by the organizers this time.[26]

With regard to communication, Barshefsky's infamous threatening announcement early on in Seattle to move the process into small group negotiations in case of lacking progress raised parties' doubts of attending a transparent and inclusive negotiation. In contrast, the explicit declaration by the new General Council Chair Bryn after Seattle to introduce more transparency and inclusiveness into the process most likely positively altered parties' perception.

In sum, the available information did not yield equal amounts of data on each indicator of a transparent and inclusive process for both negotiations. However,

24 WTO(2)-16.12.2011.
25 G-10-country(1)-15.02.2012.
26 WTO(2)-16.12.2011.

it already provides abundant evidence that negotiations were of higher transparency and inclusiveness in Geneva and Doha in 2000/2001 than in Geneva and Seattle in 1999 (for Seattle see also Bayne 2000: 139). One study even judged that the 'Doha process was more representative and more inclusive than any previous GATT or WTO meeting', while conceding that some countries still found it insufficient (Wolfe 2004: 580).

How transparency and inclusiveness influenced the summit outcomes

To what extent can we trace a causal influence of a (non-)transparent and (non-) inclusive process on the probability of agreement? As with climate negotiations, the analysis follows the four paths of (1) process and content knowledge, (2) contribution ability, (3) obstruction ability, and (4) feeling of respect (Figure 3.2).

It seems that delegations in Seattle, as in Copenhagen, lacked process and content knowledge to take an informed decision (path 1). The non-transparent and exclusive process inhibited a quicker learning about suggested solutions, as a senior negotiator acknowledged: after Seattle countries had 'two more years to understand the issues' and were thus able to commit to an agreement on the launch in Doha.[27] Turning the argument around, a more transparent and inclusionary approach may have enabled such learning already before and in Seattle. 'Countries like to have time to consider the issues in more detail', explained a WTO official.[28]

A veteran WTO colleague added that the 'fact that a lot of parties will not know is often a major impediment. It creates suspicion and fear'.[29] Delegates worry about accepting a proposition when they are in fact unsure of its benefits for their country – a very uncomfortable position to be in as they need to report 'home' about progress and results. In these cases 'no' is 'the easiest, safest option' for countries, according to former DG Moore (Moore 2003: 122). Thus, low transparency disadvantages the poorly staffed delegations of many developing countries even further (see also Narlikar 2004: 424).

Moreover, scarce information and exclusion create suspicion about the neutrality of organizers. This becomes even more important for delegations with less capacity. Least developed countries can often only afford sending two or three delegates with scarce real time support from the capital during the summit; around thirty WTO members do not even have permanent representatives in Geneva to closely follow the salient non-ministerial negotiations during preparation time.[30] These disadvantages render comprehensive information on the

27   EU-country(1)-29.11.2011.
28   WTO(1)-16.12.2011.
29   WTO(2)-16.12.2011.
30   G-10-country(2)-16.02.2011.

state of negotiations by the organizers even more important 'to explain what is going on'.[31] Otherwise, the lack of information can eventually cause 'a break-down of trust... You cannot realize an outcome without process', asserted a developing country negotiator.[32] Without trust, parties may then lose any willingness to agree. Moreover, how legitimate is a process where a large number of participating member states does not know about the key developments in process and substance? Numerous excluded developing countries had expressed their rejection of any deal on these process grounds in Seattle (Bayne 2000: 135).

Regarding contribution ability (path 2), one can imagine dynamics similar to those detected for climate negotiations, such as creating a more comprehensive negotiation text and greater ownership through a wider inclusion. While some elements in the chronology hint at this, there was not much data available to substantiate this path here. Apart from objective, content-driven disadvantages, a non-transparent and exclusive process provides the possibility to obstruct on mere process grounds (path 3). As in climate change, this is frequently owed to political–economic ideologies that oppose any further trade liberalization that is promoted by the industrialized world. A long-time WTO official suspected that this is the motivation behind the process-based resistance of several countries with socialist–authoritarian tendencies. Cuba, Venezuela, Ecuador and Bolivia, for instance, have constantly raised process complaints in trade talks, such as on transparency and inclusiveness.[33] A developing country negotiator concurs, and additionally mentioned Nicaragua. Some delegations 'were like a small child who was not able to put his hand into the cookie jar... Their manner is very strong. They have a very strong foreign policy. This is for political-ideological reasons. There is an anti-Washington consensus amongst them.'[34] The striking similarity to climate negotiations in terms of countries and strategy speaks for an interpretation that these countries take the negotiations hostage on process grounds beyond the actual negotiation substance as part of a wider ideological struggle. Whichever the motivation, process shortcomings provide a tool to obstruct negotiations.

Finally, the expectation of what would constitute respectful treatment had changed massively between the end of the Uruguay Round and Seattle (path 4). The major trade powers were accustomed to the 'GATT world', where a few delegations dominated, and agreement between the 'Quad' of the US, EU, Canada and Japan meant a new deal.[35] Although the Kennedy and Tokyo Rounds were *multi*national negotiations most parties were still 'very silent', according to a WTO veteran.[36] By the end of the 1990s though, countries vocally demanded

31 WTO(2)-16.12.2011.
32 ACP-country(1)-15.12.2011.
33 WTO(1)-16.12.2011.
34 ACP-country(1)-15.12.2011.
35 EU-country(1)-29.11.2011, EU-country(2)-16.02.2012.
36 WTO(1)-16.12.2011, ACP-country(1)-15.12.2011.

more transparency and inclusiveness in the process, and would only then feel more respected: 'Now, [developing countries] have taken a more aggressive posture ... there is a need to quickly formalize these informal decisions', said a negotiator describing the new dynamic.[37]

In Seattle, Moore and Barshefsky had followed the 'traditional' secretive format of small group negotiations. The mostly excluded developing countries were more outraged than ever before: 'They still think the WTO is a club. They still think 20 countries can decide for the rest of us,' expressed a Latin American negotiator (Odell 2009: 286). Many delegates bitterly opposed the exclusive Green Room meeting of Seattle's last night. The result of the exclusion was great frustration from the lack of respect, made even worse by the presence of ministers: 'If you have 150 ministers in the room and had five or six ministers that tried to make a deal somewhere else, they got to be frustrated as they have also other things to do. Then they have to wait for half a day.'[38] As at the Copenhagen climate summit, the Seattle approach led delegations to announce the blocking of any outcome the small group would achieve regardless of its content, on the grounds of an appalling process.

For instance, the African Group had been excluded from the last night's Green Room meeting in Seattle. They declared on the morning of the final day before any substance of the Green Room compromise was released: 'There is no transparency in the proceedings and African countries are being marginalized and generally excluded on issues of vital importance for our peoples and their future ... We will not be able to join the consensus required to meet the objectives of this Ministerial Conference' (Odell 2009: 286). A Latin American veteran of 30 years of trade negotiations echoed that:

> This is absolutely the worst – the worst – organized international conference there has ever been ... Mrs. Barshefsky is intent on forcing the process and having a declaration at all costs, almost as if it doesn't matter what the rest of the countries think about it. Well, that is not going to happen. The WTO does not belong to the United States.
>
> (Paulsen 1999)

Such a de-coupling of substance and process is a dynamic detected in previous trade negotiations, and well-known in social relations in general according to social psychology scholarship (with myriad further sources: Albin and Young 2012: 40). For trade, an 'old hand' of the WTO described that the continuous informing of delegates on the text development 'makes it much more possible for them to buy in. The feeling of exclusion might even bring them away from the objective economic rationale.'[39]

---

37   ACP-country(1)-15.12.2011.
38   G-10-country(1)-15.02.2012.
39   WTO(2)-16.12.2011.

In contrast, the explicit raising of transparency and inclusiveness of small group meetings during 2000 before Doha is said to have increased countries' willingness to cooperate (Odell 2009: 289). One reason probably was that they felt respected again. Meetings in Doha were more transparent and thereby limited frustration among delegates.[40] The salience of a transparent and inclusive process also became clear from the evidence of changes undertaken since then. One developing country negotiator, for instance, underlines that the recent creation of the G-11[41] has raised the degree of participation as it better represents the major regions in trade negotiations with official mandates and regular reporting on progress.[42]

To conclude, evidence from interviews and secondary sources demonstrates that dynamics in paths 1, 3 and 4 have also been at work in trade negotiations culminating in Seattle and Doha. There was scarce material on path 2, but circumstantial evidence suggests this is only owed to the lack of data, not of its applicability. So, increased process and content knowledge, less obstruction ability, and a greater feeling of respect all contributed to reaching the agreement to launch trade talks in Doha, and had the reverse effect in Seattle. In Moore's summarizing words on Doha: 'transparency and inclusiveness...helps to explain why Member governments were more prepared and more willing to reach agreement' (Moore 2003: 105).

Capability of organizers

Mistaking moderation for negotiation, or 'the art of neutrality'

The indicators of the capability of the organizers mirror that of the climate analysis to ensure comparability. Despite slight differences in leadership positions between climate and trade negotiations, they are fairly similar in the chosen periods. Since the creation of the WTO in 1995, there are two key organizers of trade negotiations that take place in Geneva: the WTO DG and the General Council Chairperson. The latter is an ambassador of a (usually smaller and more neutral[43]) country to the WTO with a one-year term (WTO 2012). A third key organizer is added when the biannual Ministerial Conference is held outside of Geneva: the minister of the host country then serves as Conference Chairman, who steps into the role of the General Council Chairperson during the summit (see also Narlikar 2004: 417).

There is one main difference to climate negotiations. The position of the annual President of the climate negotiations is split for trade summits outside Geneva. In that case, the General Council Chairperson focuses on the prepara-

40   G-10-country(1)-15.02.2012.
41   The G-11 consists of the US, EU, Japan, Canada, Australia, China, India, Brazil, Argentina, South Africa and Mauritius.
42   ACP-country(1)-15.12.2011.
43   EU-country(1)-29.11.2011.

tory negotiations and the Conference Chairman presides over the summit, yet with the General Council Chairperson still supporting.[44] With these two people and the Director-General already occupying central facilitative positions, this study will not examine the lead administrative official of the host country (and so depart from the climate analysis). This is not to say that the quality of his or her support also influences the performance of the host country.[45] But this would also apply to the chairs of the working groups that affect the progress of negotiations. Often, they work on salient issues over a long period of time.[46] Yet, this book focuses on the top and most influential leadership level to maintain a clear scope. There is academic consent to study this level's influence, e.g. in the research on the 'role of the chair' (e.g. Odell 2005, 2009; Wolfe 2004: 579).

The capability of these lead organizers is assessed by the same four indicators as before, depending on the availability of data: (1) cultural and organizational or personal fit to the negotiation circumstances, (2) expertise on negotiation process, and (3) content. Organizers' alignment (as dimension 4) assesses the relation between the organizers (i.e. host country and WTO Secretariat including its General Council Chair and the DG; Figure 1.4).

Let us start with the Geneva–Seattle organizers. They had a problematic cultural and organizational-personal fit to the negotiation circumstances. Moore's origin from New Zealand as a rich, developed country was one driver of the DG succession fight. In addition, some felt that Moore had proved too close to the US in the past. After decades of domination by industrialized nations, many developing countries demanded one of their representatives to finally lead the WTO (Jawara and Kwa 2003: 187, 190). At the same time, several developing countries backed Moore (Moore 2003: 95). General Council Chair Mchumo of Tanzania sided with him, and was thus partially seen as 'betraying' developing countries, turning his original cultural fit into a disadvantage (similar: Wolfe 2004: 580). These internal tensions among WTO members reduced the organizational fit of the Secretariat and its leadership at a critical point shortly before the next Ministerial Conference.

Regarding personal fit, US Conference Chair Barshefsky showed little personal fit for the short and heated negotiation days of Seattle. Evidence from the chronology and the following examples for the remaining process variables indicate that she showed a relatively low level of empathy. Similarly, one study quotes comments on Moore as being overly straightforward, not diplomatic, and 'very rough around the edges' (Jawara and Kwa 2003: 191–2, 196). In short, data indicate that lead organizers as institutions and individuals had a low fit for the circumstances in 1999.

As for process expertise, the American hosts in Seattle appeared surprisingly poorly prepared for the pitfalls of a major conference. Already the opening of the

44   See also Odell (2009: 279).
45   G-10-country(2)-16.02.2011.
46   EU-country(1)-29.11.2011.

negotiations proved to be detrimental: a WTO veteran, who had been to summits for decades, put it harshly: 'Americans did a terrible process in Seattle. They didn't even get the conference badges for delegates organized. It was a shocking scandal. The Brazilian minister, for instance, could not get in. The handling got even worse later.'[47] On the first day, Secretariat officials couldn't access their offices as the police were unable to deal with the massive protests outside. Reportedly, someone had tried to break into the conference buildings at night, so hundreds of delegates and NGOs were held up in one hotel outside the venue.[48] The police only significantly intervened after the conference had been brought to a near standstill, despite the fact that organizers had been aware of the plans months before (Bayne 2000: 136). It was a chaotic site-management that was unable to keep the conference running regardless of the protests (Odell 2009: 286). Moore considered Seattle 'the worst-organised conference ever' (Moore 2003: 98).

In addition, there seem to have been scarce planning for later on into the conference, for instance if negotiations would not come to an agreement within the allotted time. Instead of allowing for an extra day to strike a last minute compromise, the venue had been booked for a subsequent conference of optometrists (Odell 2009: 287). When the South African trade minister demanded the Conference Chair in the Green Room on the last afternoon to arrange for the likely event that no agreement would be found, it is said that Barshefsky paid only scant attention.[49] Many regarded the non-existent option to keep the venue for another day as 'lousy backup of the organizers'.[50] This casts doubts on the process understanding of the hosts.

Lack of neutrality further indicated low process expertise. Barshefsky was unable 'to play the chair's role'.[51] She repeatedly negotiated on behalf of the US while she was instead supposed to moderate the discussion (Odell 2005: 432). One example was the first Seattle Green Room meeting, where she started negotiating on the services draft on behalf of the US after having dismissed the proposal of parties.[52] Clinton's petition to include the contested issue of labour rights was another incident of this lacking neutrality. WTO officials summarized that 'it was as badly managed as any conference could be imagined,'[53] and simply 'a catastrophic process'.[54]

Which of these indications of low American process expertise also hold for the WTO? The chaotic logistical organization and security shortcomings, as well as the lacking neutrality of US facilitators, remain within the realm of the host

47   WTO(2)-16.12.2011.
48   WTO(2)-16.12.2011.
49   WTO(2)-16.12.2011.
50   G-10-country(1)-15.02.2012.
51   G-10-country(1)-15.02.2012.
52   WTO(2)-16.12.2011.
53   WTO(2)-16.12.2011.
54   WTO(1)-16.12.2011.

country. The WTO may have wanted to double-check that sufficient logistical fall-back options were provided, for instance the option for an extra negotiation day. Nevertheless, this is primarily the responsibility of the host who arranges for the conference site. On the other hand, Moore was completely new as DG, and did thus probably not have the highest process expertise in his role either (see also Wolfe 2004: 580). With 'two months into the new job [h]e didn't know what went on', commented a lead WTO official.[55] This is close to always true also for the General Council Chairperson. Given the term is only one year, Mchumo would have needed tremendous prior experience to compensate for this structural disadvantage. In short, the entire leadership can hardly be characterized as possessing abundant process expertise at this point.

With respect to content expertise, all head organizers before and during Seattle possessed at least some prior experience in trade negotiations. Moore had participated in GATT negotiations in the 1980s. Mchumo had been Trade Minister, and later ambassador for Tanzania at the UN in Geneva for years (Common Fund for Commodities 2012). Barshefsky, in particular, possessed deep content expertise as she had served as deputy and then US Trade Representative since 1993. So, as in climate negotiations, content expertise was largely present.

There is scarce data on the alignment of organizers (i.e. of the host country US and the WTO Secretariat). One study indicates that Barshefsky sought very little exchange with Moore (Odell 2005: 432). Moore himself concedes that a closer working relation of his team with General Council Chairman Mchumo would have been fruitful for Seattle (Moore 2003: 115). Moreover, some interviews nurture the suspicion that the WTO Secretariat had diverging views from how the Americans approached facilitation in Seattle. Taken together, this hints at a far from perfect cooperation between the lead organizers.

By and large, organizers in the Geneva–Doha negotiations were of higher capability, and managed to leave the chaos of Seattle behind them. With respect to the cultural and organizational-personal fit, the effect of Moore being from New Zealand and the industrialized world had faded with the passing of over two years since the succession fight. Further, developing countries seemed to be more at ease with him as it was Moore's last year in office before his Thai successor would take over. Besides, one study quotes delegates who found Moore had moved out of the US-EU corner (Jawara and Kwa 2003: 194). Overall, this allowed for a better cultural–personal fit of the DG as a person in his second ministerial. Regarding the WTO Secretariat, no organizational quarrels of the kind of the pre-Seattle year were reported for 2001.

Moreover, the origins of the General Council Chairs Bryn and Harbinson provided no reason for suspicion. Bryn's home country, Norway, had been traditionally known as a good mediator with all the required cultural-personal skills. Furthermore, Hong Kong–China is usually not accused of a developed country

55   WTO(2)-16.12.2011.

bias even though Harbinson was socialized in the former British colonial administration. On a personal level, many voices attributed abundant patience, listening skills, and sympathy for transparency and inclusiveness to Harbinson (Jawara and Kwa 2003: 74).

Finally, Qatari Conference Chairman Kamal proved to be of great cultural-personal fit for the given situation. It seems consensus to laud his 'great personality' and 'natural charm' that allowed him to effectively deal with ministers (Jawara and Kwa 2003: 90). He was further described as 'steady, humorous, [and] sharp', and that all this allowed him to play a 'central' role (Moore 2003: 128). Moreover, given his origin from the Middle East, Kamal had a vastly better position vis-à-vis developing countries than his predecessor from the US, Barshefsky.

Regarding process expertise, the organizers of Doha showed a better understanding on a number of points. In contrast to the street chaos of Seattle, the summit in Doha went on mostly undisturbed. The Qatari hosts had gone to the other extreme by prohibiting most demonstrations up-front. Unlike the Americans, they were also prepared to extend the availability of the conference venue should the summit not reach agreement before the deadline (Odell 2009: 291). They had used the experience of Seattle and other multilateral summits. In addition, they provided summit facilities lauded as superb. DG Moore described the process performance of the hosts as 'a benchmark of excellence in organization, security, and hospitality' (Moore 2003: 127).

Conference Chair Kamal was also highly held in his process expertise, to the surprise of many. One veteran negotiator found that Kamal 'proved to be very good, which no one knew before'[56] (similar: Wolfe 2004: 580). He did not push for Qatari positions as the Americans did in 1999.[57] Instead, Kamal kept himself back much more than Barshefsky. He was even regarded by one WTO veteran as a 'weak' chair.[58] One senior negotiator contradicted, perceiving him as 'firm' in his chairing style.[59] It is uncontested though that he was not as dominant as his predecessor, who irritated many delegates with the pushiness of her approach. As a result of this self-restraint, Kamal was not accused of lacking neutrality and was not put into the corner of industrialized countries (despite Qatar's wealth from the country's rich endowment with natural resources). If anything, he showed himself to be a supporter of developing countries.[60] The perception of neutrality of the trade negotiation organizers resembled the pattern at climate negotiations with scepticism towards the very proactive European Denmark and with sympathy for the more restrained Latin American Mexico.

As for the WTO, DG Moore had collected two more years of experience in his new position, greatly increasing his process expertise. 'He now knew what it

56   EU-country(1)-29.11.2011.
57   WTO(2)-16.12.2011.
58   WTO(2)-16.12.2011.
59   G-10-country(1)-15.02.2012.
60   EU-country(1)-29.11.2011.

was all about,' asserted a WTO insider close to him.[61] 2001 General Council Chair Harbinson proved equally capable in process terms. It is said that Harbinson and his predecessor Bryn enjoyed great respect among parties and contributed significantly in preparing the crucial draft text for the final ministerial declaration (Wolfe 2004: 580).[62] Overall, we can detect higher evidence of process expertise of organizers in 2000 and 2001, than in 1999.

The content expertise of organizers appeared to be overall on par with that of 1999. On the WTO side, it was probably slightly higher in 2001. Moore had gathered deep insights as DG, and General Council Chair Harbinson had been Hong Kong's ambassador to the WTO since 1994, before becoming even the DG's chief of staff after Doha (European Centre for International Political Economy 2012). Regarding the host country, Kamal had dealt with trade as minister since 1998 and was thus also familiar with the core issues (Qatari Ministry of Foreign Affairs 2012), albeit probably not as much as Barshefsky with her long experience as US Trade Representative.

Finally, there is evidence of a closer alignment of the organizers before and in Doha, than during the Seattle process. According to Moore, he and Kamal had a good relationship (Moore 2003: 128), which avoided clashes among the organizers.[63] The fact that Kamal did not take on an overly pushy approach supports this statement. It left all key organizers sufficient room to fulfil their roles. Finally, Moore describes that he was also well aligned with General Council Chairmen Bryn and later Harbinson (Moore 2003: 119). There is no evidence that would contradict the DG's perception.

In sum, the available data suggests that the overall capability of organizers was relatively higher by all indicators for the 2000 and 2001 negotiations in Geneva and Doha, compared to Geneva and Seattle in 1999. Only content expertise appeared at an equal level between both years, which is in line with the finding for climate negotiations.

How capability influenced the summit outcomes

Let us now examine to what extent we can trace decision making along the three paths identified for climate negotiations: (1) institutional effectiveness, (2) process navigation, and (3) access of the organizers to people (Figure 3.3). Regarding institutional effectiveness (path 1) the internal strife on the WTO side to choose a new DG cost precious time which would have been needed to facilitate the process. The previous comparable drafting process for the launch of the 1986 Uruguay Round had taken 18 weeks, whereas the succession quarrel left organizers and parties with a mere eight weeks before Seattle in 1999 (Odell 2009: 285). Next, the only loose cooperation between Moore, Mchumo, and

---

61   WTO(2)-16.12.2011.
62   WTO(2)-16.12.2011.
63   WTO(2)-16.12.2011.

Barshefsky as key organizers was an additional constraint for an effective facilitation. As a result, one 'key lesson from Seattle' was that they would 'have to work as one', stated Moore in hindsight (Moore 2003: 115). Accordingly, this was done decidedly differently by Moore with Mchumo's successors Bryn and Harbison before Doha.

The low capability of organizers severely undermined the smooth navigation of the process towards an agreement in Seattle (path 2). This was especially true for Conference Chair Barshefsky who did not apply situation-appropriate tools. In Seattle, Barshefsky's rude and undiplomatic chairing style reduced her authority among parties. For instance, raising pressure on delegates in Seattle, she warned that she would move negotiations to smaller circles if working groups would not make any progress. This threat to resort to opaque and exclusive venues as in the 'old GATT days' became an infamous statement cited by many (Narlikar 2004: 421; Odell 2009: 286). Her approach contrasted with the smooth chairing style of the Qatari Chairman Kamal, which helped the conference to move towards an agreement, according to a veteran negotiator.[64] It made delegates more willing to follow the Chair's suggestions and thereby allowed him a more effective steering.

The General Council Chairmen of both years also applied rather different facilitation tools. For example, their draft texts for the ministerial declaration greatly varied from the Seattle process. In 1999, the outcome of the 'lost summer' had been a late and largely bracketed text. General Council Chairman Mchumo had presented the lengthy draft of 32 pages, which was full of competing proposals, only shortly before the summit. The lack of clear leadership on the text as crucial tool to create a focal point for negotiators probably resulted from the lower process expertise of the 1999 General Council Chairman: as one study argues, his 'cautious tactic' even invited parties to insist on their demands (Odell 2009: 284, 285). In consequence, the chair was unable to show parties a zone of possible agreement, which they could slowly move to during the summit.

Learning from this mismanagement, the text for Doha had been prepared under tighter leadership by the organizers. By the summit's opening, the key elements of the draft were 'nearly finished' according to a WTO veteran. This laid the ground for much smoother negotiations for the short time available: 'The biggest difference was that we went to Doha with a great preparation.'[65] A developing country negotiator spoke in the same vein, underlining that the text seemed to be a 'fait accompli' when the Doha Ministerial started. Only 'superficial' changes in terminology were made until its adoption by the end of the summit.[66]

Regarding the match of original strategy and negotiation realities, the Seattle organizers had not prepared a sufficient plan to counter the expected massive

64   EU-country(1)-29.11.2011.
65   WTO(2)-16.12.2011.
66   ACP-country(1)-15.12.2011.

demonstrations. The failure to keep the 30,000 demonstrators to a level that still allowed delegates to continue negotiations cost nearly the entire first day (ICTSD 1999a). The 'uprising' of NGOs was considered a key factor by many participants[67] and a veteran trade negotiator found that the massive demonstrations had 'a bigger impact than on any other negotiation.'[68] Only a few voices were doubtful as to how much the protests effectively undermined agreement at the summit (Bayne 2000: 136; Wolfe 2004: 579). Yet the loss of one out of five days equals 20 per cent of the summit period, and means an enormous infringement given the multitude of complex, open questions.

In addition, the inability of the organizers to effectively handle the situation soured the tense atmosphere further. An old WTO hand reported that the chaotic process got ministers 'really fed up', who for instance waited in vain for Barshefsky and Albright to open 'Seattle'.[69] The tension from the outside turmoil was felt even more intensely through the exclusion of so many delegates from final negotiations. With abundant time on their hands, the chaotic circumstances became even more obvious to this group of delegates: 'They were occupied with protesters. They were more worried with their own survival when getting from A to B.'[70] In contrast, negotiators lauded the 'good orchestration' of the Doha conference that impacted positively on the mood of delegates.[71] Furthermore, the tranquillity of the venue allowed delegates to better navigate the summit and negotiate, while it reduced the otherwise often constructive input and pressure from civil society.[72]

As for strategic flexibility, the possibility of the need for an extra day could have been envisioned and organized by the well-resourced US government beforehand. This is especially true in light of the importance of the conference for the US and world trade. One veteran WTO official hinted at sub-optimal preparations inside the US administration.[73] Numerous participants asserted that a bit more time in Seattle may have allowed the conference to successfully reach an agreement, and not to fail completely. After all, the extra day in Doha allowed the conference to reach an agreement two years later.

Moreover, the lack of neutrality by the US hosts 'created a bad atmosphere', which many emphasized as salient factor.[74] Negotiators underlined that they would have to be able to recognize the Conference Chair as an honest broker. Otherwise, the Chair cannot gain leverage and thereby influence the progress of the summit.[75] Hence, Barshefsky's bias 'didn't help', as a veteran negotiator

67   WTO(1)-16.12.2011.
68   EU-country(1)-29.11.2011.
69   WTO(2)-16.12.2011.
70   G-10-country(1)-15.02.2012.
71   G-10-country(1)-15.02.2012.
72   WTO(2)-16.12.2011.
73   WTO(1)-16.12.2011.
74   G-10-country(1)-15.02.2012, WTO(1)-16.12.2011.
75   G-10-country(2)-16.02.2011.

asserted, stressing the importance of the chair.[76] Clinton's statement further soured the atmosphere and impinged on the willingness of developing countries for consensus on this negotiation round facilitated by the US.[77] The approach of the hosts was 'inacceptable'[78] for them.

Let us turn to the role of good access to people needed to enable facilitation and build bridges across groups (path 3). There was low cultural and organizational–personal fit and poor process expertise of the Seattle organizers. This leads to suspecting that Barshefsky, Mchumo and Moore (in his first ministerial conference as a DG) did most likely not have abundant access to a comprehensive and representative range of developed and developing country delegations. For instance, the battle of the DG's succession had severely handicapped the relations of Moore and Mchumo with many developing countries. This was not different for Barshefsky whose aforementioned attitude had put off the large majority of delegates. The access of Seattle organizers to delegations was thus at least lower than that of Kamal and Harbinson, but also of Moore in 2001. Kamal's and Harbinson's cultural-personal fit most likely opened up delegates to them, and also Moore is said to have been much better connected by 2001 (Wolfe 2004: 580). The moderate amount of data leads to suspect that the varying capability of organizers in Seattle and Doha impacted on their ability to facilitate and build bridges between dissenting delegations, which altered the chances of reaching an agreement.

To conclude, the evidence allows tracing the influence of the capability of the organizers on the likelihood of an agreement along the same three paths as for climate negotiations: institutional effectiveness, process navigation, and probably also the access to people. To be sure, less detailed material is available on these effects than for climate negotiations. Yet the accessible data of this shorter case study points in that direction.

Authority of the lead organizers

The metamorphosis of the leadership

To what extent were the lead organizers able to establish authority among negotiators? As with climate negotiations, overall trust by the large majority of key negotiators in the lead organizer in his negotiation role indicates authority here. Yet, who is the lead organizer in the case of WTO trade negotiations whose facilitation efforts parties accept or ignore?

Some see the WTO DG in this role. The higher institutionalization of trade negotiations, e.g. the regular chairing of Green Room negotiations in Geneva by the DG, makes this plausible. A senior WTO official underlines the DG's salient

---

76   EU-country(1)-29.11.2011.
77   EU-country(1)-29.11.2011, see also: Odell (2009: 286).
78   G-10-country(2)-16.02.2011.

facilitator role during the long time between Ministerial Conferences.[79] Further, the DG usually has at least one four-year term to become acquainted with the subtleties of the system. In contrast to the DG, the main responsibility of the General Council Chair to deal only with the day-to-day business in Geneva and the short, one-year term grant him little leeway.[80] However, evidence suggests that, depending on the personality and circumstances, he can make a difference before and during a summit. For example, while Mchumo did not seem to have any major role in Seattle,[81] Harbinson had a greater leverage in Doha. Nevertheless, Harbinson also remained in the background for most of the negotiations.[82] Finally comparing the DG with the Conference Chair (i.e. usually a host country minister), the latter can be influential if the summit is of heightened importance. This was the case with Qatari minister Kamal in Doha when the launch of the next trade round was at stake.[83] The same challenge and hence salience was given for Seattle with Barshefsky as Conference Chair. The strong institutional role suggests though that the DG usually has at least as much influence as the Conference Chair, as one veteran negotiator suggests,[84] which naturally varies with circumstances and personalities.

The decisive question to determine the lead organizer is what 'authority' is supposed to achieve. Following the climate analysis, the lead organizer's authority can influence parties' goodwill towards a draft text, his leeway to move negotiations forward, and the blockade potential and readiness of parties. For example, the lead organizer in a trade Ministerial Conference would propose a single negotiation text, centrally facilitate negotiations, and take decisions in key plenaries. This excludes the General Council Chair. As an ambassador of a country, he usually does not facilitate in a lead role and certainly does not preside over the meetings of ministers.[85] This is done by the host country minister as Conference Chair or the DG.[86] This leaves us with two lead organizers for the trade cases with largely equal status: the DG Moore and the Conference Chairs Barshefsky and Kamal.

Let us first turn to the Conference Chairs. From the beginning of the Seattle summit, Conference Chair Barshefsky undermined her authority in a series of instances of lacking diplomatic feel. In the first meeting that Barshefsky opened, she immediately suggested that all ambassadors should leave the room given the poor preparation of the draft text so far.[87] From now on, she expected instead to

79   WTO(2)-16.12.2011.
80   EU-country(1)-29.11.2011, WTO(1)-16.12.2011, WTO(2)-16.12.2011, ACP-country(1)-15.12.2011.
81   WTO(2)-16.12.2011.
82   G-10-country(1)-15.02.2012.
83   EU-country(1)-29.11.2011.
84   EU-country(1)-29.11.2011.
85   WTO(2)-16.12.2011.
86   WTO(2)-16.12.2011.
87   WTO(2)-16.12.2011.

have ministers providing clear political guidance. This was a blunt offence against all ambassadors constituting the vast majority of participants. It put developing countries at a disadvantage whose ministers often do not have the professional support or expertise. Consequently, a storm of applause broke out when Barshefsky's suggestion was widely rejected.[88] It demonstrated her dwindling authority among parties.

A comparable incident in a subsequent Green Room meeting aggravated this loss. She brushed aside the proposal on tariffs on services as 'absolutely useless' despite the support of several parties, according to a participant.[89] Negotiators under the leadership of the Tanzanian minister had developed the draft, who was the first to present in the Green Room. One delegate simply described her as 'not subtle enough'.[90] A senior WTO official commented that 'she irritated everybody from the first minute' and that he could 'not think of a worse performance'.[91] Subsequently, Barshefsky had lost most authority among delegates and ended up with very little support from anyone.[92]

This was in stark contrast to her successor as Chair during the Doha Ministerial Conference. With his calm and subtle approach, Qatari minister Kamal was able to acquire authority among most negotiators, assessed an 'old hand' of the system who has been in trade negotiations for 30 years.[93] Judging further from the myriad highly positive comments on the capability question, it seems fair to attribute higher acceptance of authority among delegates to him compared to Barshefsky.

Regarding the WTO DG, Moore was in charge during both summits. In Seattle, he had lost the trust of many delegations after the bitter succession fight for the DG, according to negotiators of the time (Odell 2009: 284). Given the depth of division, numerous developing countries were probably suspicious of him. Finally, the American dominance during the summit did not leave any space to Moore to substantially rebuild his authority.[94] After Seattle, conditions changed decisively over the course of two years. Moore's very different approach to negotiation management was lauded by many delegates. Besides, he enjoyed a more prominent role after the summit with only the General Council Chair next to him. The framing of the 2001 summit by some is telling of Moore's bolder presence and thereby probably also authority among delegations: he finally 'celebrated his victory' in Doha,[95] found a long time trade delegate.

In sum, none of the key organizers in Seattle enjoyed a substantial degree of trust by the large majority of key negotiators. Organizers were instead 'booed in

88   WTO(2)-16.12.2011.
89   WTO(2)-16.12.2011.
90   G-10-country(1)-15.02.2012.
91   WTO(2)-16.12.2011.
92   G-10-country(1)-15.02.2012.
93   G-10-country(1)-15.02.2012.
94   G-10-country(1)-15.02.2012.
95   G-10-country(1)-15.02.2012.

open session', as one study reports (Bayne 2000: 131, 139). In Doha, the available evidence indicates greater confidence in Moore and Kamal as lead organizing figures.

How authority influenced the summit outcomes

Let us now examine observations for the three paths that possibly connect authority and agreement also during trade negotiations: (1) parties' goodwill, (2) the lead organizers' leeway, and (3) parties' blockade potential (Figure 3.4). The low authority level of Barshefsky in Seattle undermined parties' goodwill (path 1). 'People were not willing to make a difference for her' commented a lead WTO official and compared Barshefsky to Danish Prime Minister Rasmussen at the Copenhagen climate summit.[96] In contrast, the authority of Conference Chair Kamal augmented parties' readiness for an agreement. 'He seemed to have been able to convey the seriousness of the conference and the need to agree to parties,' according to one lead delegate.[97] A developing country negotiator affirms that lacking confidence into the DG decreases the odds of an agreement, illustrating it with the efforts of current DG Lamy to gain trust through extensive travelling.[98] As an effect of lower credibility and authority it becomes more difficult for the DG to 'us[e] his good offices, to foster convergence, to isolate key issues'.[99]

Delegates also indicated the overall dynamics of path 2 for trade negotiations. A long-time negotiator stressed that host country and minister must establish 'credibility' to fulfil its facilitation role,[100] as does probably the DG. This authority, which is largely based on trust, then translates into sufficient leeway to carry out the core tasks of facilitation. Trade negotiation organizers possess varying degrees of leeway depending on the prevailing attitude towards them. One negotiator described this dependence: 'The Conference Chair can do something but negotiations only work if it is a good climate.'[101] A WTO veteran illustrated the dynamic with the different styles of the GATT organizers when closing the Uruguay Round. The Irish Peter Sutherland 'mastered' the process and was perceived as a 'very attractive and jovial figure'.[102] This high capability created trust and authority. The latter equipped him with leeway to counter blockades and take difficult decisions. Sutherland was able to push delegates into a problem-solving mode, and to rally parties around a final agreement, as an eyewitness of the day recalled.[103]

96   WTO(2)-16.12.2011.
97   G-10-country(1)-15.02.2012.
98   ACP-country(1)-15.12.2011.
99   ACP-country(1)-15.12.2011.
100   G-10-country(1)-15.02.2012.
101   G-10-country(2)-16.02.2011.
102   WTO(2)-16.12.2011.
103   WTO(1)-16.12.2011.

Finally, it is easier for parties to block progress if organizers lack wide support (path 3). In Seattle, delegates did not feel obliged to show much respect for the lead organizers, at least for Barshefsky. They saw little need to be cautious not to threaten their public image should they block progress. That was most likely different in Doha in 2001, by which time Moore and Kamal had gained the respect of most parties so that a blunt rejection of their facilitation efforts would have been politically costlier.

It needs to be emphasized that while there was sufficient material on the authority of key organizers, less evidence was available for substantiating the causal influence for these specific summits. Nevertheless, we find at least some indications that the authority of lead organizers of the trade negotiations in Seattle and Doha affected the reaching of an agreement through the paths of goodwill, leeway of the organizers, and the blockage potential of parties.

Negotiation mode

The return of constructive arguing

The negotiation mode of parties is the last factor organizers can, at least partially, influence. As described for climate negotiations, parties take on negotiation modes on a continuum between arguing (or problem-solving/integrative bargaining) and bargaining (or positional/distributive bargaining). While they exchange information on their underlying interests in arguing and look for the jointly best possible outcome, they distribute an assumed fixed set of gains and burdens by only referring to their positions when they bargain. Parties vary between the modes during negotiation phases and fora. There are limits to how much organizers can influence this negotiation mode. As in climate negotiations: when parties simply do not want any progress on an issue, they resort to bargaining, as most developing countries with regard to negotiations on the sectoral liberalization of industrial goods, for example.[104] However, organizers can convene sessions that create the setting for more arguing, or establish a process that generates mutual trust and thereby increase an open exchange, as seen for climate negotiations.

Negotiations in the run-up and during the summit in *Seattle* contained many traits of pure bargaining. Regarding the type of discourse, the key groups of parties exchanged on their contradictory positions showing little willingness to compromise (for a concise overview see Bayne 2000: 141–6). They took their respective priority issues hostage by negotiating only on the condition that their focus area would be satisfyingly dealt with first, ranging from developing countries' implementation issues to the demands of agricultural export countries for further liberalization, to name only two areas (Odell 2009: 285). This did not improve in the more secluded realm of Green Room meetings: parties repeated

104 G-10-country(2)-16.02.2011.

their statements in pure positional fashion, according to participants (*ibid.*). Their conflictive behaviour indicated a zero-sum view of the situation. Data from a key study on these negotiations qualified them as distributive negotiation strategies (*ibid.*: 283), which would fall under 'bargaining' as defined here. The evidence collected from negotiations reported in the chronology above has demonstrated this lack of concessions and the sticking to maximum positions for the major parties and issues. One insider concluded that 'there was no real negotiation' during the Seattle process (Bayne 2000: 146).

In Doha, countries behaved less conflictively and were readier to compromise (Moore 2003: 123). The US and the EU were seen to pull much more in one direction. At one point, Zoellick left a meeting and even declared that EU Trade Commissioner Lamy would speak for him.[105] The first two days though were still characterized by pure bargaining and no will to yield to the other side. The negotiation mode changed in the second half of the summit. Numerous concessions were made to developing countries to get them on board. This concern was also reflected in the organizers' text drafting: 'We bent over backwards to accommodate developing countries,' according to one WTO veteran.[106] The US, for example, made early concessions on textile and later backed down to allow a re-negotiation of anti-dumping rules and of TRIPs with regards to health. All these areas were important to developing countries. Other parties followed with concessions: Japan and the EU on agriculture, and developing countries on accepting the broad scope of the agenda (Odell 2009: 291). After intense facilitation by the DG and several ministers, India gave in at the last minute on accepting the possibility to negotiate a liberalization of investment regulations.[107] As defined above, such compromises are no proof of, but at least indicate, integrative rather than mere positional bargaining.

How negotiation modes influenced the summit outcomes

The negotiation mode seemed to have impacted on the agreement likelihood of trade negotiations along similar paths as in the climate field. It altered the extent of information exchange, the provision of facts and rationales, the breadth of issues considered, and the openness for new solutions (Figure 3.7). We start with indications for paths 1 and 2. The prevalence of arguing up to and in Doha provided more information for parties. For instance, the organizers had arranged for 'mini-ministerial' meetings of around 20 ministers preceding the massive Doha summit with over 3,000 negotiators. Their set up was similar to the Greenland and Petersberg Dialogues in climate negotiations with a comparable effect according to participants (Odell 2009: 290). The encounters built trust among negotiators. The sheltered atmosphere of this venue allowed a frank

---

105   WTO(2)-16.12.2011.
106   WTO(2)-16.12.2011.
107   G-10-country(1)-15.02.2012.

exchange on the interests underlying the positions of parties. The disclosure enhanced the understanding of each other's backgrounds to ease the reaching of a joint zone of agreement. 'I heard some say, "Well, I don't like what you are doing and don't agree, but I hadn't quite thought of it that way"', recalled one negotiator who found these meetings were necessary to reach success at all (*ibid.*).

Looking at the Seattle negotiation mode, we find evidence that the prevailing bargaining prohibited any openness for new solutions, as foreseen by path 4. No novel ideas arose as compromises that would bridge gaps between parties and across major issues. Instead, delegates retained their pre-determined views until the collapse of the meeting. Openness seems particularly important in case of new negotiation areas where the well-known principle of reciprocity is less suited than it used to be for trade in goods. The exchange of percentage points of tariffs reductions on goods during GATT negotiations was more straightforward to quantify and thus easier to bargain.[108] Yet, already the GATT contained areas where bargaining led to difficulties when searching for new solutions. The design of the dispute settlement system during the Uruguay round, for instance, was more of a public good that benefited from arguing as the joint endeavour to find the best system.[109] Negotiating tariffs on less tangible areas in Seattle such as services, intellectual property, or implementation rules for example, made positional bargaining even more prone to block progress.[110] Here, the joint development of approaches through arguing would have been even more important as their share of the trade negotiation agenda has increased.

To conclude, there is plenty of evidence from primary and secondary sources on the negotiation modes in Seattle and Doha. Over the course of these negotiations, bargaining was slowly substituted by more arguing towards the end of Doha. There is less data on the process that causally connected negotiation mode and agreement in these trade negotiations, such as on path 3. Nevertheless, all information that is available supports the climate negotiation findings.

Explanations of trade outcomes beyond negotiation management

Let us now examine explanations beyond negotiation management. To what extent do they suffice to account for the difference in outcomes of these two trade negotiations? Like the case pair on climate change, the brief period between the Seattle and Doha years suggests that structural factors are probably, by-and-large, constant. This assumption is also supported by the findings from earlier studies on these trade cases (Odell 2009: 275). I will now scrutinize these factors in more detail.

108   WTO(2)-16.12.2011: 'Tariffs [on goods] just are about bargaining. Literally, negotiations were down in 10,000s of shirts.'
109   WTO(2)-16.12.2011.
110   EU-country(1)-29.11.2011; similar: WTO(1)-16.12.2011.

Interests: Growing world trade while considering the disadvantaged

Regarding structural explanations, the interests of negotiating countries form the basis of any agreement, in climate as well as in trade negotiations (Bayne and Woolcock 2011: 21). Have these interests changed then between the Seattle and Doha years? There were no major shifts at least in the principal negotiating countries, which could have influenced the interpretation of their interests. Given their economic stake in global trade, domestic business groups frequently have a significant influence on countries' positions, especially in the US with a special process to consult business on trade issues.[111] Yet, their attitudes on trade did not change in the main trade blocs between 1999 and 2001, as shown in detail in Odell's study (Odell 2009: 276). This constant domestic factor can therefore not explain the change in outcomes. Those stakeholders affected by further liberalization knew that agriculture and service negotiations would start in 2000 anyway, so there was no incentive to change lobbying in favour (or against) new negotiations.[112] One WTO insider though suspected that the US administration, as one key player, had little interest in launching a new round with concessions that could prove detrimental domestically shortly before the Presidential election campaign of 2000.[113] Yet, Seattle would have only started a new round with first negotiations during 2000. There would have been no urgency for a US delegation to yield any substantial ground before the elections. Domestic considerations thus fall short of an explanation.

The same is true for economic interests on a global scale. In 2001, the world economy had gone into downturn. An opening of markets through a new trade round would have offered slight remedy, which opened some governments to cooperation.[114] However, already in 1999, annual benefits of US$400 billion were estimated from a deal, a number hardly negligible for most countries independent of the state of their economies (Odell 2009: 275). Thus, the fundamental economic incentive from a continuous opening of markets did not change either.[115]

But there is one political incident, which may have changed interests: the Al-Qaeda terrorist attacks on New York and the Pentagon on 11 September 2001. How far have they transformed the global political attitude towards trade? For numerous parties a successful trade summit would lend itself as a symbol of

---

111   WTO(2)-16.12.2011.

112   WTO(1)-16.12.2011.

113   WTO(1)-16.12.2011.

114   EU-country(1)-29.11.2011.

115   As in climate negotiations, massive doubts have been expressed by negotiation veterans as to how much delegations fully know the costs and benefits of comprehensive deals – an insight that would form the basis for any rational interest-rooted decision, e.g. by WTO(2)-16.12.2011 ('I have never seen such a convincing calculation on this.'), G-10-country(2)-16.02.2011 ('[The ministers] would often maybe not accept would they know the exact benefits and costs. Negotiations are not a science.'). This illustrates bounded rationality well.

functioning international cooperation despite the 'threat of terrorism',[116] and regardless of an unknown level of aggression and uncertainty.[117] In addition, many Western countries argued that poverty sows the seeds for terrorism in developing countries, which growing trade could start to counter.[118] The symbol would be even bigger with a new round launched in the Arab world, found a WTO official.[119] 'Success was imposed' by 9/11, felt one delegate.[120]

Does 9/11 then explain the launch of Doha Development Agenda? While it probably raised the willingness of some countries, it seemed to be partially an argumentative 'construct of the West', expressed a lead developing country negotiator.[121] It was reportedly used to raise the pressure on some developing countries not to object to a new round (Jawara and Kwa 2003: 117; Odell 2009: 294). Plus, developing countries had their own interests to negotiate the adjustment of imbalances from the Uruguay Round.[122] This had been their demand for many years independent of 9/11. Probably most importantly, much of the political compromise and the behind-the-scenes movement by the US and the EU had been accomplished in Geneva by the end of summer 2001, and hence prior to terrorist action (Odell 2009: 294). The intermediate draft text by General Council Chair Harbinson and DG Moore was released only two weeks after 9/11, and had been announced in July. Given the extreme complexity of the drafting and the interdependence of the positions of so many countries it is very unlikely that 9/11 substantially changed the document so fast. Finally, it is economically doubtful that any immediate, tangible impact on poverty alleviation was accepted by the mere launch of a new round.[123] In sum, 9/11 surely raised the willingness of some parties, yet it only added to a process that was already moving towards conclusion, a judgment also made later by DG Moore (Moore 2003: 130).

The only significant alteration of interests was the novel eagerness to save WTO negotiations as the forum for trade talks by reaching agreement in Doha.[124] The threat of its ongoing erosion with a further shift to bilateral and regional trade agreements loomed large. This trend would disadvantage weaker countries in bilateral negotiations with the economic superpowers. For many, only the WTO's strong institutionalization provided a reliable insurance against unilateral or regional protectionism (Odell 2009: 288). The desire to save the process is said to have added to pushing parties to compromise in the final crucial Green Room meeting. Odell (ibid.: 292) quoted one participant who spoke in the Green Room: 'Look guys, we all know this meeting has got to be a success. Another

116 EU-country(1)-29.11.2011.
117 WTO(2)-16.12.2011; similar: ACP-country(1)-15.12.2011.
118 G-10-country(1)-15.02.2012.
119 WTO(1)-16.12.2011.
120 G-10-country(1)-15.02.2012.
121 ACP-country(1)-15.12.2011.
122 ACP-country(1)-15.12.2011.
123 Along these lines see also Odell (2009: 293).
124 G-10-country(2)-16.02.2011.

breakdown would be terrible.' To this end, the scope of the proposed agreement was slightly changed to make agreement easier. General Council Chair Harbinson pushed to leave some of the fundamental problems to be resolved in future meetings.[125] The suggested outcome thereby kept the impact on the interest of countries at an acceptable level – a technique also applied by the organizers of the Copenhagen and Cancún climate negotiations.

In sum, fundamental political and economic interests remained mostly constant between Seattle and Doha, or had only a slight impact, such as 9/11, as they came too late in the process. As in climate negotiations, only the diplomatic and personal interest in sparing the multilateral trading system from another failure contributed significantly to reaching an agreement.

Power and other alternative explanations

Next to interests, we need to examine additional structural and other alternative explanations. As in climate negotiations, power is one such widely accepted variable also for trade (Woolcock 2007: 18). The *power structure* of the global trading system remained largely constant between 1999 and 2001. The US and the EU were still by far the largest trading blocs. The system could therefore be characterized as a Western hegemony, albeit with two powers, yet largely aligned in ideological trade terms. In such a set-up, one would expect an agreement if both principal players advocate for it. The US even chaired the Seattle summit and surely did not want a massive failure as host. With continuous liberalization inside the EU, the Europeans also favoured the launch of a comprehensive round. Despite this hegemonic support for a new round, the Western world was unable to ensure agreement between the participating countries in Seattle. In Doha though, agreement was reached despite a constant power structure, which can thus not explain the variation in outcomes (for a similar line of argument see Odell 2009: 275).

The use of power may, however, have influenced the outcome. Some suspect that several developing countries were nearly coerced to give their agreement in Doha by closing side deals in bilateral meetings with the bigger players, beyond the multilateral trade regime. An in-depth study details allegations of such a coercion of developing countries by the US and the EU (Jawara and Kwa 2003: ch. 6). Accordingly, they applied a mix of threats and incentives on a personal and a country level, often outside the multilateral trade agenda. Instruments were the 'blacklisting' of an ambassador, the withdrawal from bilateral preferential trade agreements and of technical assistance. Finally, it was often ministers who were said to have finally given up the positions that had long been held by their ambassadors. The authors argue that this behaviour went far beyond the accepted multilateral 'give-and-take' of such negotiations, or the normal form of side-deal.

---

125   G-10-country(1)-15.02.2012. See also Narlikar (2004: 421).

DG Moore declares rumours of 'arm-twisting' of developing country delegations a 'cruel self-serving lie' by some observers, and points at the straightforward approval of the negotiation management by developing country ministers, as quoted above (Moore 2003: 134). Given the breadth of evidence though, it seems unlikely that such strategies were not partially applied by the most powerful players. Nevertheless, the constellation of interests and power had not changed since Seattle. It would be difficult to explain why such 'carrots and sticks' were not applied in Seattle as well, and why they only worked in Doha and not two years earlier with the nearly identical set of players. In this sense, the strategic use of power can most likely not explain the difference in results between both years.

Regarding other alternative explanations, parties built on the work of the preceding negotiations of Geneva and Seattle in 1999 when they took up negotiations in early 2000.[126] They had exchanged large amounts of information in negotiations throughout 1999, which had enhanced their understanding of mutual preferences and different options. Did these insights serve as a 'stepping stone' for parties on their way to an agreement, like in climate negotiations where the Mexican Presidency built on the progress reached during the Danish Presidency?[127] It seems not as the situation was different from Copenhagen. Parties of the climate negotiations in Copenhagen had resolved many technical but also political issues, so that many substantial elements of the Cancún Agreements had been prepared. This was different in the trade cases at hand. Seattle had achieved very little, and the great political concessions to reach compromise were only reached in Doha, as were many of the more technical solutions. In this sense, there was not too much that Doha could use from Seattle, at least for the salient areas. Furthermore, all major powers had publicly committed to an agreement by proposing the Copenhagen Accord, which they felt largely bound by one year later. Such a guiding document did not exist from Seattle.

Let us briefly reiterate two final alternative explanations from the climate negotiation analysis. Regarding changes in the negotiation strategies of parties, there is no obvious data on any shift of behaviour, except for the move from bargaining to arguing. As discussed above, this can be attributed to the choice of parties *and* to the different negotiation management of the organizers. The same is true for an influence of individual negotiators that interviews and secondary sources in the literature have only indicated for the good personal relationship between Zoellick and Lamy (Moore 2003: 123; Wolfe 2004: 580). This certainly added to the outcome but mostly reflects the largely converging interest of the US and Europe in a new round. Summarizing, there is no evident alternative explanation that challenges the influence of negotiation management. The interest to save the negotiation process increases the likelihood of an agreement in a complementary way, but does not contradict the role of process.

126 G-10-country(2)-16.02.2011.
127 Cf. climate negotiations for the difference to learning.

Preliminary finding

The trade cases reveal striking similarities to the findings in climate negotiations. In both fields, negotiation management adds the missing factor in multilateral negotiations to explain the initial failure and following success of the negotiations. All four negotiation management elements correlated with the reaching of a trade agreement: transparency and inclusiveness, capability of organizers, authority of the lead organizer(s), and the negotiation modes of arguing and bargaining. Furthermore, process-tracing reveals evidence for a causal connection. The available data for the tracing is slightly limited for authority and negotiation mode. Given the much smaller scope of the trade negotiation case pair, however, it provides at least a few first solid indications that all seem to confirm the hypotheses tested in climate negotiations. So, negotiation management also played a key role in the trade regime.

This is not to forget that negotiation management alone is not sufficient to determine the outcome. The conditions of consensus-based decision making and an initial narrow overlap of interests of countries are prerequisites for it to make a decisive impact. One veteran delegate put it bluntly: 'Those that build the deal in trade are the member states. If they don't want and don't take responsibility, then nothing happens.'[128] A colleague concurs that 'Process factors can help... But however brilliant they are, if countries like the US, India, or Brazil don't want Doha progress then you can't shift this.'[129] Nevertheless, the study has shown that these interests interact with negotiation management factors. In the words of a developing country negotiator: 'There must be an overall desire for an agreement. Yet, they [interests and process] are still mutually reliant on each other.'[130] Above all, we have seen that these interests (and other structural factors) remained largely constant, and are thus necessary but not sufficient to explain the different outcomes.

Last but not least, the data-gathering showed additional trade negotiations with hints at process influence. For example, the WTO Ministerial Conference in Cancún in 2003 failed dramatically. It was meant to operationalize the issues on the agenda as a basis for closing the Doha Round. The organizers received much blame for their approach to managing the negotiations, such as Mexican Conference Chair Luis Ernesto Derbez (Narlikar 2004: 423; Odell 2005: 443). Supachai Panitchpakdi as new WTO DG was also rather inexperienced to steer the process.[131] The summit was eventually even termed '"the Copenhagen" of trade talks', referring to the negotiation management of the Danish climate Presidency in 2009.[132] Only one year later, parties made important progress and agreed on the 'July Framework' in Geneva in 2004. The key organizers had

---

128 EU-country(2)-16.02.2012.
129 EU-country(1)-29.11.2011.
130 ACP-country(1)-15.12.2011.
131 Wolfe (2004: 280, footnote 4) hints at a similarly poor performance of leadership for Cancún.
132 G-77(3)-19.07.2011.

changed, or grown in experience (like DG Supachai). Transparency and inclusiveness had been further augmented, with the inclusion of additional developing countries in the key negotiating circles. This altered 'procedural justice' had made a decisive difference, argued a focused case comparison (Albin and Young 2012: 54, 55). This case pair of Cancún and Geneva serves as an additional hint at a pattern of process influence that stretches from multiple climate talks to a series of trade negotiations, and possibly also to biosafety, which we will examine in the next chapter.

References

Albin, Cecilia, and Ariel Young. (2012) Setting the Table for Success – or Failure? Agenda Management in the WTO. *International Negotiation* 17: 37–64.

Bayne, Nicholas. (2000) Why Did Seattle Fail? Globalization and the Politics of Trade. *Government and Opposition* 35: 131–51.

Bayne, Nicholas, and Stephen Woolcock. (2011) *The New Economic Diplomacy: Decision-Making and Negotiation in International Economic Relations*. Global Finance Series. 3rd edn. Farnham: Ashgate.

Common Fund for Commodities. (2012) *Managing Director's Biography*. Amsterdam: Common Fund for Commodities. Available at www.commonfund.org/organization/the-managing-director (accessed 19 September 2012).

European Centre for International Political Economy. (2012) *Stuart Harbinson*. Brussels: European Centre for International Political Economy. Available at www.ecipe.org/people/stuart-harbinson (accessed 19 September 2012).

ICTSD. (1999a) *Bridges Daily Update* 1 December. Geneva: International Centre for Trade and Sustainable Development. Available at http://ictsd.org/i/wto/19064 (accessed 7 September 2012).

ICTSD. (1999b) *Bridges Daily Update* 2 December. Geneva: International Centre for Trade and Sustainable Development. Available at http://ictsd.org/i/wto/19087 (accessed 7 September 2012).

ICTSD. (1999c) *Bridges Daily Update* 3 December. Geneva: International Centre for Trade and Sustainable Development. Available at http://ictsd.org/i/wto/19090 (accessed 11 September 2012).

ICTSD. (1999d) Final Update: New Trade Round Postponed; Ministerial Meeting Suspended. *Bridges Daily Update* 3 December. Geneva: International Centre for Trade and Sustainable Development. Available at http://ictsd.org/i/wto/19064 (accessed 7 September 2012).

ICTSD. (1999e) Seattle Fails to Launch New Round; WTO Ministerial Negotiations Suspended. *Bridges Weekly Trade News Digest*. Geneva: International Centre for Trade and Sustainable Development. Available at http://ictsd.org/i/news/bridgesweekly/96117 (accessed 11 September 2012).

ICTSD. (2001a) *Bridges Daily Update* 10 November. Geneva: International Centre for Trade and Sustainable Development. Available at http://ictsd.org/i/wto/4566 (accessed 11 September 2012).

ICTSD. (2001b) *Bridges Daily Update* 11 November. Geneva: International Centre for Trade and Sustainable Development. Available at http://ictsd.org/i/wto/4569 (accessed 11 September 2012).

ICTSD. (2001c) *Bridges Daily Update* 12 November. Geneva: International Centre for Trade and Sustainable Development. Available at http://ictsd.org/i/wto/17142 (accessed 11 September 2012).

ICTSD. (2001d) *Bridges Daily Update* 13 November. Geneva: International Centre for Trade and Sustainable Development. Available at http://ictsd.org/i/wto/17160 (accessed 11 September 2012).

ICTSD. (2001e) *Bridges Daily Update* 14 November. Geneva: International Centre for Trade and Sustainable Development. Available at http://ictsd.org/i/wto/17178 (accessed 11 September 2012).

ICTSD. (2001f) Singapore 'Mini-Ministerial' Moves Doha Agenda Forward. *Bridges Daily Update*. Geneva: International Centre for Trade and Sustainable Development. Available at http://ictsd.org/i/news/bridgesweekly/6650 (accessed14 September 2012).

Jawara, Fatoumata, and Aileen Kwa. (2003) *Behind the Scenes at the WTO: The Real World of International Trade Negotiations*. 2nd edn. London: Zed Books.

Moore, Mike. (2003) *A World Without Walls: Freedom, Development, Free Trade and Global Governance*. Cambridge: Cambridge University Press.

Narlikar, Amrita. (2004) The Ministerial Process and Power Dynamics in the World Trade Organization: Understanding Failure from Seattle to Cancún. *New Political Economy* 9: 413–28.

Odell, John S. (2005) Chairing a WTO Negotiation. *Journal of International Economic Law* 8: 425–48.

Odell, John S. (2009) Breaking Deadlocks in International Institutional Negotiations: The WTO, Seattle, and Doha. *International Studies Quarterly* 53: 273–99.

Paulsen, Monte. (1999) New World Disorder: Beyond the Barricades, WTO Collapsed under Its Own Weight. *The Austin Chronicle* 31 December: www.austinchronicle.com/news/1999-12-31/75334.

Qatari Ministry of Foreign Affairs. (2012) *His Excellency Yousef Hussain Kamal Minister of Economy and Finance*. Doha: Ministry of Foreign Affairs. Available at http://english.mofa.gov.qa/get_gov_info.cfm?id=38 (accessed 19 September 2012).

Stiles, Kendall. (1996) Negotiating Institutional Reform: The Uruguay Round, the GATT, and the WTO. *Global Governance* 2: 119–48.

Wolfe, Robert. (2004) Crossing the River by Feeling the Stones: Where the WTO Is Going after Seattle, Doha and Cancun. *Review of International Political Economy* 11: 574–96.

Woolcock, Stephen. (2007) Theoretical Analysis for Economic Diplomacy. In *The New Economic Diplomacy: Decision-Making and Negotiation in International Economic Relations*, edited by Nicholas Bayne and Stephen Woolcock. Aldershot: Ashgate.

WTO. (1999a) *WTO Briefing Note: Ministers Start Negotiating Seattle Declaration*. Geneva: World Trade Organization.

WTO. (1999b) *WTO Briefing Note: Ministers Consider New and Revised Texts*. Geneva: World Trade Organization.

WTO. (1999c) *WTO Briefing Note: 3 December – the Final Day and What Happens Next*. Geneva: World Trade Organization.

WTO. (1999d) Director-General's Message: Seattle Ministerial Conference Must Deliver for the Poorest, Says Moore. Available at www.wto.org/english/thewto_e/minist_e/min99_e/english/about_e/02dg_e.htm (accessed 10 September, 2012).

WTO. (2001) *The Doha Ministerial: Culmination of a Two-Year Process*. Geneva: World Trade Organization.

WTO. (2012) *Understanding the WTO: The Organization; Whose WTO Is It Anyway?* Geneva: World Trade Organization.

Chapter 6

Biosafety negotiations
The rocky path to the Cartagena Protocol

So far, we have seen that negotiation management in multilateral negotiations plays significant roles in the areas of climate change and world trade. I now expose these preliminary findings to a third test: multilateral negotiations in the realm of biosafety. Similarly to climate change and trade, biosafety negotiations collapsed in Cartagena (Colombia) in 1999, before they reached a successful conclusion in 2000 in Montreal (Canada). These two rounds of negotiation serve as the third case pair. A finding that process is also a decisive factor in this field would fortify the notion that negotiation management matters in complex multilateral negotiations, irrespective of the specific sub-field (Figure 6.1). I begin by telling the story of the biosafety negotiations, before I apply the negotiation framework with its four management elements and explore alternative explanations.

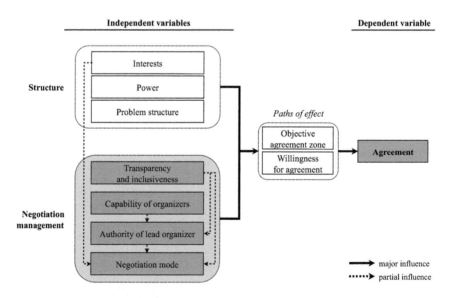

Figure 6.1 Applying the negotiation framework to biosafety negotiations

The hurricanesque Cartagena chaos and the historic agreement in Montreal

The crafting of a Protocol 'blueprint' and its Caribbean demise in 1999

In 1992, the 'Earth Summit' in Rio de Janeiro included the conservation of biodiversity as one of its key environmental goals in the final declaration. The summit adopted the Convention on Biological Diversity (CBD) whose preamble recognized nothing less than 'the importance of biological diversity for evolution and for maintaining life sustaining systems of the biosphere', and thus the foundations of human life on earth. During the 1990s, science and businesses had made significant progress in the development of living modified organisms (LMOs), also referred to as genetically modified organisms (GMOs; WHO 2012). This new trend divided countries in the ensuing negotiations. Biotechnology advocates aimed to increase agricultural yields, improve specialty chemicals, mitigate health problems, and much more. The opposing camp was more cautious about the ramifications of this novel and still unknown innovation, which potentially carried ecological and health risks (Zedan 2002: 23).

In this situation, COP-2 of the Biodiversity Convention in Jakarta, Indonesia, in 1995 provided a negotiation mandate for a Protocol to the Convention, aimed at reconciling these interests for a sustainable use. The essential issues of the negotiations already surfaced in negotiating the mandate: countries exporting LMO-based commodities wanted to ensure that the economic potential was safeguarded. For them, significant business opportunities were at stake should a restrictive regulatory regime come into place with serious hurdles to trade in LMO commodities. Especially North America had advanced far on agricultural biotechnology and countered any stiff constraints to LMO trade. They were later joined by a few economically more advanced developing countries with a strong agricultural-technological sector (La Vina 2002: 35, 41).

At the same time, importing countries in Europe and most of the developing world insisted on the precautionary principle as a safeguard against possibly great harms to the environment and human health (Falkner 2002: 5). EU delegates faced significant pressure from the European public with the first imports of LMO food from North America in the late 1990s (Bail et al. 2002a: 167). Poorer developing countries had long pushed for the protocol also for socio-economic reasons. They were afraid of threatening their agricultural foundations by the release of imported LMOs into their ecosystems, and of a seismic shift in the agricultural industry through biotechnology from 'the West' that could push entire agricultural sectors in the developing world out of business. This posed an existential risk for developing countries, which already suffered from food shortages.

Respecting both sides of the debate, delegations had to specify how LMO commodities could be traded while ensuring the recipient country would be able to take an informed decision on its permission before the organism became much more difficult to control after its release into the environment. A prior assessment of the commodity was therefore crucial to most countries, later known as the advance informed agreement procedure (AIA). After heated debates in Jakarta, the mandate not only included negotiating the transboundary movement of LMOs, but also their domestic handling and use, as demanded by developing countries. Developing countries succeeded in reaching a wide scope of the mandate including socio-economic, liability, and compensation issues (La Vina 2002: 40).

Based on this mandate, parties gathered for negotiations in the Ad Hoc Biosafety Working Group (BSWG) to begin drafting a protocol in July 1996 in Aarhus (Denmark). Veit Köster of the host country Denmark was elected as chairman and remained in this position throughout the entire process. The working group met another four times in Montreal, the seat of the Biodiversity Secretariat, over the course of two and a half years. The early meetings were marked by a broad discourse on the scope of the Protocol and general conceptual issues. Negotiations about the essential elements only started in 1998 (Falkner 2002: 3). By that time, the quickly expanding trade in LMOs, especially genetically modified agricultural commodities such as soya beans and maize, had significantly raised awareness of the talks (*ibid.*: 5). This rising economic importance and the ongoing scientific uncertainty regarding the ramifications of LMOs on biodiversity rendered negotiations more contentious (*ibid.*: 4).

The structure of the draft protocol emerged during BSWG-3 in 1997 and contained four elements, which translated into the following negotiation groups (Köster 2002: 52): Sub-Working Group 1 (SWG-1) on the regulatory regime (e.g. AIA procedure); SWG-2 on all remaining issues (e.g. handling, transport and labelling of LMOs, the clearing house mechanism); Contact Group 1 on definitions; and Contact Group 2 on financial and institutional matters. A first, vastly bracketed, protocol text was drafted. During the subsequent BSWG-4 and 5 meetings in 1998, negotiations became more adversarial. Parties ensured keeping their positions in the draft, which resulted in an astounding 450 brackets on 32 pages by the end of BSWG-5[1] (Köster 2002: 47).

A total of 138 countries convened for the BSWG-6 meeting in Cartagena, on the Caribbean coast of Colombia, from 14 to 22 February 1999, which included three days of running overtime (Köster 2002: 51). The expert working group was meant to conclude the draft text and forward it to the political summit of the Extraordinary Conference of the Parties to the Convention of Biological Diversity (ExCOP). The ExCOP was then supposed to adopt the Protocol to the Convention. A series of areas remained contested. Parallel to the four negotiation bodies, several informal groups and a 'Friends of the Chair' group were created to resolve the hardest issues (*ibid.*: 16).

On 17 February, the plenary handed over all outstanding issues to the 'Friends

1   UNEP/CBD/BSWG/6/2.

of the Chair'. In an evening stocktaking plenary, BSWG-6 Chair Köster announced that he would propose a single negotiation text as a compromise, as parties still seemed unable to agree on a joint text. Given the lack of progress, Köster eventually dared to take this controversial step on 18 February. Supported by the CBD Secretariat and several delegates, he compiled the text by 8 am (Köster 2002: 57). Mistakes and technical problems delayed its distribution until later in the afternoon. Upon its release, numerous parties complained that their positions were no longer contained in Köster's draft, and that one day was lost as the document needed major revisions due to its many errors (IISD 1999a).

Köster's effort notwithstanding, the 'Friends of the Chair' could not find a compromise when discussing the newly released draft. Entering the weekend, BSWG-6 now ran overtime, so that Juan Mayr Maldonado, Colombian Minister of the Environment and Chair of the fast-approaching ExCOP, intervened in support of the process on February 20. While existing groups continued negotiations, Mayr formed a small informal group ('Friends of the Minister') consisting only of the representatives of the three main coalitions (Miami Group, EU, and Like-Minded Group). No further delegates were allowed as observers (Bail *et al.* 2002a: 176). Mayr wanted to 'better understand the different views... [and] attempt to reach some compromise', as his adviser explained (Samper 2002: 65). The 'Friends of the Minister' negotiated for two days and nights, yet without breakthrough.

So the chair's text, corrected for mistakes, was introduced to the final BSWG-plenary at 3 pm on 22 February.[2] Deeply unsatisfied with the content and intransparent drafting process numerous countries were far from accepting the document (IISD 1999a). At this point, the exhausted Köster lost his 'instinct' as a chair for a moment and 'gavelled' his draft 'through', as he conceded (Köster 2002: 58). Observers described an ensuing 'deluge of dissatisfaction' in the plenary (IISD 1999a). 'The text was thrust down delegates' throats without any discussion', seethed a Mauritian delegate (*ibid.*). The US negotiator saw it as 'a surprise to all'. The text, which was 'acceptable to no one[,] was gavelled through posthaste' (Enright 2002: 99). A Like-Minded Group member called it 'very swift gavel work' (Nevill 2002: 151). Officially adopted by the BSWG-6, the text now served as a basis for the commencing ExCOP.

The ExCOP in Cartagena lasted from Monday 22 to Wednesday 24 February, with ministers arriving to seal the agreement on a new Protocol. In light of the stalemate, Chair Mayr encouraged a re-grouping of parties according to their interests rather than their regional grouping (Falkner 2002: 17). The major coalitions became the LMO-embracing Miami Group (e.g. US, Canada, Argentina, Chile), the Like-Minded Group containing most developing countries, the EU, the Central Eastern European Group, and the small Compromise Group of several OECD countries aiming to facilitate middle ground (e.g. South Korea,

2 UNEP/CBD/BSWG/6/L.2/Rev.2.

Mexico, Norway, Switzerland). With the deadline fast-approaching, Mayr called on a 'Group of 10' to take on the crucial unresolved areas on the first day of the ExCOP. The group consisted of a limited number of spokespersons of the newly-formed groups, while other delegates were only allowed to observe (IISD 1999a). The small group convened in the evening and negotiated nearly around the clock until the end of the conference.

The summit neared a breakdown during the night before the last day. At this point, the EU stepped in and proposed a package with 'gives' and 'takes' for all major groups: the decision on the AIA procedure for LMO commodities and on differentiated LMO documentation would be postponed (for the Miami Group), but would still be up for regulation at a later point (for the Like-Minded Group); the 'savings clause', which would have prescribed a precedence of, inter alia, the WTO trade regime over the Protocol, would be deleted (for the EU) (Falkner 2002: 18). More than 130 countries grudgingly accepted the compromise. Nevertheless, the Miami Group rejected at 4 am, despite last minute mediation efforts by Mayr and UNEP Executive Secretary Klaus Töpfer (Bail et al. 2002a: 178). The Miami Group claimed that the compromise avoided resolving essential questions, such as on LMO commodities (Falkner 2002: 18). According to them, the suggested text was merely a 'political statement' with central rules which were unclear or impossible to fulfil (Enright 2002: 101). So, the Cartagena negotiations ended without a Protocol in the final plenary on 24 February. With parties calling for a quick resumption of talks, Mayr only suspended the ExCOP to conclude a deal by no later than COP-5, in May 2000.[3]

The Viennese rebirth of the 'Cartagena' Protocol and its Montreal conclusion in 2000

After Cartagena, parties resumed consultations, first briefly in Montreal in July, and then for a longer meeting at the UN in Vienna, from 15 to 19 September 1999. They identified and started addressing those highly controversial issues that had remained unresolved at the summit (Samper 2002: 69). Eventually, three areas of primary concern crystallized during informal consultations: the application of AIA procedures to commodities (such as LMOs used for feed, food, or processing, and thus not meant for release into the environment), the relation of trade and biosafety rules, and the scope of the protocol about which LMOs to include (ibid.: 70). No tangible progress was achieved in Vienna, granted senior negotiators from the Miami Group (Enright 2002: 102) and the Compromise Group (Akasaka 2002: 202). It was useful though in clarifying the positions of countries on the remaining core issues (Mayr 2002: 225) and in attaining the political commitment for a protocol by all parties (Gupta 2000: 206). Regarding procedure, Chair Mayr managed to get all delegates to agree to

3   EM-I/1.

continue using the novel 'Group of 10' format for the central questions. Unlike in Cartagena, each of the five coalitions participating 'at the table' now had an equal number of two representatives, and the meeting continued to be open for all other delegates as observers (Samper 2002: 70).

In the aftermath of Vienna, organizers attempted to further learn about true reservation points of parties on the different issues through intense contacts up to the highest levels, as the latter could signal potential flexibility. As a result of these informal consultations, Chair Mayr sent out a compromise draft serving as a focal point for parties several weeks before the last informal session in Montreal in mid-January 2000 (Samper 2002: 71). In the meantime, the WTO summit in Seattle had collapsed in December, which raised the pressure for a successful conclusion of the next multilateral talks, which were on biosafety. At the same time, the trade summit in Seattle did not pre-empt a decision on trade in LMOs, so it was left for biosafety negotiators to decide (Mayr 2002: 225). At the informal session in Montreal, parties reacted positively to the chair's 'non-paper' and focused on the core remaining questions (Samper 2002: 73).

Negotiations continued straight into the Montreal summit. It was the resumed ExCOP, taking place from 24 to 29 January 2000, one year after Cartagena had failed. Attendance had now nearly doubled to around 750 negotiators from 133 government delegations, in addition to myriad observers and the media (Depledge 2000: 160; IISD 2000). It was still small compared to the thousands of participants in the climate or trade talks, but sufficient to turn the public spotlight onto Montreal. Mayr had been very active to ensure a 'mass presence' of environment ministers, whom he considered essential for reaching agreement (Mayr 2002: 226). After a short opening plenary on Monday, the two contact groups on LMO commodities and scope of the agreement met instantly at the nearby Delta Hotel. Organizers postponed the groups on trade and myriad other outstanding issues to focus delegates on the core areas (Samper 2002: 74). They maintained the 'Vienna setting' for these informal consultations since delegates had praised it as an appropriate blend of transparency and informality (ibid.: 72).

Unexpectedly, the groups on LMO commodities and scope (allowing only a narrow exclusion of some LMO types) made quick progress (Samper 2002: 73). As a result, the third contact group on trade-related issues had already begun their work on 25 January. Negotiations had now shifted into round-the-clock gear for the rest of the summit. On 27 January, organizers broadened the mandates of existing groups, and even established new ones, to address the remaining outstanding challenges early enough, such as the precautionary approach and socio-economic issues. These aspects were too salient for numerous countries to be left unresolved until the last hours of the ExCOP (Samper 2002: 73). Numerous environment ministers now began to support facilitation on these crucial issues of trade, the precautionary principle, and the details of LMO commodities (Falkner 2002: 21).

After significant progress had been reached in the joint negotiations of the 'Vienna setting', organizers issued a revised draft with only a few brackets left at

2am in the morning of the last day, Friday 28 January. Throughout the remaining night, delegations now met bilaterally and especially with Chair Mayr in his hotel to bridge the last differences, as Canadian and EU politicians recalled (Anderson 2002: 239; Wallström 2002: 248). In a late morning stocktaking session, Mayr informed delegates that organizers would start compiling a final compromise draft under his guidance as Chair in case parties were unable to produce a joint text (IISD 2000; Samper 2002: 74). Informal facilitation by Mayr continued during the day, especially on the precautionary approach and on the relation of the biosafety and trade regimes, with ministers trading political concessions. Results were woven into Mayr's final text, which was distributed at 7.20pm (Akasaka 2002: 205; Wallström 2002: 247).

The ensuing examples illustrate some of the key compromises (for the following see Samper 2002: 74). The transit and use of LMO commodities (for food, feed and processing) do not fall under the AIA but only under a 'lighter' procedure. Pharmaceuticals remain outside the scope of the Protocol. Both decisions were regretted by the Like-Minded Group. The ambiguous preamble entails several provisions on the relationship of the Protocol to trade rules, which as a compromise are partially even contradictory. Among others things, they state that the Protocol is on par with existing other regimes (like WTO-trade rules), which is a part formulated against the wish of the EU and the Like-Minded Group to give biosafety priority. Finally, the Protocol contains the precautionary approach as demanded by the Like-Minded Group and the EU, against the will of the Miami Group.

The final plenary began at 11:40pm on Friday, but had to be suspended only a little later. The Miami Group still fought with the EU (supported by the Like-Minded Group) over whether and how to identify and document those shipments of commodities, which potentially contain LMOs. In an attempt to resolve the deadlock, a small contact group of organizers and around ten expert delegates, who were representative of all regions, debated the risk of whether such a new regulation would disrupt transportation systems (Bail *et al.* 2002a: 184; Samper 2002: 75). They negotiated in vain from around 2 to 3am (*ibid.*: 75). The successive, heated bilateral meeting of the Miami Group and the EU brought the breakthrough on this final Gordian knot: at 4am, their negotiators eventually agreed on a compromise suggestion by the Miami Group. Countries would only need to document the possibility that LMOs are part of a shipment ('may contain'), with details to be decided by a COP in two years (Bail *et al.* 2002a; Samper 2002: 185). The Canadian Environment Minister David Anderson then needed to remove the last hurdle for the Miami Group by transgressing his delegation's original 'red line' (Anderson 2002: 242). Finally, the Like-Minded Group, excluded from this essential bilateral, had to be brought on board. They were dissatisfied with this ultimate unfair step of the process. The group nevertheless agreed reluctantly to the deal as one of their spokespersons, Tewolde Egziabher of Ethiopia, was adamantly advocating in favour of the compromise (Anderson 2002: 242). In the early morning of 29 January, the ExCOP plenary adopted the Cartagena Protocol on Biosafety.

The agreement was widely welcomed and considered a success across negotiation blocs and civil society groups (Bail et al. 2002b: 516; Gupta 2000: 224). The Cartagena Protocol on Biosafety created rules for the transboundary movement, transit, handling and use of LMOs (Article 4). Among its core provisions are the AIA procedure in combination with the precautionary principle. The operationalization of this principle in a multilateral environmental agreement signifies a global premiere (Bail et al. 2002b: 516). It grants LMO-importing countries the right to decide on allowing a LMO into its territory after it has assessed its potential consequences. For example, the export of genetically modified maize must now be notified to the government of the importing country. The Biosafety Clearing-House supports governments in this endeavour by providing information on the LMO commodity, such as on the modified maize. Combined with capacity-building, the Protocol enables especially developing countries to better control the impact of LMOs on their territories. For exporting countries, the regulations averted overly high practical hurdles to their flourishing LMO trade.

The Protocol entered into force on 11 September 2003, upon its 50th ratification.[4] Despite the non-ratification by some major exporting countries, such as Canada and the US (as a non-CBD party, the US cannot sign), the Protocol works nonetheless. It provides greater legal certainty and capacity-building for LMO-importing countries, irrespective of the ratification by the exporting country (Falkner 2009: 117).

To what extent did the collapse of Cartagena and the subsequent success in Montreal depend on the difference in negotiation management? The latter has its largest influence under two conditions, which are both given in our cases. First, the biosafety negotiations follow the consensus principle (Article 29 CBD), just like the climate change, trade and most other economic or environmental regimes of the UN. Given that regulations bind all participating states, no delegation wanted to subscribe to actions they were not prepared to undertake. This decision rule impedes the reaching of agreement in the negotiations, and thereby raises the importance of negotiation management.

Second, agreement before both summits was neither impossible nor certain. By the start of Cartagena, the rapidly expanding trade in LMO commodities had raised stakes for exporting and importing countries alike to regulate a swiftly evolving economic and ecologic reality. This need for a regulatory framework can be considered as at least a narrow overlap of interests. At the same time, the wide gaps in positions on the substance itself made an agreement highly uncertain before Cartagena.

Convergence had slightly grown by the second summit, the resumed ExCOP in Montreal in 2000. Rising public interest and the political pressure to succeed after the first breakdown served as additional motivation for parties.

4   EM-I/3.

Nevertheless, agreement could not be taken for granted. It is reported that 'many delegates gave . . . a 50:50 chance' (Falkner 2002: 20). The Miami Group lead negotiator recalled that 'many observers were predicting another impasse' (Ballhorn 2002: 112). Lead EU delegates perceived the success chances 'not better than even' (Bail *et al.* 2002a: 180). Several academic analyses concurred by finding that 'prospects for success looked bleak' (Depledge 2000: 158) and seeing a 'spectre of uncertainty' (Gupta 2000: 217). The conditions for a decisive impact of negotiation management were thus fulfilled. Let us now address the core question of which factors influenced the creation of the Protocol.

Transparency and inclusiveness

Rebuilding trust through the 'Vienna setting'

The familiar pattern of indicators determines the degree of transparency and inclusion (Figure 1.3). The set-up of small group meetings before and during Cartagena was neither transparent nor inclusive. During the Cartagena preparation, parties complained about small group exclusiveness: they did not feel represented by the four delegates drafting the text in one of the salient working groups (SWG-1 at the BSWG-3 meeting). This was different to SWG-2: which maintained an open-door policy (Falkner 2002: 11). During the BSWG-6 meeting in Cartagena, Köster used the 'Friends of the Chair' as key support for his facilitation. They were at least nominated by regional groupings and not hand-picked by the organizers as at the climate COP-15 (*ibid.*: 16). Nevertheless, the new circle did not reflect the respective regional sizes and led to a 'disproportionate representation', as many negotiators complained (IISD 1999b; Nevill 2002: 150).

Even less transparent and inclusive was the weekend meeting of the successive small group during the BSWG-overtime, the 'Friends of the Minister' with incoming ExCOP Chair Mayr. They tried to revise the chair's compromise text, which the 'Friends of the Chair' had been unable to agree on. It began as a 'closed negotiation session' with the EU, the Like-Minded Group, the Miami Group and Japan only, according to US and EU participants that conceded its lack of transparency (Bail *et al.* 2002a: 176; Enright 2002: 100). The ensuing frustration outside the small room led Mayr to open the meeting later on for the excluded groups. This process was heavily criticized in the BSWG-6 closing plenary by parties for its lack of transparency and its exclusiveness (IISD 1999a).

With the start of the ExCOP in Cartagena, Mayr aimed at enhancing small group transparency and inclusiveness (Samper 2002: 67). Mayr wanted to depart from the 'Friends of the Chair' format, which he found had 'an excluding, discriminatory connotation that leads to conflict' (Mayr 2002: 223). He introduced what was later named the 'Vienna setting' for small group meetings, which continued beyond Cartagena in the Vienna and the resumed Montreal ExCOP negotiations. Ten spokespersons represented the five coalitions, distributed according to their respective size (Samper 2002: 67).[5] Delegates were seated at a round table to 'see one other as they spoke...All those wanting to follow the negotiations could enter the room and observe for themselves the dialogue among the delegations', explained Mayr (Mayr 2002: 227). The small group remained open to delegates as observers without the right to intervene (Bail *et al.* 2002a: 177). In sum, the new small group setting was much more transparent and inclusive as everyone could follow its negotiations and all coalitions had spokespersons at the table. Yet, after years of preparations and nine days of BSWG-6 negotiations with serious shortcomings of transparency and inclusiveness, the change in process in the remaining two days was insufficient to alter the general characteristic of these negotiations on balance.

This was different for the ensuing Vienna–Montreal process. Mayr continued negotiations under the more transparent and inclusive format with the slight alteration that the five coalitions would now have two representatives each (Falkner 2002 19). The 'Vienna setting' could now start taking full effect and shape the perception of delegates with regard to the negotiation process. In addition, organizers further advanced inclusiveness in Vienna by enhancing the equal treatment of negotiation groups. During informal consultations in the 'Vienna setting', they allowed a 'random determination of interventions by the groups' by the drawing of coloured balls from a bag (Samper 2002: 70, 73). This practice continued at the Montreal ExCOP with toy teddy bears substituting the coloured balls. A seemingly minor point led to greater fairness of the speaking order and augmented the goodwill of delegates.

Only the final day and night of the Montreal ExCOP negotiations casts a shadow on small group transparency and inclusion. A mere handful of organizers, ministers, and expert negotiators participated in resolving the last contested issues during the 17 hours between the Friday morning stocktaking session and the closing plenary at 4:40am on Saturday. All the other hundreds of delegates were excluded from these negotiations and from any information about their state, except for the announcement of three postponements of the closing plenary (IISD 2000). One developing country negotiator compared the situation to that of the BSWG-6 meeting in Cartagena. He described the exclusion 'at this vital final stage' in Montreal as 'incredibly frustrating, not to say unrepresentative and undemocratic' (Nevill 2002: 146). The Canadian Environment Minister conceded that they had been 'behind closed doors the whole time', especially for the final bilateral of the Miami Group and the EU: for 'those outside, particularly those in the Like-Minded Group, it was unquestionably highly unsatisfactory to their sense of fair process' (Anderson 2002: 242).

Again, we cannot qualify the Vienna–Montreal process simplistically in one way or another. The last day was without doubt neither very transparent nor inclusive. However, that was true for each of the final days of the climate and

5   Samper recorded the following distribution: EU (1), Central and Eastern Europe (1), Compromise Group (1), Miami Group (2: one 'North', one 'South'), Like-Minded Group (5).

trade negotiations studied. Importantly though, all the other 14 days of net time of preparatory negotiations in Vienna and Montreal, and of negotiations at the resumed ExCOP followed the transparent and inclusive 'Vienna setting'. Taken together, this allows treating this second year of small group negotiations as comparatively transparent and inclusive. As negotiators themselves stated: 'Still, numerous Like-Minded Group colleagues approved of the "Vienna setting"' (e.g. Salamat 2002: 159).

After this small group analysis, let us now turn to the creation of the Protocol text itself. Parties developed the draft text largely in a bottom-up fashion during the BSWG meetings leading up to BSWG-6 in Cartagena. Throughout the five meetings Köster helped guide the process, but refrained from suggesting a single negotiation text. Instead, delegates assembled the building blocks of the protocol text (Köster 2002: 49–51), which even contained a fair amount of civil society input (Bail et al. 2002b: 514). The result of this mostly transparent and inclusive text evolution was a highly bracketed draft by the beginning of Cartagena.

With no agreement in sight towards the scheduled end of the BSWG meeting, Köster turned to compile a compromise proposal during the night from 17 to 18 February. The base was the original draft text from the beginning of Cartagena and additional elements created during BSWG-6. Numerous people participated in the drafting, such as around ten individual negotiators, who did not represent any regional group but aimed to support the chair with their expertise (Köster 2002: 58). In addition, CBD-Secretariat officials contributed by crafting text from elements that had emerged from the negotiation groups they supported. Köster with 'his' group of delegates and the Secretariat then scrutinized the respective proposals, with the chair finally deciding on their inclusion (ibid.).

Given the rather random selection of the delegates supporting Köster during that night, one can barely speak of a transparent and inclusive text drafting phase. Lead EU negotiators confirmed the lack of 'any formal consultation with the negotiating groups or the key negotiators' (Bail et al. 2002a: 175). A Jamaican delegate described that it 'was ... extremely difficult to understand how the chair arrived at the final text for submission to the ExCOP' (Fisher 2002: 125). For another developing country representative the text came 'out of the blue' since the names of the authors were unclear, as well as their regional origins (Nevill 2002: 150).

The post-Cartagena evolution of the draft text proceeded in a more transparent and inclusive manner. In Vienna, parties continued substantive discussions on the Cartagena draft. The outcomes were summarized by Chair Mayr in a 'non-paper'. This revised draft was sent out several weeks before the informal negotiations in Montreal preceding the ExCOP. This process provided parties with sufficient time to familiarize themselves with its content ahead of the next summit (Mayr 2002: 226). At the resumed summit, the text continued to be revised through the work of all groups. Mayr summed up the progress of negotiations in draft texts at 2 am and 7 pm on the last Friday, yet close to all of the key elements had been the result of negotiations in the open 'Vienna setting'.

Therefore, the text evolution in its entirety received less criticism than in the previous year.

The third element of information on the negotiation schedule and progress yields a similar picture. Especially during the hectic and chaotic last days of BSWG-6 in Cartagena, delegates heavily criticized organizers for not informing about schedule and progress. During 'overtime', the small groups of 'Friends of the Chair' around Köster were substituted by 'Friends of the Minister' of Mayr. At the same time, working groups continued negotiations, and it seems that most were fairly unenlightened about the state of the meeting as a whole.

The Montreal ExCOP stood in marked contrast. Chair Mayr paid great attention to fully informing all delegates about the negotiation schedule and progress (for the following see Mayr 2002: 227). Any changes in the schedule of working groups were announced in detail regarding the new place and time. Even consultations of the chair with a subset of countries, usually only one group, were made public to ensure full awareness of the process for all delegates. This focus on duly informing all delegates reminds of the Cancún climate negotiations' approach.

Let us now turn to the inclusiveness of the two negotiation rounds. Small group inclusiveness was already discussed above. Next, the integration of negotiation levels showed a rather low inclusion in Cartagena. Expert negotiators continued their year-long negotiations during overtime until the end of BSWG-6. In parallel, Mayr started the minister-dominated process with his 'Friends of the Minister' group. Their efforts were largely disconnected from the expert negotiations. While the minister group did not reach any suggestion and thus did not jeopardize the product of the expert negotiations, their lacking integration did also not help to use the political lever at the expert level itself. As observers noted, 'one participant characterized the competing discussions as operating in "parallel universes", colliding only while in line for fresh juices and Colombian coffee' (IISD 1999a).

For the ExCOP in Montreal, organizers aimed at a wide attendance of ministers to guarantee the political clout for last-minute compromises beyond the original mandate of delegations (Samper 2002: 72). Indeed, the summit's result was moulded more by ministers, who managed to strike the necessary final compromises (Ballhorn 2002: 114; Wallström 2002: 247). At the same time, EU negotiators and the EU Commissioner report that while ministers took the necessary political decisions in crucial bilateral meetings on the last Friday, they did not interfere with the formal negotiation process and 'left the details to the officials' (Bail et al. 2002a: 182: see also Wallström 2002: 247). In sum, negotiation levels in Montreal did not work in complete mutual isolation. Rather, the work-sharing appears more integrated with a functioning distribution of responsibilities and communication between the political and expert levels.

Data are scarce on the difference between the years for the last two elements of the analysis. We can cautiously infer from the chronology above that Mayr and his team put a slightly greater emphasis than Köster on reaching out to all countries when they deliberated compromise solutions for the deadlocked negotiations. It was they who widened the small group set up to a more inclusive format, which means a greater reach-out to countries that had been more neglected so far.[6] There exists little, but more explicit, data for the differences in communication about transparency and inclusiveness. After the anger of the final BSWG-6 hours, Mayr explicitly departed from the former negotiation scheme to transform the process. This became a recurring theme of the new organizers until the end of the Montreal ExCOP. It provided a greater sense of transparency and inclusiveness.

In sum, transparency and inclusiveness were much higher in Vienna and Montreal than in Cartagena before them. To be sure, the levels of differences varied among indicators, and the amount of available data faced certain constraints. Nevertheless, the overall picture is clear and undisputed among delegates, organizers, and observers.

How transparency and inclusiveness influenced the summit outcomes

As with climate and trade negotiations, we now turn to the question of whether we can find causal mechanisms next to mere correlation. We will follow the four paths identified for the other negotiations: process and content knowledge, contribution ability, obstruction ability and the feeling of respect (Figure 3.2). The varying process designs influenced parties' knowledge about the content and process of negotiations (path 1). ExCOP-Chair Mayr considered the change in format 'one of the major lessons learnt from this process' as it 'provide[d] a better understanding among the parties and thereby a more representative, realistic and practical agreement' (Mayr 2002: 219). An opaque process 'generates suspicion and distrust among those who have been excluded. And, as shown [at the WTO summit] in Seattle, exclusion, suspicion, and distrust are determinant factors in the failure of the negotiation process' (ibid.: 226). The 'ties of trust' among delegates contributed to reaching agreement during decision time in the last hours of the Montreal ExCOP with 'despair and stress' omnipresent (ibid.: 227). One recent study on 'Lessons Learnt' in environmental negotiations echoes that restored trust from a transparent and inclusive process was a crucial success factor of the biosafety talks (Davenport et al. 2012: 45). In addition, the emphasis on informing diligently about negotiation schedule and progress ensured a good understanding of the process for all participants, which Mayr found a 'further important part of facilitating the negotiations' (Mayr 2002: 227).

One may argue though that the maturing of issues was first required to reach agreement (Depledge 2000: 161). Yet, the fact that parties were at the end of an intense year-long negotiation process already in Cartagena speaks against the notion of insufficient information and expertise at that point. EU delegates

---

6   The use of another element of the variable (small group inclusiveness) as indicator is of course limited, as it does not fully co-vary with 'breadth of deliberation'.

confirmed such abundant knowledge in 1999: 'Issues were well known' to parties by that time (Bail *et al.* 2002a: 174). To be sure, this is difficult to measure with precision, but a year-long deep exchange on these recurring issues weakens the argument that learning was needed first by parties. Counterfactually, more transparent and inclusive negotiations in Cartagena would have accelerated mutual learning on delegates' positions and personal acquaintance to use informal contacts. The Miami Group's head negotiator described how a greater mutual familiarity of positions and people during the Montreal ExCOP was one salient factor (Ballhorn 2002: 114).

Regarding contribution ability (path 2), the new format beyond traditional UN negotiation blocs allowed the parties to ally in groups that better reflected and articulated their joint interests in negotiations in Vienna and Montreal (Mayr 2002: 222). This clear-cut advocacy for positions ensured that draft texts maximized the comprehensiveness of positions. It enhanced the ownership across parties that had all contributed to the outcome (see also Davenport *et al.* 2012: 44). Contribution was further increased by the effective integration of the numerous environment ministers in negotiations. This was held as another crucial factor in Montreal. Ministers raised the pressure on expert negotiators to progress. Their active participation allowed them to exercise their political clout to attain the final compromise (Bail *et al.* 2002a: 185; Mayr 2002: 226).

Parties in the first year did not feel treated with the respect they expected, leading to their greater aversion against an agreement (path 3). Cartagena partly failed because many countries perceived that 'they were excluded from key meetings and decisions at Cartagena', found the former G-77 Chair of the negotiations on the mandate of the Protocol in Jakarta (La Vina 2002: 43). The exclusiveness of the 'Friends of the Minister' group at the end of BSWG-6 brought 'strong criticism', as a key adviser to Mayr admitted (Samper 2002: 65). He further recalled that on the last BSWG-6 day many delegates waited with 'growing frustration' for the final plenary that was repeatedly postponed, while the small group had negotiated nearly around the clock for two days. The new format of the ExCOP then came too late to make up for the ill will that had accumulated. A US negotiator from inside the small group meetings conceded that the change to include those left out was 'so late in the day in Cartagena that it did little to promote consensus building' (Enright 2002: 100). One study agrees that given the high number of complaints about 'closed doors' Mayr's opening of the small group was 'only in the last few days of Cartagena' (Depledge 2000: 161).

The atmosphere really changed by Vienna and Montreal. One biosafety researcher reported from 40 interviews with decision-makers in Cartagena and Montreal that the negotiators only 'felt represented' with the introduction of the 'Vienna setting'. Before, a 'large number of countries and major groups' had sharply criticized the non-transparent manner of the Cartagena process (Gupta 2000: 217). The altered design was 'widely credited' with reaching agreement in Montreal, concluded the study. Further analyses yielded similar results. The new 'Vienna format' was broadly welcomed by negotiators (Depledge 2000: 161;

Falkner 2002: 19), and 'undoubtedly contributed to the wide acceptance of the final agreement', found a comprehensive study (Bail *et al.* 2002b: 514). A senior US negotiator conceded that the setting 'helped to reduce the frustration felt by many delegations over the previous lack of transparency' (Enright 2002: 100).

This is not restricted to poorer developing country delegates. The lead Swiss negotiator stated that if Switzerland was 'to be part of the contracting parties, we would not accept exclusion in any round of negotiations ever again' (Nobs 2002: 187). The delegate underlined the 'utmost importance' of the process: 'nothing can compare to the value and usefulness of the 'Vienna setting'. Its transparency and fairness to all parties had no equal' (*ibid*.: 192). A lead delegate from Central and Eastern Europe echoes that 'the 'Vienna setting' was an important step in the negotiations ... assur[ing] the equal opportunity for participation by all parties (Nechay 2002: 212).

To be sure, the Vienna setup still excluded those few countries that did not belong to any of the five groups (Ballhorn 2002: 111). Besides, disappointment grew at the Montreal ExCOP including within the groups officially represented in the small group talks. Some spokespersons exchanged less and less with the delegates they were chosen by, expressed a frustrated Like-Minded Group negotiator with regard to their Ethiopian representative Tewolde Egziabher (Nevill 2002: 152). Yet as discussed before, the new format of the 'Vienna setting' still achieved a much higher degree of inclusiveness than all previous forms. This allowed restricting access at least somewhat in the final hours given negotiators had not been left out before (similar: Davenport *et al.* 2012: 45). This study therefore concurs with one seasoned biosafety facilitator in that one 'major reason' for the success in Montreal was the more transparent and inclusive 'Vienna setting' (La Vina 2002: 43). This supports and complements research on the role of 'fair process' across disciplines.

Capability of organizers

Blending Colombian intuition with growing process intimacy

Moving to the second lever of negotiation management, what role did the capability of organizers play in the biosafety negotiations? The set-up of the principal organizers slightly differed from climate and trade. Nevertheless, the core structure was similar enough to maintain a comparable analysis across regimes. Danish official Veit Köster chaired the year-long preparative process in the BSWG towards Cartagena as it first gathered in Aarhus, Denmark, in 1996. Colombian Environment Minister Juan Mayr succeeded by the end of the Cartagena talks to chair the first ExCOP and remained in this position until the end of the process. On the UN side, Hamdallah Zedan facilitated negotiations as the Executive Secretary of the Biodiversity Secretariat in both rounds.

Similarly to climate negotiations, there was always one key political facilitator from the host country (Köster followed by Mayr), and one from the UN side.

The main difference is that the first 'round' did not have one constant chair, but ended with the ExCOP in Cartagena where Mayr took over from Köster, albeit only for the two days of the ExCOP. Given that Köster presided over negotiations from 1996 to 1999, and that Mayr joined the process so late, we may consider Köster as *de facto* head of the first 'round' of the case pair.

Last but not least, there is neither strong indication nor sufficient data to include the main officials aiding Köster and Mayr as facilitators. Köster received key support and advice from the 'extended Bureau' of the BSWG, which entailed the co-chairs he had chosen (Köster 2002: 53). Contrary to the Bureau members sent by the regions, 'Köster's co-chairs' were more independent and interested in bringing the process to a conclusion. They thereby fulfilled a function similar to that of the lead host country facilitator on the administrative level for the climate negotiations (e.g. de Alba in Cancún) and that of the General Council Chair in trade talks during the summit (e.g. Harbinson in Doha). For the ExCOP, Christián Samper was mentioned as one of Mayr's closest advisers on the administrative level during both ExCOP meetings, who had substantial previous CBD experience (Samper 2002: 63). Yet, as there are only scarce hints as to their exact roles, I will refrain from including advisers in this short assessment of the biosafety organizers, and compare Zedan, Köster and Mayr for 'round one' with Zedan and Mayr in the resumed negotiations along the well-known indicators of capability (Figure 1.4).

Veit Köster was a senior official in the Danish Environment Ministry. He served as BSWG Chair during the entire protocol negotiation process and was later named 'the architect of the protocol' by ExCOP-Chair Mayr. There was not much evidence from secondary sources on Köster's cultural-personal fit. His process and content expertise in turn seems quite high. Köster collected abundant experience (co-)chairing biosafety meetings during the Biodiversity Convention negotiations, such as one Ad Hoc Working Group during the initial CBD negotiations in 1988 to meetings at CBD COP-1 in 1994 (Köster 2002: 44).

Juan Mayr was Chair of the ExCOP in Cartagena and Montreal. Delegates from all main groups describe him as having a very high cultural and personal fit for the situation: a 'considerable charm, wit and persuasiveness and ... seemingly endless reserves of goodwill, stamina and, most of all, patience' (Nevill 2002: 152). EU lead negotiators also emphasized Mayr's charisma (Bail *et al.* 2002a: 179). His special 'dedication' to the process was underlined by the Miami Group head delegate (Ballhorn 2002: 114), as were his 'special efforts', cited as an important success factor by a Like-Minded Group delegate (Salamat 2002: 159). Analysts attribute Mayr with an 'engaging leadership style' (Depledge 2000: 161) and with the ability to work 'the empathy angle' (Davenport *et al.* 2012: 45).

His process expertise entails several facets. He was acquainted with the biosafety process, albeit only from participating as NGO representative for the preparations of the Rio 'Earth Summit' in 1992. Mayr had only been in office as Environment Minister since August 1998, and thus a mere six months before chairing the ExCOP in February 1999. He considered himself 'unfamiliar with formal United Nations operational procedures' and took on his role as a chair with 'mixed feelings' (Mayr 2002: 220). Yet, while his experience with multilateral processes was limited, he had collected experience as 'peace negotiator' and was 'accustomed to placating warring factions' (IISD 1999a). He had become familiar with good process design before when resolving local conflicts in Colombia (Mayr 2002: 222). He 'imported' the local mediation format into the biosafety negotiations as the 'Vienna setting'. So, Mayr possessed facilitation expertise, even if not in a multilateral arena. The content itself was 'quite new' to him, as he conceded (*ibid*.: 220). When negotiations resumed though, Mayr had accumulated biosafety-specific experience from the intense days of the Cartagena process. So by Montreal, he had substantial capability in all dimensions.

The Secretariat of the Convention supported the Cartagena and Montreal years of the negotiations with Hamdallah Zedan of Egypt as *Executive Secretary*. By the beginning of the crucial BSWG meeting in Cartagena, Zedan had been Executive Secretary for just a few months and never attended a BSWG-meeting in this role. He had accompanied BSWG meetings as UNEP's head of the biodiversity programme since 1996 where he also acquired high content expertise with biosafety issues. However, regarding the ins and outs of the Executive Secretary's role in process matters at heated, final BSWG-meetings, Zedan was probably at a low to medium level of expertise when compared to others holding such a position for longer. This capability naturally increased over the following year of negotiations until Montreal, so Zedan reached a higher level in this respect by 2000. Regarding the cultural–personal fit of the Executive Secretary, there are indications that Zedan was able to gain 'trust and reputation... in particular from the developing world' (Siebenhüner 2007: 270). His Egyptian origin may have contributed to this. Zedan improved the organizational fit of the CBD Secretariat as he invested a lot of energy into reforming its internal management, reported one study (*ibid*.). As this organizational endeavour most likely lasted for more than a few months, the effect of greater capability due to this change can only be counted for the resumed ExCOP at the earliest, and not for Cartagena.

The alignment between organizers gives a mixed picture during the Cartagena round. Regarding Zedan and Köster, the latter recalled a largely harmonious relationship between him as BSWG Chair and the CBD Secretariat (Köster 2002: 54). A few weeks before Cartagena, for instance, Köster met with the Secretariat to jointly outline two potential protocol texts, defining the range from a minimal to a maximal solution (*ibid*.: 57). However, in Köster's entire account of the negotiations, he does not report a single interaction with CBD Executive Secretary Zedan, which raises at least doubts about an overly intense working relationship. With respect to Mayr and Köster, their handover appeared harmonious ('my good friend Köster'), with the two deliberating on the best strategy once the BSWG had passed its work on to the ExCOP in Cartagena (Mayr 2002: 220). At the summit itself, doubts arose on a seamless cooperation. Incoming ExCOP Chair Mayr picked up informal consultations in parallel to Köster's efforts to get parties to adopt his compromise draft on the final weekend of the BSWG-6 meeting. Köster had commented on these days in nebulous terms: it 'all belongs to history now and will soon be forgotten' (Köster 2002: 58). While there are no explicit accounts that this had been due to a clash between the chairs, the set-up of parallel streams and Köster's comment raise suspicion.

With regard to the Vienna and Montreal negotiations, decent alignment between the Chair's team and the Secretariat seemed in place. When Mayr had special logistical requirements for the 'Vienna setting' at the Montreal ExCOP, for which the usual ICAO building was not fitting, the CBD Secretariat in Montreal showed 'cooperation and understanding' by providing the Delta Hotel opposite the ICAO area as an additional venue (Mayr 2002: 226). Mayr also lauded the 'dedication and support' for the process by UNEP Executive Director, Klaus Töpfer, and by the CBD Secretariat (ibid.: 228). This indicates a good working relationship between the team of the ExCOP Chair and the UN. Again though, Zedan of the CBD Secretariat is not mentioned by Mayr in his account of the two summits, and mirrors Köster's report on this point. It could imply an only loose cooperation between Mayr and Zedan.

In sum, we find evidence of high process and content expertise on Köster, while we lack evidence on his personal-cultural fit. Mayr was at low expertise regarding biosafety issues and multilateral processes (but had a rich background in general facilitation) in his first year, and had higher knowledge in the following one. He received abundant praise on the personal–cultural side. Zedan is similar to Mayr with moderate process expertise in his first year and improved expertise in the second, as well as positive mention of his personal-cultural fit. His content expertise was constantly high.

So overall, we find a high degree of process expertise when reaching an agreement, with Köster as the only exception so far. We may also state that a good personal-cultural fit came alongside the reaching of agreement, with the caveat that we know little on this about Köster as a central actor. Content expertise correlated only in the second year but not in the first one. This confirms earlier findings that content expertise is not sufficient on its own. The organizational fit of the Secretariat was higher in the second year, when agreement was attained. Finally, the alignment of organizers is uncertain given the scarce data. Evidence, though, hints at a stronger relationship in the second year of the successful summit. In short, high capability of the organizers was present, by and large, when the parties reached agreement at the biosafety negotiations.

How capability influenced the summit outcomes

On a causal level, the varying degrees of the capability of organizers may have affected the outcome along the three familiar paths of institutional effectiveness, process navigation, and people access (Figure 3.3). We find evidence for most of the mechanisms, which shows the parallel dynamics across regimes. The looser alignment leads to the assumption that institutional effectiveness was lower in the first round of negotiations (path 1). First, Zedan's managerial improvements of the Secretariat led to enhanced trust by governments in the Executive Secretary 'as leader of a well organised bureaucracy', which provided him with a greater lever in negotiations (Siebenhüner 2007: 270). It probably also helped to empower Secretariat staff to better fulfil their supporting role in the negotiations. Overall we find, albeit scarce, indication of the effect of the institution's capability on the biosafety protocol. Second, no major Copenhagen-like clashes occurred inside and between the organizing institutions. Yet the parallel small group structures, which Köster and Mayr had created in the final Cartagena negotiations, and the only loose cooperation with Zedan, undermined the efficient use of time and possibly staff motivation. To be sure though, little empirical evidence is available to substantiate these theoretically likely consequences.

Let us now turn to process navigation (path 2). Köster used his rich process and content expertise to eventually compile a chair's text in Cartagena before it was too late. Was this the most appropriate tool for the situation at hand? The possible counterfactual is that countries would have concluded the BSWG-6 closing plenary without forwarding a text to the summit. Köster's text instead provided a very helpful focal point for negotiations, as a delegate conceded (Fisher 2002: 125). ExCOP Chair Mayr also underlined that the text was an 'extremely useful way out because it helped to bring clear understanding of how the protocol could be developed positively and of its remaining gaps.' He conceived of it as important for the final success: 'Without this text it would have been extremely difficult to reach agreement on several substantive aspects' (Mayr 2002: 221). So, the creation of a chair's text was appropriate.

Highly problematic though was the 'gavelling through' of the text by Köster against wide resistance by parties in the closing plenary, as described above. Köster possessed sufficient process experience to normally refrain from such measures. He showed himself surprised about his own action and the 'loss of instinct' (Köster 2002: 58). So maybe it was a lack of personal fit to take appropriate action in such a decisive situation under utmost pressure? Either way, it caused major irritation among parties at a critical juncture of the process, and thereby heavily impeded on their readiness to reach agreement in the few remaining hours of the ExCOP.

In a similar way, the lower multilateral process expertise of Mayr possibly led to the creation of an initially exclusive circle of 'Friends of the Minister'. The resulting offence to delegations rendered this an inappropriate tool in the already heated atmosphere of deadlock during BSWG-overtime. Further, probably the minor experience in his new role inhibited Zedan from providing better support for Köster and Mayr in the navigation of the last days of Cartagena.

Finally, the key organizers of both years seemed to have been aware of the importance of neutrality for process navigation. Köster refrained from influencing the substance of negotiations by all means, describing lack of neutrality as a great risk for any chair (Köster 2002: 53, 56). He cautiously stayed at arm's length from his colleagues of the EU, and thereby successfully avoided being accused of bias. There also seems to be a general recognition for the Secretariat in its behaviour as a 'credible and balanced facilitator', with no differentiation between both years (Siebenhüner 2007: 267). Lacking neutrality did therefore not seem to be an issue.

Turning to the third path, Mayr's warm-hearted and humorous personality ensured significant people access to open delegates up for his facilitation and bridge-building (path 3). As Mayr had arrived late in the process, he could only make full use of it after Cartagena. His empathy made delegates feel at ease to openly discuss the tough questions at hand. To illustrate with a few examples from Montreal, which Mayr himself recorded: he used coloured teddy bears to determine the speaking order in the small room, which 'added a significant and much-needed note of warmth and humour'; he made all the hundreds of delegates hold hands at one time as a 'symbol of unity that helped to relax the atmosphere'; and abundant tropical flowers at the centre of the round table were meant to remind people of unity and biodiversity (Mayr 2002: 227). What appear to be small details reportedly worked to smooth the atmosphere and to broaden the access to delegates for the chair. Observers reported from conversations with numerous participants that Mayr's 'bearing' provided 'levity and hope', and even 'comic relief' (IISD 2000: 11). This style is reminiscent of the warm-hearted, humorous, and empathetic approaches of the Mexican climate negotiation facilitators de Alba and Espinosa. Finally, one analyst points to Mayr's engaging style as a chair, which instilled 'common purpose' among delegates, and was seen an additional success factor (Depledge 2000: 161). Rallying parties around a common goal serves as a critical means to build bridges between conflicting groups.

In sum, the capability of organizers affected the progress of biosafety negotiations and thereby adds another piece to the research on the role of institutions and individuals in international politics. The evidence revealed that the second year benefited above all from higher institutional effectiveness and the unique access of its organizers to people, especially by lead organizer Mayr. In contrast, the Cartagena summit carried the burden of one great mistake in process navigation by its chair Köster, when he forced the agreement upon delegates in the final BSWG plenary of expert negotiators. This led to a massive backlash for the ensuing ExCOP as high-level ministerial negotiation, which eventually broke down.

Authority of the lead organizers

Of the swift loss – and cumbersome gain – of trust

Apart from the capability of organizers, the related critical question is what degree of authority among negotiators the lead organizer was able to establish? Mirroring the previous cases, overall trust by the large majority of key negotiators in the lead organizer in his negotiation role indicates authority (Figure 1.5).

Among the organizers of the two negotiation rounds towards Cartagena and Montreal, the respective Chairs Köster and Mayr carried the heaviest burden, and are thus considered as lead organizers for this study. No accounts could be found that attributed this responsibility to the CBD Executive Secretary instead. This reflects the finding of the climate and trade negotiations with the respective host ministers as lead organizers, plus the WTO Director-General for trade, who held an equally important role owing to the deep institutionalization of the world trade system.

BSWG Chair Köster played a central role in the biosafety negotiations. As noted above, ExCOP Chair Mayr dubbed him 'architect' of the Protocol. Köster reported that he needed to excel in countless roles as 'spiritual advisor or psychologist (weeping delegates!) through being a manipulator or seducer to the other extreme of being a dictator' (Köster 2002). This required a minimum level of acceptance as delegates needed to trust him to fulfil these roles.

Nonetheless, it seems that Köster had lost this support among parties towards the end of the process. He suffered a serious blow to his authority on the final days of the pivotal BSWG Cartagena meeting. On the last official day his compromise text was released, but the number of errors required a major revision that cost one entire day of scarce negotiation time. This came combined with insufficient communication from Köster's side, noted observers: participants 'wandered around the conference centre looking for official word from the Chair' (IISD 1999a).

The parallel negotiations by incoming Chair Mayr did not fortify Köster's authority. Instead, it may have conveyed the notion that Köster was no longer in full control of proceedings. An indication for this is a comment in Köster's own summit account. He wrote that he would describe neither the events of the 'Friends of the Chair' group nor those from 19 to 22 February (with the release of 'his' text and Mayr's intervention): 'It all belongs to history now and will soon be forgotten. Moreover, the present account of the process should in no way be seen as a kind of apologia' (Köster 2002: 58). He conceded that he needed to gavel his 'draft through' in the closing plenary. By the end of the process, he did not enjoy sufficient authority, or else it would have been easier to take such a difficult decision without causing the ensuing storm of criticism.

In contrast, ExCOP Chair Mayr was widely held in high esteem, as also laid out in the capacity section, which was the base for his broad acceptance by delegates. There were more than frequent positive comments, such as 'Mayr's distinctive and skilled chairmanship' by then British Environment Minister Michael Meacher (Meacher 2002: 231), and that 'without Mayr's consistently skilful and imaginative approach in the process to the final showdown, we would not have succeeded' by EU Environment Commissioner (Wallström 2002: 244). This praise of Mayr's capability includes observers from civil society: he 'mesmerized us all' (Reifschneider 2002: 277). To illustrate with one example from the penultimate day of the Montreal ExCOP: Mayr dared and managed to have all delegates of the meeting in the 'Vienna setting' 'to stand, clasp hands, and ponder how to move the process forward' (IISD 2000). The fact that delegates across parties followed his unusual suggestion, as they had done earlier when using the coloured bears to determine the speaking order, speaks for the authority he had accumulated by then.

To be sure, data on the authority of the lead organizers are scarcer than for climate and trade negotiations. Nevertheless, the available evidence on balance still points in a distinct direction in both cases. After his initial acceptance by delegates, Köster suffered a significant loss of authority by the end of the BSWG-6 process in Cartagena. Mayr in turn was widely held in high esteem during the year of the Vienna and Montreal negotiations. Authority therefore correlated with agreement in both years.

How authority influenced the summit outcomes

Let us now examine whether the three paths, which connected authority and agreement for climate and trade negotiations, also hold for biosafety: parties' goodwill, the lead organizer's leeway, and the blockade potential of parties (Figure 3.4). What does the available evidence suggest for biosafety negotiations? The goodwill of parties in Cartagena was at the lower end anyway, and Köster's reduced authority did not help in this regard (path 1). Parties reacted very angrily, when they realized the need to broadly revise the chair's text on the last official BSWG day due to the many mistakes it contained. They may have taken it more lightly in case of a widely accepted BSWG Chair presiding over the negotiations. Or, when Köster eventually proposed to adopt the final compromise on the last day of overtime in Cartagena, parties showed very little willingness to lower their reservation points. Their loud protest against the Chair's contested decision to adopt the draft nevertheless, further indicates the low goodwill Köster was faced with at this point. Mayr in contrast was able to push parties to a compromise in the final hours of Montreal, despite the weighty concessions which each of them had to make.

Next, the chair of the biosafety negotiations could counter procedural blockade much more easily when he possessed sufficient leeway (path 2). For instance, EU lead negotiators stressed the salience of the 'political clout' ExCOP Chair Mayr held. This leeway was one of Mayr's pivotal assets to bring negotiations to a successful end in Montreal after the breakdown in Cartagena (Bail et al. 2002a: 179). Mayr was said to have been able to develop 'good working relationships with all negotiators', which was mentioned as one vital factor also by a Miami Group head delegate (Ballhorn 2002: 114). It provided him with sufficient leeway to counter blockades in the final Montreal days.

Last but not least, there was insufficient authority by Köster to deter parties from derailing a last minute compromise at the Cartagena BSWG meeting (path 3). There was no evidence that would have shown that parties were concerned about their public image in case they would not cooperate with the Chair to reach an agreement. It was decidedly not such that Köster's stainless authority pushed parties into accepting major compromises. In contrast, all available evidence on Mayr suggests the accumulation of abundant respect for him in his role as ExCOP-Chair in Montreal. It does not seem implausible that delegates at least took into consideration not to openly offend Mayr in his role as widely accepted chair by blocking last minute suggestions for compromise.

In sum, the analysis on authority during the biosafety negotiations rests on lesser available data than for the other case pairs. Nevertheless, direct and circumstantial evidence paints a picture, which is tellingly similar to climate and trade negotiations: the authority among delegates of the lead organizer affected the likelihood of an agreement. This is further empirical material that supports research that sees a salient role for chairs of negotiations.

Negotiation mode

The swift-swinging pendulum between constructive drafting and positional fighting

The last factor, which is partially open to the influence of organizers, is the nego-tiation mode of parties. The analysis follows the approach taken for the climate and trade negotiations (Figure 1.6). We start with the prelude to the Cartagena summit. As the field of biosafety used to be largely unchartered territory for most, parties adopted an arguing-mode during the initial negotiations on the mandate for a Protocol in Jakarta in 1995. A constructive atmosphere prevailed in this opening phase and for the following two years of BSWG meetings (La Vina 2002: 39). The mode transformed to positional bargaining by BSWG-4 in 1998. Options had emerged more clearly and parties had become aware of their specific, national interests. They insisted on their suggestions and left the draft mostly unchanged until the final meeting. Chair Köster describes 'a reluctance of almost every delegation to give up anything that had the slightest potential of being used as a bargaining chip at the very end' (Köster 2002: 47). The Miami Group lead negotiator concurred that parties still 'talked at, if not past, one another' at the informal consultation in Montreal in August 1998, only half a year before the expected conclusion of talks in Cartagena (Ballhorn 2002: 107).

This continued into the Cartagena BSWG meeting. The available data suggests that the negotiation mode did never significantly shift to the arguing end of the spectrum. For instance, the atmosphere between the influential Miami Group and the African Group was very tense. A lead developing country nego-tiator recalled: 'The senior US delegate, in his arrogance, blundered in and clearly expected the Africans to cave in under the force of his presence... We left the meeting furious, and it set a very negative tone at the beginning of BSWG-6' (Nevill 2002: 149).

There are some hints that delegates seemed to have moved back closer to arguing at the two-day-and-night 'Friends of the Minister' meeting on the last weekend of BSWG-6 in Cartagena. Mayr's adviser spoke of 'very frank questions and answers on the issues'. 'We spent hours... trying to understand the concerns of others in a very informal and constructive setting' (Samper 2002: 65). The US negotiator recalled an 'unfettered debate' (Enright 2002: 100), and EU delegates found that 'a real negotiation process started' only then (Bail *et al.* 2002a: 176). The frankness of the discourse seemed to have abandoned the mere exchange of positions, and thus bargaining.

Yet this does not stand up to closer inspection. Lead EU delegates contradicted such an interpretation. They recalled that the Miami Group was talking about their myriad demands for the modification of the text on a 'take-it-or-leave-it basis'. The Miami Group's spokesman allegedly 'insisted on his position and showed little interest in compromise' (Bail *et al.* 2002a: 177). The account seems plausible given that it was also the Miami Group that later rejected the proposed compromise in Cartagena as the only country grouping. Hence, while the discussion in the 'Friends of the Minister' group may have been candid, the discourse mode by the Miami Group rather indicates a positional than integrative bargaining.

Köster's controversial decision to state consensus on his draft in the final BSWG-6 plenary aggravated the adversarial climate for the remaining summit ExCOP days. Many delegations took on 'rigid' positional bargaining along their group lines, recalled a senior US negotiator (Enright 2002: 99). According to the Miami Group head negotiator, the G-77 rejected exchanging informally with the Miami Group at all in Cartagena (Ballhorn 2002: 109). At the same time, several negotiators reported that the Miami Group was adhering to all of its demands in the small group meetings under Mayr during the ExCOP (Bail *et al.* 2002a: 177; Nevill 2002: 150). Furthermore, they were said to have offered nothing in return to Africa's or the EU's offers. In any case, we cannot find indications that arguing prevailed in these last two days.

Parties seemed to have shifted to a more conciliatory tone in the ensuing Vienna and Montreal negotiations after the collapse of Cartagena, indicating more of an arguing approach. The Vienna consultations took place in such a 'much calmer and friendlier atmosphere' (Falkner 2002 19), and were 'frank exchanges among delegates' in an informal setting (Depledge 2000: 161). Mayr's key adviser described that groups had agreed to 'focus on concepts and possible solutions, instead of drafting text' (Samper 2002: 70). This implies a move towards the 'arguing' end of the spectrum of negotiation modes. A senior US negotiator supports this notion by recalling them as 'constructive' (Enright 2002: 102), as did a lead developing country delegate (Nevill 2002: 152).

Unfortunately, very limited data have been brought to light by secondary sources on the negotiation mode at the Montreal ExCOP itself. This leaves us with tentative inferences on this part of the second round. Delegates had largely negotiated in an arguing mode in the preparatory talks in Vienna. The likelihood is high that this style continued into the Montreal ExCOP. There were no incidents eroding the ambience between negotiators, so they probably arrived in Montreal prepared to maintain the spirit of the Vienna talks. One developing country negotiator confirms this continuous 'sense of accommodation' (Salamat

2002: 159). Moreover, the 'Vienna format' for a constructive discourse remained in place, which gave delegates no incentive to alter the negotiation mode granted they were in the same forum speaking to the same people. Also, Montreal suffered from no major process disruptions, which in other cases resulted in an altered negotiation mode.

The only significant change came on the long final day of the summit, when altered small group constellations and bilaterals substituted for the 'Vienna format'. However, the privacy and last-minute character of these secluded talks, often only with a few delegates and chair Mayr, could also imply arguing. It is this setting and moment, when parties, often facilitated by the chair, finally reveal extensive information on their positions to enable a compromise, such as under the minister-pairs at the Cancún climate summit and the small group meeting at the Doha trade ministerial. The extent of ground parties ceded in these last hours also indicates their willingness for compromise and an understanding of a win–win situation.

In sum, positional bargaining dominated the first round of biosafety negotiations before and during Cartagena, except for the very beginning of talks when parties were familiarizing themselves with this new area of global concern. Arguing prevailed during post-Cartagena negotiations in Vienna, and we can infer from circumstantial evidence that it continued at the Montreal ExCOP. The dominance of arguing over bargaining was therefore given when parties reached agreement in the second year.

How negotiation modes influenced the summit outcomes

I will now trace the causal connection between negotiation mode at the biosafety negotiations and the likelihood of an agreement. Due to the nature of the secondary material though, we have to collect the few available hints from the chronology above to illustrate the four paths of information exchange, provision of facts and rationales, breadth of consideration of issues, and the openness to new solutions (Figure 3.7). We start with the prelude to the Cartagena summit, which gives evidence for most paths. The arguing mode of the early years, such as during the negotiations on the mandate in Jakarta, helped parties to take first big steps towards making an agreement possible at all. The scarce knowledge about the field of biosafety of many delegates made them exchange information very openly, provided plenty of new facts for all, and led to a broad consideration of all potential issues. This allowed the parties and Chair Köster to devise the general structure of a Protocol.

The switch to positional bargaining during the Cartagena summit entailed the mere repetition of positions by parties, which Köster had already complained about during the end of the preparatory talks. At that point delegates were only eager about keeping their positions as laid down in the draft (Köster 2002: 47). By and large, this attitude blocked any of the four paths towards nearing an agreement. The recitation of well-known positions did neither provide new information and rationales, nor broaden the view for further issues and new solutions. As delegates maintained this mode during the brokering attempts by incoming Chair Mayr during the BSWG-6 overtime, it is no surprise that no compromise was reached in Cartagena.

The well-documented change to arguing in Vienna went hand in hand with greater information from delegates about their underlying interests and the provision of rationales of why they had been suggesting certain solutions for so long. One Vienna participant assured that the bolder emphasis on concepts instead of mere bargaining and the more informal setting helped to better provide facts and rationales behind the position of parties (Nevill 2002: 152). That had been the idea of Chair Juan Mayr when explaining that the informal nature of his 'Vienna setting' intended that arguments 'flow more smoothly and to concentrate the participants' energy on listening to each group's position and analysing common understandings and differences (Mayr 2002: 222).

While various voices ascertained that Vienna did not bring tangible progress in terms of 'issues resolved', negotiators comments give fair evidence that the mutual understanding, and thereby options for compromise, had increased. It served as the basis for the quick progress in the two main groups at the resumed ExCOP in Montreal. The different negotiation mode meanwhile continued to impact on negotiations, as one lead negotiator from the Like-Minded Group assured. He conceived of the less conflictive approach as one main reason for success in Montreal (Salamat 2002: 159).

In sum, we found positional bargaining when the deadlock at the Cartagena round occurred, and a greater share of arguing in the Vienna and Montreal negotiations when agreement was reached. Process-tracing has now provided indications, albeit only from secondary sources, that the four paths of influence of negotiation mode on outcome were also at work during the biosafety negotiations. It thereby adds cases to constructivist and negotiation scholarship that show the relevance of discourse and negotiation modes.

Explaining biosafety outcomes beyond negotiation management

Before reaching a conclusion on the influence of negotiation management, we must examine alternative ways of explaining the different outcomes of these biosafety negotiations. To what extent do interest and power account for the variance in outcomes between Cartagena and Montreal? Can we find other explanations, such as the role of preparatory work which facilitates agreement one year later? Let us examine these alternatives in detail now.

Interests: the promises and risks of living modified organisms

We start with a rationalist account by analysing the political economy underlying the biosafety negotiations. Biosafety involved countless interests of

developed and developing countries, as indicated for the various country groupings above. Similarly to the climate and trade cases, the crucial question is
whether these interests changed between the two negotiations rounds of
Cartagena and Montreal in 1999 and 2000. The temporal proximity of the cases
suggests that they remained largely constant, but does this hold up under closer
examination?

Which concrete interests were at stake? Benefits from LMOs in food and feed
supply, in pharmaceuticals, and in other areas promised substantial economic
gains for producing countries, but also potential upsides of greater access to nutri-
tion and enhanced health care worldwide. In consequence, those countries most
advanced in agricultural biotechnology proposed only loose regulations, as they
already enjoyed or soon expected significant new business. As this development
had rapidly picked up speed in the late 1990s, the stakes became even higher.
The exporters were united in the Miami Group of a handful of developed and
developing countries.

Against this stood the threats to the environment and human health from an
artificial intervention into the genetic pool of nature, about which science had
only scarce knowledge so far. Furthermore, a looming dominance of agricultural
biotechnology put the traditional agriculture of developing countries, which still
formed the centrepiece of the economy in many countries, at risk of redundancy.
The Like-Minded Group of most of the developing countries (except for those
more advanced in biotechnology, such as Argentina and Chile) and the EU
largely articulated those concerns on the environment, health, and economic
structures. The partial convergence of their preferences was one determining
factor in both years. It bridged the North–South divide, which had largely been
unheard of in multilateral fora so far.

So, overall, tremendous economic interests clashed with environmental and
health concerns in the biosafety talks. The emphasis naturally depended on the
respective point of view. One US official concluded that this 'is not an environmental negotiation. This is about trade' (La Vina 2002: 42). As a result, the
Miami Group consisted of a high number of foreign affairs and trade officials. How
much it was about environment for others, however, illustrated the composition
of the EU delegation with mostly 'environmental' officials (Bail et al. 2002a: 167).

The long-term and far-reaching nature of these fundamental environmental,
health and economic interests did not change within the one year between
Cartagena and Montreal. This was even true for the Miami Group, which had
blocked the Cartagena negotiations and agreed to compromise one year later.
Their most vocal proponents were Canada and the US. The Canadian government was still driven by domestic incentives not to constrain the opportunities
of its biotechnology business (Anderson 2002: 238). The country had become a
significant exporter of LMOs and was party to the Convention. The situation
was comparable in the US (although a non-party) where the general political set
up was steady for both years with the Clinton administration in power and the
biotechnology industry of continuing stellar interest to the government.

While basic interests remained largely constant, the domestic discourse to shape parties' preferences had slightly changed. In the US, the increase in civil society activities after the deadlock of trade negotiations in Seattle had raised pressure on politicians to adopt a protocol (Depledge 2000: 160; Falkner 2002 19). Polls in 1999 found '80 per cent of American consumers' in favour of labelling of LMO food, according to Mayr (2002: 224). Yet, we do not know what their share was before Cartagena. Nonetheless, several analysts suggested that the 'non-issue' of LMOs had moved further into the public consciousness in the US after Cartagena (Depledge 2000: 160; similar: Gupta 2000: 218). It is therefore conceivable that the altering public discourse lowered the resistance against the Protocol by the Miami Group. Yet, less than twelve months were most likely not sufficient to change the US position, which was also still influenced by the massive business interests.

Domestic discourse on the interests of their countries was different from the US and its allies in the other major groups. In case of the EU, the framing of 'biosafety' as a major concern by NGOs and parts of the scientific community had let European delegates take a much more proactive stance in negotiations by the late 1990s (Falkner 2009: 118). By the peak of the Protocol development in 1999 and 2000, a growing number of people in Europe had started opposing genetically modified food imports from North America. Yet, the transformation of the European discourse occurred over a longer period of time. Hence, the LMO-cautious mindset of European negotiators was already in place by Cartagena. It hardly changed further by Montreal. Finally, the interests and positions of the Like-Minded Group proved fairly constant. It had been the developing countries who had brought the concern about biosafety onto the international agenda in the first place, and maintained this stance throughout the negotiations. In sum, this constructivist reasoning helps to explain the existence of the *general* precondition for a protocol, which is also the result of an altered discourse over the 1990s. However, these preconditions did not fundamentally change between Cartagena and Montreal. As we have seen, the perception of interests stayed mostly constant for the principal negotiating groups. Thus, neither the constellation of structural interests nor discourse can explain why countries did agree in Montreal in 2000, and not earlier, or later.

Even so, while underlying interests remained constant the content of the suggested compromise text may have changed decisively by the ExCOP in Montreal. One could argue that in this case, pay-offs on the constant interests of parties would then have altered and could explain the different behaviour. For example, one lead US negotiator portrayed the objection in Cartagena as mainly based on the failure to regulate one core question of the agreement: the AIA procedure for LMO commodities (Enright 2002: 101). Yet, the Montreal ExCOP also postponed some key details related to this question: the final compromise prescribed that a later COP would decide on the precise regulation of the AIA procedure. In this respect, one pivotal issue for the US still remained fairly vague, so pay-offs for the Miami Group did not change on this point. The same holds for the second argument that only the 'imprecise' wording enabled the break-through in Montreal (citing Aarti Gupta: Siebenhüner 2007: 266). As illustrated by the climate and trade cases, 'ambiguity' is a traditional compromise tool in multilateral negotiations. Nothing could have stopped parties from resorting to this technique earlier in Cartagena, had they chosen to do so. Finally, similarly to climate and trade negotiations, many parties were very unsure about the exact consequences of biosafety and its proposed regulations for their countries. The lack of capacity, especially of the poorer developing countries, rendered this task nearly impossible (Muller 2002: 140). As a result, delegations hardly knew to what extent a proposal was objectively more in the interest of their countries from one year to another. Given the high similarity between the Cartagena and Montreal proposals, the change in positions based on the realization of very different pay-offs is barely conceivable. In sum, the change in outcome was not owed to a better match of the proposed agreement with the interests of countries.

Let us finally turn to one changed interest, known from the climate and trade analysis: most delegations were keen to preserve biosafety negotiations by avoiding another spectacular collapse. As with the infamous breakdowns of the climate and trade talks in Copenhagen and Seattle, the deadlock of the summit in Cartagena was echoed in global media (Falkner 2002: 18). It brought the so far technical topic into the international spotlight and raised pressure on governments to succeed, as myriad lead negotiators and organizers asserted, such as from China, the EU, and Switzerland (Bail et al. 2002a: 185; Lijie 2002: 160; Mayr 2002: 225; Nobs 2002: 190). The Miami Group's head of delegation described how countries had 'only one' more chance to reach an agreement after the Cartagena 'wake-up call' (Ballhorn 2002: 113). The collapse of the WTO trade summit in Seattle only weeks before the Montreal ExCOP accelerated this dynamic[7] (Bail et al. 2002a: 180; Salamat 2002: 159). Many delegations strove to demonstrate that multilateralism can successfully address critical issues of globalization (Falkner 2009: 119).

Lead delegates and ministers emphasized that the political costs would now be too high for one country to block a deal (Muller 2002: 142: Wallström 2002: 248). As the Miami Group had been isolated in its rejection of the compromise proposal during Cartagena's last night, it had received much blame for blocking the agreement (Depledge 2000: 158; Mayr 2002: 223–4). A developing country negotiator concurs that the 'avalanche of criticism, particularly of the Miami Group' weakened their position (Salamat 2002: 159). EU negotiators concurred in the interpretation of 'public pressure' on the Miami Group (Bail et al. 2002a: 181). The group did probably not want to repeat this situation, especially as many had blamed the US already for the WTO failure in Seattle. Taken together, this enhanced interest of delegates in reaching an agreement impacted on the second round.

7   There, Miami Group members had tried to bring the transboundary movement of LMOs under the WTO roof, according to EU negotiators.

In sum, fundamental interests remained constant during both years and can therefore not explain the different outcomes. Moreover, the suggested outcomes were also fairly comparable, and did thus not better match the interests of countries in one year or another. The only clear novel interest was to avoid a second spectacular collapse, with the world watching.

Power and other alternative explanations

To what extent had power structures altered between the Cartagena in February 1999 and Montreal in January 2000 to explain the difference in outcome? Starting with the most powerful players, the US as largest producer of LMO crops participated as part of the Miami Group (even as a non-party to the CBD parent agreement), jointly with the other large agricultural producers (Ballhorn 2002: 106). Economically, the EU was even bigger than the US in GDP terms. The developing world in turn suffered from the segregation of some of their more advanced economies that sided with the Miami Group. Yet this split, which had led to the creation of the Like-Minded Group, had already occurred seven months before the Cartagena summit, in July 1998. It thus influenced the dynamics of both negotiation rounds. The economic power fundamentals of the key country groupings did therefore not change. A constant power structure with unaltered preferences of the mightiest players though is unable to explain a variance in outcome. Moreover, the result of Montreal even ran contrary to realist thinking, as the wishes of the US as political–economic hegemon of the late 1990s. In the end, the US was unable to inhibit the Protocol, or at least to significantly weaken its substance (Falkner 2009: 114). This speaks against hegemonic theory which would have expected the most powerful country to enforce its main interests.

Maybe the use of power by the dominating delegations had changed? A seasoned developing country negotiator described how pressure was exercised by 'big powers' on developing states, using means such as high-level political channels circumventing the official negotiation forum, bilateral incentives including beyond biodiversity, and even direct personal pressure by discrediting individual delegates (Muller 2002: 142). A lot speaks for this account to be at least partially true as we find the same allegations for climate and trade negotiations from numerous other sources. Nonetheless, it remains doubtful that these uses of power made the difference. If interests and power structures were steady, why should power-based means have worked in Montreal, and not already in Cartagena?

One additional alternative explanation was the work accomplished in Cartagena, which had a stepping stone effect. The Miami Group head delegate described how they were able to build on those concepts in Montreal, which they had developed for 'all the main and secondary issues' during the Cartagena negotiations (Ballhorn 2002: 114). This preparation was a stepping stone for the successive round of negotiations. However, the mere fact that delegations had thought through issues before and prepared propositions in a more profound way did not render an agreement a 'fait accompli'. Similarly to climate and unlike the trade negotiations, there was at least a rough 'blueprint' for an agreement from Cartagena, in which the core structure of the Protocol had been laid out already. In this way, Köster's draft text from Cartagena continued to serve as focal point and base for further negotiations (Mayr 2002: 224; Wallström 2002: 247). Yet, as Cartagena had shown, the mere existence of his text at the outset of the ExCOP did not inhibit the collapse of the summit. Further, the adoption of the text in Montreal was still all but certain, as illustrated by the chronology above. In other words, work from preceding negotiation as such was not a sufficient or necessary condition, but nevertheless increased the chances of agreement.

Another explanation could be the changed negotiation strategy by country groupings. The account of a senior US negotiator described how the Miami Group reached out to the Like-Minded Group after Cartagena during 1999 to find common ground before the next ExCOP (Enright 2002: 102–4). This included a meeting of both groups in Ethiopia. Accordingly, the visit improved the mutual understanding of interests, helped to build personal relations, and generated ideas for solutions. Taken together, it allegedly facilitated negotiations on contested central issues like the information requirements for LMO commodities and the scope of the Protocol at the Montreal ExCOP. The Canadian top negotiator shared this view (Ballhorn 2002: 110).

Yet accounts of the other major groups contradicted this perspective by Miami Group delegates. The spokesperson of the Like-Minded Group from Ethiopia, who had invited the Miami Group to Africa, linked the Montreal breakthrough more to the 'negative public reaction in North America against the Miami Group's blatant disregard of human and environmental safety', which 'weakened its stance substantially' (Egziabher 2002: 117). A glimpse of the anger of the Like-Minded Group about US negotiation behaviour is still visible in hindsight, when its chairman commented that the US 'was foolishly given the undeserved right to take part in negotiating the biosafety protocol, even though it did not intend to be a party to it' (ibid.: 119). Another developing country negotiator also portrays the negotiating camps differently from the Miami Group's (but also from her chairman's) interpretation: industrialized countries bridged their differences and left 'developing countries to fend for themselves' in the end (Muller 2002: 145). This last perception however is contradicted by a fellow Like-Minded Group negotiator who saw their Group opposing the Miami Group jointly with the EU (Salamat 2002: 156), a view overall shared by lead EU negotiators (Bail et al. 2002a: 181–2).

The varying evidence renders it difficult to arrive at a broadly accepted interpretation, and to identify with confidence altered strategies of alliance building after Cartagena. If anything, there is a slight tendency to see the EU and the Like-Minded Group in one camp, based on their common preference for a more robust protocol. One could therefore also trace the eventual adoption back to their influence as a united group of middle-power countries, which pushed for the further evolution of the regime (a 'k-group' under liberal theory; Falkner 2009: 116). However, EU–developing country proximity had not significantly altered between Cartagena and Montreal. The continuity in alliance building can thus barely account for the difference in outcomes.

Finally, some participants described a variance in negotiation behaviour by the Compromise Group. This small group had formed by the end of the Cartagena negotiations and comprised OECD countries outside the 'big groups' (cf. the chronology outlined in 'The hurricaneseque Cartagena chaos and the historic agreement in Montreal' earlier in this chapter). EU negotiators found that they had become a 'major player' due to their facilitative efforts during the Vienna meeting in 1999 (Bail *et al.* 2002a: 179). By the Montreal ExCOP they played a 'pivotal role', added a Like-Minded Group negotiator (Salamat 2002: 156). Their facilitation created mutual understanding and a middle ground. They centrally aided Mayr, for example, to draft his compromise 'non-paper' before the Montreal ExCOP, which included verbatim parts of their suggestion on the vital issue of LMO commodities (Ivars 2002 198). They also contributed to the vital last-minute compromise on LMO commodities during the final night (Akasaka 2002: 206). Chair Mayr recalled that the group 'propose[d] ingenious ways to overcome difficult moments in the meetings held after Cartagena' (Mayr 2002: 223). In sum, the Compromise Group was the only coalition which was newly formed for the 'second round' of negotiation in Vienna and Montreal. A variety of sources suggests that this novel actor played a very helpful role in reaching the final compromise.

To conclude, the structure and uses of power are unable to account for the different results as they were largely steady during 1999 and 2000. The non-structural factor of the availability of the previous work of the Cartagena summit increases the likelihood of agreement, although it is not sufficient as Köster's draft text was already in the hands of delegates when the first ExCOP collapsed. Only the Compromise Group appearance as a new actor on the scene in Vienna and Montreal convincingly accounts for some of the difference, and complements the influence of negotiation management.

Preliminary finding

The biosafety negotiations revealed the same dynamics as for climate and trade talks. The negotiation framework has thus held in a third regime of world politics. This strengthens the confidence that negotiation management can make a decisive difference in international relations. Several studies provided abundant material with first-hand accounts of participants, particularly the volume edited by Bail, Falkner and Marquard (*The Cartagena Protocol on Biosafety*, Earthscan, 2002). Further, the available evidence uncovered parallels to climate and trade that go as far as nearly verbatim quotes on how a specific negotiation management factor increased the probability of the Cartagena Protocol. The data therefore sufficiently supports the third case and its conclusions.

To briefly recap what we have seen in detail for the biosafety talks: organizers significantly increased the transparency and inclusiveness of the process with the 'Vienna setting' format in the second year; the capability of the organizers showed rich process expertise in the second year, and a high personal-cultural fit of ExCOP Chair Mayr, though overall there was less dissimilarity between Cartagena and Montreal than in the trade and climate cases; further, Mayr enjoyed greater authority among parties than Köster, especially towards the decisive end of the resumed round; and arguing had a much larger share over bargaining during the Vienna and Montreal meetings. While negotiation management changed between the years, structural factors of interest and power, again, were largely constant. The fear of another failure though, and surge of the novel facilitating actor of the Compromise Group also accelerated the dynamic towards agreement.

The Cartagena Protocol of 2000 was, of course, only a first step on the long way to an efficient global regime of biosafety. Yet, it marked an important beginning, which pioneered salient innovations in international environmental regulation, such as the concrete application of the precautionary principle. Similarly to climate change and trade though, implementation remains a core challenge for the arduously negotiated regulations. As for biosafety, 164 countries had signed up to the Cartagena Protocol by 2012. Members have developed new regulations on response measures in the case of damages from LMOs under the supplementary Nagoya Protocol of 2010. Generally speaking, implementation for biosafety is on a promising course.

To conclude, the two rounds of the Biosafety Protocol negotiations with their summits in Cartagena and Montreal harden the case that negotiation management alters the probability of a successful conclusion. Moreover, it can even make the decisive difference in regime building, when interests only narrowly overlap in the beginning and negotiations require consensus. The outcome casts substantial doubts on the singular use of structural theories on interests and power, at least as far as they would aim at explaining short- to mid-term developments as such a sequence of negotiations. Pivotal elements of this finding are reflected in the words of ExCOP Chair Mayr:

> Global negotiations...need to be undertaken in a transparent and participative manner and sometimes require innovative techniques of negotiation. I hope the small innovations made in Montreal on this manner will flourish during the twenty-first century and help achieve...multilateral agreements.
>
> (Mayr 2002: 228)

References

Akasaka, Kiyo. (2002) Compromise Group: Japan. In *The Cartagena Protocol on Biosafety: Reconciling Trade in Biotechnology with Environment and Development*, edited by Christoph Bail, Robert Falkner and Helen Marquard. London: Earthscan.

Anderson, David. (2002) Environment Ministers: Canada. In *The Cartagena Protocol on Biosafety: Reconciling Trade in Biotechnology with Environment and Development*, edited by Christoph Bail, Robert Falkner and Helen Marquard. London: Earthscan.

Bail, Christoph, Jean Paul Decaestecker and Matthias Jørgensen. (2002a) European Union. In *The Cartagena Protocol on Biosafety: Reconciling Trade in Biotechnology with Environment and Development*, edited by Christoph Bail, Robert Falkner and Helen Marquard. London: Earthscan.

Bail, Christoph, Robert Falkner and Helen Marquard. (2002b) Conclusion. In *The Cartagena Protocol on Biosafety: Reconciling Trade in Biotechnology with Environment and Development*, edited by Christoph Bail, Robert Falkner and Helen Marquard. London: Earthscan.

Ballhorn, Richard. (2002) Miami Group: Canada. In *The Cartagena Protocol on Biosafety: Reconciling Trade in Biotechnology with Environment and Development*, edited by Christoph Bail, Robert Falkner and Helen Marquard. London: Earthscan.

Davenport, Deborah, Lynn M. Wagner and Chris Spence. (2012) Earth Negotiations on a Comfy Couch: Building Negotiator Trust through Innovative Processes. In *The Roads from Rio: Lessons Learned from Twenty Years of Multilateral Environmental Negotiations*, edited by Pamela S. Chasek and Lynn M. Wagner. Abingdon: Routledge.

Depledge, Joanna. (2000) Rising from the Ashes: The Cartagena Protocol on Biosafety. *Environmental Politics* 9: 156–62.

Egziabher, Tewolde B. G. (2002) Like-Minded Group: Ethiopia. In *The Cartagena Protocol on Biosafety: Reconciling Trade in Biotechnology with Environment and Development*, edited by Christoph Bail, Robert Falkner and Helen Marquard. London: Earthscan.

Enright, Cathleen A. (2002) Miami Group: United States. In *The Cartagena Protocol on Biosafety: Reconciling Trade in Biotechnology with Environment and Development*, edited by Christoph Bail, Robert Falkner and Helen Marquard. London: Earthscan.

Falkner, Robert. (2002) Negotiating the Biosafety Protocol: The International Process. In *The Cartagena Protocol on Biosafety: Reconciling Trade in Biotechnology with Environment and Development*, edited by Christoph Bail, Robert Falkner and Helen Marquard. London: Earthscan.

Falkner, Robert. (2009) The Global Politics of Precaution: Explaining International Cooperation on Biosafety. In *Cooperating without America: Theories and Case Studies of Non-Hegemonic Regimes*, edited by Stefan Brem and Kendall W. Stiles. Abingdon: Routledge.

Fisher, Elaine. (2002) Like-Minded Group: Jamaica. In *The Cartagena Protocol on Biosafety: Reconciling Trade in Biotechnology with Environment and Development*, edited by Christoph Bail, Robert Falkner and Helen Marquard. London: Earthscan.

Gupta, Aarti. (2000) Creating a Global Biosafety Regime. *International Journal of Biotechnology* 2: 205–30.

IISD. (1999a) Highlights from BSWG-6 and the First Extraordinary COP of the CBD, Monday, 22 February 1999. *Earth Negotiations Bulletin* 9(116).

IISD. (1999b) Highlights from the Sixth Session of the BSWG-6, Thursday, 17 February 1999. *Earth Negotiations Bulletin* 9(113).

IISD. (2000) Report of the Resumed Session of the Extraordinary Meeting of the Conference of the Parties for the Adoption of the Protocol on Biosafety to the Convention on Biological Diversity. *Earth Negotiations Bulletin* 9(137).

Ivars, Birthe. (2002) Compromise Group: Norway. In *The Cartagena Protocol on Biosafety:*

Reconciling Trade in Biotechnology with Environment and Development, edited by Christoph Bail, Robert Falkner and Helen Marquard. London: Earthscan.

Köster, Veit. (2002) The Biosafety Working Group (BSWG) Process: A Personal Account from the Chair. In *The Cartagena Protocol on Biosafety: Reconciling Trade in Biotechnology with Environment and Development*, edited by Christoph Bail, Robert Falkner and Helen Marquard. London: Earthscan.

La Vina, Antonio G. M. (2002) A Mandate for a Biosafety Protocol. In *The Cartagena Protocol on Biosafety: Reconciling Trade in Biotechnology with Environment and Development*, edited by Christoph Bail, Robert Falkner and Helen Marquard. London: Earthscan.

Lijie, Cai. (2002) Like-Minded Group: China. In *The Cartagena Protocol on Biosafety: Reconciling Trade in Biotechnology with Environment and Development*, edited by Christoph Bail, Robert Falkner and Helen Marquard. London: Earthscan.

Mayr, Juan. (2002) Environment Ministers: Colombia. In *The Cartagena Protocol on Biosafety: Reconciling Trade in Biotechnology with Environment and Development*, edited by Christoph Bail, Robert Falkner and Helen Marquard. London: Earthscan.

Meacher, Michael. (2002) Environment Ministers: United Kingdom. In *The Cartagena Protocol on Biosafety: Reconciling Trade in Biotechnology with Environment and Development*, edited by Christoph Bail, Robert Falkner and Helen Marquard. London: Earthscan.

Muller, Bernarditas C. (2002) Like-Minded Group: Philippines. In *The Cartagena Protocol on Biosafety: Reconciling Trade in Biotechnology with Environment and Development*, edited by Christoph Bail, Robert Falkner and Helen Marquard. London: Earthscan.

Nechay, Gábor. (2002) Central and Eastern Europe. In *The Cartagena Protocol on Biosafety: Reconciling Trade in Biotechnology with Environment and Development*, edited by Christoph Bail, Robert Falkner and Helen Marquard. London: Earthscan.

Nevill, John. (2002) Like-Minded Group: Seychelles. In *The Cartagena Protocol on Biosafety: Reconciling Trade in Biotechnology with Environment and Development*, edited by Christoph Bail, Robert Falkner and Helen Marquard. London: Earthscan.

Nobs, Beat. (2002) Compromise Group: Switzerland. In *The Cartagena Protocol on Biosafety: Reconciling Trade in Biotechnology with Environment and Development*, edited by Christoph Bail, Robert Falkner and Helen Marquard. London: Earthscan.

Reifschneider, Laura M. (2002) Industry: Global Industry Coalition. In *The Cartagena Protocol on Biosafety: Reconciling Trade in Biotechnology with Environment and Development*, edited by Christoph Bail, Robert Falkner and Helen Marquard. London: Earthscan.

Salamat, Mohammad Reza. (2002) Like-Minded Group: Iran. In *The Cartagena Protocol on Biosafety: Reconciling Trade in Biotechnology with Environment and Development*, edited by Christoph Bail, Robert Falkner and Helen Marquard. London: Earthscan.

Samper, Christián. (2002) The Extraordinary Meeting of the Conference of the Parties. In *The Cartagena Protocol on Biosafety: Reconciling Trade in Biotechnology with Environment and Development*, edited by Christoph Bail, Robert Falkner and Helen Marquard. London: Earthscan.

Siebenhüner, Bernd. (2007) Administrator of Global Biodiversity: The Secretariat of the Convention on Biological Diversity. *Biodiversity and Conservation* 16: 259–74.

Wallström, Margot. (2002) Environment Ministers: European Commission. In *The Cartagena Protocol on Biosafety: Reconciling Trade in Biotechnology with Environment and Development*, edited by Christoph Bail, Robert Falkner and Helen Marquard. London: Earthscan.

WHO. (2012) *20 Questions on Genetically Modified Foods*. New York: World Health Organization.

Zedan, Hamdallah. (2002) The Road to the Biosafety Protocol. In *The Cartagena Protocol on Biosafety: Reconciling Trade in Biotechnology with Environment and Development*, edited by Christoph Bail, Robert Falkner and Helen Marquard. London: Earthscan.

Chapter 7

Conclusion

We began by asking whether (and, if so, how) negotiation management influences the outcome of multilateral negotiations, a question to which we now have a robust answer: there is a 'power of process' which can make a decisive difference to the ability to reach global cooperation. Coming to the end of this book, the summary of the key negotiation dynamics of the climate, trade and biosafety cases may provide useful policy insights for the organizers of future negotiations. Based on this account, two questions guide the synthesis of the academic findings in the following section:

- What have we learnt to answer the initial questions posed by this book?
- What is its contribution to the theory of international relations?

I will finally suggest how future research could take this work forward.

Policy insights for the organizers of future negotiations

There are astonishing parallels between the impact of negotiation management on negotiations in the regimes of climate change, world trade and biosafety. It played a significant role in each of the case pairs, culminating in the summits on climate change in Copenhagen and Cancún in 2009 and 2010, on world trade in Seattle and Doha in 1999 and 2001, and on biosafety in Cartagena and Montreal in 1999 and 2000. Organizers applied the respective process levers in very similar ways across these regimes. The findings may therefore serve as 'lessons learnt' for the organizers of future negotiations. What should be avoided? What has worked well in the past? Let us first revisit why interests and power may deserve less attention from organizers than is usually expected.

Interests and power taking a backseat

The findings suggest that organizers of future organizers may want to avoid exclusively focusing on interests and power. The interests of countries as one traditional determinant in negotiations remained constant in all three case pairs.

This was mainly due to the fundamental nature of the stakes involved. Regarding climate change, tremendous environmental, economic and social risks around the globe stood against the stellar challenge to fairly distribute the economic burden of mitigation and adaptation among parties. Nothing less than an economic revolution is required for states to transform into low carbon economies. These conditions of climate change remained unchanged from 2009 to 2010. Negotiations on a new trade round touched upon interests, which were equally fundamental. Developed countries pushed for a further liberalization of trade in areas of their competitive advantage, such as investment and services. In contrast, developing countries demanded to first adjust provisions of the most recent agreement creating the WTO, which they considered highly unbalanced. Besides, they called for more accessible and fairer agricultural markets. Rich countries should terminate their subsidies in one of the rare sectors where 'the South' enjoyed partial advantages. Again, these economic drivers underlying the positions of countries were unaltered between 1999 and 2001. Finally, the stakes in the biosafety negotiations evolved during the 1990s as the field enormously gained in economic significance. By the Cartagena summit, the principle coalitions were fully aware of their economic opportunities from export on one side, and the environmental, economic, and health risk from importing on the other. While public pressure continued growing in Europe but also in North America, no profound redefining of national interests took place between the summits in 1999 and 2000, neither among the exporting Miami Group nor among importing countries. So across three regimes, constant fundamental interests cannot explain the outcomes, where success followed failure within only a brief period of time.

We see a comparable picture for the role of power in these case pairs. All principal countries supported the final climate compromise in Copenhagen, which had been crafted by the US and the largest emerging economies (which comprise the BASIC group). This late but unanimous coalition of great powers notwithstanding, the summit took only note of their suggestion. With very similar power structures in place, the agreement was then adopted in Cancún, and so one year later than a pure power-based account would have predicted. Power structures in trade in the late 1990s also remained constant between Seattle and Doha. The 'Quad' of the US, EU, Canada and Japan was still the mightiest group in share of world trade, despite its hegemonic position beginning to weaken due to a greater number, and growing self-confidence of, emerging economies in the WTO. Hegemonic power notwithstanding, the 'Quad' pushed in vain for the launch of a new round of trade liberalization in Seattle. When parties reached agreement in Doha two years later, the power of the launch-favouring 'Quad' had, if anything, decreased in the wake of the financial crisis. Once more, political–economic might revealed itself as a weak predictor of regime evolution. This was not much different for biosafety negotiations. How can power-based theories explain the collapse of talks in Cartagena in 1999 and the adoption of an agreement one year later, when the power structures were largely constant?

The dominating biotechnological exporters comprised major economies, such as the US, Canada and several vibrant emerging countries. Despite their resistance throughout both years, these powerful exporters were unable to avert the creation of the Protocol on biosafety in Montreal.

In sum, observations from three regimes speak against an exclusive focus on hegemonic countries by organizers when facilitating agreement in these kinds of multilateral negotiations. Power shows explanatory shortcomings similar to those of interests. This is not to say that structural theories of interests and power over-all may not well explain broader *long-term* regime evolution, such as the scarce progress in climate protection, where the US and China as the most powerful players showed little ambition over more than one decade now. In this sense, structural and negotiation management theory may complement each other in their different perspectives on the object of study. The sole focus by organizers of multilateral negotiations on the 'big players' and allegedly rational interests, however, may prove detrimental.

Negotiation management tipping the scales

Instead, rich evidence from negotiations across the fields of climate change, trade and biodiversity revealed that organizers hold four levers of negotiation manage-ment in their hands. The following section illustrates the key lessons learnt by summarizing how six sets of organizers tipped the scales at multilateral summits with their respective negotiation management, towards breakdown or agreement. Jointly with the details of the preceding chapters of this book, they may serve as input for a checklist of the dos and don'ts of future negotiation management.

Transparency and inclusiveness

The Danish Presidency of the climate talks has become a show case of a negoti-ation process that lacked in transparency and inclusiveness vis-à-vis most delegations. The Danes had prepared a compromise draft behind the scenes, which became infamously known as the 'Danish text'. It infringed upon parties' prerogative to develop their own negotiation text. Moreover, the exclusive composition of the small group of 30 leaders hammering out the final deal offended the excluded 90 heads of state and government. It all peaked in the secretive session of major powers of the US and BASIC countries. Their compro-mise was vocally objected to on process grounds by many of the excluded countries. The summit ended in deadlock, merely taking note of the major powers' suggestion.

Learning from Copenhagen, the Mexican Presidency and the UN Climate Secretariat profoundly altered the process. Organizers reached out widely to all countries, including those much neglected in the past, such as the Latin American ALBA coalition. The hosts refrained from drafting their own compro-mise texts and cautiously reiterated the mantra that there was 'no Mexican text'.

An open-door policy avoided any repetition of the closed small circles that had irritated so many in the year before. Parties could join the small informal rounds on key outstanding issues under the facilitation of the organizers at any time. Welcoming this transparency and inclusiveness, delegates adopted the Cancún Agreements.

We find the same pattern for two pairs of salient trade negotiations. Similar to Copenhagen, the organizers of the Seattle talks chaired a process that was still dominated by the exclusive style of the GATT days when the 'Quad' of the US, EU, Canada, and Japan largely negotiated the outcome among themselves. The so-called Green Room of the WTO Director-General had become the symbol of this approach to resolve key issues in a small circle of major trade powers. In addition, the US Conference Chair did not reach out intensively to small and middle powers to reduce their worries of exclusion. The emerging large developing countries however no longer tolerated this lack of transparency and inclusiveness in Seattle and raised stern objections against any outcome from such a negotiation process. In the end, the conference reached a stalemate.

In the aftermath of the Seattle collapse, the chief trade negotiation organizers in Geneva made the process explicitly more transparent and inclusive. WTO General Council Chair Bryn and Director-General Moore enhanced the information flow on essential steps of the negotiations and opened up Green Room meetings to all major coalitions. Having been excluded from key talks before, African representatives were now invited to the small group negotiations in Doha. Director-General Moore carefully built contacts to a range of developing countries by wider travelling than any of his predecessors. Many negotiators and observers considered it the most transparent and inclusive trade negotiations ever. As a result, countries broadly endorsed the process and its outcome in Doha, launching a new round of trade negotiations.

The dynamics of the biosafety negotiations seemed to be little different. The open-ended preparatory talks transformed into the exclusive circles of the 'Friends of the Chair' and later the 'Friends of the Minister' at the Cartagena summit under Chair Köster and his successor Mayr. Parties vocally protested against this kind of process with the vast majority left in the dark during the decisive final days of negotiations on the Biosafety Protocol. Again, dozens of ministers were neither included in trying to solve the outstanding issues, nor fully informed about progress made. This created suspicion and ill will against text coming out of these secretive circles. So the Cartagena summit eventually had to be suspended without a result.

In striking parallel to the shifts in the climate and trade talks, the new COP President Mayr announced the introduction of a new negotiation format that would guarantee each party the participation in, or at least observation of, small group negotiations. This so-called 'Vienna setting' gave the five major negotiation groups, which reflected all principal interests, a seat at the round table. It allowed all others delegates to follow the negotiations from the back of the room. Parties warmly welcomed this profoundly changed procedure and maintained it during the Vienna and Montreal talks. In addition, Chair Mayr made a conscious point in reaching out to as many delegations as possible in person. Hardly anyone felt excluded, and negotiators in Montreal eventually agreed on the Protocol on biosafety.

For policy-makers, one could summarize the findings as follows:

- Provide sufficient information on small group negotiations.
- Inform broadly about the origin, evolution, and conclusion of the compromise text.
- Inform diligently about both overall negotiation progress and schedule.
- Design an inclusive selection process for small group negotiations.
- Ensure the integration of workstreams across several negotiation levels.
- Reach out broadly to parties when facilitating compromise.
- Augment the perception of transparency and inclusiveness by 'branding' negotiations accordingly.

Capability of organizers

We find a similar picture with regard to the capability of the host country and the respective supporting Secretariat as organizers. Capability entailed dimensions such as the personal–cultural fit of lead officials, their process and content expertise, and the alignment of the organizers. The Danish Presidency started out with a team from the Danish Climate Ministry that had high expertise in the process and content of climate negotiations. Intense rivalries between the ministry and the Prime Minister's office broke out in the run-up to the politicized summit. They led to the resignation of climate insider Becker only a few weeks before the COP, who served as principal adviser to Climate Minister Hedegaard. The new leading team of Danish Prime Minister Rasmussen, however, had a much smaller network among negotiators and scarce experience in multilateral processes. The most revealing moment was the pitiful statement of Rasmussen as COP-President in the crucial hours of the closing night of Copenhagen. Having called for a vote on the compromise proposal (against core provisions of procedure), he acknowledged in front of all delegates that he did not know 'your rules'. Danish woes with UNFCCC Executive Secretary de Boer aggravated the situation further and undermined any possibility of a joint last minute effort to rescue the summit.

In light of the Copenhagen breakdown, Mexican President Calderón resolved early rivalries among the Mexican ministries. He chose the foreign ministry to lead the facilitation, while the environment ministry would provide expert input on substance. Foreign Minister Espinosa and her chief adviser de Alba were both seasoned diplomats who knew the multilateral system inside out. Moreover, they were highly empathic personalities combined with a non-directive attitude and good sense of humour. This stood in contrast to the more direct Danish form of communication and granted the Presidency wide access across negotiation groups. Such access provided rich insights on parties' motivations, essential to finding eventual common ground. Relations of the host country with the UN also improved tremendously with new UN climate head Figueres. Unlike her predecessor de Boer, Figueres preferred a cooperative, behind-the-scenes support of the Presidency. Their alignment paved the way for Cancún's success.

The story of the Seattle organizers mirrors that of the Danes: it proved to be full of strife, lack of process expertise and empathy. The long-lasting fight between developed and developing countries over the succession of the WTO Director-General paralysed preparations of the ministerial summit in Seattle. The controversy also weakened the position of incoming Director-General Moore. Moreover, the US approach to its Conference Chairmanship hampered any progress. Chair Barshefsky ignored minimum facilitation standards. She negotiated on behalf of the US while simultaneously trying to facilitate talks as chair. Negotiators accused her of a crude and directive chairing style, when she bluntly rejected carefully drafted proposals by key delegates. Finally, the US proved incapable of ensuring access to the conference venue for many delegates in the face of thousands of anti-trade demonstrators, so one of only a few days was lost to find a compromise.

The capability of the Doha organizers was the opposite of that of Seattle. Director-General Moore had built much stronger relations with developing countries, and had gained experience over two years of running the process. The support of Harbinson as General Council Chair, an old-hand of trade negotiations from Hong Kong–China, served him as a vital asset. Harbinson was one of the key drivers behind compiling a single negotiation text from parties' inputs on time. The document remained largely unaltered in Doha and served as the basis for the launch of the trade round in Doha. The network and skilful leadership of Moore and Harbinson was complemented by the behind-the-scenes approach of the Qatari chairmanship of the Doha summit. Mirroring the empathic and indirect style of Espinosa and de Alba, host Chair Kamal achieved a seamless cooperation with his fellow organizers of the WTO. His high process expertise surprised many, and so he maintained neutrality in his chairing and never obviously pushed for Qatari interests – in marked contrast to the Americans.

Despite less available data, the biosafety talks appear in a very similar light. Köster of Denmark had accumulated abundant content and process experience by the time he chaired the Cartagena expert negotiations. Köster refrained from a clear violation of neutrality, yet he eventually forced the text through despite the still vehement objection by many parties. It was therefore hardly surprising that agitated parties had lost any goodwill to still reach a compromise in Cartagena. This directive and pushy chairmanship approach reminds of Köster's counterparts as chairs at the Copenhagen and Seattle negotiations. This negative dynamic could barely be compensated by the head of the Biodiversity Secretariat Zedan, as he had taken up his position merely a few months before. Besides, little evidence is available that would show a deep cooperation between Köster and Zedan. Even worse, Köster and Mayr worked in two parallel small groups ('Friends of the Chair' and 'Friends of the Minister'), which raised suspicion of divergences between key organizers in the decisive hours of Cartagena.

Incoming Colombian Chair Mayr was in some respect the personal–cultural mirror image of Köster. Negotiators across the board praised his empathy, sense of humour, creativity, and the less directive form of communication. He began rebuilding trust into the leadership and process after the controversial negotiations had come to standstill by the end of Cartagena. His approach is reminiscent of the Mexican climate facilitators Espinosa and de Alba, with whom he interestingly shares a Latin American cultural background. The more indirect form of communication was also true for Kamal, the Qatari chair of the trade negotiations. These parallels support the importance of the right personal–cultural fit. Finally, Mayr brought process expertise from previous political assignments, and both he and Secretariat head Zedan had one year after Cartagena to expand on this before they successfully facilitated agreement on the new Protocol in Montreal.

For policy-makers, one could summarize the findings as follows:

- Ensure organizational fit of institutions to the specific negotiation situation (e.g. internal unity of the organizing institution, clear responsibilities inside the Presidency, continuity of officials with core positions).
- Ensure cultural fit of individuals to the specific negotiation situation (e.g. maintain neutrality, communicate in a not too directive way, keep any activism to a moderate level, create an inviting, unthreatening atmosphere).
- Ensure personal fit of individuals to the specific negotiation situation (e.g. lead organizers to be empathic, approachable, open to listening, modest, humorous, able to steer confidently).
- Ensure rich process expertise of individuals in the dynamics of complex multilateral negotiations and the available facilitation 'toolkit'.
- Establish and nurture good working relations between the Presidency and treaty Secretariat (e.g. a non-competitive interaction between the principal facilitators, limited rivalry for publicity).

Authority of the lead organizer

The chair of a summit negotiation fulfils elementary functions for moving negotiations forward and for bringing them to a successful conclusion in the often delicate moments of a closing plenary. Broadly accepted authority among the large majority of key negotiators is therefore a vital element for succeeding in this task. Climate Minister Hedegaard had gained a fair amount of trust in her person as first President of the Copenhagen summit. It was undercut by the leakage of the 'Danish text' in the first week and the Presidency's reaction to it. With the start of the pivotal high-level segment, the 'disappearance' of Hedegaard, as many perceived it, and the takeover of Prime Minister Rasmussen proved disastrous. A mere few months into office, Rasmussen lacked prior multilateral experience and showed only minor empathy for the situation. The Danish Prime Minister soon reached the lowest authority levels possible. Hardly any lead delegate accepted him in his role as Conference President, as indicated by some unquotable comments. This poor standing among major delegations deprived him of any meaningful lever to steer Copenhagen to a successful outcome.

The contrast to Mexican Foreign Minister Espinosa could not have been greater. Her year-long multilateral experience and strong empathy quickly created trust among delegates who were still haunted by the experiences of the final days in Copenhagen. A great relief about her chairing style was noticeable in the room when Espinosa held plenary stocktaking sessions during the two weeks in Cancún. With increasing goodwill, parties forgave process mistakes that may have otherwise caused an outrage during the Danish Presidency. The close to unanimous support for Espinosa culminated on Cancún's last day: negotiators gave minute-long standing ovations after she had released the compromise text, and one senior Secretariat official described the appreciation of her as that of a 'rock star' in an interview. This broad authority with all parties was pivotal when Espinosa faced the sole opposition of Bolivia to the final package during the night of the closing plenary. In what was a borderline decision to overrule the explicit objection of one party, Espinosa gavelled consensus on the adoption of the Cancún Agreements. It is difficult to imagine that parties would have accepted such a decision by Rasmussen given his long record of process violations.

In contrast to climate, two lead organizers steer the trade negotiations in the more institutionalized WTO system: the Conference Chair of the host country and the WTO Director-General. In Seattle, the lack of neutrality and empathy by US Conference Chair Barshefsky largely undermined her authority among delegates. She offended expert negotiators from the start by asking them to leave the room as she was unsatisfied with their preparatory work. Ministers should now take over to give political guidance. Her suggestion was rejected, which delegations celebrated vocally. At the summit, the US organizers were even booed in open session against any diplomatic convention. WTO Director-General Moore of New Zealand faced initially low authority among many developing countries after his succession fight with Supachai Panitchpakdi of Thailand. Sidelined by the preponderance of the American hosts, Moore had no opportunity to rebuild his authority during the few days of the Seattle Ministerial. Overall then, neither of the two summit heads was accepted widely enough to provide essential leadership.

These conditions improved a lot by Doha. Over more than two years, Moore was able to nurture the trust of delegates. His explicit inclusion of delegations formerly marginalized in WTO negotiations earned him the sympathy of many developing country negotiators. His greater experience as Director-General improved his process navigation and thereby increased his authority among delegates. In contrast to Barshefsky, Qatari Conference Chairman Kamal applied a greater behind-the-scenes approach and proved less prone to offending delegations. Many negotiators appreciated his calm but skilful facilitation. They accepted Kamal as open-minded mediator even more, as he showed neutrality in chairing the summit. In sum, Moore and Kamal could rely on their well-established authority in steering Doha towards a successful outcome.

The biosafety talks mirror this pattern of low versus high levels of authority in their failures and successes. Danish official Köster had chaired expert negotiations over several years. Yet when they culminated in Cartagena, he suffered severe blows to his authority. Köster paid dearly for the use of the exclusive 'Friends of the Chair' group, formed in the old spirit of the GATT days. This undercut his trust and authority among delegates. When it became obvious that he tried to push through the adoption of the Protocol draft to be forwarded to the political summit in Cartagena, he further lost significant goodwill among delegates. His authority reached a new low point in these decisive final hours.

This was in astonishing contrast to Colombian Environment Minister Mayr. Coming in just before the high-level summit in Cartagena, he suffered a bumpy start when convening the small and exclusive 'Friends of the Minister' group to rescue the Cartagena talks at the last minute. The meeting ended without result and offended excluded delegates. Yet, he slowly regained the confidence of delegates with his quick turn to the transparent 'Vienna setting', an innovation which they credited Mayr for. His empathetic attitude contributed to the sympathy delegates had for him. One expression of this was the acceptance by negotiators of continuing to use Mayr's negotiation format until the Protocol was adopted in Montreal. They also followed suit with several other of his nonconventional suggestions, such as the holding hands of all delegates at one point, or the use of coloured teddy bears in Montreal to determine the speaking order of the principal groups. This trust gave him broad access to negotiators, which provided critical information on a possible middle ground between parties, finally enabling the Cartagena Protocol.

For policy-makers, one could summarize the findings as follows:

- Overall, be aware that attaining a high authority level is a fragile endeavour requiring a cautious, steady build-up of political capital over an often lengthy period of time.
- Continuously watch for the interaction between parties' reaction to the design of the negotiation process and the acceptance of the Conference leadership.
- Ensure high capability of the lead organizer, or the perception thereof (e.g. delegates gain trust when the organizer masters the process well and interacts in an inoffensive, open and neutral way).
- Maximize the transparency and inclusiveness of the process as lead organizer (e.g. parties gain trust in the lead organizer when they are kept informed about key steps and when they can express their interests).

Negotiation mode

Organizers have partial influence over the negotiation mode of parties. They foster open-ended arguing and the search for a joint solution through the creation of sheltered and stress-reducing negotiation settings and a trust-generating, neutral chairmanship. Or else, organizers tilt parties towards defensive, positional bargaining with a mere exchange of positions based on a zero-sum understanding. While the mode varies from phase to phase, positional bargaining dominated in Copenhagen overall. Parties were fighting for their positions in a high pressure situation with the fear of possibly losing out in a far-reaching agreement. They made very little progress until the high-level segment opened. In contrast, the US and BASIC-countries negotiated in a greater arguing mode in their exclusive small group meeting of the last day and thereby achieved at least a political compromise on core issues. Yet as we have seen, their last minute proposal reached the thousands of other delegates too late, who were moreover offended by the opaque process.

On the way towards Cancún, the organizers had therefore placed prominent emphasis on creating a substantive and frank exchange between parties. To this end, they convened workshops during the year on all pivotal negotiation issues, such as on finance and on the monitoring of commitments. Based on the same idea were exchanges in other fora, such as the Petersberg Dialogue and the Cartagena Dialogue. They were all meant to enhance understanding between the groups and to generate innovative ideas. This spirit of arguing and a more conciliatory attitude continued in Cancún. In the last week of the summit, the inclusive consultations on selected core issues led by ministers from a developing and a developed country each contributed to a constructive, interest-revealing mode. Their political guidance helped expert negotiators to climb out from their long-held trenches: they now exchanged more on the actual interests underlying their positions, instead of merely fighting for the greater gain or avoidance of costs in a tit-for-tat fashion.

Negotiations for the launch of a new trade round were already characterized by mere positional exchanges in the run-up to Seattle. This did not improve during the summit. Countries held the entire process hostage insisting on first dealing satisfactorily with their respective priority issues. Even the more exclusive Green Room meeting in Seattle, which often enhances arguing, did not shift parties away from bargaining. Participants of these meetings reported fierce positional strategies. Parties seemed to conceive of a new trade round as a win-lose situation and were thus unwilling to employ conciliatory strategies to trade on differences in interests. The chaos, stress, and deep dissatisfaction with the negotiation management of the organizers did not improve the goodwill of parties to take more creative approaches either.

Doha also saw a rough start with little movement on any side of the different groups. Yet soon, the negotiation mode altered towards more arguing. The US and EU established a much more constructive relationship, not least based on the excellent understanding between their lead negotiators Zoellick and Lamy. The positive dynamic extended to other groups and when the summit reached half time, the behaviour of countries indicated a greater sense of arguing. All major groups started making concessions, from developed countries such as the US, EU and Japan, to developing countries. As stated before, yielding also occurs in positional bargaining, but it is much more likely to be the result of integrative arguing. There, parties identify the varying values they place on specific issues and then compromise by trading on their differences. This integrative, arguing approach contributed to the launch of the Doha trade round.

Negotiations on biosafety began with a long arguing phase to identify the core issues for a protocol and the negotiation agenda. In the year before Cartagena however, parties hardened their positions and moved to mere bargaining. The realization of the high stakes by exporting and importing countries accelerated this dynamic: from opportunities for the biotechnology industry to economic, environmental and health risks. In this mood, delegations no longer engaged in any substantive debate and repeated their positions mantra-like by the start of Cartagena. African Group negotiators and the G-77 limited any exchange with the Americans after furiously leaving a first meeting with US negotiators due to the attempt by the latter to dictate conditions of an agreement one-sidedly. Last minute efforts by Köster and Mayr to extract concessions in a more open-minded, small group setting did not move parties to a more constructive mode. As Köster pushed the Protocol draft through on the last day of expert negotiations, parties maintained their positional style until the political summit also ran into deadlock.

Post-Cartagena, Mayr tried to get parties back to exchanging in a frank and constructive way, using the negotiation format of the 'Vienna setting' as one salient tool. A small circle of only ten delegates of all negotiation coalitions gathered around the table, and anyone else interested sat at the back as observer. The format built trust through transparency and thereby opened up delegates to speaking more freely. At the same time, the restricted number of negotiators created space to effectively exchange about everyone's interests. The lower level of stress and the sheltered environment gradually enabled parties to focus more on concepts and argument than on pure bargaining. This spirit of Vienna remained during the summit in Montreal, while the positional exchange about concessions also continued of course, especially in bilateral negotiations in the last hectic days of Montreal. Nevertheless, the EU–US bilateral during the night of the closing plenary considered the underlying interests of most parties involved, indicating a decent degree of arguing. Participating negotiators eventually crafted the decisive elements of the compromise for the Cartagena Protocol.

For policy-makers, one could summarize the findings as follows:

- Consider that delegates choose their negotiation mode partly based on the negotiation management by the organizers.

- Maximize trust into the organizers so that delegates are less anxious about small group negotiations, and more open-minded to arguing – and do not perceive it to be safer to stick to their initial positions.
- Create informal settings outside the official negotiations ahead of a summit to provide arguing space without the pressure of an outcome, and through a non-public set up and a less crowded atmosphere.
- Create small informal groups also at summits, but handle them very carefully as too much exclusiveness destroys the trust of non-participating delegations.

To conclude, abundant evidence across regimes advises the organizers of future negotiations to carefully consider the four levers of negotiation management they hold in their hands. These factors frequently contribute to the failure and success of negotiations. Developing a detailed checklist of core negotiation management requirements, like mediators would do in a much less complex family or business mediation, may prove fruitful for facilitating agreement. Let us finish by outlining the remaining drivers affecting the outcome.

Initial failure and the 'stepping stone' effect

Two vital factors that come with the 'passage of time' between two negotiations emerged from the analysis across all cases: the effects of initial failure and of groundwork from preceding summits. The first negotiation round of each case pair had originally been supposed to reach convergence in the respective regime, but ended in initial failures: a comprehensive climate agreement on mitigation and adaptation in Copenhagen, the launch of a new trade round in Seattle, and a set of biosafety rules for the movement of living modified organisms in Cartagena. Their breakdowns raised pressure to succeed at the following attempt and warned delegates not to endanger the multilateral negotiation forum of the regime, as numerous interviewees revealed.

The second explanation for a greater probability of agreement is the 'stepping stone' effect. Climate delegations had negotiated for long hours in Copenhagen resolving myriad details. Leaders eventually crafted the political compromise of the Copenhagen Accord. So in Cancún, negotiators could build on this foundation and accelerate agreement. A similar dynamic occurred in the biosafety talks, where difficult compromises had been struck and the Protocol had been largely developed before Cartagena collapsed. Delegates in Montreal could therefore move forward much more quickly. Only the Seattle trade talks turned out to be so chaotic and adversarial that little preparatory output was left over for negotiators in Doha two years later.

Both explanations carry explanatory power. Many delegates affirmed extraordinary urgency to succeed after the initial, grand failure. Previous groundwork assisted negotiators extremely well and allowed proceeding at a faster pace in the second negotiation round. But are these alternative factors always necessary or at least sufficient to reach agreement? This seems rather unlikely. Long preceding negotiations to develop abundant detail of negotiation substance do not suffice by themselves. In all cases studied here, negotiators already had extensive content available after negotiations over several years. So, it is at least difficult to say that it was exactly this one additional round (like Cartagena for biosafety) that created the missing bit of input. Similarly, if an initial, grand collapse was always needed, we would never see an agreement at the round when it is expected. While this was true for the three cases studied here, the Kyoto Protocol, for instance, was adopted without the prior collapse of a summit. Other cases are easily conceivable.

Nevertheless, the availability of advanced negotiation material and greater motivation for an agreement do complement negotiation management factors (without being necessary or sufficient on their own). They can even interact with process factors, as a greater willingness for success opens delegates up to compromise in an arguing mode. Moreover, advanced negotiation material also allows a greater exchange on content in arguing terms as issues are better understood. So, rather than being mutually exclusive process factors increase the likelihood of agreements jointly with these two alternative explanations.

Finally, this study could *not* find substantial evidence for an influence of alternating negotiation strategies by countries or outstanding individual nego-tiators that made a difference from one year to another. This is not to say that they remained constant or never influenced an outcome, but that this cannot be shown across all three cases. The only clear-cut exemption was the biosafety talks where the Compromise Group of small and middle powers contributed to facilitation as a new actor in the second negotiation round in Vienna and Montreal. They helped ease the tension between the adversarial camps.

In sum, organizers of upcoming negotiations may want to use the insights from these astonishing parallels between the dynamics of environmental and economic negotiations. The detailed documentation of the core chapters could serve as a resource for developing a checklist for designing future negotiation management. Organizers may also heighten their awareness that a sole focus on power and interests has frequently proven short-sighted. Overall, it may hope-fully contribute to facilitate agreement in the multiple global challenges ahead of us.

Significance of results for international relations and negotiation analysis

Moving on to the academic relevance of this book, I will now examine how these findings answer the initial question posed by it, and how they contribute to the wider theory of International Relations and Negotiation Analysis. Empirical data and analysis across three regimes have shown that good negotia-tion management favoured the successful conclusion of the summits in Cancún,

Doha and Montreal for cooperation on climate change, trade, and biodiversity. It also revealed how a dismal process worsened the likelihood of success, contributing to the collapses of Copenhagen, Seattle, and Cartagena. As results varied despite constant interests, power, and problem structure only the altered negotiation management could explain the difference. This confirms the core hypothesis, which holds that effective management of a multilateral negotiation by the organizers increases the probability of an agreement (Figure 7.1). The four steps of correlation, process-tracing, examination of alternative explanations, and the comparison across three regimes allow us to state with confidence that negotiation management caused a significant delta in probability of agreement.[1]

This narrows the explanatory gap left by structural theory for the three case pairs of negotiations on the salient global issues of climate change, world trade, and biosafety. It discovers and details causal relationships between independent and dependent variables of regime building (George and Bennett 2005: 26, 27). These findings hold political importance as another round of negotiations with disastrous negotiation management would most likely have inhibited

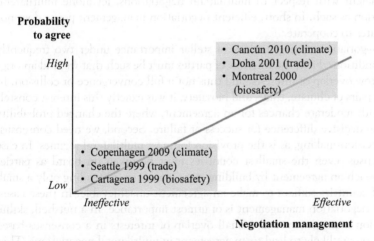

Figure 7.1 Negotiation management and the probability of agreement

Note: The summit names represent the process management of all organizers (host country and Secretariat) during the whole year of each respective Presidency, not just during the summit.

1   It would have been helpful to quantify to what extent probability was altered, as discussed at the outset of this book. However, the dynamics of 'multilateral negotiations' as a highly complex social object of study do not allow attributing simplistic statistical values to these variables.

agreement on demanding multilateral challenges once more. The delay in action would have cost many countries dearly in environmental, economic and social terms.

Can we say that negotiation management is necessary or sufficient for any agreement in multilateral negotiations? Necessity requires that agreement is *only* possible when effective negotiation management is given. This appears inconceivable from a simple scenario. Let us imagine a negotiation where interests of countries fully converge. In this case, parties would hardly be bothered about the kind of negotiation management. They would be prone to agree to meet their common interests, and would probably conclude their talks successfully. In such a case, effective negotiation management would not be necessary.

Let us change the scenario to examine sufficiency. Interests of parties are now fully opposed to each other at the outset. If negotiation management was a sufficient variable, a perfect process would *always* lead to agreement, despite these clashing interests. Our thought experiment will now demonstrate that this is unlikely. In our case of this absolute lack of congruence of interests, even the best managed negotiation cannot move delegates to an agreement. Parties will remain in opposition to each other and the negotiation will collapse. An effective process is therefore no guarantee for success. In sum, negotiation management has the important limitation that it is, by itself, neither necessary nor sufficient with respect to multilateral negotiations, let alone multilateral cooperation as such. In short, efficient negotiation management per se does not cause states to cooperate.

Yet negotiation management is of stellar importance under two frequently given conditions. First, the interests of parties must be such that we find an original narrow overlap of interests, and thus not a full convergence or collision. In the case pairs of climate, trade, and biosafety, it was exactly this interest constellation with moderate chances for an agreement, where the changed probability made the decisive difference for success or failure. Second, we need consensus-based decision-making, as is the provision for most multilateral regimes. In case of consensus, even the smallest countries must be taken on board as parties cannot reach an agreement by building mere majorities. Offending only a small group of countries suffices to make an agreement unachievable. In these cases, efficient negotiation management is of utmost importance. In a nutshell, skilful negotiation management *and* a small overlap of interests in a consensus-based negotiation are likely to lead to an agreement in multilateral negotiations. This, at least, has been the constellation and result across the three regimes studied here.

The findings also support the hypotheses on the four elements of negotiation management (1.1 to 1.4): transparency and inclusiveness, capability of organizers, authority of the lead organizer, and negotiation mode affected the probability to find a compromise inside the zone of objective agreement that meets the core interests of everyone, and to create the subjective willingness of negotiators to agree additional to a pure interest-based analysis of costs and benefits

(Figure 7.2).[2] Effective negotiation management led to the successful conclusion of a multilateral negotiation through these objective and subjective levels, in our cases the Cancún Agreements on climate change, the launch of the Doha Round on trade, and the Cartagena Protocol on biosafety. So, negotiation management with its four elements can tip the balance in favour or against an agreement under certain circumstances, and thereby alter the likelihood of multilateral cooperation.

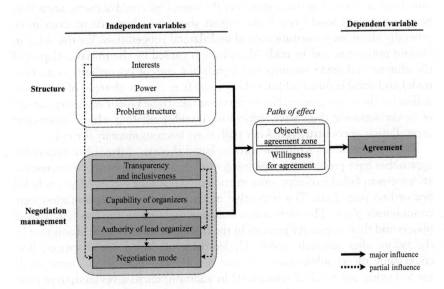

Figure 7.2 Negotiation framework probed in three regimes

2   All four elements of negotiation management had by and large the same shape in the cases of failure, and the opposite shape in the cases of success. This evidence does therefore not allow determining exactly how many of them need to be given for negotiation management to be considered 'effective' versus 'poor'. It could be all of them; it could be fewer; but we cannot say how many or which of them, as all four elements were always present. It is easily conceivable that a multilateral negotiation reaches agreement in the absence of one of the elements of negotiation management, despite only a small overlap of interests and consensus-based deci- sion-making, and so in an event when effective negotiation management is hypothetically most needed. Yet, borrowing from the idea of family resemblance in social science concepts (Goertz 2006), we may still be able to qualify a negotiation management in a negotiation as 'effective' if only a subset of 'm of n' elements is found to be 'good' (e.g. only one lead organ- izer had not a high capability). Finally, as the four negotiation management elements partially influence each other, the odds are high that most of them are either given or not. Their mini- mum number thus needs to be identified in future work.

How does this finding relate to the wider theory of international relations and negotiation analysis? The variable of negotiation management complements traditional structural international relations theories in cases where they failed to explain the outcomes. As we have seen, all three case pairs cast substantial doubt on the neorealist thinking of the role of power in regime building. In none of the negotiations were the most powerful countries able to push only their interests through. At the climate summit of Copenhagen, the US and China with their mighty allies had reached a compromise, yet it was rejected by a group of small countries. During the biosafety talks, the Protocol was even created against the initial wish of the US as the hegemon of the time. One could of course argue that many neorealists would not bother about short time horizons or even more generally about such institutionalized multilateral cooperation. Yet the delay in climate mitigation and in trade liberalization caused by the initial collapses of the climate and trade summits had significant current opportunity costs (e.g. trade) and sizeable future additional expenses (e.g. climate change) of billions of dollars for the major powers. Neorealists that take these salient economic aspects of power seriously then have difficulties in substantiating why a hegemonic constellation of countries could not push their interests *instantly* through.

We find a similar picture for interest-based theories. Liberal institutionalist approaches have problems in explaining why countries with constant interests in an agreement failed to compromise in one year while they successfully concluded one or two years later. The respective incentives for regime cooperation were continuously given. The same is true for game theorists, as the constellations of players and their respective pay-offs in the three case pairs were held constant by the before–after research design. Under these unaltered circumstances, how could game theory substantiate why one negotiation ended in stalemate, while the following one reached agreement? In addition, micro-level analysis of delegates as executing actors of the strategies of their countries revealed abundant evidence that decisions in the final heated days and nights of a summit were not only rational, but the result of highly subjective processes. This raises doubts about the applicability of rationalist theory to regime creation through multilateral negotiation processes.

In sum, these traditional structural international relations theories could hardly explain the difference in outcome. This is at least true for the short- and mid-term evolution of such negotiations and their regimes. As noted earlier, however, systemic approaches may still be well-equipped to account for broader and longer-term developments of cooperation, such as the standstill of the Doha Round on trade for over a decade before its conclusion in 2013, or the limited progress on substantial climate protection given the low support of some major powers. In this sense, structure and process *complement* each other when looking at the entire short- to long-term cycle of multilateral cooperation. Jointly, they form a comprehensive negotiation framework.

Filling the explanatory gap left for the salient multilateral negotiations studied here, this book makes two major contributions to the field of international relations and negotiation analysis. The first contribution is of an empirical and theoretical nature: based on the collection and analysis of abundant first-hand data, the book strengthens the position of 'process', which complements traditional structural international relations theory. Regarding the unique empirical evidence, this research has created a database comprising all structural and process factors. It allows for a numerical and structured analysis of each of these variables, while accounting for the origin of respondents and their coalition membership (such as a UNFCCC official, or a BASIC group delegate). The file contains material from 60 expert interviews with all principal actors of the in-depth study of the climate but also the trade negotiations (such as the current and former UNFCCC Executive Secretaries, lead officials of the Danish and Mexican climate Presidency, and chief negotiators from key countries). I was able to cross-check the data through my participant observation as member of a lead European delegation to the UN climate summit in Doha in 2012. This provided unique insights into confidential negotiations and bilateral meetings otherwise closed to observers, as well as to the negotiation strategy of a national delegation. I further draw on observation of the climate summits of Cancún and Durban in 2010 and 2011, and of the trade ministerial talks in Geneva in 2011.

With respect to the theoretical nature of this first contribution, the book supports and refines international relations theories that emphasize process. Its evidence illuminates that they were able to capture the key drivers behind the climate, trade, and biosafety negotiations in a more comprehensive way. This is not to say that structure does not matter. As detailed above, a small overlap of interests is one condition for negotiation management to make its greatest difference. But, as we have seen, structure alone does not get us very far in explaining outcomes of a sequence of negotiations. Let us now highlight to which specific theories this research contributes.

The findings support and refine existing scholarship of *constructivism* in multilateral negotiations on one side (Deitelhoff and Muller 2005; O'Neill *et al.* 2004; Risse and Kleine 2010; Ulbert *et al.* 2004; Zürn and Checkel 2005) and of negotiation literature on *arguing and bargaining* more specifically within and beyond international relations on the other side (Hopmann 2010; Odell 2010; Sebenius 1992; Thompson 2009; Wagner 2008). The collected evidence finds that the hypothesized dynamics of constructivist and negotiation theory were mostly in place. This research departed from constructivist tradition by not focusing on selected, *specific* lines of discourse (such as the evolution of the debate on REDD+ forest protection in climate mitigation). It rather took an overall view of discourse in each negotiation and operationalized negotiation modes by borrowing from negotiation literature, which had detailed the concepts of arguing and bargaining in all kinds of negotiations previously (e.g. Thompson 2009). The book thereby built on the few approaches that explicitly connect constructivism and negotiation theory for multilateral negotiations (e.g. Odell 2010).

This research finds that discourse in a constructivist sense is enabled through the negotiation mode of arguing, in contrast to positional bargaining where no profound exchange occurs. Substantive exchange about an issue (i.e. constructivist discourse) develops and possibly transforms the understanding of preferences of a country. This could eventually lead to a change of positions that can make the decisive difference for reaching an agreement. The book adds detail to this still only vaguely answered question of through which paths such a change in preferences exactly occurs in a multilateral negotiation. Evidence from climate, trade, and biosafety demonstrated that the choice of negotiation mode between arguing and bargaining and the kind of discourse affected the likelihood of an agreement. So overall, the negotiation management element of 'negotiation mode' supports and refines the central hypotheses of constructivism on discourse and of negotiation literature on arguing and bargaining.

Next, recent scholarship on institutions and the function of 'the chair' posited that bureaucracies and individuals can make a large difference in reaching international cooperation (Biermann and Siebenhüner 2009; Blavoukos and Bourantonis 2011; Depledge 2007; Odell 2005; Tallberg 2010). The results of this book affirm this notion, as also argued by works on agency beyond unitary states, such as by transnationalism, bureaucratic theory, and foreign policy analysis. This research found that especially the lead organizers (often from the host country) and their interaction with the respective regime Secretariat played central roles in facilitating agreement. Their agency must be considered next to states and to abstract structural categories of interest and power. Moreover, this book refined existing approaches by providing a detailed operationalization of leadership through negotiation organizers based on the collected evidence. Two related variables stood out: the capability of organizers and the authority of the key organizer in negotiations. Indicators for the capability of negotiation organizers entailed the personal-cultural fit, process and content expertise, and institutional alignment. The book also drew a precise picture of the causal pathways from the capability and authority of organizers to the negotiation outcome.

Finally, the interdisciplinary research on transparency and inclusiveness is supported and further refined by this work. It serves to bring this process element closer to the attention of international relations theory. Despite gaining growing attention across fields of international relations, such as in conflict, trade and climate change studies, as well as beyond international relations (Albin and Young 2012; Davenport et al. 2012: 45, 53; Müller 2011; Odell 2009: 284), the process element of transparency and inclusiveness is still only scarcely studied. This book developed a nuanced concept of transparency and inclusiveness in multilateral negotiations based on the findings of the in-depth study of the climate change case pair. The breakdown into seven indicators allows for its empirical examination across regimes, such as for trade and biosafety. Further, this research also highlighted how this process variable causally affected the outcomes. We eventually find that transparency and inclusiveness has been a principal element of negotiation management and may serve well in future research on multilateral negotiations. To conclude on its first contribution, this work uncovered new, strong empirical evidence for the importance of process next to structure in international relations theory. Theoretically, it supported and refined a series of specific theories on individual negotiation management factors.

This brings us to the second major contribution of this book. In the spirit of regime theory to strive for inclusionary explanatory frameworks (Bayne and Woolcock 2011; Biermann and Pattberg 2012; Keohane and Victor 2011; Odell 2010; Osherenko and Young 1993), it went beyond strengthening and complementing existing particular process approaches: it provides a comprehensive framework of multilateral negotiations, which integrates structural and negotiation management variables, and their detailed paths of effect on outcome; the latter requires an objective alignment of interests with the suggested outcome, and a subjective willingness by delegates to agree. For this framework construction, the research (1) extracted key variables of negotiation management from scholarship and primary data, and integrated them into a holistic framework, (2) detailed its causal mechanisms that connected negotiation management and outcome for climate negotiations, and (3) probed the entire approach in two additional case pairs of the trade and biosafety regimes.

The negotiation framework overcomes the approach to examine only one or two of these factors in isolation, which proves overly restrictive in light of the multiple analytical lenses, myriad levels, and agents – such as structural versus non-structural; domestic versus multilateral; individual versus government versus state aggregate. The collected data demonstrated the high value of a comprehensive model. It yielded a holistic picture of the events by looking at structural circumstances *and* at the entire set of negotiation management factors. It leaves us with a better understanding why the initial summits of climate change, trade, and biosafety collapsed, and why they succeeded one or two years later. To be clear: the second contribution is not about replacing existing individual strands of negotiation management research. Instead, this work supports, refines and integrates them into one comprehensive negotiation framework that rests on strong empirical evidence.

To conclude, scholars of political science and negotiation analysis may consider this negotiation framework for future work. When they set out to explore the reasons behind the outcomes of regime building through multilateral negotiations, the framework could provide a more holistic tool to cover all relevant aspects. So far, the data show that negotiation management by the organizers was a major factor in the creation of the Cancún Agreements on climate change, the launch of the Doha Round on trade, and the Cartagena Protocol on biosafety. It revealed the 'power of process'. To close with a comment by former UNFCCC Executive Secretary Yvo de Boer, made after Copenhagen: 'Good negotiation management is absolutely critical.'[3]

3 Personal interview in London in 2011, exact date anonymized.

The research road ahead

This finding suggests further research on the role of negotiation management. Empirically, it would be valuable to apply the novel framework to additional instances of regime building to further test and refine its use. This could be done vertically within one regime by studying other major successes and failures, such as the 20 years of climate negotiations. This adds a deeper contextual dimension to the focused study of the case pair of the Danish and Mexican Presidencies. A horizontal approach could also be developed, which would reach beyond the trade and biodiversity cases of this book. The caveat here is to remain within consensus-based regimes and to ensure a comparably complex problem structure. Negotiations such as on the Montreal Protocol on the ozone layer for example, dealt with a much narrower problem than the three regimes of this research. In these instances of lower complexity, negotiation management might also be of lesser importance.

Another empirical approach would be to strengthen the hypothesis by individual level experimental design. Building on the approaches and insights of interdisciplinary negotiation analysis (jointly with social and individual psychology, and economics for instance), a controlled experiment could test negotiation management theory in a larger n-situation through multiple runs of a negotiation simulation. The design would mirror the conditions of a complex, multilateral negotiation, which would require multiple players and at least a one or two-day game period. The set up would create dynamics that contain the four negotiation management factors in question, and then collect data on the behaviour of participants. Such a probably student-based simulation can help in filling the data gap that the secrecy of real-world negotiations leaves, even in cases where participant observation within a national delegation is possible: how exactly do delegates act in salient bilateral meetings? How do they come to the eventual decision of the delegation on the agreement in the final hours?

One collateral empirical finding of this research hints at the importance of a closer examination of the individual level. The same people often negotiate on the various issues. For example, some delegates and ministers at the biosafety talks also participated in climate negotiations, such as Bernarditas de Castro Muller of the Philippines and Jan Pronk of the Netherlands; trade negotiators became facilitators on climate change, such as Steffen Smidt of Denmark; previous trade *and* climate change summit delegates later went into biosafety negotiations, such as Kiyo Akasaka of Japan. These examples of lead negotiators of their respective countries could be continued endlessly. This illuminates why social psychological dynamics at place in one realm of negotiations would also apply to similar (or even identical) people in another regime, if the latter is comparable in its setting as a huge, complex and consensus-driven multilateral negotiation. The biosafety negotiations chair, Juan Mayr, wrote on the salience of negotiation management *across* regimes: 'I consider this matter to be of great significance in the present context of multilateral negotiations on trade and environment, which is characterized by mistrust and limited participation' (Mayr 2002: 219). Taken together, additional empirical evidence may strengthen the finding that these dynamics occur in very similar fashion across multilateral regimes.

Without speculating as to which kind of conceptual refinements these added data would lead, two aspects deserve special consideration. First, negotiation management variables are interlinked with some degree of co-variation. For example, high capability of organizers is often (but not necessarily) correlated with greater acceptance of the lead organizer. Future study may discover stronger indication for a co-variation and may eventually lead to a simplification of the theory by the merging of process variables. Next, the emphasis of this research was on levers (mostly) in the hands of the organizers, understood as negotiation management factors. In contrast, we found only minor indications of the influence of process factors under the control of parties on the outcome (e.g. negotiation strategy, individual negotiators). It may be promising to more rigorously assess the connection between process variables of organizers and of parties. For instance, how does negotiation management by the organizers influence the choice of negotiation strategy by parties?

Finally, while negotiation management helps in explaining the outcome of a negotiation, it sheds only a dim light on the successive evolution and implementation of the agreement. Climate and trade regimes have been moving extremely slowly despite interim negotiation successes. For instance, the Doha trade round was launched in 2001 and yet an agreement with new binding rules only materialized in 2013. Granted, addressing implementation is too vast to be included here. It is studied by an entire sub-field of regime research. Nevertheless, one may draw attention to an interesting connection between negotiation management and implementation: a more transparent and inclusive process, which is also based on thorough arguing, is likely to produce better accepted and more comprehensive outcomes, with a higher ownership of the agreement. Chances are then greater for a smooth implementation. This section briefly outlined potential avenues for future research. It would be exciting to see empirically where and under which conditions the negotiation framework holds. It would furthermore be conceptually intriguing to continue refining the framework towards a parsimonious and still inclusive theory of regime building.

For now, I conclude that negotiation management can make the decisive difference in reaching multilateral cooperation on salient global challenges of today, such as climate change, trade and biosafety. The organizers of future multilateral negotiations may want to take this finding to their hearts.

References

Albin, Cecilia, and Ariel Young. (2012) Setting the Table for Success – or Failure? Agenda Management in the WTO. *International Negotiation* 17: 37–64.

Bayne, Nicholas, and Stephen Woolcock. (2011) *The New Economic Diplomacy: Decision-*

Making and Negotiation in International Economic Relations. Global Finance Series. 3rd edn. Farnham: Ashgate.

Biermann, Frank, and Philipp Pattberg. (2012) *Global Environmental Governance Reconsidered*. Cambridge, MA: MIT Press.

Biermann, Frank, and Bernd Siebenhüner. (2009) *Managers of Global Change: The Influence of International Environmental Bureaucracies*. Cambridge, MA: MIT Press.

Blavoukos, Spyros, and Dimitris Bourantonis. (2011) Chairs as Policy Entrepreneurs in Multilateral Negotiations. *Review of International Studies* 37: 653–72.

Davenport, Deborah, Lynn M. Wagner, and Chris Spence. (2012) Earth Negotiations on a Comfy Couch: Building Negotiator Trust through Innovative Processes. In *The Roads from Rio: Lessons Learned from Twenty Years of Multilateral Environmental Negotiations*, edited by Pamela S. Chasek and Lynn M. Wagner. Abingdon: Routledge.

Deitelhoff, N., and H. Muller. (2005) Theoretical Paradise – Empirically Lost? Arguing with Habermas. *Review of International Studies* 31: 167–79.

Depledge, J. (2007) A Special Relationship: Chairpersons and the Secretariat in the Climate Change Negotiations. *Global Environmental Politics* 7: 45–68.

George, Alexander L., and Andrew Bennett. (2005) *Case Studies and Theory Development in the Social Sciences*. Bcsia Studies in International Security. Cambridge, MA: MIT Press.

Goertz, Gary. (2006) *Social Science Concepts: A User's Guide*. Princeton, NJ: Princeton University Press

Hopmann, P. Terrence. (2010) Synthesizing Rationalist and Constructivist Perspectives on Negotiated Cooperation. In *International Cooperation: The Extents and Limits of Multilateralism*, edited by I. William Zartman and Saadia Touval. Cambridge: Cambridge University Press.

Keohane, Robert O., and David G. Victor. (2011) The Regime Complex for Climate Change. *Perspectives on Politics* 9: 7–23.

Mayr, Juan. (2002) Environment Ministers: Colombia. In *The Cartagena Protocol on Biosafety: Reconciling Trade in Biotechnology with Environment and Development*, edited by Christoph Bail, Robert Falkner and Helen Marquard. London: Earthscan.

Müller, Benito. (2011) *UNFCCC – the Future of the Process: Remedial Action on Process Ownership and Political Guidance*. Oxford: Climate Strategies.

Odell, John S. (2009) Breaking Deadlocks in International Institutional Negotiations: The WTO, Seattle, and Doha. *International Studies Quarterly* 53: 273–99.

Odell, John S. (2005) Chairing a WTO Negotiation. *Journal of International Economic Law* 8: 425–48.

Odell, John S. (2010) Three Islands of Knowledge About Negotiation in International Organizations. *Journal of European Public Policy* 17: 619–32.

O'Neill, Kate, Jörg Balsiger, and Stacy D. VanDeveer. (2004) Actors, Norms, and Impact: Recent International Cooperation Theory and the Influence of the Agent-Structure Debate. *Annual Review of Political Science* 7: 149–75.

Osherenko, Gail, and Oran R. Young. (1993) *Polar Politics: Creating International Environmental Regimes*. Cornell Studies in Political Economy. Ithaca, NY: Cornell University Press.

Risse, Thomas, and Mareike Kleine. (2010) Deliberation in Negotiations. *Journal of European Public Policy* 17: 708–26.

Sebenius, James K. (1992) Negotiation Analysis: A Characterization and Review. *Management Science* 38: 18–38.

Tallberg, Jonas. (2010) The Power of the Chair: Formal Leadership in International Cooperation. *International Studies Quarterly* 54: 241–65.

Thompson, Leigh L. (2009) *The Mind and Heart of the Negotiator*. 4th ed. Boston: Pearson Education.

Ulbert, Cornelia, Thomas Risse, and Harald Müller. (2004) Arguing and Bargaining in Multilateral Negotiations. Paper presented at the Conference on Empirical Approaches to Deliberative Politics, European University Institute, Florence.

Wagner, Lynn M. (2008) *Problem-Solving and Bargaining in International Negotiations*. International Negotiation Series, vol. 5. Leiden: Martinus Nijhoff Publishers.

Zürn, Michael, and Jeffrey T. Checkel. (2005) Getting Socialized to Build Bridges: Constructivism and Rationalism, Europe and the Nation-State. *International Organization* 59: 1045–79.

Main features of the Copenhagen Accord and Cancún Agreements

	Copenhagen Accord[a]	Cancún Agreements
Mitigation	• Limit global temperature increase to 2°C • Shift from specified, binding top-down emission reduction goals to a voluntary bottom-up system • Annex I parties: commit to voluntarily quantified emission targets for 2020, submitted by 31 January 2010 • Non-Annex I parties: commit to voluntary mitigation actions, submitted by 31 January 2010 • Two blank appendices with mitigation tables for Annex I and II parties • Concede longer time frame for emission peaking in developing countries	• Limit global temperature increase to 2°C • Work to identify global goal for substantially reducing emissions by 2050 • Annex I parties: considering submitted quantified emission targets, urges parties to increase ambition to meet IPCC recommendations; avoid gap between Kyoto Protocol commitment periods; continue option to use emissions trading and project-based mechanisms • Non-Annex I parties: increase ambition to reach at least some mitigation relative to business-as-usual by 2020 • Work to identify time frame for emission peaking
MRV/ICA	• Annex I parties: emission reduction and financing monitored, reported, and verified • Non-Annex I parties: mitigation actions reported through national communications every two years. Internationally unsupported mitigation subject to domestic MRV and ICA; supported mitigation to international MRV	• Annex I parties: enhance reporting on emission reduction and provision of financial, technology and capacity-building support • Non-Annex I parties: enhance reporting on mitigation and support received. Guidelines for the MRV/ICA of two mitigation forms to be developed: internationally (un)supported mitigation

Finance	• Annex I parties: joint commitment for new resources for adaptation and mitigation in developing countries: a) US$30 billion for 2010–2012; b) mobilize US$100 billion a year by 2020; funding coming from a wide variety of public and private sources • Copenhagen Green Climate Fund: shall be established as operating entity of the financial mechanism • High-Level Panel under the COP- to study financing implementation	• Annex I parties: invitation to submit information on resources for fast-start and long-term financing to Secretariat by May 2011, 2012, and 2013 • Green Climate Fund (GCF): is established as operating entity of the financial mechanism • GCF-governance: governed by 24 board members (equal share of developed and developing countries); administered by World Bank as interim trustee • Standing Committee under the COP to assist in examining financing implementation
Technology and capacity-building	• Technology Mechanism: shall be established to accelerate technology development and transfer for adaptation and mitigation	• Technology Mechanism: shall be established to accelerate technology development and transfer for adaptation and mitigation • This includes: Technology Executive Committee and a Climate Technology Centre and Network • Capacity-building support: to be enhanced
Others	• No official UNFCC COP-decision • Level of detail: 3 pages (w/o appendices) • Review: assessment of the implementation of this Accord to be completed by 2015 • REDD+: immediate establishment of a mechanism and financial mobilization from developed countries	• Official UNFCCC COP-decisions • Level of detail: 27 pages (w/o appendices) • Review: periodically check adequacy of long-term global goal and progress, to be completed by 2015 • REDD+: further measures detailed • Cancún Adaptation Framework and Adaptation Committee: established to promote implementation of enhanced action • Response measures: work programme established to consider economic and social consequences of measures

Note: a. Analysis of *both* outcomes draws also on UNFCCC documentation and IISD (2009) 'Summary of the Copenhagen Climate Change Conference', *Earth Negotiations Bulletin* 12(459).

Questionnaire to organizers of the UNFCCC negotiations

Date: ....
Place: ....
Interviewee: ....
Professional position (current and previous related position): ....
Email: ....

– All answers will be treated anonymously –

I.   **What role did you have at the COP-15 and 16 negotiations?**

II. **Generally comparing negotiations and outcomes during the Danish and Mexican Presidencies of the UNFCCC climate negotiations in 2009 and 2010.**

Negotiation phase of COP-15 and 16
1. Why did you not get an agreement at COP-15 in Copenhagen?
2. Which were critical moments in the year leading up to *and* during COP-15?
3. How did you get to an agreement at COP-16 in Cancun?
4. Which were critical moments in the year leading up to *and* during COP-16?
5. How well aligned was the interaction between host country and UNFCCC-Secretariat during 2009 and 2010?

Preparation phase for COP-15 and 16
6. To determine countries' position which role did the following criteria play?
    a. Was it enough to approximate the *absolute* gains or losses for a country? Or, did the gains or losses matter only *compared* to those of other countries?
    b. In this sense what was at stake for countries, e.g. what size was the financial impact?
    c. Did the power distribution among countries matter to reach an outcome, and if so, how?
    d. How did domestic factors play a role to determine countries' positions?

III. Specifically, what role did these conditions play for the outcome of COP-15 AND 16?

7. **Transparency and inclusiveness** of the negotiation process
   a. Did all parties know the crucial moves and steps before and at COP negotiations?
   b. How were parties included in the negotiations?
   c. Did this kind of transparency and inclusion have an influence on whether they agreed to the proposal?
8. **Capability** of Conference Presidents (Hedegaard & Rasmussen / Espinosa), **host head negotiators** (Lidegaard / de Alba), **UNFCCC Executive Secretaries** (de Boer / Figueres)
   a. In hindsight, what was done well or not so well by you and these organizers? E.g. on process and content matters at the COP.
   b. How did that influence the reaching of an agreement?
9. **Acceptance of authority**: Conference Presidents (as above in question 8.)
   a. Did you manage to establish full authority in your negotiation role among parties?
   b. Did that influence parties' rejection or acceptance of the proposal, e.g. in the final nights when accepting the overruling of Bolivia at COP-16?
10. **Negotiation mode: Arguing and problem-solving vs. bargaining**
    a. Did you see open-ended *arguing and problem-solving* about content ["constructive discourse which is open to a change of minds based on facts and logical insights in order to find a joint solution"]? This would be in contrast to *bargaining* ["discuss the distribution of an assumed fixed set of gains and burdens, based on merely stating countries' positions"].
    b. Did this negotiation style get parties closer to or further away from an agreement? How?
    c. In which negotiation setting did arguing or bargaining happen?
11. **Which other variables** played a role for reaching an outcome from your perspective?
    a. Why did those that objected in Copenhagen no longer reject the agreement in Cancun?
    b. Were there any non-climate related side agreements at COP-15 or COP-16?
    c. Which impact had the "failure" of COP-15 non-agreement on COP-16?
12. Who would you recommend to interview further?

Thank you very much for your contribution to this research.

Note: This is the semi-structured questionnaire developed after the first phase of exploratory interviews. Questionnaires for delegates and observers were adapted to their perspective on the capability and authority of the organizers for question 8 a. and 9 a.

Interview list on climate negotiations

Names and positions of interviewees have been withheld for the sake of anonymity.

Country/organization	Interview location	Interview date
Antigua and Barbuda	Cancún	04.12.2010
Australia	Cancún	30.11.2010
Bolivia	Bonn	17.06.2011
Brazil	Cancún	04.12.2010
Brazil	London–Brasilia, phone	08.07.2011
Brazil	Bonn	15.06.2011
Democratic Republic of Congo	London	22.07.2011
Denmark	Cancún	02.12.2010
Denmark	Bonn	16.06.2011
Denmark	Copenhagen	11.08.2011
Denmark	Copenhagen	12.08.2011
Denmark	Copenhagen	12.08.2011
Denmark	Brussels	09.02.2012
Denmark	London–Geneva, phone	16.02.2012
European Union	London	27.01.2011
European Union	London	16.08.2011
Germany	London–Brussels, phone	20.01.2010
Germany	Cancún	03.12.2010

Country/organization	Interview location	Interview date
Germany	Berlin	16.03.2011
Germany	Berlin	26.05.2011
Germany	Durban	10.12.2011
India	Bonn	16.06.2011
Japan	Bonn	04.07.2011
Japan	London	27.07.2011
Mexico	London–Mexico City, phone	02.02.2011
Mexico	London–Mexico City, phone	08.02.2011
Mexico	Bonn	15.06.2011
Mexico	Bonn	16.06.2011
Mexico	Bonn	07.07.2011
Netherlands	London	17.02.2011
New Zealand	Cancún	07.12.2010
Nicaragua	Durban	09.12.2011
Philippines	Bonn	13.06.2011
Saudi Arabia	Durban	08.12.2011
Singapore	London–Singapore, phone	19.07.2011
South Africa	Hamburg–Pretoria, phone	16.03.2012
Switzerland	Bonn	09.08.2011
United Kingdom	London	20.11.2010
United Kingdom	London	04.05.2011
United Kingdom	London	05.05.2011
United Nations	Bonn	28.04.2010
United Nations	Cancún	04.12.2010
United Nations	Cancún	08.12.2010
United Nations	London	17.05.2011
United Nations	Bonn	14.06.2011
United Nations	Bonn	16.06.2011
United Nations	Bonn	03.08.2011

Country/organization	Interview location	Interview date
United States	London–Washington, phone	20.04.2011
United States	London–Boston, phone	02.06.2011
United States	Bonn	14.06.2011
Yemen	Cancún	04.12.2010
Zimbabwe	Bonn	14.06.2011
Daily Telegraph	Cancún	06.12.2010
IISD and Earth Negotiations Bulletin	Cancún	08.12.2010
WWF	Bonn	16.06.2011

Questionnaire to delegates of the WTO trade negotiations

Date: ....

Place: ....

Interviewee: ....

Professional position (current and previous related position): ....

Email: ....

– All answers will be treated anonymously –

I.   What role did you have at trade negotiations so far?

II. <u>Generally</u> comparing negotiations of Seattle (1999) / Doha (2001) / Cancun (2003)

[3rd 4th 5th WTO ministerial conference on the agenda for a new trade round]

Negotiation phase of Seattle / Doha / Cancun

1.   Why did you <u>not</u> get an agreement in Seattle in 1999?
2.   Which were critical moments before and in Seattle?
3.   Why <u>did</u> you get to an agreement in Doha in 2001?
4.   Which were critical moments before and in Doha?
5.   Why did you <u>not</u> get to an agreement in Cancun in 2003?
6.   Which were critical moments before and in Doha?

Preparation phase for negotiations

7.   To determine your countries' position, what mattered most to you?
8.   In addition to what you mentioned, which role did the following criteria play?
   a.   Was it enough to approximate the *absolute* gains or losses for your country? Or, did the gains or losses matter only *compared* to those of other countries?
   b.   In this sense what was at stake for your country, e.g. what size was the financial impact?
   c.   Is an agreement only possible with the support of the most powerful countries?
   d.   How did domestic factors play a role to determine your position?

III. Specifically, what role did these conditions play for the outcome of trade negotiations?

9. Negotiation style: Arguing and problem-solving vs. bargaining
   a. Did you see open-ended problem-solving and arguing about content? ["constructive discourse which is open to a change of minds based on facts and logical insights in order to find a joint solution"] This would be in contrast to bargaining ["discuss the distribution of an assumed fixed set of gains and burdens, based on merely stating countries' positions"].
   b. Did this negotiation style get you closer to or further away from an agreement? How?
   c. In which negotiation setting did arguing or bargaining happen?
10. Transparency and inclusiveness of the negotiation process
   a. Do you think you always knew what happened before and at COP negotiations?
   b. How was your input to the negotiations being asked for?
   c. Did your kind of inclusion have an influence on whether you agreed to the proposal?
11. Capability: Conference Chair [host country minister] (SEATTLE: Mrs Barshefsky, US; DOHA: Mr Kamal, Qatar; CANCUN: Mr Derbez); WTO Director-General (SEATTLE and DOHA: Mike Moore, NZ; CANCUN: Supachai Panitchpakdi); WTO General Council Chair (SEATTLE: Ali Mchumo, Tanzania; DOHA: Kare Bryn, Norway / Stuart Harbinson, HK-China; CANCUN: Mr Pérez del Castillo, Uruguay)
   a. How capable did you perceive them on process and content matters?
   b. How did that influence the reaching of an agreement?
12. WTO Director-General / Conference Chair: degree of acceptance of their authority
   a. Did they establish full authority in their negotiation roles towards you as a party?
   b. Did that influence your acceptance of the proposal in the final nights?
13. Which other variables played a role for reaching an outcome from your perspective?

IV. Concluding

14. Did a difference in negotiation management cause the (non-)agreement?
15. In which other negotiations did process play a major role?
16. Who would you recommend to interview further?

Thank you very much for your contribution to this research.

Note: Questionnaires for organizers were adapted to their perspective on the determination of the position of countries, the capability and authority of the organizers for question 7, 11, and 12.

Interview list on trade negotiations

Names and positions of interviewees have been withheld for the sake of anonymity.

Country/organization	Interview location	Interview date
United Kingdom	London	29.11.2011
Denmark	London–Geneva, phone	16.02.2012
St. Lucia	Geneva	15.12.2011
Switzerland	Hamburg–Geneva, phone	15.05.2012
Switzerland	Geneva	16.12.2011
WTO	Geneva	16.12.2011
WTO	Geneva	16.12.2011

Index

For product safety concerns and information please contact our
EU representative GPSR@taylorandfrancis.com Taylor & Francis
Verlag GmbH, Kaufingerstraße 24, 80331 München, Germany